Transatlantic Scots

D1614593

Transatlantic Scots

Edited by
Celeste Ray

Foreword by
James Hunter

THE UNIVERSITY OF ALABAMA PRESS

Tuscaloosa

Typeface: ACaslon

∞

The paper on which this book is printed meets the minimum requirements of American
National Standard for Information Sciences—Permanence of Paper for Printed Library
Materials, ANSI Z39.48–1984.

Library of Congress Cataloging-in-Publication Data

Transatlantic Scots / edited by Celeste Ray ; foreword by James Hunter.
p. cm.
Includes bibliographical references and index.
ISBN 0-8173-1473-3 (alk. paper) — ISBN 0-8173-5240-6 (pbk. : alk. paper)
1. Scottish—North America—History. 2. Scottish—North America—Social life and
customs. 3. Scottish—North America—Ethnic identity. 4. Regionalism—North America.
5. Transnationalism. 6. Scotland—Emigration and immigration—History. 7. North America—
Emigration and immigration—History. 8. North America—Ethnic relations. I. Ray, R. Celeste.
E49.2.S3T73 2005
305.891′63073—dc22

2005004046

Editor's Note: All British and Canadian spellings have been retained in
chapters by British or Canadian authors.

Contents

Illustrations

Foreword

James Hunter

In a crofting township on the Hebridean island of Skye, I was scheduled some years back to attend a public meeting held on a January evening of the sort that ensures Skye will never rival Florida as a winter destination for vacationers. It was, as it had been since 3:00 P.M., pitch-dark; a gale howled off the nearby ocean; the rain was ice-cold, needle-sharp, and unrelenting.

Out of the storm, and into the township's community hall where people were gathering, there stepped an elderly crofter. With water cascading from his clothing, he looked at me in a less than friendly fashion. "You're the man," he said accusingly, "who's always writing about the Highland Clearances."

I admitted as much—several of my books having touched on that grim period in the nineteenth century when thousands of Scots families, often by way of prelude to their eviction, were ejected forcibly from their homes.

"Well," said this wet, wind-battered crofter, "my only regret about the Highland Clearances is that the [expletive deleted] landlords didn't finish what they started. If they had, I might be growing oranges in California."

Had things gone differently for my own family, if they'd done what many other Scottish families did, they might easily have become Americans—or Australians, Canadians, New Zealanders, or South Africans. But they didn't. So, like that disgruntled crofter, I'm not an orange-growing Californian but a Scot—a Scot who lives in Scotland, a Highlander who works in our Highlands and Islands.

I'm glad, indeed I'm proud, that's so. However, my being a Highlander who's resident in the Highlands makes me, I reckon, something of a statistical anomaly. If it were possible (which it isn't) to take everyone living in the Highlands and Islands at the time, say, of the Battle of Culloden (in 1746) and to trace each of those folk's descendants, more (and I think many more) such descendants would be found outside our part of Scotland than would be found within it.

No one knows the exact number, but it's certainly the case that since Culloden, hundreds of thousands of people have left the Highlands and Islands. It's also the case that most Highlands and Islands emigrants were glad to have had the chance to set up home elsewhere.

Sometimes that's not appreciated in Scotland. Often in Scotland we dwell on the negative aspects of the emigrant experience; on the often dreadful circumstances in which the decision to leave was made; on the pain of parting from friends, neighbours, and homeland; on the hazards of pioneering on some distant frontier. And because in Scotland we focus on those things, we're prone to imagine our emigrant kin as deeply unhappy people forever wishing themselves back home. Nothing could be further from the truth.

Recently I was taken to see a tombstone adjacent to Old Bethesda Presbyterian Church in North Carolina's Cape Fear River country. This tombstone commemorates Colin Bethune, who came, very probably, from the Isle of Skye—source of many of the Cape Fear country's eighteenth-century settlers and a locality where Bethune, or Beaton, remains a common surname. His place of birth, however, mattered less to Colin than the country where he'd made his home. "Colin Bethune," his tombstone reads. "Died 1820, aged 74. An honest man. A native of Scotland by accident, but a citizen of the U.S. by choice."

Something of the emotions behind that most assertive of inscriptions became clear to me as a result of what I was shown of Old Bethesda's surroundings by my good friend Dr. Alex C. McLeod. Alex, who lives in Nashville, Tennessee, was raised in Old Bethesda's vicinity. By profession, Alex is a physician. He's also president of the Associated Clan MacLeod Societies, on whose behalf I'm presently writing an account of our worldwide Highlands and Islands diaspora as exemplified by the history of this single clan.

Alex's great-great-great-grandmother, Effie McLeod, sailed from Skye in August 1802. Like thousands of Skye folk before her, Effie was bound for the Cape Fear River country, where, in time, she was joined by her husband, Murdoch.

With this emigrant couple's present-day descendant, Alex McLeod, I visited the site of Murdoch's and Effie's homestead. The site is now part of Fort Bragg Military Reservation. Murdoch's fields, it follows, have reverted to forest, and nothing remains of the log cabin where he and Effie lived. All that's preserved of their presence is the tiny family graveyard where those Skye-born pioneers were buried more than 150 years ago.

Nearby, however, you can still find the house that Effie's and Murdoch's son, John McLeod, built at the time of his marriage in 1831 to Flora Johnson. Exploring this house in the company of John's great-great-grandson, Alex, I was impressed immediately by its spaciousness. In the early 1830s, when John and Flora McLeod were starting life together and beginning to raise a family of seven boys and six girls, John's cousins back in Skye would have been inhabiting single-roomed, thatched, and perennially damp hovels of the kind then standard in the Highlands and Islands. John McLeod, in contrast, owned a one-and-a-half storey, timber-framed home that ran to six sizeable rooms. And at a time when his Skye relatives would have been the (wholly insecure) tenants (if they were lucky) of four or five acres of inferior soil, John McLeod was the outright possessor of two thousand acres of North Carolina farmland. On this farmland, John pastured a large herd of cattle; on it, too, he grew maize, cotton, and tobacco.

Still in North Carolina and still in Alex's company, I also visited the houses built by John's son, Alexander, another farmer, and by Alexander's son, Robert, a lumber merchant. Just as John's home was more substantial than Murdoch's log cabin, Alexander's was bigger than John's, Robert's an advance on Alexander's. Taken together, or so it seems to me, this hundred-year-long sequence of McLeod family residences is nothing less than the realisation, in timber, brick, and stone, of what in the nineteenth century began to be called the American Dream.

To believe in the American Dream was to be convinced that to get to the United States from Europe was instantly to liberate oneself from the Old World's hardships and injustices. Simply by crossing the ocean, it was thought, men and women—who, had they remained in the countries of their birth, would have been condemned to lifelong poverty and exploitation—could gain the ability to shape their own lives, fulfill their potential, and gain a good income.

In reality, to be sure, matters were never that simple. Many people who left the Highlands and Islands for America didn't even get there—dying on overcrowded, leaking, filthy, disease-ridden emigrant ships. And of those who made it across the Atlantic, by no means all did as well as Murdoch and Effie McLeod, their sons, their grandsons, and their great-grandsons. As this single family's story makes clear, however, there were plenty of emigrants—from the Highlands and Islands as from the rest of Europe—who managed to make the American Dream come true. This was not because people like Effie and Murdoch acquired new talents, new capacities, in the United States. It was down to that country's more open, more democratic society that enabled Murdoch,

Effie, and their numerous counterparts to do things in the Cape Fear River country they never could have done in Skye. That is why, from the late eighteenth century onward, America features in Gaelic songs and poems as a place of almost fabled opportunity and freedom; a country where (and this was the big thing) there were no evicting landlords; a country where, as was then impossible in Scotland, a working family could acquire a home, a farm, of their own.

Which is not to say emigration had no downsides. Yes, emigration was a generally enriching experience from the standpoint both of emigrants themselves and of the societies that received them. But in the places North Carolina's Scottish settlers came from—Skye, for example—emigration's consequences were unremittingly, absolutely, almost terminally negative. The thousands of Skye families who took themselves across the Atlantic constituted, from a North American perspective, a huge gain in human capital. To Skye, on the other hand, those same families represented a massive loss—of talent, manpower, and capacity. Making good that loss has not been easy. But today we are at last beginning to create circumstances that are attracting folk to the Highlands and Islands in much the same way as Murdoch and Effie MacLeod were long ago attracted to North Carolina.

The consequences of this success are readily apparent in Skye. Forty years ago, the island's population had been falling for more than a century, and that trend seemed set to continue. Instead the opposite has happened. Present-day Skye, its population up by nearly 50 percent since the 1960s, has thousands of new residents, hundreds of new homes. The island's economy has diversified enormously. As a result, Skye is home to several high-tech businesses, a college delivering higher education through the medium of Gaelic, flourishing arts and heritage centres, first-rate hotels, and The Three Chimneys—which an international panel has voted twenty-eighth best restaurant in the world.

I am convinced that in Skye and in much of the rest of the Highlands and Islands, positive developments of this sort will continue. That is ultimately because new communications and other technologies are enabling us to envisage a much more dispersed pattern of economic activity than the one familiar to us since the industrial revolution. Age-old barriers of distance and remoteness are starting to break down. Globally, the most advanced, the most exciting businesses are beginning to be located in places where their owners and workforces can simultaneously earn a good living and have immediate access to natural heritage—to coastal or mountain landscapes—of the very highest quality. Hence the current success of American regions like the Pacific North

West or Colorado. Hence my belief that where those American localities have led, the Highlands and Islands can readily follow.

To those of us trying to help with the emergence of a new Scotland, the Scottish diaspora can be a source of endless aggravation. Don't you realise, we ask our North American cousins, that Scotland has moved on; that it's no longer the country your ancestors left; that there's much more to our twenty-first-century nation than castles, clan chiefs, kilts, Highland games, and thatched cottages? But if Americans of Scottish ancestry can legitimately be accused of misunderstanding modern Scotland, so we Scots are guilty of failing to come to terms with the fact that Scottish Americans are the product of a history that is not ours.

Just as Scotland did not become frozen in time the moment your ancestors left it, neither did your forebears cease to evolve and develop when they crossed the Atlantic. You have been shaped by your North American, as well as by your Scottish, heritage. We, on our side, need to understand that. After all, it has to be from a Scottish standpoint a huge asset, given that we are a tiny country of just five million people, to have many times that number of folk out there—in countries like Canada, Australia, New Zealand, and South Africa as well as the United States—believing they share kinship with us. If we are to make the best of what you can do for Scotland, we need to come to terms with who you are, with why you think and feel and act the way you do. This wholly admirable book will help us do that—which is why it's hugely to be welcomed.

Transatlantic Scots

Introduction

Celeste Ray

Most Americans have no idea that April 6 is National Tartan Day and would probably have to be told that "tartan" is what they might call plaid. Those who know are avid in their knowledge. Scottish Americans organize tartan balls, bagpipe parades (the ten thousand pipers strutting through New York City in 2002 were hard to miss), and "Scottish heritage weeks" (the St. Andrew's Society of Baltimore, Maryland, declared a "Scottish-American History and Heritage Month" for April 1999). Local Scottish-American heritage societies put on "Kirkin's of the Tartan" (church services) like that I attended on Tartan Day 2003 in Chattanooga, Tennessee.

The venue was Chattanooga's First Cumberland Presbyterian Church, an imposing modified gothic structure of local quartzite. After receiving a few welcoming hugs from tartan-draped acquaintances, and having resisted their inducements to participate in similar garb, I slipped into one of the back pews just before 11 A.M. As the local bagpipe band played "Highland Cathedral," members of the city's Scottish society solemnly processed down the central aisle carrying pieces of their clan tartans. After a roll call of the clans represented, the congregation was reminded that whatever their ethnic origins, all are part of "Clan Dia," the children of God. The remainder of the worship service was decidedly typical of the sedate Cumberland Presbyterian denomination (originating in 1802 in Scots- and Scots-Irish-settled Tennessee and Kentucky).

The minister's main reference to the aberration in that Sunday's liturgy was to note, with some amusement, that the Chattanooga event had been mentioned the previous evening "on the BBC in London." That a Chattanooga happening would be of interest to Londoners surprised many participants who have had much more exposure to British marketers peddling a tartan heritage

Fig. 1. An outdoor Kirkin' of the Tartans at the Grandfather Mountain Highland Games in North Carolina (Photo courtesy of Hugh Morton)

than to Scottish (and English) criticisms of their penchant for the same. Most were unaware that their claims to a hyphenated identity would be met with anything but goodwill, that they would be part of what the British media dubs "America's Tartaneers,"[1] or of the debate churning in the British newspapers and journals over North Americans' use of Scottish symbols in the name of heritage.[2]

Having monitored or engaged in these debates, the contributors to this volume are academics from the disciplines of history, anthropology, folklore, sociology, and literary criticism. Most have pursued the subjects they cover for over a decade, and some for three. Our conversations began with a panel I organized at the American Anthropological Association meetings in San Francisco in 2000.[3] Considering different facets of the Scottish heritage movement in the United States and Canada, and often from opposing viewpoints, the product of our discourse is not a united perspective. Our shared interests lie in examining the public performance and creation of tradition as well as the renegotiation of history and cultural memory into heritage. We seek to understand the ways in which historical moments are selected to shape identity

and how the Scottish heritage movement relates to the wider surge of interest in ethnicity in North America since the 1960s. In this introduction I
wish to provide a brief summary of scholarship on Scots in North America
and to discuss the challenges of studying those who will read what we write
about them.

Transatlantic Scots as Subjects

If Scottish accounts of hyphenated Scots abroad have recently become more
voluminous and critical, Scottish Americans and Scottish Canadians have been
the subjects of domestic, if mostly filiopietistic, scholarship for at least a century
and a half. President Woodrow Wilson famously remarked that "every line of
strength in American history is a line colored with Scottish blood." Prior to the
ethnic revivals of the 1960s and 1970s, few other ethnic groups had received
as much scholarly, or popular, attention.[4] By the mid-nineteenth century, North
American scholars had begun to document Scottish influences on their respective nations. In the United States in 1856, George Chambers published one of
the first, and much emulated, works on "the Principles, Virtues, Habits and
Public Usefulness" of the Scots-Irish settlers of Pennsylvania. Intellectual accounts of Scots in British North America proved popular by 1880. In that year
Sir James MacPherson LeMoine delivered a paper to the Literary and Histori-
cal Society of Quebec titled "The Scot in New France: An Ethnological
Study," and William Jordan Rattray published the first of three volumes titled
The Scots in British North America.[5]

The long tradition of examining the seemingly disproportionate influence of
Scottish and Scots-Irish intellectual thought on North American culture and
politics includes Charles A. Hanna's *The Scotch-Irish (or the Scot in North Britain, North Ireland and North America)* (1902); Wilfred Campbell's *The Scotsman in Canada* (1911); George Fraser Black's *Scotland's Mark on America*
(1921); John H. Finley's *The Coming of the Scot* (1940); James A. Roy's *The Scot
and Canada* (1947); and T. J. Wertenbaker's *Early Scottish Contributions to the
United States* (1945), to name but a few. These volumes provide long lists of
Scottish inventors, scientists, millionaires, celebrities, and politicians of Scottish origins: thirty-one U.S. presidents are claimed to have some documented
Scottish ancestry; as are twenty-one of the fifty-six signers of the Declaration
of Independence (only two being native Scots, John Witherspoon and James
Wilson); and two-thirds of the first thirteen governors of states.[6] The repeat-
ing motif of such publications is America's intellectual and cultural debt to
Scotland.[7]

Similarly, in March 2003 the Presiding Officer of the Scottish Parliament, Sir David Steel, could recite a similar litany of Scottish influences in Canada during a talk with Scottish community representatives in Ottawa: "over 4 million people, or 13% of the Canadian population, list themselves as being of Scots descent in the census . . . Not only should we acknowledge our shared history, we must celebrate it . . . The first governor in what is now Canada was Sir William Alexander of Scotland . . . The first two Canadian Prime Ministers were both native-born Scots," and so on. Stories of influential Scots are similar in other former British colonies, and while their influence was not always benign regarding native inhabitants, their successes have allowed diasporic communities to put a bright face on the traumas of exile and immigration (Harper 2003; Calder 2003; Hewitson 1998; Reid 1976).

In Canada, recent publications on "notable Scots" and their roles in Canadian history include Jenni Calder's *Scots in Canada* and Matthew Shaw's *Great Scots!: How the Scots Created Canada* (both 2003). Those popular with hyphenated Scots across the continent include Duncan Bruce's hagiographic *The Mark of the Scots: Their Astonishing Contributions to History, Science, Democracy, Literature, and the Arts* (1996); Stewart Lamont's *When Scotland Ruled the World: The Story of the Golden Age of Genius, Creativity, and Exploration* (2001); and Arthur Herman's *How the Scots Invented the Modern World* (2001). (Herman's book has been much debated in the media on both sides of the Atlantic, but especially in Scotland—perhaps as Scots, harboring a lingering Presbyterian fear of pride, hate to be admired.[8]) In the United States, Billy Kennedy's *The Making of America: How the Scots-Irish Shaped a Nation* (2001) and Michael Fry's *"Bold, Independent, Unconquer'd, and Free": How the Scots Made America Safe for Liberty, Democracy, and Capitalism* (2003) appear at Scottish-American community events.

The last, by Fry, is the most recent installment crediting Scots for inspiring American independence. Much has been made of the influence of Scot John Witherspoon (first president of Princeton University) on the Declaration of Independence. (He did get Thomas Jefferson to remove a condemnation of "Scotch and other foreign mercenaries" from a draft.) In *Inventing America: Jefferson's Declaration of Independence* (1978), Garry Wills suggested that the document drew more on the Scottish than the French Enlightenment (Howe 1989, 572). Similar arguments followed Wills. Archie Turnbull (1986) suggested that despite his aversion to "Scottish Tories," Thomas Jefferson modeled the Declaration of Independence on the 1320 Scottish Declaration of Arbroath.

Yet, contrary to the celebrated influence of Scottish thinkers, Scots in

America were often reviled in the colonial period. Jacob Price noted that in the tobacco-growing Chesapeake, Scots were disliked for their business success and the influence of Glasgow firms on the tobacco trade in Virginia and Maryland (1954, 198–99; see also Brock 1982, 48–49; and Devine 1975). Margaret Sanderson and Alison Lindsay assert, "It could almost be said that Scotland 'exported' administrators to the American colonies. The Scots Governors and Lieutenant Governors, generally efficient and hard-headed, were no more beloved as a rule than their merchant fellow-Scots" (1994, 4). During the American Revolution, a Williamsburg pamphleteer, "Scotus Americanus," wrote acidly about Scottish Highlanders and their reasons for emigrating to remind them why they should not be Loyalists (as so many Highlanders were) (Meyer 1957, 144). Andrew Hook notes that "the American revulsion against the Scots lasted at least as long as the war." From a statute passed by the Georgia Assembly in August 1782, Hook quotes, "the People of Scotland have in General Manifested a decided inimicality to the Civil liberties of America," and as a result, "no Scot was to be allowed to settle, or carry on any kind of trade, in Georgia, unless he had supported the patriotic side" (1975, 69). In view of the popularity of all things Scottish in the United States today, this strong resentment against the Scots might seem surprising; especially when it is considered that Georgia was the state where Scots constituted the highest proportion of the population.

By the close of the War of 1812, however, anti-Scottish sentiment had mellowed to the point that Sir Walter Scott's "Hail to the Chief" was played to honor the end of hostilities and the late George Washington. The Scottish song has announced the arrival of the American chief executive to formal occasions since 1828.[9] How did Scots, so maligned as economically grasping, unpatriotic, and "supporters of tyrants" in the eighteenth century, become idealized for their contributions to American independence and culture less than a century later? A partial answer to this question lies in understanding the contrasting experiences of the three different Scottish ethnic groups who came to the colonies (Highland, Lowland, and Ulster Scots). While in British North America the Ulster Scots were simply known as "Irish," in the United States they became "Scots-Irish." As I will detail in chapter 2, for the United States, each group had different settlement patterns, cultural traditions, and politics. In Scotland at the end of the eighteenth century and during the nineteenth century, Highland imagery had come to represent the Scottish national identity, so that by the time Chambers wrote of the Scots-Irish "public usefulness" and "virtues" in 1856, he was writing for an audience well versed in Sir Walter Scott's novels and notions of things Scottish as romantically Highland; an audience that had begun to perceive their Highland, Lowland, and Ulster Scots ancestors as collectively and similarly Scottish in a fashion their ancestors might not have recognized. When Scottish contributions to early American life began to be examined academically, the ethnic divisions so important in that time period had long since diminished or been forgotten. By this time, too, "more foreign" immigrants were arriving on U.S. shores, making Scots seem very American indeed.

In 1954 the *William and Mary Quarterly* devoted an issue to examining links between Scotland and America. Providing a survey of writings in Scottish-American history, George Shepperson noted that to examine the Scottish contribution to American development "may seem, at first, a well-worn theme" (1954, 163). Shepperson would perhaps not be surprised that five decades later, scholars of many disciplines still debate the subject as if it were fresh.[10] This collection's novelty lies in addressing popular perceptions of Scottish heritage and the shape of transatlantic Scottish communities as indicative of the meaning of ethnicity in an age of multicultural awareness and globalization.

Cultural Relativism at "Home"

Much of the analysis in this book considers how history and heritage diverge. However, we do not critically examine the heritage lore of hyphenated Scots as a hollow exercise in deconstruction; instead we wish to explore how heritage is created and why some historical events, rather than others, shape public ritual and familial memories. That a tradition is invented does not detract from its present meaning to those who emotionally invest in its practice. While historians Eric Hobsbawm and Terence Ranger (1983) prompted a scholarly fad in debunking "the invention of tradition," all traditions are invented at some point and are continually reinvented in different contexts (see Giddens 1991, 150). Rather than simply highlight the inventiveness of symbolic ethnicities, and of multiculturalism more generally, we strive to examine the reasons behind the selection of traditions and hyphenated identities.

Maintaining objectivity is perhaps easier when examining the cultures of "others" far from home, and offering a neutral analysis of cultural viewpoints within our own cultures has been a challenge for contributors. The interdisciplinary and international team of authors in this volume have varied reasons for becoming interested in Scottish heritage movements (as will readers). While all ideas of culture and ethnicity are to some extent reified, some contributors write with objections to the particular style of reification and objectification of their national or regional identity. What the Scottish diaspora conceives as

Scottish can be excruciating for Scots. While we research a common subject, our disciplinary training and approaches do sometimes position us in opposing camps. For example, some contributors (Vance, Hook, McArthur) contest the applicability of "diaspora" in referencing the transatlantic Scottish experience, while those contributors who emphasize fieldwork, especially with descendants of Highland, Gaelic-speaking Scots (Basu, Bennett, Dembling, Ray), are more likely to describe transatlantic Scots as they describe themselves, as a diaspora. Some contributors write with the judgment and critical viewpoint of historians, but none are apologists, and most strive for the respect folklorists grant their subjects.

Until recently, anthropological ethnographers had remained reticent about studying "at home," and scholars, largely from literary criticism, began studying "our culture" without the fieldwork methods or cultural relativism of anthropology. "Culture Studies" developed in the 1980s with perceptive scholars who wanted to examine culture without spending the time ethnographic fieldwork demands. Cultural critics, who are often trained as literary critics, try to avoid what in literary study has been called "the intentional fallacy"—the fallacy being the assumption that the meaning of a text could be discovered by determining the author's intention. Cultural critics "trust the tale, not the teller," while ethnographic fieldworkers particularly seek the intentions and experience of those performing and participating in public rituals.[11] Rather than document ethnic boundary markers employed in the claiming of identity and then condemn or condone cultural practices and beliefs according to what we think we know about such symbols, ethnographic fieldwork requires that we ask with an open mind what those who employ symbols believe themselves to be communicating. To write about cultural events as if they were "text" and to trust only the tale and not the teller can be an exercise in mythmaking itself. Historians rightly question the value of sources relying on secondhand material, and anthropologists likewise question cultural studies scholars' reliance on Web sites and second- or third- or fourth-hand reports without "being there in the field" (see Nugent and Shore 1997; Knauft 1996). It is perhaps more appealing to be "in the field" when one is a novelty in another culture and so certainly marginal. Respectfully studying the "bizarre" beliefs and practices of one's own neighbors (with whom one is presumed to share some common cultural ground and expectations and therefore with whom one may become more readily frustrated or annoyed) is a different type of challenge.

Scholars, and perhaps westerners in general, are more willing to be tolerant of folk beliefs of "other" people. We also tend to be intrigued and charmed by folk beliefs in our own societies of other periods ("folk" usually implying pre-modern). We are interested in arguments such as Alexander Carmichael's that songs and poetry modeled on a "Celtic" liturgy survived in the Western Isles into the nineteenth century (1992). We are amazed that John Lorne Campbell recorded tales from the Fenian Cycle on South Uist in the 1950s (D. Smith 2001, 36; Campbell 1990). We allow ourselves to be fascinated by antiquarian accounts of "fairy belief" surviving in Britain and Ireland into the twentieth century. However, we are dismissive, embarrassed, and even outraged at what we could call "folk beliefs" about heritage in our own societies today. After almost two decades of academic "deconstruction," we self-righteously determine to disabuse people of their beliefs. Story collectors of one hundred, or even forty, years ago took delight in "finding" the most isolated of people in their own societies and learning about how they perceived the world. What makes the difference?

Unlike the folklore collectors of the nineteenth and early twentieth centuries, today we assume that there is *always* a political, perhaps even "racist," reason for the creation of heritage lore and urban legends. Perhaps because of our own privileges of education, technology, and exposure to the media, we expect unemotional rationalism of everyone in our own societies—it is obligatory. Any belief—for example, in fantastic ancestral origins—that seems "retrograde" or unsupported by contemporary scholarship is assumed to be held for ill-intentioned motives; hence the invective against "white ethnics" in the 1960s and 1970s and the righteous tone of many "whiteness" studies in the 1990s. Or perhaps scholars become so irritated at those "like themselves" who choose to believe, for example, that Native Americans never crossed the Bering Strait but were created in the Grand Canyon,[12] that Mexico's Olmecs and their monuments are really African in origin, or that Clan Gunn discovered America,[13] because of the pseudo-academic language and style in which such stories are often presented. Perhaps scholars are more skeptical because the medium of communication is no longer the local storyteller at a hearth, but more often the seemingly legitimacy-granting Internet. Perhaps having the luxury of sitting around thinking about and critiquing others' thoughts, we cannot imagine believing as they do and cannot imagine why anyone "like us" would either. Each generation of scholars refashions history, yet the lag between popular culture and "the truth," as academics currently preach it, can frustrate attempts at relativism in the study of heritage and identity politics (see Englund 2002; Baron and Spitzer 1992; and Jenkins 2002).

Before literacy was common and before ethnographies were read by their subjects, storytellers imitated others they most respected. It is therefore no surprise that today's storytellers imitate the academic style adopted by money-making television networks that purport to be educational (for example, The Learning Channel or The Discovery Channel). How much time do academics spend in the classroom undoing the "scholarly" television productions on pseudo-science fantasies like those of Barry Fell (who claimed that Egyptians, Celts, Libyans, and Basques colonized America by 800 B.C.) or of those who are still looking for an Atlantis that Plato invented as a model Utopia. And what scholar has not groaned at such a production in his or her field only to hear colleagues in other disciplines remark on how fascinating they found it?[14] As in the past, the more fabulous the tale, the more often people want to hear it.

Scholars and culture critics critique contemporary conceptions of heritage as inauthentic, fallacious, or even absurd, yet heritage is not history nor even necessarily historical. Heritage may make history happy, grievance-ridden, or appealingly tragic, but it is always in flux; it is difficult to pin down and, like expressions of ethnic identity, it varies according to context. Why do people want to believe in a particular vision of heritage? Perhaps for some it is a belief that their origins are superior to all others; for some this belief may become political and may structure their alliances and social activities. Sometimes ethnic identities are primarily political and need to be examined as such. However, except in the case of ethnic supremacists and nationalists, ethnic identities are not always political, but endure or revive to fill other needs (for familial harmony, for a sense of self, for community, for the pleasure and fun that their celebration brings). For many, having any sort of "ancient origins" is emotionally appealing—even if they be tribal, a-literate, supposedly battle-mad, origins of an agro-pastoralist Highland clan. Commenting on representations of Scottishness in the film *Braveheart* (which has sparked debates about Scottish identity as if it had been a documentary rather than a movie), Tim Edensor noted "it may be emotional authenticity rather than historical accuracy that satisfies audiences" (2002, 156; for more on the use and abuse of *Braveheart,* see McArthur 2003).

At the Kirkin' I described in the beginning of this introduction, I was asked to walk with a family member of the local Scottish society's president and carry their clan tartan (our surnames being similar). While I felt complimented that he should ask and wish to involve me in this way, any pleasure in parading and being on display faded with my last tap solo in junior high school. Even had I not been raised a "back row Baptist" (a dancing one at that), I often have a difficult time convincing Scottish Americans that I am repeatedly present at their gatherings to observe, not as a hyphenate myself. While I have not been tempted to "go native," I have had to suspend criticism of "the tale" to appreciate the deeply held beliefs and worldviews of "the tellers." As I remind my students, cultural relativism begins at home. Of what use is it for a North American to claim to appreciate the finer points of Zen Buddhism and yet refuse to try to understand one's fundamentalist Pentecostal neighbor?

Tolerance or respect is much easier to extend at a distance. Cultural relativism was the chief anthropological ethic for the generations trained in the mid-twentieth century, when a goal in fieldwork was to impact the culture one studied as little as possible. As humans observing other humans, relativism has limits. We obviously lack cross-cultural agreement on what constitutes "human rights;" for many societies such rights are still limited, even ideologically, to sex, caste, color, or class. Increasingly, some cultural studies scholars are willing to critique customs that violate human rights, while others still attempt to defend them in the name of sacred, reified culture or hallowed tradition. However, culture is not always good; in fact all cultures basically rot—each in its own particular way. Culture keeps some people in positions of power and others powerless. It is often easier to be a cultural relativist about what is least familiar, novel, and not actually impinging on one's self or loved ones. "At home" one must sometimes be reminded to balance the unquestionable value of historicist inquiry with accounts not only of the "spectacular and historic," but also with a respectful focus on the quotidian aspects of popular culture (Edensor 2002, 10; see also A. Jackson 1987 and Glassberg 2001). Historians Marjory Harper and Michael Vance (1999, 37) paraphrase a particularly salient line from David Lowenthal: "ancestral loyalties often 'rest on fiction as well as truth,' we must learn to face its fictions."

Intentions and Case Studies

While some cultural studies scholars and anthropologists (especially those leaning toward ethnopoetics) would privilege what people *believe* about their past, the historian privileges "facts" and the deconstruction of myths.[15] If not through individual essays, then as a whole, this volume attempts to balance a respect for both and to complement the "natives'" perspectives with those of the outside observer. No cultural phenomenon can be understood without a diachronic perspective—without historical background. It *does* matter that two hundred people were evicted in a particular clearance of a Highland clachan rather than the one thousand of folklore. This collection does not seek to validate myths nor to insult those who hold them dear, but to understand how historical events are mythologized and why people want to believe, or uncritically repeat, mythic visions of history cast as heritage.[16]

While some authors are more critical of the heritage movement than others, most, but perhaps not all, of us would agree with anthropologist Anthony Cohen's suggestion that "it is less important . . . to cast academic aspersions on the authenticity of a group's putative lineage than to attempt to understand why a distinctive . . . identity should be so compelling to its members (some of whom are only voluntary affiliates)" (1986, 341–42; see also A. Smith 1998). This volume compares the development of hyphenated Scottish identities in the United States and Canada, and, by considering both transatlantic Scots for whom a Scottish ethnicity is symbolic and voluntary and those for whom an awareness of a Scottish heritage is familial and transgenerational, more generally examines the legacy of diasporas and the multiple levels of meaning invested in ethnic identities.

In the next chapter, I examine the meaning of ethnic identity in popular and scholarly discourse and consider Scottish Americans as an ethnic group. In two subsequent chapters Canadian historian Michael Vance and I consider Scottish immigration to North America and Scottish ethnic organization in both the United States and Canada as an introduction to contributors' essays that examine the regional expressions of Scottish heritage movements.[17] Scottish folklorist and ethnologist Margaret Bennett examines the evolution of Hebridean identities in Canada's Eastern Townships from "Quebec-Hebrideans" to "les Écossais-Québecois" and the French style of Scottish events and commemorations there (see also Bennett 1998). Michael Vance examines the appeal of a Scottish identity in Nova Scotia and how a sentimental vision of Scottishness has come to symbolize the region and subsumed other ethnic identities in the area (Mi'kmaq, Acadian, and African). As he has done elsewhere (1975; 1999), Scottish literary critic Andrew Hook examines the tension between a rosy, heritage-based vision of Scottish contributions to American life and the actual experience and reception of Scots in colonial America. Hook focuses on the negative influences of perceptions of "Scottish" heritage on American culture and also recounts the appeal of Scottish motifs for neo-Confederate and American extremist groups. My chapter on "Bravehearts and Patriarchs," examines masculinity "on the pedestal" in hybrid celebrations of a Highland Scottish and southern regional identity. Robin Cohen (1997) has noted that the creation of hybrid cultures is typical of the diasporic experience. While the large numbers of Scottish and Scots-Irish immigrants to the colonial South helped shape what it means to be southern, today's heritage enthusiasts are "Scottish" in a southern fashion.

Cohen describes diasporas as dispersals from a homeland to two or more foreign lands. Such emigration is often traumatic, or may be for colonial purposes or for economic betterment (1997, 118–37). He notes other characteristics of diasporas considered through essays in this volume: the maintenance of transnational relationships and the desire to "return" to the homeland. Two essays consider the nature and social roles of transnational tradition; its invention and renegotiation; its transmission and performance.[18] Scottish sociologist Grant Jarvie, who has written about the nineteenth-century re-creation of Highland games in Scotland (1991), examines the role of the games in producing social capital and fostering local and transatlantic communities. American anthropologist Jonathan Dembling discusses assertions that Cape Breton Gaelic language, dancing, and musical traditions are more "authentic" than those in Scotland itself and considers the current trend for learning Cape Breton music and dance in Scotland. He argues that Scots learning Cape Breton styles are participating in a wider debate about what it means to be Scottish now.

Considering heritage pilgrimage to the homeland, British anthropologist Paul Basu and American anthropologist John Sheets describe efforts by the Scottish diaspora to reestablish connections to particular hills and glens and develop friendships with their current inhabitants. Sheets writes of the transatlantic network between American and Canadian descendants of emigrants from Colonsay with the island's current community. Heritage tourists' knowledge of clan-specific history allows them to achieve a certain intersubjectivity with their real or presumed ancestors at sites featured in clan lore. Basu considers "roots-tourists" and respectfully explores hyphenated Scots' experience of place as an anchor for identity.

Considering Scottish influences on North American politics and culture, Scottish historian Ted Cowan examines Scottish responses to Tartan Day celebrations. A Canadian invention, Tartan Day is now celebrated by hyphenated Scots across the continent. Wanting a day designated in honor of Scots' contributions to Canadian history, Jean Watson led a personal campaign to have the first Tartan Day ratified in Nova Scotia in 1987.[19] Other Canadian jurisdictions followed in the first half of the 1990s, including Ontario (1991) and New Brunswick (1993), and even Quebec had passed an act proclaiming Tartan Day in time for the 2004 event. April 6 was chosen as the anniversary of the 1320 Scottish Declaration of Arbroath.[20] Following the Canadian lead, several American states began proclaiming Tartan Days in the mid-1990s (Tennessee in 1996 and North Carolina in 1997). In March of 1998 the U.S. Senate passed Resolution 155 making April 6 "National Tartan Day," (also approved by the House of Representatives on March 9, 2005).

At first Scots in Scotland seemed bemused, but it was not long before journalists initiated cringing over the flamboyance of events and before critics began to question possible motives behind such a holiday (McArthur 1998; Ray 2001; Hague 2002a, 2002b). The Scottish diaspora is far larger than the current population of Scotland (just over five million), and as Scotland has recently regained its own parliament (1999) and tries to revise its national imagery, the diasporic celebration of Tartan Day is of significant interest if not concern. Cowan suggests the best way for Scots to reconcile themselves to the events is to stop feeling responsible for them and see Tartan Day as a North American phenomenon, not a Scottish one. In 2004 the Edinburgh newspaper *The Scotsman* featured editorials about whether Scottish politicians should make appearances at Tartan Day festivities in North America (which they do). On April 6 the paper also published a letter from Robert More of the Clan Muir Society in Coos Bay, Oregon, in which he informs the readership, "We couldn't care less if Scottish politicians want to join the fun . . . The event has already taken on a life of its own, and will continue to grow in this country." Indeed it has.

In his concluding piece, Scottish media scholar and culture critic Colin McArthur ruminates on a question he has considered for over two decades: why such a limited repertoire of images and tropes about Scotland continues to resonate through the centuries and throughout the international Scottish diaspora. Commenting on how narratives of the past shape cultural identities, Stuart Hall (1990) has noted that different cultural identities develop according to whether we passively receive narratives of the past or whether we position ourselves within these narratives through individual agency. Using Hall's distinction and favoring determination over agency, McArthur posits a "Scottish Discursive Unconscious," a "preexisting and hegemonic *bricolage* of images, narratives, subnarratives, tones, and turns of phrase" that hinders novel perspectives on Scottishness. His essay challenges other contributors' emphases on transatlantic Scots' agency in negotiating their heritage and reminds us that as Scots increasingly debate their own identity, they will increasingly scrutinize and contest that of the Scottish diaspora.

Trading on Highland motifs, imagery, and what McArthur calls the Scottish Discursive Unconscious, the North American Scottish heritage movement of the past half-century has only gained momentum in the last decade. While this has benefited the Scottish tourism industry, the images on which it thrives hardly represent, or please, Scots themselves. As debates over Scotland's contested national identity continue to unfold in the twenty-first century, will transgenerational (as well as relatively new and carefully constructed) transatlantic links endure? Only the next few decades will reveal if hyphenated

Scots continue to revere the tartan monster and shortbread tin imagery, or if transatlantic connections keep the diaspora from perceiving the past as home and the new Scotland as a foreign country.

Notes

For patient help in the reference department of the University of the South library, I wish to thank Heidi Syler, Wayne Maxson, and Kevin Reynolds. I appreciate draft reading and thoughtful comments from Richard O'Connor, Michael Vance, Ted Cowan, John Sheets, Eric Lassiter, and Donna Murdock. The contributors thank Tammy Scissom for wrangling with bibliographic styles of international scholars from several disciplines. Thanks also to former students Jill Birdwell, Ben Marsee, Tom Smythe, Chris Ramsey, Chris Brooks, Reagan McRae, Mead Ferris, Hannah Schremser, Carrie Parris, and Blake Smith for draft reading and checking bibliographies.

1. If journalist George Rosie did not coin the term, he was one of the first to write about America's star-spangled "tartaneers."

2. In this volume "North America" refers to both Canada and the United States; "Scottish Americans" refers to residents of the United States; and "British North America" refers to Canada.

3. Michael MacDonald, Euan Hague, and Stevan Jackson also participated in this panel, and Jane Nadel-Klein added thoughtfully to discussion. Michael Newton and John Gibson were also a part of developing exchanges.

4. In 1969 Maldwyn Jones noted this about the Scots-Irish (1969, 46).

5. Thanks to Michael Vance for these Canadian benchmarks.

6. Such celebratory publications have remained popular in the second half of the twentieth century and beyond: see Charles Walker, ed. (1988) *A Legacy of Scots: Scottish Achievers* (Edinburgh: Mainstream); Ian Fellowes Gordon (1988), *Famous Scots* (London: Shepheard-Walwyn); Bill Fletcher (1995), *Baxter's Book of Famous Scots Who Changed the World* (Glasgow: Lang Syne Publishers); Elspeth Wills (1985), *Scottish Firsts: Innovation and Achievement* (Edinburgh: Mainstream); June Skinner Sawyers (1996), *Famous Firsts of Scottish Americans* (Gretna, LA: Pelican); and echoing the arguments of Bruce (1996) and Fry (2003), but in a far less scholarly fashion, Robert Galvin (2002), *America's Founding Secret: What the Scottish Enlightenment Taught Our Founding Fathers* (Lanham, MD: Rowman and Littlefield).

7. While many books on the subject feature hyperbole, Scottish resistance to the English was familiar to American colonials. George Washington's will mentions a box "made of the oak that sheltered the great Sir William Wallace after the battle of Falkirk" that had been given to him by the Earl of Buchan.

8. Like any other ethnic group celebrating its heritage, the Scottish-American community glosses less savory Scottish influences and exports. By tradition, Pontius Pilate was born in Fortingall, Perthshire, where his father was on military service. The last man beheaded in the United Kingdom was a Scot (Simon Fraser, 11th Lord Lovat in 1747). The pirate Captain Kidd was also Scottish, although none of these men of

course make it onto "our ancestors" boards displayed in clan society tents at Highland games. Not all clan chiefs were as admirable as they are idealized in clan lore today—many were the reason for their clansfolks' emigration, yet this part of history is downplayed in heritage lore, and clan chiefs are frequently honored guests at Highland games. Edinburgh's fame as a center of medical learning is justified, and Americans frequently sought medical training there in the eighteenth and nineteenth centuries, but it was also the home of William Burke and William Hare, who, not content with robbing graves to supply bodies for Edinburgh's medical school, turned to murder (sixteen times between 1827 and 1828). The brutal Ugandan leader Idi Amin retained his own kilted pipe band, at one point called his mansion "Holyrood House," and himself "the Last King of Scotland." The lynch law in America may have had Scottish origins (Shepperson 1954, 164), and the Fiery Cross, which inspired the Ku Klux Klan's use of the same, remained in use in Scotland until the 1820s (Pittock 1991, 112) and was revived as the title of a neo-Jacobite journal in the early 1900s (Pittock 2001, 99). Scots also invented some things we might be better off without: single malt whisky, television (John Logie Baird, 1888–1946), and cloned sheep. However, compared with the long lists of positive Scottish contributions to the world, the list of notorious Scots is remarkably short. For such a small population (5,119,200 in 2003), the Scots do seem freakishly overachieving, managing to be first with the steam engine, fingerprinting, nylon, the postcard, the telephone, metal detectors, antiseptic (Joseph Lister, 1867), cornstarch, and adhesive postage stamps, to list just a few inventions. Perhaps the Scottish proclivity for innovations relates to the Scots' historic emphasis on education—even prior to the Enlightenment (Sloan 1971). Scotland required compulsory education for sons of freeholders by 1496, had four universities for its tiny population by 1583, and established parish schools by a government act in 1696. Yet, Scots have an abiding "Crisis of Confidence" (see Craig 2003).

9. The lyrics for the song are from stanza XIX of the second canto of Scott's *The Lady of the Lake.* Published in 1810, the book was tremendously popular during the War of 1812. The chief in Scott's story, Roderick Dhu, was a defender of Clan Douglas who was killed by King James V.

10. For an excellent summary of scholarship on the history of Scottish settlement and intellectual exchange between Scotland and America (one that would have saved me considerable work had I known of it earlier!), see Richard Sher's introductory essay in *Scotland and America in the Age of Enlightenment* (1990).

11. Thanks again to John Grammer for explaining the intentional fallacy.

12. This was one argument advanced in attempts to prevent scientific analysis of a nine-thousand-year-old skeleton from the state of Washington (known as "Kennewick man"). Under NAGPRA (the Native American Graves Protection and Repatriation Act), a local federation of Native Americans tried to have the body buried without scientific study, claiming DNA and other analysis would insult his remains and yield no information about immigration of early Native Americans, as they "never immigrated." Because the skeleton exhibited unusual features for a Native American, a neo-Viking group also tried to claim the body as a peripatetic ancestor. In an age of multiculturalism, the fantastic ideas that humans had never crossed the Bering Strait

and that something like a Viking culture existed eight thousand years before the Viking period were both advanced as serious claims to obtain the body.

13. Clan Gunn literature often claims that its forebears were "Discoverers of America." The story is detailed at the Clan Gunn Heritage Center in Latheron, Caithness, and is mentioned on the Web site of the Scottish Executive (the devolved government for Scotland). A Scottish nobleman, Sir Henry Sinclair (sometimes called Prince Henry), is thought to have sailed to Nova Scotia in 1398 with a fleet of twelve ships. Some interpret him to be the legendary figure known as Glooscap among the Micmac Indians—a figure who told them of Jesus, Jack and the Beanstalk, and how to roll dice. In 1954 an amateur archaeologist identified what is known at "the Westford Knight," a stone carving of "a fourteenth-century knight" in Westford, Massachusetts. The "carvings" are thought to represent the arms of the ancient Clan Gunn on a knight's shield, what the Clan Gunn Heritage Center interpretive boards deem "the earliest known example of Gunn Arms." That small groups could have crossed the Atlantic at the time is certainly plausible; that they would have encountered native societies on what were perhaps accidental visits and then had had an impact on them is not likely and quite different from the historical accounts of castaways in the Age of Exploration.

14. Being trained in archaeology, I've been asked by brilliant PhDs in psychology, biology, and political science how the Celts built Stonehenge and what "ancient Celtic" rituals "the Druids" perform there at the summer solstice today. (Stonehenge is of course a Neolithic monument, not Iron Age, and the "Druids" of today are a nineteenth-century romantic development without recourse to the ancient Celtic Druids' unrecorded, oral tradition.)

15. For more discussion of ethnographic/folkloric approaches to history as reality and to reflexivity in the collection of folkloric data, see Tonkin 1990; Stewart 1996; Bendix 1997; Kirshenblatt-Gimblett 1998; and Stoeltje, Fox, and Olbrys 1999.

16. For more on memory, mythmaking, and the evolution of history into heritage, see Kammen 1991; Hoelscher 1998; Lowenthal 1996, 1985; Samuel and Thompson 1990; Tonkin 1990; Brundage 2000; Bendix 2000; Lipsitz 1990; Brown 1998.

17. We have not intentionally ignored the Midwest or West. At the time of organizing this collection, we simply could not locate potential contributors working with contemporary hyphenated Scots (rather than immigration history) in western Canada or in the West or Midwest of the United States. For more on the history of Scots in these areas, see Harper 2003; Calder 2003; Evans 1965, 1969; Szasz 2000; T. Jackson 1968; Kerr 1976; McGregor 1982; Le Roy 1978; and Hunter 1996. Vance provides sources for Scottish settlement in Canada in his introduction to Canadian hyphenates.

18. For more on the performance of heritage, see Carole Trosset (1993) *Welshness Performed: Welsh Concepts of Person and Society* (Tucson: U of Arizona P) and Felicia Hughes-Freeland (1998), *Ritual, Performance, Media* (London: Routledge). Also see Steven Hoelscher's 1998 book *Heritage on Stage* (Madison: U of Wisconsin P) and his essay "Where the Old South Still Lives: Displaying Heritage in Natchez, Mississippi," in Celeste Ray, ed. (2003), *Southern Heritage on Display: Public Ritual and Ethnic Diversity within Southern Regionalism* (Tuscaloosa: U of Alabama P), 218–50.

19. Tartan Day was first celebrated by the Federation of Scottish Clans in Nova

Scotia in 1986. Australia and New Zealand celebrate Tartan Day on July 1 as the anniversary of the date in 1782 when the Repeal Proclamation annulled the Act of Proscription of 1747, which had made wearing tartan an offense after Culloden.

20. The declaration was a letter dated April 6 to Pope John XXII with the seals of eight earls and thirty-one barons condemning the perfidy of the English Edward I and confirming Robert I as the rightful king of an independent Scottish nation. Ted Cowan provides further details in chapter 12.

Works Cited

Baron, Robert, and Nicholas Spitzer, eds. 1992. *Public Folklore.* Washington, DC: Smithsonian Institution Press.

Bendix, Regina. 2000. "Heredity, Hybridity, and Heritage from One Fin de Siécle to the Next." In *Folklore, Heritage Politics, and Ethnic Diversity,* ed. Pertti J. Anttonen, 37–52. Botkyrka, Sweden: Multicultural Centre.

———. 1997. *In Search of Authenticity: The Formation of Folklore Studies.* Madison: U of Wisconsin P.

Bennett, Margaret. 1998. *Oatmeal and the Catechism: Scottish Gaelic Settlers in Quebec.* Montreal: McGill-Queen's UP.

Brock, William. 1982. *Scotus Americanus: A Survey of the Sources for Links between Scotland and America in the Eighteenth Century.* Edinburgh: Edinburgh UP.

Brown, Callum. 1998. *Up-helly-aa: Custom, Culture, and Community in Shetland.* Manchester: Mandolin.

Bruce, Duncan. 1996. *The Mark of the Scots.* New York: Citadel.

Brundage, W. Fitzhugh, ed. 2000. *Where These Memories Grow: History, Memory, and Southern Identity.* Chapel Hill: U of North Carolina P.

Calder, Jenni. 2003. *Scots in Canada.* Edinburgh: Luath.

Campbell, John L. 1990. *Songs Remembered in Exile.* Aberdeen: Aberdeen UP.

Carmichael, Alexander. [1900] 1992. *Carmina Gadelica.* Edinburgh: Floris.

Cohen, Anthony. 1986. "Comment on Celtic Ethnic Kinship and the Problem of Being English." *Current Anthropology* 27, no. 4 (Aug.–Oct.): 341–42.

Cohen, Robin. 1997. "Diasporas, the Nation-State, and Globalisation." In *Global History and Migrations,* ed. Wang Gungwu, 117–44. Boulder, CO: Westview.

Cowan, Ted. 1999. "The Myth of Scotch Canada." In *Myth, Migration, and the Making of Memory: Scotia and Nova Scotia c. 1700–1990,* ed. Marjory Harper and Michael E. Vance, 49–72. Halifax, Nova Scotia: Fernwood.

Craig, Carol. 2003. *The Scots' Crisis of Confidence.* Edinburgh: Big Thinking.

Devine, Tom. 1975. *The Tobacco Lords: A Study of the Tobacco Merchants of Glasgow and Their Trading Activities, 1740–90.* Edinburgh: John Donald.

Edensor, Tim. 2002. *National Identity, Popular Culture, and Everyday Life.* Oxford: Berg.

Englund, Harri. 2002. "Ethnography after Globalism." *American Ethnologist* 29, no. 2: 261–86.

Evans, E. Estyn. 1969. "The Scotch-Irish: Their Cultural Adaptation and Heritage in the American Old West." In *Essays in Scotch-Irish History*, ed. E. R. R. Green. London: Routledge and Kegan Paul.

———. 1965. "Cultural Relics of the Ulster Scots in the Old West of North America." *Ulster Folklife* 11: 33–38.

Fry, Michael. 2003. *"Bold, Independent, Unconquer'd, and Free": How the Scots Made America Safe for Liberty, Democracy, and Capitalism.* Ayr, Scotland: Fort Publishing.

Giddens, Anthony. 1991. *Modernity and Self-Identity: Self and Society in the Late Modern Age.* Stanford, CA: Stanford UP.

Glassberg, David. 2001. *Sense of History: The Place of the Past in American Life.* Amherst: U of Massachusetts P.

Hague, Euan. 2002a. "National Tartan Day: Rewriting History in the United States." *Scottish Affairs*, no. 38 (winter): 94–124.

———. 2002b. "The Scottish diaspora: Tartan Day and the appropriation of Scottish identities in the United States." In *Celtic Geographies: Old Culture, New Times,* ed. David Harvey, Rhys Jones, Neil McInroy, and Christine Milligan, 139–56. London: Routledge.

Hall, Stuart. 1990. "Cultural Identity and Diaspora." In *Identity: Community, Culture, Difference,* ed. J. Rutherford, 222–38. London: Lawrence and Wishart.

Harper, Marjory. 2003. *Adventurers and Exiles: The Great Scottish Exodus.* London: Profile.

Harper, Marjory, and Michael E. Vance. 1999. *Myth, Migration, and the Making of Memory: Scotia and Nova Scotia, c. 1700–1990,* ed. Marjory Harper and Michael E. Vance. Halifax, Nova Scotia: Fernwood.

Herman, Arthur. 2001. *How the Scots Invented the Modern World.* New York: Three Rivers.

Hewitson, Jim. 1998. *Far Off in Sunlit Places: Stories of the Scots in Australia and New Zealand.* Edinburgh: Cannongate.

Hobsbawm, Eric, and Terence Ranger, eds. 1983. *The Invention of Tradition.* Cambridge, Eng.: Cambridge UP.

Hoelscher, Steven. 1998. *Heritage on Stage.* Madison: U of Wisconsin P.

Hook, Andrew. 1999. *From Goosecreek to Gandercleugh: Studies in Scottish-American Literary and Cultural History.* East Linton, Scotland: Tuckwell.

———. 1975. *Scotland and America: A Study of Cultural Relations, 1750–1835.* Glasgow: Blackie.

Howe, Daniel Walker. 1989. "Why the Scottish Enlightenment Was Useful to the Framers of the American Constitution." *Comparative Studies in Society and History* 31, no. 3 (July): 572–87.

Hunter, James. 1996. *Scottish Highlanders, Indian Peoples: Thirty Generations of a Montana Family.* Helena: Montana Historical Society Press.

Jackson, Anthony. 1987. *Anthropology at Home.* London: Tavistock.

Jackson, Turrentine. 1968. *The Enterprising Scot: Investors in the American West after 1873.* Edinburgh: Edinburgh UP.

Jarvie, Grant. 1991. *Highland Games: The Making of the Myth.* Edinburgh: Edinburgh UP.

Jenkins, Richard. 2002. "Imagined but Not Imaginary: Ethnicity and Nationalism in the Modern World." In *Exotic No More: Anthropology on the Front Lines,* ed. Jeremy MacClancy, 114–28. Chicago: U of Chicago P.

Jones, Maldwyn. 1969. "Ulster Emigration, 1783–1815." In *Essays in Scotch-Irish History,* ed. E. R. R. Green, 46–68. London: Routledge and Kegan Paul.

Kammen, Michael. 1991. *The Mystic Chords of Memory: The Transformation of Tradition in American Culture.* New York: Knopf.

Kerr, William Gerald. 1976. *Scottish Capital on the American Credit Frontier.* Austin: Texas State Historical Association.

Kirshenblatt-Gimblett, Barbara. 1998. "Folklore's Crisis." *Journal of American Folklore* iii, no. 441 (summer): 281–327.

Knauft, Bruce. 1996. *Genealogies for the Present in Cultural Anthropology.* New York: Routledge.

Lamont, Stewart. 2001. *When Scotland Ruled the World: The Story of the Golden Age of Genius, Creativity, and Exploration.* London: HarperCollins.

Le Roy, Bruce. 1978. *Lairds, Bards, and Mariners: The Scot in Northwest America.* Tacoma: Washington State Historical Society and the Center for Northwest Folklore.

Lipsitz, George. 1990. *Time Passages: Collective Memory and American Popular Culture.* Minneapolis: U of Minnesota P.

Lowenthal, David. 1996. *Possessed by the Past: The Heritage Crusade and the Spoils of History.* New York: Free Press.

———. 1985. *The Past Is a Foreign Country.* Cambridge, Eng.: Cambridge UP.

McArthur, Colin. 2003. *Brigadoon, Braveheart, and the Scots: Distortions of Scotland in Hollywood Cinema.* London: I. B. Tauris.

———. 1998. "Scotland May Rue the Day." *The Scotsman* (April 5), 13.

McGregor, Alexander Campbell. 1982. *Counting Sheep: From Open Range to Agribusiness on the Columbia Plateau.* Seattle: U of Washington P.

Meyer, Duane. 1957. *The Highland Scots of North Carolina, 1732–1776.* Chapel Hill: U of North Carolina P.

Nugent, Stephen, and Cris Shore, eds. 1997. *Anthropology and Cultural Studies.* London: Pluto Press.

Pittock, Murray. 2001. *Scottish Nationality.* London: Palgrave MacMillan.

———. 1991. *The Invention of Scotland: The Stuart Myth and the Scottish Identity, 1638 to the Present.* London: Routledge.

Price, Jacob. 1954. "The Rise of Glasgow in the Chesapeake Tobacco Trade, 1707–1775." *William and Mary Quarterly,* Scotland and America, 3d ser., ii, no. 2 (April): 179–99.

Ray, Celeste. 2001. *Highland Heritage: Scottish Americans in the American South.* Chapel Hill: U of North Carolina P.

Ray, Celeste, ed. 2003. *Southern Heritage on Display: Public Ritual and Ethnic Diversity within Southern Regionalism.* Tuscaloosa: U of Alabama P.

Reid, W. Stanford, ed. 1976. *The Scottish Tradition in Canada.* Toronto: McClelland and Stewart.

Samuel, Raphael, and Paul Richard Thompson, eds. 1990. *The Myths We Live By.* London: Routledge.

Sanderson, Margaret, and Alison Lindsay. 1994. *The Scots in America: Historical Background, List of Documents, Extracts and Facsimiles.* Edinburgh: Scottish Record Office.

Shepperson, George. 1954. "Writings in Scottish-American History: A Brief Survey." *William and Mary Quarterly,* Scotland and America, 3d ser., 11, no. 2 (April): 163–78.

Sher, Richard, and Jeffrey Smitten, eds. 1990. *Scotland and America in the Age of the Enlightenment.* Princeton, NJ: Princeton UP.

Sloan, Douglas. 1971. *The Scottish Enlightenment and the American College Ideal.* New York: Teachers College Press.

Smith, Anthony. 1998. *Nationalism and Modernism: A Critical Survey of Recent Theories of Nations and Nationalism.* London: Routledge.

Smith, Donald. 2001. *Storytelling Scotland: A Nation in Narrative.* Edinburgh: Polygon.

Stewart, Kathleen. 1996. *A Space on the Side of the Road.* Princeton, NJ: Princeton UP.

Stoeltje, Beverly, Christie Fox, and Stephen Olbrys. 1999. "The Self in 'Fieldwork': A Methodological Concern." *Journal of American Folklore* 112, no. 444 (spring): 158–82.

Szasz, Ferenc. 2000. *Scots in the North American West, 1790–1917.* Norman: U of Oklahoma P.

Tonkin, Elizabeth. 1990. "History and the Myth of Realism." In *The Myths We Live By,* ed. Raphael Samuel and Paul Thompson, 25–35. London: Routledge.

Turnbull, Archie. 1986. "Scotland and America, 1730–70." In *A Hotbed of Genius: The Scottish Enlightenment, 1730–1790,* eds. David Daiches, Peter Jones, and Jean Jones, 137–53. Edinburgh: Edinburgh UP.

1

Transatlantic Scots and Ethnicity

Celeste Ray

In the last half century, amid the growing discourse about globalization, the concept of "ethnicity" has supplanted other ways in which we used to describe human differences. Many scholars, and the media, seem to consider this innovative. While concern about ethnic divides on the global scale may be new, multiethnic societies are not—the first state-level societies of the Middle East were multiethnic. Interethnic relations and assimilation have likewise been a concern of state governments since their beginnings. Joshua Fishman notes that attempts to instill a sense of shared identity, rather than multiple ethnicities, has "definite Alexandrian . . . Roman . . . Western Christian . . . and Islamic precursors" (1985, 494), to which we could add Chinese and South and Central American examples as well. Yet today, less than 10 percent of nation-states are anything close to ethnically homogeneous. Ethnic differences within societies have simply taken on a different importance in post-Enlightenment times— once nation-states began to overtly embrace the notion of meritocracy; since scholars began studying power differentials relating to class, race, and gender; and perhaps after sociologists and anthropologists, among others, began investigating ethnicity as a phenomenon. Some of the interest in ethnic diversity across Europe, Australia and New Zealand, and North America relates to critiques of colonialism (and the irony of the same when immigration from former colonies impacts the societies of former colonizers). For scholars in the United States, a significant factor in our interest in ethnicity is not merely our changing expectations of immigrants (evolving from models of assimilation to pluralism to multiculturalism), but America's superpowerdom.

Partly in response to demographic changes with the immigration reform bill in 1965, and certainly by the mid-1970s, ethnicity became interesting. Heritage tourism to ancestral homelands, ethnic celebrations, and an interest in ethnic music, foodways, and material culture have become an increasingly accepted part of American life. Marilyn Halter notes that when Congress passed the Ethnic Heritage Act in 1974 to support the funding of initiatives that promote the distinctive cultures and histories of the nation's ethnic populations, the philosophy of cultural pluralism had become the "reigning paradigm" at the highest levels of government (2000, 5). Spurred by America's bicentennial celebrations and books such as Alex Haley's *Roots,* genealogy is now one of the fastest-growing hobbies in the United States. Even those whose families have been in America for over three hundred years are looking for origins and "reclaiming" what they perceive as ancestral traditions from nations where they would never be considered "hyphenated" or anything other than American.

This chapter considers the meaning of ethnicity in scholarly and popular consciousness and how it relates to Scottish Americans. Eighteenth-century Scottish immigrants were unquestionably ethnic in colonial America; are their descendants ethnic today?

Ethnicity, Symbolic Ethnicity, and Race

So, what is ethnicity? The idea of ethnicity comes from the Greek *ethnos,* meaning "people" or "nation." Herodotus flexibly described the Ionians, Dorians, Ephesians, and Kolophonians as *ethne* according to what festivals they celebrated, their mythic genealogies tracing group origins to an eponymous ancestor, shared language or dialect, and sometimes residence (Hall 1997). Today, anthropologists likewise define ethnic groups as having shared customs, religious practices, linguistic traditions, geographical origins, and, sometimes, common descent. Ethnic groups might also exhibit similar inheritance patterns and gender roles. After Frederik Barth (1969; 2000), anthropologists studying ethnicity look for recognized social boundaries between groups and describe "ethnic boundary markers" (possession of a distinctive language or dialect; a particular style of dress, music, cuisine, and religious expression), although no one of these alone defines an ethnic group. Membership in an ethnic group *may* relate to kinship and descent, but not always. Even when a belief in shared ancestry is involved in ethnic identity formation, it can be what anthropologists call "fictive kinship," and it is often mythic. As George De Vos noted, while ethnic identities can be "past-oriented," the actual history "often trails off into legend or mythology" (1975, 8–9; see also Ardener 1989 and Cannadine 2002). Ethnic groups may relate to residence, but when speaking of an ethnic group as a "community" today, we more often mean Benedict Anderson's sense of an imagined community with geographically dispersed members (1983).

Ethnic identities evolve over time and, far from being "primordial," are often quite voluntary. When an ethnic identity is claimed, those who assert it form an ethnic group. When an ethnic identity is imposed from the outside (generally on a minority group), it is an ethnic category. Occasionally an ethnic category goes through "ethnogenesis" and becomes an ethnic group—as with the labels "Hispanic" or "Latino." In eighteenth-century America, "Scottish" was an ethnic category. The ethnonym "Scotch-Irish" (Scots-Irish) was first employed to distinguish Patriot Ulster Scots from Highland Scots (mostly Loyalists) and later to distinguish between Protestant Scots from Ulster and the Catholic "Famine Irish." The American development of this ethnic group is another kind of ethnogenesis. In the late eighteenth and early nineteenth centuries, "Scots-Irish" was an "emergent ethnicity." The Scottish-American ethnic group of today may be called "resurgent," as its "ethnic identification, organization, or collective action is constructed around . . . historical identities" (Nagel 1998, 260).

While many people may reject an ethnicity they learn as children, others actively embrace one their parents, grandparents, or more distant ancestors abandoned. Whether or not someone emphasizes an ethnic identity may depend on context (the home as opposed to the office; a religious holiday as opposed to a regular worship service). A person may hold more than one ethnicity simultaneously and play on overlapping sets of loyalties and multiple identities depending on the situation, the company, or one's goals and the prestige and power, or lack thereof, connoted by an identity (see Okamura 1981). The "situational selection of ethnic identity" has been a feature of anthropological studies since E. E. Evans-Pritchard's *The Nuer* (1940; in which Dinka become Nuer) and Edmund Leach's *Political Systems of Highland Burma* (1964; in which the Kachin become Shan) (Jacobson 1979, 437). Situational selection of ethnic identity can be different from what Herbert Gans (1979) and Richard Alba refer to as "'symbolic ethnicity,' a self-conscious attempt to 'feel ethnic,' to the exclusion of 'being ethnic'" (Alba 1990, 76). However, these ideas often relate in the Scottish heritage movement. One may emphasize one's Mexican ancestry on Mexican Independence Day or even Cinco de Mayo, and also learn a song in Gaelic or practice for competitions in Scottish athletics, but otherwise live a "non-ethnic" life. One might even dress to signify a personal creole combining a sombrero and a kilt. More recently Marilyn Halter has called such expressions of identity "convenience ethnicity," an identity expressed at festivals rather than something that is overt on a daily basis (2000, 9). Affiliating with an ethnic group voluntarily may involve acquiring ethnic shibboleths or rediscovering those devalued or discarded by one's ancestors.[1]

Symbolic ethnicity is often a "nostalgic reclamation of an ethnic identity already lost." However, Richard Alba (1990), Mary Waters (1998), and Michael Hughey (1998) make a hyperbolic judgment when they claim that symbolic ethnicity categorically lacks any "reality," and that it is a "lightly worn aspect of personal identity" (Hughey 1998, 8). This denies the deep emotional investment people make in voluntary or "reclaimed" identities. While scholars may view ethnic identities as constructions or as symbolic, those who claim them often do perceive them as "primordial" or as "voices in the blood" (Gil-White 1999; Ray 2001, 13, 80–84). While those claiming a particular identity may not materially mark their ethnicity to outsiders on a daily basis, scholars cannot simply assume it is not incorporated as part of their worldview or that it is detached, or even tangential, to their daily, non-festival realities. What should be clear through discussion of empowered ethnic groups (contrasted with disempowered ethnic categories), of ethnogenesis, of emergent and resurgent ethnicities, of convenience and symbolic ethnicities, is that such identities are flexible and permeable. Ethnic identity is not set for all time. As a cultural phenomenon, ethnicity is dynamic, evolves over time, and is renegotiated in different contexts and periods (Barth 1969; Hannerz 1976; Aronson 1976; Binderman 1977; Keefe 1989; Hall 1990; Stern and Cicala 1991; Gillespie 1995; Ray 2001 and 2003). The relationship of ethnicity to other aspects of one's identity is also mutable. Currently, ethnicity is most often misassociated with "racial" identity.

Ethnicity does not mean "race." Members of different so-called races can and do belong to the same ethnic group. In the media and on government forms, the word "ethnicity" is incorrectly used interchangeably with "race." "Ethnicity" refers to cultural and social aspects of identity, not biological aspects or phenotype (physical appearance), which is the most common meaning of "race" in the United States.[2] "Race" formerly connoted "kind" or "lineage" (Banks 1996, 162). It also used to be shorthand for culture, nation, language, or people, often in connection with the spurious idea that there could be any biological predisposition to cultural distinctiveness. In the nineteenth and even early twentieth century, "race" often referred to national or regional origins: "the Scottish race" or "the Highland race" or "the house and race of Douglas." With our different histories and experiences, the British, the Canadians, and Americans use the shared English term "race" quite differently. The British still frequently employ "race" in an antiquarian sense, often referring to nationality as well as to color, but color schemes are different in Britain than in the United

States. People from India or the Middle East may be called "black" in Britain, when such a designation seems inappropriate to African Americans (see Bonilla-Silva 2003, 278). Based on cultural assumptions about physical appearance, "race" is socially constructed rather than biologically valid (see Harrison 1995 and Baker 1998). As a species, we are too evolutionarily recent to have discrete "racial" populations. (While physical human variation is arrayed on a continuum, it is impossible to disrupt that continuum into three or six or nine or more discrete groups as scholars such as Johann Herder [1744–1803] attempted to do in the Linnaean drive for classification.) We have only superficial markers on the human genome relating to aspects of appearance such as hair form and melanin production for skin and eye color, but not enough to distinguish separate subgroups one could call races. Social classifications of "race" focus predominantly on phenotype and have done so since the ancient Egyptians divided the world's people into "red" for Egyptian, "yellow" for people to the east, "white" for those to the north, and "black" for Africans from the south (Gossett 1963, 4). However, since the writings of the ancient Greeks, "ethnicity" has properly referred to identity and culture.

As we have become more aware of the repercussions of the idea of "race," through the horrors of the Nazi regime that sought to define society through racist ideology and through the struggles of the American civil rights movement to overcome racist practices (to name just two obvious examples), "ethnicity" has often been used as a more polite—or politically correct, but not actually correct—word when an author or speaker really means "race."[3] Anthropologists began using the term in the 1970s instead of "tribal," when "tribal" became perceived as negative. "Tribal" implied "isolated, primitive-atavistic, and non-Western," while "ethnic" implies "nonisolated, contemporary and universally applicable" (R. Cohen 1978, 384; see also Jenkins 2002; wa Wamwere 2003, 20).[4] Perhaps also in reaction to globalization today, scholars of many disciplines use "ethnic" or "ethnicity" when they might have employed "cultural" or "subculture" a quarter of a century ago. "Ethnicity" has come to mean distinctiveness, if variously defined.

We may dismiss any biological validity of the race concept and distinguish ethnicity as a purely cultural form of identity, but this is not how either is discussed in the media or popular culture. As geographer Wilbur Zelinsky notes of ethnic groups, sometimes "cultural commonalities believed to define the group are regarded as racial in origin. The fact that there is no anthropological basis for such a belief is irrelevant. Perception is what counts" (2001, 44). Popular culture commonly misperceives race as ethnic identity. The twentieth-century conflation of "race" with ethnicity has yielded some remarkable developments. In the United States, as Howard Winant has noted, the panethnicity of the post–civil rights era led to the racialization of what had once been recognized as distinct cultural groupings. For example, he notes that prior to the late 1960s there were no "Asian Americans." "In the wake of the civil rights movement, distinct Asian ethnic groups, primarily Chinese, Japanese, Filipino, and Korean Americans, began to frame and assert their common identity as Asian Americans. This political label reflected the similarity of treatment that these groups historically encountered at the hands of state institutions and the dominant culture at large" (1998, 200). Creating solidarity among the distinct ethnic groups of Asian origin entailed suppression of the significant historical, cultural, and linguistic differences between them in favor of a racialized identity. The social conflation of ethnicity with race is sometimes purposeful and sometimes a linguistic habit, but scholars of ethnicity have argued, in Henny-Penny-like proclamations, that it is unavoidable. The following section examines the perspectives of scholars on ethnicity in a climate of political correctness.

Ethnic Studies and Scholarly Correctness

As anthropologist Ronald Cohen remarked in 1978, "Quite suddenly, with little comment or ceremony, ethnicity is an ubiquitous presence. Even a brief glance through titles of books and monographs over the past few years indicates a steadily accelerating acceptance and application of the terms 'ethnicity' and 'ethnic' to refer to what was often subsumed under 'culture,' 'cultural,' or 'tribal'" (1978, 379). This is even truer now across disciplines. Anthropologists and sociologists may have approached ethnicity through an interest in tribes, cultures, and societies, and political scientists and historians have addressed ethnic identities through their focus on nationalism, but in the last decade we have increasingly been exploring the same subjects.[5] In the process, we are reinventing each others' wheels, failing to communicate across disciplines and self-righteously debating the supposed rights and wrongs of claiming ethnic identities in a climate of multiculturalism.[6]

Not long after the inception of America's post–World War II "ethnic revival," scholars began documenting and arguing over the cultural phenomenon. Nathan Glazer and Daniel Moynihan (1963) were among the first to point out the persistence of ethnicity despite the assimilation model. They later noted that the first dictionary appearance of "ethnicity" was in *Webster's Third New International* (1961) and that the *Oxford English Dictionary's 1972 Supplement* traces the first recorded usage of the term in recent times to David Riesman in

1953 (1975, 1). However, Werner Sollors suggests that "ethnicity" appears as early as 1941 in a study of Newburyport, Massachusetts, by W. Lloyd Warner and Paul Lunt (Sollors 1986, 23). Actually, sociologist Max Weber (1864–1920) discussed the concept by name much earlier (see his classic essay "Ethnic Groups," published posthumously in 1922 in his magnum opus *Economy and Society* and reproduced in Hughey 1998).

While approaches to ethnicity have greatly varied across disciplines, anthropologist Frederik Barth is the most frequently cited scholar of ethnicity. Barth has discussed ethnicity as a cultural identity rooted in descent and place, yet has argued that ethnicity endures, not as a static identity produced in isolation, but as a dynamic identity constantly renegotiated through time. Barth's work asserts that the consciously maintained boundaries of ethnic groups are what remain even while the ethnic identity itself may evolve (1969). Like Barth, George De Vos argued in 1975 that "how and why boundaries are maintained, rather than the cultural content of the separated group, are what one must examine in the study of ethnic relations" (6). Their works have influenced social scientists' perspective of ethnicity as political. But those who have taken this approach have largely ignored Barth's other points that ethnic identities are not necessarily exclusionary, but can include "overlapping sets of ascriptive loyalties" that make for multiple identities (1969, 20–23). Ethnicities often are, but need not solely or only be, constructed vis-à-vis another group's hegemonic identity. As Cohen also noted, interethnic relations are not always based on inequities between groups, and "anthropological data do not support the notion that ethnicity is simply an aspect of social stratification" (1978, 394; see also Hartigan 2003, 96). In other disciplines, ethnicity has most commonly been discussed as a political identity in relation to class, racial, or other potential social conflicts and viewed as negative when embraced by a privileged group and viewed positively as "resistance" when embraced by an unprivileged group.

Class and power differentials exist within ethnic groups as well as between them. Ethnicity used to be associated with the lower classes. In her book *Shopping for Identity*, however, Marilyn Halter examines consumerism and the commodification of ethnicity and argues that "ethnic identification has become an indicator of economic success and integration . . . Getting ahead financially and getting back to one's cultural roots are perfectly compatible personal aspirations in America today" (2000, 10; see also Wells 1990). In fact, she goes on to quote the work of Lawrence Fuchs (1997), that among whites, "a complete reversal has occurred in the relationship of ethnic identification to social class." The 1990 U.S. census indicated that those who identified as "American" rather than being of an ethnic background had higher rates of poverty, and only 10 percent had a college education, compared with 25 percent of those who reported a specific ancestry (Halter 2000, 11). That Americans could check more than one ethnic identity in the 2000 census made the news, but increasingly Americans are identifying not only as ethnic but as multiethnic. And Scottish Americans not only celebrate Scottish roots but may also claim to be German-, Italian-, African-, or Mexican-Scottish Americans.

For those perceiving ethnicity as primarily political, the failure of the melting pot was considered a problem—"an ethnic problem." The 1960s and 1970s then witnessed a move from assimilationist models for immigrants to ideas of pluralism. In the 1980s and 1990s, Americans discarded pluralism (a coexistence and toleration of difference) for multiculturalism (a celebration of difference). Today the idea of ethnicity is cozier and more user-friendly than it was a quarter of a century ago. Americans now buy ethnic foods in grocery stores, wear ethnic clothes, decorate their homes in international ethnic pastiches, and often assume that multiculturalism means nonracism as if ethnicity meant "race."

Among the scholars tracing revivals of ethnic identities were, and are, those willing to grant legitimacy to some but not others. Some ethnic movements are deemed a triumph over repression, and others are judged a negative and racist response to the civil rights movement (rather than consonant with the spirit of the times). One of the especially amusing and moralistic condemnations of what authors called "white ethnics" was offered by Howard Stein and Robert Hill as a "psychosocial study of the white ethnic cultural movement" in which European ethnicities are defined as "self-deception" and "delusional" (1977, 9). Introducing their volume, Weston La Barre compares their work to "salvage ethnography" (collecting the remains of tradition before it disappears) and notes that such study in Europe and among European Americans is "hardly worth fieldwork" (ix). La Barre praised Stein and Hill: "What a satisfaction to find the word *ironic* properly used!" (ix). However, they did not realize the irony of their own arguments. Their views reflect the ultimate ethnocentric and Eurocentric perspective of the anthropological lens as valid only for the study of the "other" (for Stein and Hill, non-Europeans). They would be willing, as many social scientists remain willing, to adopt a quite WASPy definition of ethnicity, critiqued back in 1976 by Ulf Hannerz for implying that ethnicity is a quality "which is absent among Anglo-Saxons; which . . . increases among Americans of European descent as you pass over the map of Europe from the northwest toward the southeast; and which is very strong among people of non-European ancestry" (431).[7] Hannerz notes that while their relationships to the common societal arena might differ, no group of people is any more or any less ethnic than any other. In the contemporary sociopolitical climate, Americans are happily and purposefully exoticizing their perceived identities to demonstrate just how ethnic they can be. In their conclusion Stein and Hill claim, "Anthropology, like American culture in general, is woefully misguided if it embraces ethnicity as the wave of the future" (287)—yet, almost thirty years after their publication, ethnic movements remain more vibrant than ever.[8]

I give this lengthy example from the 1970s because it largely characterizes the scholarship about European ethnic revivals in America of that period. When pluralism was a newly discovered answer to the assimilationist model, scholars critiqued the celebration of ethnicity by those they considered "non-ethnic" whites. Although anthropologists and historians have since deconstructed notions of Eurocentrism, otherness, and "the exotic," these ideas still arise in more recent studies of European-American identities, most often with the judgment-implicit label of "whiteness studies."[9] The very concept of "white ethnics," employed perhaps first by Novak in 1972 (and also Stein and Hill 1977; Alba 1990; and Ignatieff 1993, 8) and subsequent "whiteness studies," simply reinforces Eurocentric notions that "white" is the unchanging norm and only nonwhites can legitimately be ethnic. While Canadians chose the metaphor of a "mosaic" to describe their ethnic mix, Americans (perhaps being more obsessed with food) unfortunately chose the salad. I say unfortunately because "who actually likes salad?" and also because the assumption within the metaphor is that "white people" are all lettuce (and not interesting romaine, mesclun, endive, or arugula, but iceberg).

Today's multiculturalism is not simply an extension of cultural pluralism. As sociologist Michael Hughey has remarked:

> Cultural pluralism advocated a kind of ecumenical framework in which ethno-racial identities would be tolerated and valued as different but still fellow worshipers at the altar of Americanism. Multiculturalism, at least in some versions, so exalts group identities that it offers no program or framework for the integration of groups into a larger unity.
>
> Multiculturalism finds expression both as an ideological romanticization and exaltation of minority group identities and as an assertion of minority claims against the traditional Anglo-Protestant majority by virtue of an aggressive devaluation of its culture as inherently oppressive. In pursuit of this agenda, for example, multiculturalists cultivate a linguistic moralism or etiquette of public discourse (one aspect of "political correct-

ness") in which all ethno-racial identities are proclaimed to be equally positive, all valuable and cherished possessions (except for the Anglo-Protestant). (1998, 7; see also Devine 1996 and Wood 2003)

Whiteness studies of the last decade are in some ways a return to the 1970s critique of "white ethnics." Sociologist Mary Waters believes symbolic ethnicity "persists because of its ideological 'fit' with racist beliefs," but she suggests this only for northern European symbolic ethnicities (1998, 273). She proposes that claims to identity are always in response to social threats or change. Undoubtedly some are; the nativist development of Protestant Orange Lodges in North America and their discriminatory politics in response to Irish Catholic immigration are mentioned later in this chapter. Symbolic ethnicities are often past-focused. When we choose to remember a selected past in a similar way, we celebrate our unity, but in doing so we emphasize what divides us from all of those with other memories or perhaps a different memory of the same selected past.[10] Surely some involved in ethnic revivals were attempting to redefine themselves in a new way in response to social changes resulting from the civil rights movement or the militancy of the Black Power movement. As Joshua Fishman noted: "The rising tide of Black pride should not be ignored as a stimulant for the white ethnic revival, but neither should it be overstressed" (1985, 508). To view ethnic revivals as simply mechanistic responses to race relations is absurdly reductionistic. Yet, anthropologist Roger Sanjek has written of his remarkable epiphany that "white ethnic persistence was a hoax," and that he "was delighted with the title of Richard Alba's revisionist paper 'The Twilight of Ethnicity among American Catholics of European Ancestry'" (1994, 9).[11] Identity movements cannot be studied in a vacuum; they respond to multiple factors. To say that "white ethnics" are simply asserting an ethnicity as a "backlash to multiculturalism" is to ignore several interesting facets of identity; first, these ethnics are attempting to avoid being identified as majority WASPs; second, American history has been punctuated by cyclical patterns of ethnic awareness and celebration; third, assertion of hyphenated identities in our particular time period relates to the high American profile globally; and lastly, some so-called white ethnics do have a transgenerational sense of distinctive origins and heritage.

In his book *Racial and Ethnic Groups*, sociologist Richard Schaefer claims, "The ethnicity of the 1990s embraced by English-speaking whites . . . does not include active involvement in ethnic activities or participation in ethnic-related organizations" (1996, 127). The following accounts of Scottish Americans and Canadians focus on North Americans of European descent who actively celebrate their ethnic awareness through centuries-old, and brand-new, heritage societies and organizations. Hyphenated Scots maintain transnational links with the homeland through genealogical research, educational exchange, and heritage tourism. They follow Scottish rules and standards for ethnic events and competitions in expressive cultural forms, and bring teachers and judges across from Scotland to facilitate the same. They also maintain transatlantic connections by importing Scottish speakers, ministers, and traditions such as the Highland games, invented or reinvented in Scotland after their ancestors left. The ethnic revival of the 1960s and 1970s is not the "last gasp of white ethnicity," as many social scientists forecasted (Stein and Hill 1977; Patterson 1979; Steinberg 1981; Bausinger 1983; Fishman 1985). On nearly every weekend of the summer and fall, a Scottish Highland games, with its accompanying clan gatherings, *ceilidhs* (evening socializing and singing), dancing and piping, harp and fiddle competitions, happens somewhere in America and Canada. These events draw thousands of participants; one weekend games event at Grandfather Mountain in North Carolina sees well over thirty thousand participants annually—hardly a "gasp."

Over ten million Americans claim to be of Scottish descent. For many, a Scottish-American identity is recently reclaimed (a symbolic or resurgent ethnicity). However, we cannot dismiss the very real sense of fellowship and community provided to hyphenated Scots in the hundreds of thousands through local, regional, and national heritage organizations, regular gatherings, and print literature (such as society newsletters and community-wide newspapers). The Scottish-American community may be imagined in Benedict Anderson's sense, yet it has physical actualization not only at ethnic festivals but through the forging of new communities based on shared interests. Scottish ethnic and heritage revivals respond to postmodern phenomena, but in many locations settled by Scottish immigrants, they also draw upon centuries-old transmission of cultural traditions. While ethnicity may be "optional" for many Americans, the selection of identities and their renegotiation is revealing, not only of how Americans perceive each other, but of our particular moment in history.

Scottish Americans

The hyphenated Scottish community is difficult to stereotype. It consists of liberals and conservatives, members of varied socioeconomic backgrounds and occupations, Christians and neo-Pagans, retirees and teenagers, and those with multiple ethnic backgrounds, who, despite their diverse political and religious perspectives, nevertheless feel linked through a sense of kinship and love of things Scottish. Heritage events and ethnic organizations involve Americans and Canadians with a transgenerational awareness of their Scottish ancestry who have learned about their Scottish roots from their families, and also those who have not even had a Scottish surname in their family for five generations. Some become involved in Scottish heritage because their spouse has a Scottish surname, or because someone in her or his ancestry did. Others have no discernible Scottish links and simply join out of interest, yet choose a tartan and a clan society or heritage group to join. A hyphenated Scottish ethnicity often relates to one's family tradition, but for many, specifically affiliating with a particular clan heritage (or joining several clan societies) just as often adds an optional dimension to an "inherited" identity.

While sporadic commemoration has existed in Scots-settled communities that maintain a strong sense of roots, the spectacular latter-twentieth-century growth of the Scottish heritage movement means that many participants are seeking a symbolic ethnicity.[12] For those with links to one of the colonial Scottish settlements or who otherwise know family immigration histories, swapping tales of ancestral origins in Scotland is a typical conversation starter at heritage events. When two MacNeils meet, introductory exchanges may involve noting if one's MacNeils were from Barra or South Uist. "My MacKinnons are from Mull," "Mine are from Skye" will be followed with place-specific lore (and perhaps a comment or two about the Macleans who also lived in these areas and with whom both groups of MacKinnons regularly feuded.) These types of exchanges often leave the Smith or the Clerk or the Forrester (or those with other occupational names found throughout Scotland, Ireland, Wales, and England and who are just happy to be "Scottish") at a loss, but not without a tartan.

Newly reborn Scots tend to place a special emphasis on the long loss of "tradition" and ancestral grievances. Those claiming Scottish origins after discovering a Scottish surname in their genealogies also tend to display tartan with more enthusiasm than those with a transgenerational awareness of their Scottish ancestry. Part of the appeal of the heritage movement is perhaps that Scottish Americans are one of the few groups of European Americans who can trace their tribal origins, albeit selectively. The Highland clans were a chiefdom-level society, but informants liberally use the term "tribal" in describing their ancestral past. As "ethnicity" replaced the term "tribal" in academia, "tribal" acquired currency in popular culture.

Each of the last few centuries have witnessed reactions through expressive culture to new socioeconomic developments. Partly in response to the new industrialism in the late eighteenth century, romanticism flourished in the arts and literature; while the nineteenth century witnessed a drive for "progress," it also saw the Pre-Raphaelite Brotherhood, the Arts and Crafts Movement, and Highlandism. In the heart of the technological age, a "modern primitives" movement began in North America and Europe (see also Berger, et al. 1973; Lears 1981; Vale and Juno 1989; Giddens 1991; Latour 1993; McKay 1994; Lowenthal 1996; Institute for Cultural Research Monograph 2000). While largely urban in its origins, this very postmodern movement embraced romanticized visions of primitiveness easily transportable to everyday life, if not the office, from body piercing to music to primal screaming therapy, as expressive responses to what has been called "postmodern alienation" (a lack of community, frustration over changes in gender roles and family structures, and globalization). Such social movements often start out seeming wildly radical at the time (for example, the architect and critic Augustus Welby Northmore Pugin [1812–1852] wanting to return to Gothic architecture and the Roman Catholic church in 1840s Victorian England). However, some aspects of social movements deemed most shocking can eventually become somewhat mainstream. (Middle-aged women and "grannies" got haircuts in the 1990s that had been punk in the early 1980s; teenagers in Alpine villages now wear multiple eyebrow and nose piercings with their dirndls in saints' feast day processions). Attending a recent Highland games, I enjoyed watching a Glasgow-based drumming group named *Clann an Drumma,* whose lightly clad and luxuriantly long-haired dancing performers reminded the crowd to "Keep it Tribal."[13] As a people watcher, I could not help but be entertained by the disgust of cultural purists who were disappointed that the band attracted a larger crowd than the Gaelic *Mòd* (a competition in singing and poetry). But what I enjoyed most was watching the vigorous toe-tapping of Presbyterian ladies old enough to have been shocked by the gyrations of Elvis and the hairstyles of the Beatles.

Hyphenated Scots and a "Celtic" Ethnicity

Nineteenth-century Americans devised many and varied celebrations of Scottish origins and heritage, most commonly focusing on an Anglo-Saxon identity rather than the Celtic one embraced today. Part of the reason Scots evolved from an ethnic category to exemplary Americans was by contrast with the "foreignness" of more recently arriving immigrants of rural, peasant, unskilled, non-English-speaking, and Catholic or Jewish backgrounds.

America's nineteenth-century Protestant Orangemen sought to distinguish themselves from anything Celtic. As an ethnic group, the nineteenth-century

Scots-Irish were notoriously antiforeigner (supporting "Know-Nothing" groups), and in northern urban areas (especially Pittsburgh, Philadelphia, and New York) the Scots-Irish were leaders in the American anti-Catholic movement of the 1840s and 1850s. In response to increasing "Celtic" or "Native" (Catholic) Irish immigrants, the urban Scots-Irish imported the Orange Order to American cities (the first lodge began in 1867 in New York; others soon developed in Boston, Philadelphia, and Pittsburgh (Berthoff 1953, 190–91; see also McCauley 1990).[14]

In 1928, when North Carolina's governor Angus McLean unveiled a monument to the MacNeills in the town of Red Springs (in the heart of a colonial Highlander settlement), he referred to them as "a branch of the great Anglo-Saxon family" (Corbitt 1931, 444). However, in today's Scottish heritage movement, participants conceive of themselves as definitely NOT Anglo-Saxon, but as something quite distinct from WASPs in both American ethnic hierarchies and in relation to ancient histories of oppression—as Celts. This Celtic thesis began to gain ground in the 1970s, partly in response to critical historiography and sociology about the American experience leading up to and after the bicentennial celebrations. In the 1970s, distinguishing oneself as ethnic became not only acceptable in a pluralistic United States but interesting and desirable as well.[15]

The 1980s and 1990s have seen the latest Celtic revival of identities and expressive culture. Such revivals have been happening since at least the late 1100s in Ireland—the best known being that of the late nineteenth and early twentieth centuries inspired by nationalism, civil rights movements (for land reform, voting rights, and linguistic freedoms), and by artists and poets such as William Butler Yeats. (Luckily for Ireland it had a Yeats instead of a Walter Scott.) Scotland had its own Celtic arts revival at the same time period that partially fostered the neo-Jacobite movements of the 1890s and the pre–World War I era, but that revival never assisted the cause for nationalism in Scotland as the Celtic revival had in Ireland. Things Celtic have again become fashionable in popular culture on both sides of the Atlantic, from folk music, dance, and art to new-age constructions of "Celtic" religious rituals and beliefs (although Druidic lore was oral, not written, and therefore cannot be "revived"). At the same time as the general public actually became interested in their work, archaeologists were engaged in a passionate debate throughout the 1990s as to whether Iron Age inhabitants of Britain and Ireland were actually "Celts." Despite the survival of Celtic languages in the islands, similarities in island and continental material culture, and the fact that early medieval Irish and Welsh literature yields striking parallels with ethnographic accounts of pre-Roman continental Celts, the debate fixates on the likelihood that a Celtic elite may have invaded/ruled the islands without being representative of the population, much like the latter Normans, and on a lack of evidence for islanders having *called themselves* Celts.[16] As to any genetic legacy, Bryan Sykes and his research team at the Institute of Molecular Medicine at Oxford University have recently suggested that 99 percent of British and Irish people share an essentially Paleolithic gene pool, little impacted by later arrivals such as the Celts, Romans, Angles, Saxons, Jutes, Vikings, or Normans. Will, or how will, popular culture respond to such revelations? The lesser-known and less-romanticizable Paleolithic ancestors whose DNA still dominates the British gene pool are (so far) hardly an appealing source of identity.[17]

Antiquarian scholarship inspired the poets, novelists, and artists who popularized things Celtic in the nineteenth century, as more recent scholarship has similarly done in the latter twentieth century. Celtic imagery also had political uses in both periods' revivals, most recently for François Mitterand poignantly delivering a speech from the Iron Age fortress site at Bibracte (Crumley and Marquardt 1987); for the Irish Republican Army; for the Scottish National Party; for white supremacist groups; and for those trying to distance themselves from white supremacists in the United States (the varied political agendas of the above are not in any way paralleled here). How will scholarly denials of an Iron Age Celtic people inhabiting the islands influence today's perceptions of Celtic identities, of "the island Celts" as a colonized people, and of those constructed as the non-Celtic "other"? Throughout the last two decades, cultural "purists" have argued that one must speak a Celtic language to be a "Celt." Does one ethnic boundary marker, language, alone constitute ethnicity? Must one's Iron Age ancestors be "verified" Celts for one to claim a Celtic identity today? If, as Sykes's DNA studies suggest, neither the Celts nor the Anglo-Saxons left any substantial genetic impact on British population, does this matter for the contemporary claiming of ethnicity?[18] No. Ethnicity is about culture, not biology. Those claiming an ethnic identity may assume it has a biological component (through kinship and descent), but apparently anthropologists must still fight the racist assumption that culture is in the genes. That those claiming a Celtic identity today may not have a Celtic gene pattern matters little; culture is learned. As archaeologist Barry Cunliffe (1997) has remarked, "Perhaps the only real definition of a Celt, now as in the past, is that a Celt is a person who believes him or herself to be Celtic."[19] Culture may be an intellectual inheritance, but individuals and groups learn and renegotiate identities from day to day and century to century. In the last two decades social scientists have delighted in debunking invented traditions, granting legitimacy to some and denying the value or political correctness of others. What matters more is understanding why people embrace the visions of ethnicity that they do, how they learn them, and what roles identities and heritage play in structuring their realities in particular contexts and periods.

Ethnic Diversity among Hyphenated Scots

Since the late 1990s, English and Scottish journalists have made a genre out of articles that simplistically link the Scottish heritage movement in the United States to a white supremacists' conspiracy.[20] Celebration of a particular identity does not mechanically lead to supremacist ideologies; or what have we set ourselves up for with our well-meaning multiculturalism? Undoubtedly the celebration of any heritage can foster hatred of any "other," but the vast majority of Scottish Americans are not celebrating "whiteness." That white supremacists would be attracted to the heritage of people who happen to be white is obvious, but such creatures are not the organizers of Scottish heritage events, nor are they representative of the hundreds of thousands of participants in the Scottish heritage movement across North America.

Increasingly, ethnic celebrations focus on a fusion of identities and expressive cultures such as "Afro-Celt" music, which is popular with younger participants at Scottish heritage events. Those of multiple backgrounds are exploring the ethnic heritages not necessarily obvious by their physical appearance and tracing genealogies that were once downplayed when "racial" exogamy was considered, or even outlawed as, "miscegenation." Edward Ball's best-selling *Slaves in the Family* (1998) examines little-acknowledged or long-denied kinship links between his family and descendants of former Ball slaves. In the way that Alex Haley's *Roots* fostered America's post-bicentennial genealogy craze, Ball's work has helped to pique public interest in hidden histories and in familial relationships across the socially constructed "racial" divides that have characterized the bulk of U.S. history.

Those who on government forms or by popular classifications might be considered ethnically "African" or "Asian" are today tracing specific ethnic heritages within the European sides of their families. While bundles of hyphens become more linguistically awkward, they are becoming less socially so. While they may have been reluctant to attend twenty years ago, African-European Americans attended the 2004 annual homecoming at Long Street Presbyterian Church (founded in 1756) to remember their McArthur ancestors who were part of the Scottish Highlander settlement in North Carolina's Cape Fear Valley and to whom other, "white," participants were also related. As I have noted

Fig. 2. Xavier Allen bass drumming at the Saline
Celtic Fest, Michigan (Photo courtesy of Xavier Allen)

above, a person may have more than one ethnic identity and heritage and may share ethnic identity with those of different socially designated "races."

Many African Americans have Scottish ancestry, and they are also members of clan societies, bagpipe bands, and Scottish history reenactment societies. While participants identify themselves as "African Scots," one native of North Carolina, Xavier Allen, who is an accomplished Highland dancer and drummer for a pipe band, self-identifies as a "Caribbean Highlander." Harrison Bailey III of Easton, Pennsylvania, is a record setter in international Scottish heavy athletic competitions. First Sergeant Dwayne Farr, an African American from Detroit, Michigan, made the international news in April 2004 playing his bagpipes in Fallujah, Iraq. From Corinth, Mississippi, Gustavus Arius McLeod is of African, Scottish, and Choctaw descent and has been to the MacLeod homelands on the Isle of Skye and met the clan chief. In 1999 he became the first person to fly to the magnetic North Pole in an open-cockpit airplane. A bagpiper played at his takeoff, and McLeod wore his kilt when his aircraft was hung at the College Park Aviation Museum in Maryland (McLeod 2002, 2004).

In the American South, where I have done my fieldwork, Native American Scots may send their children to both Highland dancing competitions at Scottish games and Native American dancing competitions at powwows. The many historical links between Scots and American Indians find expression in clan tent displays at Highland games, story and song, and elaborate fusions of a Plains headdress, a Creek beadwork belt, or leather leggings with tartan.

Several generations of Mexican-Scottish Americans and other Hispanic-Scottish Americans who regularly attend Scottish events, are members of clan and heritage societies and bagpipe bands, and playfully refer to themselves as "Taco Tartans." Amy Krueger has an American mother and an Arab father and finds that her interests in her Scottish background have made her "a different person by being diversified." Because of the history of colonialism, many immigrants to the United States from India also have Scottish ancestry, and Chandra Wallace wears a sari of the colors of her clan's tartan.

As ethnic exogamy becomes more common and more accepted, the shape of ethnic heritage celebrations in the twenty-first century will no doubt be quite different from those of the 1960s and 1970s. As people examine branches of their family trees that may have been downplayed or severed, or that might not correlate in the popular imagination with their phenotype, some scholars might consider their identities a symbolic or optional ethnicity. However, the abiding interests in, and emotional commitments to, a heritage should not be so lightly dismissed.

Notes

1. For a small sampling on other enduring ethnic groups in North America, see Spickard and Fong 1995; Schultz 1994; Lindenfeld 2000; Patterson 1976; Fugita and O'Brien 1991; Petrissans 1991; Halter 1993; and Wong 1998.

2. Lawrence Fuchs has noted that "race" first appeared in the U.S. census in 1870. Prior to this, slaves (assumed to be black) were not counted, but "free persons of color" had been counted since 1820. The U.S. Census Bureau further divided this category into "white, black or mulatto" for free persons in 1850 (1997, 24).

3. Sociologist Steve Fenton (2003, 54) notes that Julian Huxley and A. C. Haddon suggested replacing the term "race" with "ethnic groups" as early as 1935 in their book *We Europeans: A Survey of "Racial" Problems* (New York: Harper).

4. "Tribe" comes from Latin "tribus meaning barbarians at the borders of the

empire" (R. Cohen 1978, 384). Now a Member of Parliament in Kenya, Koigi wa Wamwere clearly distinguishes between *ethnicity* (belonging to a particular ethnic group and having pride in that group) and *tribalism* (despising, attacking, or discriminating against others based on their ethnicity). He notes that nonacademic Africans use "tribalism" in daily conversation, while scholars (who reject "tribalism" as a racist and Eurocentric term) simply use "ethnicity" to describe both identity and hatred and bias. He advocates replacing "tribalism" with "negative ethnicity" (2003, 20–24).

5. For works on ethnicity and nationalism, see Alonso 1994; Nairn 1977, 1997; Hechter 1975; Gellner 1983; Eriksen 1993; Smith 1986, 1998, 1999, 2000; Billig 1995; A. Cohen 1985; Calhoun 1993; Gorski 2000; Jenkins 2002; McCrone 1998; Fry 2003; Ascherson 2002; Schlesinger 1992; Ellis 1998; Kellas 1998; Hearn 2000; McPherson 1999; and Thomas 1992. For a good survey of theories of nationalism, see Edensor 2002.

6. The development of ethnic identity and ethnic studies is quite different in Canada. I comment only on the United States here. Documenting the evolving debates about assimilation, pluralism, and multiculturalism are beyond the scope of any footnote and most of the books that have tried. For summarizing works about thoughts on American ethnicity, consult Nathan Glazer and Daniel P. Moynihan 1963 (an influential and much-critiqued volume, its main problem lies in only examining New York City and offering spurious generalizations to America as a nation—something subsequent writers have done much more so than the authors) and 1975; De Vos and Romanucci-Ross 1975; Hannerz 1976; Epstein 1978; Kottak and Kozaitis 1987; Sollors 1986, 1989; Roosens 1989; Alba 1990; Waters 1990; Hollinger 1995; and Zelinsky 2001. For an excellent summary of thought about race and ethnicity in both the United States and Britain, see Banks 1996.

7. In his 1972 book, *The Rise of Unmeltable Ethnics* (rereleased in 1996), Michael Novak even went so far as to define American "ethnics" as "descendants of immigrants of southern and eastern Europe: Poles, Italians, Greeks and Slavs." He further noted that American ethnics also "include, of course," Armenians, Lebanese, Slovenes, Ruthenians, Croats, Serbs, Czechs, Slovaks, Lithuanians, Estonians, Russians and Spanish, and the Portuguese completed his list (1996, 55).

8. Likewise, Joshua Fishman, before he could anticipate multiculturalism and without realizing the enduring revivals of hyphenated identities centuries in the shaping, wrote the following: "There is a vast amount of evidence pointing to the conclusion that an 'ethnic revival' of sorts occurred in the U.S.A. between the mid-sixties and the mid-seventies and that it had significantly declined by the late seventies . . . by the late 1970s and early 1980s, the 'ethnic boom' seemed to have subsided very considerably" (1985, 489–90).

9. The Irish-American experience is usually conceptualized in terms of the Irish being denied and then "achieving" "whiteness." Especially see Michael Hout and Joshua R. Goldstein (1994), "How 4.5 Million Irish Immigrants Became 40 Million Irish Americans: Demographic and Subjective Aspects of the Ethnic Composition of White Americans," in *American Sociological Review* 59, no. 1 (Feb.), 64–82; Noel Ignatiev (1995), *How the Irish Became White* (New York: Routledge); and Bronwen Walter

(2001), *Outsiders Inside: Whiteness, Place, and Irish Women* (New York: Routledge). For other readings on whiteness, see also Ware and Back 2002; Grace Elizabeth Hale (1998), *Making Whiteness: the Culture of Segregation in the South, 1890–1940* (New York: Pantheon); Beth Kolko, Lisa Nakamura, and Gilbert Rodman, eds. (2000), *Race in Cyberspace* (New York: Routledge); David R. Roediger (1991), *The Wages of Whiteness: Race and the Making of the American Working Class* (London: Verso). Italian American identities have been similarly scrutinized; see *Are Italians White?: How Race Is Made in America* (2003), ed. Jennifer Guglielmo and Salvatore Salerno (New York: Routledge).

10. As anthropologist Paul Shackel concisely puts it, "Memory can be about (1) forgetting about or excluding an alternative past, (2) creating and reinforcing patriotism, and/or (3) developing a sense of nostalgia to legitimize a particular heritage" (2001, 665).

11. Alba's paper appeared in 1981 in *Annals of American Academy of Political and Social Sciences* 454: 86–97. Another version, titled "The Twilight of Ethnicity among Americans of European Ancestry: The Case of Italians," appeared in his 1985 edited collection *Ethnicity and Race in the U.S.A.: Toward the Twenty-first Century* (London: Routledge and Kegan Paul).

12. Americans of Scottish descent retained a sense of Scottish identity through the eighteenth and nineteenth centuries. Documentable Highland games began in America in the 1830s. Scots immigrants celebrated Queen Victoria's marriage with a forty-eight-hour street party in New York in 1840 (Donaldson 1986, 12–13; Hewitson 1993, x). Almost two hundred years after a Scots Charitable Society was founded in Boston in 1657 (to ease the plight of Cromwellian prisoners), 1853 saw the founding of the first United States Caledonian Club. In 1866 in Pulaski, Tennessee, Confederate veterans of Scottish origin formed the Ku Klux Klan with rituals inspired by a variety of European romanticisms, the most infamous of which (such as the burning cross) were Scottish.

13. It is a curious point in world history when tribal peoples seek democratization while those in democracies romantically seek retribalization (at least on the weekends).

14. For an account of violent Irish/Scots-Irish ethnic conflict in New York City, see Michael Gordon (1993), *The Orange Riots: Irish Political Violence in New York City, 1870 and 1871* (Ithaca, NY: Cornell UP).

15. The idea of a Celtic identity has caught on across the country, but in the southern region it has been advanced in scholarly circles. While the following make claims for cultural continuities that anthropologists find untenable, their assertions of an ethnically "Celtic" South have appeal for some members of the general public. Forrest McDonald and Ellen Shapiro McDonald (1980), "The Ethnic Origins of the American People, 1790," *William and Mary Quarterly* 37: 179–99; Forrest McDonald and Grady McWhiney (1975), "The Antebellum Southern Herdsman: A Reinterpretation," *Journal of Southern History* 41: 147–66; Forrest McDonald and Grady McWhiney (1985), "Celtic Origins of Southern Herding Practices," *Journal of Southern History* 51: 165–82; Grady McWhiney (1988), *Cracker Culture: Celtic Ways in the Old South* (Tuscaloosa: U of Alabama P); James Michael Hill (1986), *Celtic Warfare*

(Edinburgh: John Donald); and Grady McWhiney and Perry Jamieson (1982), *Attack and Die: Civil War Military Tactics and the Southern Heritage* (University: U of Alabama P). Rowland Berthoff wrote against this school of thought in a 1986 article for the *Journal of Southern History* titled "Celtic Mist over the South" (vol. 52, no. 4: 523–46), the response from Forrest McDonald and Grady McWhiney follows on 547–48). Apart from this school, but echoing a few similar ideas that Scots-Irish identity and "mentality" derive from millennia of cultural continuity is Rodger Cunningham's (1987) *Apples on the Flood: Minority Discourse and Appalachia* (Knoxville: U of Tennessee P).

16. For the recent debate on Celtic identity (initiated by anthropologist Malcolm Chapman, 1978 and 1992), see Pittock 1999; James 1998, 1999; Cunliffe 1992, 2001; Jones 1997; Ruth and Vincent Megaw 1996, 2002; Creighton 2000; Hill 1989; Collis 1997, 2003; and Green 1999. Pittock notes that most of these debates neglect "the Celts" as an imagined community (1999, 6).

17. However, DNA studies can identify Paleolithic migrations, and in his 2001 book *The Seven Daughters of Eve: The Science That Reveals Our Genetic Ancestry,* (New York: W. W. Norton) Bryan Sykes traces all contemporary European genes back to seven women living between 45,000 and 15,000 years ago. For a fee, one can have one's DNA traced to one of these seven "tribes," and the interested public is falling into DNA genealogy with the enthusiasm of nineteenth-century phrenologists.

18. Other interpreters of genetic data (related to family, rather than Iron Age groups) hope to profit by linking genes to "family tartans." In 2004, neuroscientists from Glasgow University established a company called "Crucial Genetics," hoping to build a database with genetic patterns for different surnames. Kiltmakers and tartan shops anticipate climbing sales as they envision being able to tell North Americans which tartans they can buy. The Sobieski-Stuarts must be laughing in their graves.

19. John Collis tells us that the idea of Iron Age inhabitants of Britain being Celtic arose only in the sixteenth century and became popular in the eighteenth century though the study of linguistics. However, we do not know if language was the primary criteria used by ancient authors to define Celts. In any case, Collis and others note that the classical writers did not refer to the Celtic-speaking inhabitants of Britain as Celts (1997, 28–29).

20. For example, see Nigel Hawkes (1999) "Racists Scots in U.S. Have Links to SNP," in *The Times,* January 8; and Hamish Macdonell (2004) "Racists Target U.S.-Scots' Festivals," in *The Scotsman,* April 20 (and Macdonell has been at this for a while). See also a similar article on the Scottish National Party (1999), "Nationalists Link to U.S. Racists Claim," in *The Daily Mail,* January 9; Noel Young and Peter Laing (1999) "Ku Klux Klan 'Hijacked' Braveheart," in *Scotland on Sunday (The Scotsman),* November 28.

Works Cited

Alba, Richard. 1990. *Ethnic Identity: The Transformation of White America.* New Haven, CT: Yale UP.

Alonso, Ana Maria. 1994. "The Politics of Space, Time, and Substance: State Formation, Nationalism, and Ethnicity." *Annual Review of Anthropology* 23: 379–405.

Anderson, Benedict. 1983. *Imagined Communities.* London: Verso.

Ardener, Edwin. 1989. "The Construction of History: 'Vestiges of Creation.'" In *History and Ethnicity,* ed. Elizabeth Tonkin, et al., 22–33. London: Routledge.

Aronson, Dan. 1976. "Ethnicity as a Cultural System: An Introductory Essay." In *Ethnicity in the Americas,* ed. Frances Henry, 9–22. The Hague: Mouton.

Ascherson, Neal. 2002. *Stone Voices: The Search for Scotland.* New York: Hill and Wang.

Baker, Lee. 1998. *From Savage to Negro: Anthropology and the Construction of Race, 1896–1954.* Berkeley: U of California P.

Banks, Marcus. 1996. *Ethnicity: Anthropological Constructions.* London: Routledge.

Barth, Frederik. 2000. "Boundaries and Connections." In *Signifying Identities: Anthropological Perspectives on Boundaries and Contested Values,* ed. Anthony Cohen, 17–36. London: Routledge.

———. 1969. "Introduction." In *Ethnic Groups and Boundaries: The Social Organization of Cultural Difference,* ed. Frederik Barth, 9–38. Boston: Little, Brown.

Bausinger, Hermann. 1983. "Senseless Identity." In *Identity, Personal and Socio-cultural,* ed. Anita Jacobson-Widding, 337–45. Uppsala, Sweden: Academiae Upsaliensis.

Berger, Peter, Brigitte Berger, and Hansfried Kellner. 1973. *The Homeless Mind: Modernization and Consciousness.* New York: Random House.

Berthoff, Rowland. 1953. *British Immigrants in Industrial America, 1790–1950.* Cambridge, MA: Harvard UP.

Billig, Michael. 1995. *Banal Nationalism.* London: Sage.

Binderman, Murray. 1977. "The State and Future of a Theory of Ethnicity." In *American Ethnic Revival: Group Pluralism Entering America's Third Century,* ed. Jack Kinton, 8–27. Aurora, IL: Social Science and Sociological Resources.

Bonilla-Silva, Eduardo. 2003. "'New Racism,' Color-Blind Racism, and the Future of Whiteness in America." In *White Out: The Continuing Significance of Racism,* ed. Ashley Woody Doane and Eduardo Bonilla-Silva, 271–84. New York: Routledge.

Calhoun, Craig. 1993. "Nationalism and Ethnicity." *Annual Review of Sociology* 19: 211–39.

Cannadine, David, ed., 2002. *What Is History Now?* London: Palgrave.

Chapman, Malcolm. 1992. *The Celts: The Construction of a Myth.* London: St. Martin's.

———. 1978. *The Gaelic Vision in Scottish Culture.* London: Croom Helm.

Cohen, Anthony. 1985. *The Symbolic Construction of Community.* London: Tavistock.

Cohen, Ronald. 1978. "Ethnicity: Problem and Focus in Anthropology." *Annual Review of Anthropology* 7: 379–403.

Collis, John. 1997. "Celtic Myths." *Antiquity* 71, no. 271: 195–201.

———. 2003. *The Celts: Origins, Myths, and Inventions.* Gloucestershire: Tempus.

Corbitt, David Leroy, ed. 1931. *Public Papers and Letters of Angus Wilton McLean, Governor of North Carolina, 1925–1929.* Raleigh: Council of State.

Creighton, John. 2000. *Coins and Power in Late Iron Age Britain.* Oxford: Oxford UP.

Crumley, Carole, and William H. Marquardt, eds. 1987. *Regional Dynamics: Burgundian Landscapes in Historical Perspective.* San Diego: Academic Press.

Cunliffe, Barry. 2001. *Facing the Ocean: The Atlantic and Its Peoples 8000 BC–AD 1500*. Oxford: Oxford UP.

———. 1997. *The Ancient Celts*. Oxford: Oxford UP.

———. 1992. "Pits, Preconceptions, and Propitiation in the British Iron Age." *Oxford Journal of Archaeology* 11, no.1: 69–83.

Devine, Philip. 1996. *Human Diversity and the Culture Wars: A Philosophical Perspective on Contemporary Cultural Conflict*. Westport, CT: Praeger.

De Vos, George, and Lola Romanucci-Ross, eds. 1975. *Ethnic Identity: Cultural Continuities and Change*. Palo Alto, CA: Mayfield.

Donaldson, Emily Ann. 1986. *The Scottish Highland Games in America*. Gretna, LA: Pelican.

Edensor, Tim. 2002. *National Identity, Popular Culture, and Everyday Life*. Oxford: Berg.

Ellis, John. 1998. "Reconciling the Celt: British National Identity, Empire, and the 1911 Investiture of the Prince of Wales." *Journal of British Studies* 37 (October): 391–418.

Epstein, Arnold Leonard. 1978. *Ethos and Identity*. Chicago: Aldine.

Eriksen, Thomas Hylland. 1993. *Ethnicity and Nationalism: Anthropological Perspectives*. London: Pluto.

Evans-Pritchard, E. E. 1940. *The Nuer: A Description of the Modes of Livelihood and Political Institutions of a Nilotic People*. Oxford: Clarendon.

Fenton, Steve. 2003. *Ethnicity*. Cambridge, Eng.: Polity.

Fishman, Joshua, Michael Gertner, Esther Lowy, and William Milán. 1985. *The Rise and Fall of the Ethnic Revival: Perspectives on Language and Ethnicity*. Berlin: Mouton.

Fry, Michael. 2003. *"Bold, Independent, Unconquer'd, and Free": How the Scots Made America Safe for Liberty, Democracy, and Capitalism*. Ayr, Scotland: Fort Publishing.

Fuchs, Lawrence H. 1997. "What We Should Count and Why." *Society (Social Science and Modern Society)* 34, no. 6 (Sept./Oct.): 24–27.

Fugita, Stephen S., and David J. O'Brien. 1991. *Japanese American Ethnicity: The Persistence of Community*. Seattle: U of Washington P.

Gans, Herbert. 1979. "Symbolic Ethnicity: The Future of Ethnic Groups and Culture in America." *Ethnic and Racial Studies* 2 (January): 1–20.

Gellner, Ernest. 1983. *Nations and Nationalism*. Oxford: Basil Blackwell.

Giddens, Anthony. 1991. *Modernity and Self-Identity: Self and Society in the Late Modern Age*. Stanford, CA: Stanford UP.

Gillespie, Marie. 1995. *Television, Ethnicity, and Cultural Change*. London: Comedia.

Gil-White, Francisco. 1999. "How Thick Is Blood? The Plot Thickens . . . If Ethnic Actors Are Primordialists, What Remains of the Circumstantialist/Primordialist Controversy?" *Ethnic and Racial Studies* 22 (5): 789–820.

Glazer, Nathan, and Daniel P. Moynihan. 1970 [1963]. *Beyond the Melting Pot: The Negroes, Puerto Ricans, Jews, Italians, and Irish of New York City*. 2nd ed. Cambridge: MIT Press.

Glazer, Nathan, and Daniel P. Moynihan, eds. 1975. *Ethnicity: Theory and Experience*. Cambridge, MA: Harvard UP.

Gorski, Philip. 2000. "The Mosaic Moment: An Early Modernist Critique of Modernist Theories of Nationalism." *American Journal of Sociology* 105, no. 5 (March): 1428–68.

Gossett, Thomas. 1963. *Race: The History of an Idea in America.* Dallas: Southern Methodist UP.

Green, Miranda. 1999. "Pagan Celtic Religion and Early Celtic Myth: Connections or Coincidence?" In *Celtic Connections: Proceedings of the 10th International Congress of Celtic Studies, Volume One: Language, Literature, History, Culture,* ed. Christopher Chippendale and Timothy Taylor, 82–90. East Linton, Scotland: Tuckwell.

Hall, Jonathan. 1997. *Ethnic Identity in Greek Antiquity.* Cambridge, Eng.: Cambridge UP.

Hall, Stuart. 1990. "Cultural Identity and Diaspora." In *Identity: Community, Culture, Difference,* ed. J. Rutherford, 222–38. London: Lawrence and Wishart.

Halter, Marilyn. 2000. *Shopping for Identity: The Marketing of Ethnicity.* New York: Schocken.

———. 1993. *Between Race and Ethnicity: Cape Verdean American Immigrants, 1860–1965.* Urbana: U of Illinois P.

Hannerz, Ulf. 1976. "Some Comments on the Anthropology of Ethnicity in the United States." In *Ethnicity in the Americas,* ed. Frances Henry, 429–38. The Hague: Mouton.

Harrison, Faye. 1995. "The Persistent Power of 'Race' in the Cultural and Political Economy of Racism." *Annual Review of Anthropology* 24: 47–74.

Hartigan, John. 2003. "Who Are These White People?: 'Rednecks,' 'Hillbillies,' and 'White Trash' as Marked Racial Subjects." In *White Out: The Continuing Significance of Racism,* ed. Ashley Woody Doane and Eduardo Bonilla-Silva, 95–111. New York: Routledge.

Hearn, Jonathan. 2000. *Claiming Scotland.* Edinburgh: Polygon.

Hechter, Michael. 1975. *Internal Colonialism: The Celtic Fringe in British National Development, 1536–1966.* Berkeley: U of California P.

Hewitson, Jim. 1993. *Tam Blake & Co.: The Story of Scots in America.* Edinburgh: Cannongate.

Hill, J. D. 1989. "Re-Thinking the Iron Age." *Scottish Archaeological Review* 6: 16–24.

Hollinger, David. 1995. *Post-Ethnic America.* New York: Basic Books.

Hughey, Michael. 1998. "Introduction." In *New Tribalisms: The Resurgence of Race and Ethnicity,* ed. Michael Hughey, 1–16. New York: New York UP.

Ignatieff, Michael. 1993. *Blood and Belonging: Journeys into the New Nationalism.* New York: Farrar, Straus, and Giroux.

Jacobson, David. 1979. "Review of Urban Ethnicity." *American Anthropologist* 81, no. 2 (June): 437–38.

James, Simon. 1999. *The Atlantic Celts: Ancient People or Modern Invention.* London: British Museum Press.

———. 1998. "Celts, Politics, and Motivation in Archaeology." *Antiquity* 72, no. 275: 200–09.

Jenkins, Richard. 2002. "Imagined but Not Imaginary: Ethnicity and Nationalism in the Modern World." In *Exotic No More: Anthropology on the Front Lines,* ed. Jeremy MacClancy, 114–28. Chicago: U of Chicago P.

Jones, Sian. 1997. *The Archaeology of Ethnicity: Constructing Identities in the Past and Present*. London: Routledge.

Keefe, Susan, ed. 1989. *Negotiating Ethnicity: The Impact of Anthropological Theory and Practice*. (Napa Bulletin 8). Washington, DC: National Association for the Practice of Anthropology.

Kellas, James. 1998. *The Politics of Nationalism and Ethnicity*. 2nd ed. New York: St. Martin's.

Kottak, Conrad, and Kathryn Kozaitis. 1987. *On Being Different: Diversity and Multi-culturalism in the North American Mainstream*. New York: McGraw Hill.

Latour, Bruno. 1993. *We Have Never Been Modern*, trans. Catherine Porter. Cambridge, MA: Harvard UP.

Leach, Edmund. 1970 [1964]. *Political Systems of Highland Burma: A Study of Kachin Social Structure*. London: Athlone.

Lears, T. Jackson. 1981. *No Place of Grace: Anti-Modernism and the Transformation of American Culture, 1880–1920*. New York: Pantheon.

Lindenfeld, Jacqueline. 2000. *The French in the United States: An Ethnographic Study*. Westport, CT: Bergin and Garvey.

Lowenthal, David. 1996. *Possessed by the Past: The Heritage Crusade and the Spoils of History*. New York: Free Press.

McCauley, Timothy. 1990. "Nativism and Social Closure: A Comparison of Four Social Movements." *International Journal of Comparative Sociology* 31 (Jan./Apr.): 86–93.

McCrone, David. 1998. *The Sociology of Nationalism: Tomorrow's Ancestors*. London: Routledge.

McKay, Ian. 1994. *The Quest for the Folk: Antimodernism and Cultural Selection in Twentieth-Century Nova Scotia*. Montreal: McGill-Queen's UP.

McLeod, Alexander. 2004. January 11. Interview with author. Nashville, Tennessee.

———. 2002. "The Hawk and the Viking." *Clan MacLeod Magazine* (October): 562–67.

McPherson, James. 1999. *Is Blood Thicker than Water? Crises of Nationalism in the Modern World*. New York: Vintage.

Megaw, John Vincent Stanley, and M. Ruth Megaw. 1998. "'The Mechanism of (Celtic) Dreams?': A Partial Response to Our Critics." *Antiquity* 72, no. 276: 432–35.

———. 1996. "Ancient Celts and Modern Ethnicity." *Antiquity* 70, no. 267: 175–81.

Nagel, Joane. 1998. "Constructing Ethnicity: Creating and Recreating Ethnic Identity and Culture." In *New Tribalisms: The Resurgence of Race and Ethnicity*, ed. Michael Hughey, 237–72. New York: New York UP.

Nairn, Thomas. 1997. *Faces of Nationalism*. London: Verso.

———. 1977. *The Break-up of Britain: Crisis and Neo-Nationalism*. London: NLB.

Novak, Michael. 1972. *The Rise of the Unmeltable Ethnics*. New York: Macmillan.

Okamura, Jonathan. 1981. "Situational Ethnicity." *Ethnic and Racial Studies* 4, no. 4: 452–65.

Patterson, G. James. 1979. "A Critique of 'the New Ethnicity.'" *American Anthropologist* 81: 103–05.

———. 1976. *The Greeks of Vancouver: A Study in the Preservation of Ethnicity*. National Museum of Man, Mercury Series, Paper No. 18. Ottawa: National Museum of Man.

Petrissans, Catherine. 1991. "When Ethnic Groups Do Not Assimilate: The Case of Basque-American Resistance." *Ethnic Groups* 9: 61–81.

Pittock, Murray. 1999. *Celtic Identity and the British Image.* Manchester, Eng.: Manchester UP.

Ray, Celeste. 2001. *Highland Heritage: Scottish Americans in the American South.* Chapel Hill: U of North Carolina P.

Roosens, Eugeen E. 1989. *Creating Ethnicity: The Process of Ethnogenesis.* Newbury Park, CA: Sage.

Sanjek, Roger. 1994. "The Enduring Inequalities of Race." In *Race,* ed. Steven Gregory and Roger Sanjek, 1–17. New Brunswick, NJ: Rutgers UP.

Schaefer, Richard. 1996. *Racial and Ethnic Groups.* 6th ed. New York: HarperCollins.

Schlesinger, Arthur. 1992. *The Disuniting of America: Reflections on a Multicultural Society.* New York: Norton.

Schultz, April. 1994. *Ethnicity on Parade: Inventing the Norwegian American through Celebration.* Amherst: U of Massachusetts P.

Shackel, Paul. 2001. "Public Memory and the Search for Power in American Historical Archaeology." *American Anthropologist* 103, no. 3: 655–70.

Smith, Anthony. 2000. *The Nation in History: Historiographical Debates about Ethnicity and Nationalism.* Hanover, NH: UP of New England.

———. 1999. *Myths and Memories of the Nation.* Oxford: Oxford UP.

———. 1998. *Nationalism and Modernism: A Critical Survey of Recent Theories of Nations and Nationalism.* London: Routledge.

———. 1986. *The Ethnic Origins of Nations.* Oxford: Basil Blackwell.

Sollors, Werner, ed. 1989. *The Invention of Ethnicity.* New York: Oxford UP.

———. 1986. *Beyond Ethnicity: Consent and Descent in American Culture.* Oxford: Oxford UP.

Spickard, Paul, and Rowena Fong. 1995. "Pacific Islander Americans and Multiethnicity: A Vision of America's Future." *Social Forces* 73, vol. 4 (June): 1365–83.

Stein, Howard, and Robert Hill. 1977. *The Ethnic Imperative: Examining the New White Ethnic Movement.* University Park: Pennsylvania State UP.

Steinberg, Stephen. 1981. *The Ethnic Myth: Race, Ethnicity, and Class in America.* New York: Atheneum.

Stern, Stephen, and John Cicala, eds. 1991. *Creative Ethnicity: Symbols and Strategies of Contemporary Ethnic Life.* Logan: Utah State UP.

Thomas, Nicholas. 1992. "The Inversion of Tradition." *American Ethnologist* 19, no. 2 (May): 213–32.

Vale, V., and Andrea Juno. 1989. *Modern Primitives: An Investigation of Contemporary Adornment and Ritual.* San Francisco, CA: Re/Search Publications.

wa Wamwere, Koigi. 2003. *Negative Ethnicity: From Bias to Genocide.* New York: Seven Stories Press.

Ware, Vron, and Les Back. 2002. *Out of Whiteness: Color, Politics, and Culture.* Chicago: U of Chicago P.

Waters, Mary. 1998. "The Costs of a Costless Community." In *New Tribalisms: The Resurgence of Race and Ethnicity,* ed. Michael Hughey, 273–98. New York: New York UP.

———. 1990. *Ethnic Options: Choosing Identities in America.* Berkeley: U of California P.

Wells, Miriam. 1990. "Brokerage, Economic Opportunity, and the Growth of Ethnic Movements." In *American Culture: Essays in the Familiar and Unfamiliar,* ed. Leonard Plotnicov, 179–96. Pittsburgh: U of Pittsburgh P.

Winant, Howard. 1998. "Contesting the Meaning of Race in the Post-Civil Rights Period." In *New Tribalisms: The Resurgence of Race and Ethnicity,* ed. Michael Hughey, 197–211. New York: New York UP.

Wong, Bernard. 1998. "The Chinese in New York City: Kinship and Immigration." In *The Overseas Chinese: Ethnicity in National Context,* ed. Francis L. K. Hsu and Hendrick Serrie. New York: UP of America.

Wood, Peter. 2003. *Diversity: The Invention of a Concept.* San Francisco, CA: Encounter Books.

Zelinsky, Wilbur. 2001. *The Enigma of Ethnicity: Another American Dilemma.* Iowa City: U of Iowa P.

2

Scottish Immigration and Ethnic Organization in the United States

Celeste Ray

For many hyphenated Scots, their sense of emotional attachment to Scotland is to the Scotland of the past—the Scotland they imagine their ancestors left. The heritage tourism industry allows them to experience this Scotland through selective visitation of clan-specific sites, and the literature of ethnic organizations tends to focus on historical themes rather than current Scottish events. Curiously, the Scotland for which hyphenated Scots wax nostalgic is one rewritten through the romanticism of the late eighteenth and early nineteenth centuries—one that might be unrecognizable to the colonial immigrant ancestors of many Scottish Americans. This chapter first explores the type of identity that Scottish Americans embrace as Scottish, and why they do so. The chapter then sketches brief immigration histories of the different Scottish ethnic groups in colonial times and considers how the ethnic divides between Scots, so important in the eighteenth century, were downplayed through Scottish ethnic organizations in the nineteenth. The chapter concludes with descriptions of the Scottish-American community and ethnic organization and heritage activities today.

Scottish-American Identity

Throughout the 1990s, Scottish scholars published synergistically on the creation of a Highlandized Scottish national identity, and since Scotland regained its own parliament in 1999, more ink has spilled over the future of that identity.[1] Scotland still manifests regional cultures, some of which might be labeled ethnic within Scotland.[2] These distinct identities are largely unacknowledged in transatlantic heritage enthusiasts' celebrations of Highland Scottish imagery and identity.

Three Scottish ethnic groups settled in colonial America with different cultural backgrounds and different reasons for immigrating.[3] Lowland Scots tended to settle more as individuals and families along the eastern seaboard with the English, especially in Virginia, Maryland, and South Carolina, and were more likely to settle in urbanizing areas than the Highlanders. Often arriving in America in organized groups, Highlanders tended to settle together in communities. Just over 70 percent settled in what became North Carolina and New York, "north and south of the main English destinations" (Bailyn 1986a, 205; 1986b). The Scots-Irish initially settled primarily in Pennsylvania and then spread across the frontier. Despite the history of self-segregation among the various Scottish immigrants to America, the Scottish identity embraced by Canadian and American descendants of Highland Scots, Lowland Scots, or Ulster Scots alike is a Highland Gaelic identity that came to represent the Scots long after most ancestral immigrants left Scotland. A type of romanticism peculiar to late-eighteenth- and nineteenth-century Scotland, called Highlandism, led to the fetishism of Highland material culture and reshaped Scottish national identity in relation to English hegemony.[4] While embracing the symbols created through this power imbalance, heritage enthusiasts also posit ancestral immigration as a forced diaspora because of the same. That a heritage-lost seems forcibly lost, not just forgotten, makes its reclaiming particularly potent.

How specifically we define a heritage depends upon the social context in which, and with whom, we are "remembering" a selected past. The exodus of Scots to America has shaped Scottish-American identity today much more than Revolutionary discrimination and fighting between the Scottish ethnic groups. Although the British burned Lowland Scots and Scots-Irish Presbyterian churches in America "as sedition-shops" and "consigned Bibles with Scottish versions of the psalms to the flames as texts of rebellion" (Shepperson 1954, 174); and although Patriots burned Loyalist Highland Scots' homes; and although thousands of Highlanders fled to Canada, the Bahamas, or back to Britain in the immediate postwar period, these experiences do not feature in the creation of a unified "Scottish-American" identity. For example, the symbol of the Scottish-American Military Society (SAMS) is imagery of a Scots-Irish Patriot at the Battle of Kings Mountain, North Carolina. The battle was fought largely between Patriots and Scots Highlander Loyalists, yet SAMS members wear their society's symbol with the kilts of Highlanders. The divisions between Scots in the American colonial period are fused through heritage lore and imagery focused on Highlandism and the struggles of the Jacobites.

Attempts to restore the Stuarts to the British throne in the late seventeenth and early eighteenth centuries are known as the Jacobite Risings. The last one ended at the 1746 Battle of Culloden with the defeat of Charles Edward Stuart and his predominantly Highland army. In today's heritage lore, the postwar, anti-Highland policies of the ruling Hanoverians are remembered as "ethnic cleansing." Many see ancestral emigration as a direct result of the defeat of the Jacobites and collapse of the Highland clan system that followed.[5] Actually, more Scots were transported to America during the seventeenth-century Covenanter period and following the Jacobite Rising of 1715 than after Culloden. Abbot Emerson Smith's often-quoted figure for the number of Jacobites indentured to work as slaves in America "during the term of their natural lives" is 866. However, only 153 of the 610 who were actually transported came to the American colonies (A. Smith 1947, 200–02; Brock 1982, 76).[6] While the shiploads of political exiles of heritage lore may not have swarmed America's shores, the social, political, and economic aftermath of Culloden did drive the emigration patterns of the eighteenth and nineteenth centuries.

Immigration to America

Thomas ("Tam") Blake was one of the first Scots known to have come to America. A mercenary and adventurer, Tam was part of the Coronado Expedition in 1540 through what is now the American Southwest.[7] The number of Lowland Scots transported to Charleston, South Carolina, in 1682–1683 as Covenanters was greater than that of exiled Jacobites reaching America following Culloden, but the major thrust of Scottish immigration came in the eighteenth century, particularly between the 1760s and 1770s. Once the king had declared the colonies to be "in rebellion" (August 23, 1775), emigration from Scotland to America was made illegal (September 4), especially when it was realized that emigrants were leaving Scotland with both money and arms (Bailyn 1986a, 53).

From America's first census in 1790, it can be determined that the country included roughly 260,322 people of Scottish birth or descent (approximately 8.3 percent of the population). Those of Scottish birth or descent emigrating from the six counties that now form Northern Ireland comprised another 6 percent of the population (Brock 1982, 13). While New England (Maine, New Hampshire, Vermont, Massachusetts, Rhode Island, and Connecticut) had a distribution of Scots between 5.1 percent (in Vermont) and 2.2 percent (in Connecticut), the Middle Atlantic colonies (New York, New Jersey, Pennsylvania, and Delaware) averaged between 7–8 percent. The South had the most

Scottish settlers as a percentage of total populations, with 10.2 percent in Virginia, 14.8 percent in North Carolina, 15.1 percent in South Carolina, and 15.5 percent in Georgia (Brock 1982, 13).[8] These figures are estimated from the 1790 census and do not include those Scots who left the colonies after the Revolution. William Brock notes that the percentage of Loyalists who were Scottish and who left the colonies during and after the Revolution is conservatively figured at 19 percent, or as many as 30,400 Scots, who would have included leaders in commerce and those who had been public officeholders prior to hostilities (1982, 14).

A brief survey of the different settlement patterns of colonial Highland Scots, Lowland Scots, and the Scots-Irish provides some historical background for considering the nature of ethnic identity and what it means to be a "hyphenated Scot" in America today.[9]

Highlanders

While Highlanders had various reasons for moving to the colonies, two of the prime factors for eighteenth-century emigration were the availability of land in America (it was known as "the best poor man's country in the world") and the high rents at home. Post-Culloden social, economic, and political changes hastened the decline of the Highland clan system and substantially changed the relationship between clan chief and clansfolk. Whereas before Culloden the clansfolks' obligation to their chief was in the form of military service, after Culloden the value of clan lands lay in their ability to generate an income for the chief. The tacksmen (*daoine uaisle*) first felt the crunch when their nominal rents were replaced with higher and higher monetary obligations to the chief. The tacksmen had been military leaders and had leased land (tacks) to other clansfolk. When expecting higher rents from their underlings was futile, they often organized them for emigration instead—sometimes in groups of hundreds and often resettling together. Eric Richards notes, "The history of Highland migration contains some of the strongest images of communal clan-like movements in the history of European exoduses" (1999, 106).[10] James Hunter named his book *A Dance Called America* after a popular song by the Highland band Runrig and an account by James Boswell of emigration fever. On a visit to the Isle of Skye, Boswell described a dance in which "Each of the couples . . . successively whirls round in a circle, till all are in motion; and the dance seems intended to show how emigration catches, till a whole neighbourhood is set afloat" (Hunter 1994, 38).

These emigrations were often driven by financial need but were still largely voluntary in nature—as compared with "the Clearances" of the nineteenth century, which removed tenants more rapidly and completely so that landlords, often absentee, might graze deer or sheep in their place for sporting and economic benefits.[11] While government officials spoke of exiling whole clans after Culloden (especially the Camerons and MacDonalds), clansfolk removed *themselves* in the eighteenth century in what J. M. Bumsted has perhaps over-optimistically called "the People's Clearance" of 1770–1815 (1982, xv–xvi).[12]

After the conclusion of the French and Indian Wars in 1763, many Highland soldiers chose to settle where their regiments had demobilized and encouraged the emigration of their families there (particularly to North Carolina, New York, and Georgia). However, the five years between 1770 and 1775 (until emigration by Scots to America was banned) were perhaps the height of Highland immigration to America. Bernard Bailyn notes, "Between 700 and 800 people were reported to have left the port of Stornoway in the Outer Hebrides on a single day in June 1773, a month in which 800 emigrants on the Isle of Skye completed arrangements for their voyage to North Carolina," and in October "775 more were known to have left Stromness in the Orkneys" (Bailyn 1986a, 41). By the 1770s, the Highlanders were accounting for almost a fifth of all emigration to British North America (Hunter 1994, 43).

After the Revolutionary War, Highlanders did emigrate for North America again, but most went to Canada, especially during the nineteenth-century Clearances. Only one late-nineteenth-century group of Clearance victims from Skye sought out the North Carolina community. The British Napier Commission, set up to study and alleviate "the Highlanders' distress," invited more than forty families to emigrate in 1884 to North Carolina with the promise of shelter and employment for a year after their arrival. Not finding the "Highland," predominantly Gaelic-speaking community they would have found a century earlier, or the prosperity that the Commission had promised, many of these families returned to Scotland. Across the Highlands, between one-half and two-thirds of the rural population were uprooted in the Clearances over the course of five decades (Bitterman 1999, 254), and this legacy flavors the Scottish heritage movement in Canada just as the Jacobite period frames that in the United States.

Some of the best-known Highlander settlements include the Cape Fear Valley in North and South Carolina, the Mohawk and Upper Hudson Valleys in New York, the Altamaha Valley in Georgia, and Pictou in Nova Scotia and Prince Edward Island.[13] In some of these places a strong Scottish identity endures even today. Many Scottish Americans elsewhere claim descent from these original Scottish settlements. Descendants of Cape Fear Valley Highlanders pioneered the settlement of Alabama, Tennessee, Mississippi, and

Texas. Others, beginning with Neill McLendon and Daniel Douglas Campbell, settled "Argyle" in Florida's panhandle (near DeFuniak Springs in Walton County). They brought family and friends to form a satellite of the Cape Fear community in the 1820s when the county was established. By 1850 the census notes over 1,200 settlers there. The first settlement was "Eucheeanna," named after the twelve-mile-wide and twenty-five-mile-long Euchee Valley and the Native American tribe who seemed happily ensconced before the Scots pushed them out. A signer of the Florida Constitution, Colonel John McKinnon, was among them, as were McLeans, McCaskills, Gunns, and MacBrooms, several of whom have memorials in the Euchee Valley Presbyterian Church Cemetery.[14] Today, Argyle hosts an annual Highland games.

Highlanders also played a significant role in the creation of Georgia. David Dobson claims that the Register of Emigrants for the period 1773 to 1775 indicates that two-thirds of those who migrated directly from Great Britain to Georgia had been born in Scotland (1994, 167). Solicited by the Trustees for Establishing the Colony of Georgia, hundreds of Highlander families immigrated to the pine barrens of the Georgia coast beginning in January of 1736 to settle and protect the new British colony. First called New Inverness, their settlement became known as Darien—not to be confused with the disastrous Darien Project in Panama (see Insh 1922). The military governor, James Oglethorpe, recruited colonists as a group who would settle as a community and who were "accustomed to hardship, militant in nature, and willing to become frontier farmer-soldiers" (Parker 1997). In his detailed account of Darien, historian Anthony Parker notes that a full one-third of the Scottish immigrants to Georgia in 1735 were from the Mackay clan (1997, 33). At Darien, the Highlanders formed a society "structured around their clan leaders," especially John Mohr Mackintosh and Captain Hugh Mackay, "who acted as decision makers and adjudicators."[15] They remained distinct from other Scots and "from the rest of the inhabitants of the colony by design and, more important, by language. Gaelic was the language of the people of Darien and the plaids of the Highlands were their attire" (Parker 1997, 95; see also Ivers 1974, 100–01). When the Trustees' rule ended and the colony reverted to Crown control (1749), the Highland regiments (the Highland Rangers and the Highland Independent Company of Foot) disbanded. Limitations on land grants ended in 1752 so that Scots moved out from the original settlement to raise cattle and begin the lumber business that would remain the focus of Darien's industry until the American Civil War.

Other Scots of course came to Georgia, immigrating from South Carolina or directly from Scotland, and not all of them found the pine barrens of Georgia to their taste. Parker notes that the Lowland Scots from Glasgow and Edinburgh became known as the "Malcontents" (1997, 4). Not many of the Highlanders remained long at Darien; in fact, of the approximately 250 original settlers, almost four-fifths moved elsewhere (Parker 1997, 83). Some Highlanders left the colony of Georgia in the late fall of 1740, along with some discontented Lowland Scots from Savannah, for South Carolina (Parker 1997, 161 n.7) Yet, they pioneered the way for many later Scottish settlers in the state. Parker notes that "Scottish names are to be found throughout Georgia's continuing history in the ranks of politics and place-names . . . These Highlanders may scarcely have been missed in the glens and mountains of Scotland, but in Georgia they made a difference" (1997, 98–99). David Dobson remarks that those Scots who stayed established Scottish societies and celebrated St. Andrew's Day throughout the eighteenth century (1994, 122). Today, the town of Darien (population about 2,000) holds a "Scottish Day" in March; the John Mohr Mackintosh Pipe and Drum Band is a Grade V competition and performance band traveling the Southeast and based in Atlanta, and a living history unit called the "Oglethorpe Highlanders" (set about 1742) encamps at local schools and at Highland games across the South.

Perhaps most famous as a destination for Highlanders, North Carolina has long been called "the land of the God-blessed Macs." Highland immigration began about 1732 (some may have come to North Carolina in 1729 when North Carolina attained Royal colony status) and increased about the late 1760s, peaking in the two years before 1776 (Meyer 1961, 72). Induced by bad harvests, the social and political changes after the Jacobite disaster, and letters home from soldiers who had served in the Seven Years War, most immigrants came from the Western Highlands and Isles. As historian Whitfield Bell remarked, "[N]ot individuals only, but whole families and parishes migrated to America. Six vessels carrying twelve hundred persons from the Highlands and Isles sailed in 1770. Five hundred persons from Islay and three hundred and seventy from Skye took ship for North Carolina in 1771, and the next year two hundred left Sutherland for the same destination" (1954, 277).

The "Mayflower" of the Cape Fear Scots was a ship called the *Thistle*. Most of the 350 passengers aboard its 1739 voyage came from Argyllshire in southwest Scotland. Later Highland immigrants to the valley came predominantly from the northern areas of Ross, Sutherland, and the Isle of Skye (Graham 1956, 50; for more on immigrants to North Carolina see McLean 1919 and 1942). Estimates vary in the numbers of Highlanders who settled the Cape Fear Valley, from 30,000 total to Duane Meyer's calculation of approximately 20,000 in the eight years prior to the Revolution alone (1961, 63–64). Excluding third-generation Scottish Americans, and considering only first- or second-generation Scots, a more conservative number of 10,000 is often repeated for those living across the sandy pineland frontier of Cumberland County in 1774, just prior to the mass migrations of that year and 1775 (Bailyn 1986a, 27).

Even if more refined estimates are desirable, the size of these migrations alone is impressive. Highlanders came in large groups often organized by their tacksmen, but they also came because of the generous land grants and a ten-year tax exemption ensured by North Carolina governor Gabriel Johnston. Johnston, who governed North Carolina from 1734 until his death in 1752, was himself a native Scot. Similar offers from his successor, Governor Josiah Martin, and letters from settled immigrants to family back home further encouraged new arrivals. Martin issued Cape Fear land grants in return for an oath of loyalty to the Crown. By placing new Highland immigrants around the original settlement, he hoped that social pressure would encourage Highlanders to honor their oath in the trouble he knew was coming. Believing their loyalty unshakable, Martin actively sought Scots Highlander immigrants (as opposed to Scots-Irish or Lowland Scots) up to the beginning of the Revolutionary War.

The Highlanders originally settled what was Bladen County, North Carolina. In 1754, much of their land became a part of the newly created Cumberland County—ironically named after the duke who was infamous for hounding and slaughtering Jacobites in Scotland during the lifetime of many Highland immigrants. Today the settlement extends through Anson, Bladen, Moore, Cumberland, Richmond, Scotland, and Robeson Counties in North Carolina and portions of northern South Carolina. Cross Creek formed the center of the settlement. The area incorporated in 1762 with the name of Campbellton (the Campbells being the most powerful family in Argyllshire, from whence many immigrants hailed, but not necessarily admired by the immigrants, as the Campbells supported the Hanoverians in the Jacobite cause). By 1783 the Highlanders had become uncomfortably synonymous with Loyalism, and Campbellton acquired its present name of Fayetteville in honor of the Patriots' hero, General Marquis de Lafayette.

Hunter remarks on an eighteenth-century song that relates the popularity of the Carolinas as a destination for Highlanders and advocates "*dol a dh'iarraidh an fhortain an North Carolina*" (going to North Carolina to seek a fortune). Not all remained happy with their choice to emigrate. Many were forced to uproot again after having sided with the Loyalists in the Revolutionary War, including the Jacobite heroine Flora MacDonald and the Gaelic poet John MacRae (Iain MacMhurchaidh). Arriving in 1774, MacRae settled near McLendon's Creek "in gloomy and endless dark forests to dwell," and was among the Loyalists at

Moores Creek Bridge (also called "America's Culloden") in February of 1776. His son Murdoch died at Moores Creek, and by 1780 MacRae had long since ceased to write of the new land with hope (MacDonell 1982, 33). Loyalists who left the Carolinas after the Revolution submitted claims to the British government requesting compensation for their lost property. Their detailed inventories reveal not only their prosperity and what they had improved and built on their lands, but also ongoing communications with the homeland. Captain Angus Campbell asked for compensation for the loss of his library, including "*The Scotch Magazine* for thirty years compleat." More Highlanders remained in North Carolina than left after the war, and even today their descendants maintain a strong sense of community in the Cape Fear Valley.

As with many non-English-speaking immigrant groups, the transgenerational, public use of the "homeland" language survived longest in the religious context. Of Cape Fear descent and the first American to compete (and win) in the National Gaelic *Mòd* in Scotland, Jamie MacDonald has noted that while the use of the Gaelic language for religious services does seem to have largely ceased after the Civil War, a self-conscious use of Gaelic was occasionally heard in services in the first decade of the twentieth century (1993, 134; see also Newton 2003). Today, ministers at Cape Fear church homecomings will say a few words of welcome or read a biblical passage in Gaelic. Reenactors of Highland military units also drill in (often self-taught) Gaelic, and others learn Gaelic to sing in North American *Mòds*. While some committed hyphenates travel to Scotland for language courses, North American Gaelic-learners are variously received in the homeland (see Morgan 2000).

Cape Fear descendants have commemorated the Highland settlers through poetry, monuments, sermons, and gatherings since the nineteenth century. A succession of short-lived "Scottish patriotic" societies formed in North Carolina between the 1880s and 1920s. Transnational commemorations of local Scottish pioneers are not new in the Cape Fear Valley. When Governor Angus McLean dedicated a memorial to MacNeill pioneers in 1928 at Flora Mac-Donald College in Red Springs, "on behalf of the people of North Carolina, who appreciate the great contribution which the MacNeills have made to the building of a better and nobler commonwealth," not only was the president of the Clan MacNeill Association of America present, but so was the chief of the Clan MacNeill of Barra (Corbitt 1931, 448). Following the Great Depression, in 1939 a bicentennial celebration of the Highland settlement took place in Fayetteville. Although the event was intended to become an annual celebration, World War II intervened. In the two years of the celebration's existence, a thousand people signed their names in the visitor book, many noting their ancestry back to Scotland and adding beside their names that of an immigrant ancestor five generations removed. Many Cape Fear residents today can still recite these genealogies, still attend the churches their immigrant ancestors founded in the mid-eighteenth century, and some still farm the land settled by the same. Dame Flora MacLeod (the first female clan leader recognized by the Lord Lyon) also visited the Cape Fear Valley in her 1953 American tour. (On this tour she made her famous plea to Scottish Americans to "Come back to Scotland," perhaps not surprising, as her travels were sponsored by the British Travel Association.) She visited the Flora MacDonald College and attended a homecoming and "Gathering of the Clan" at Old Bethesda Presbyterian Church in Moore County that drew an estimated fifteen hundred people. The 1950s also saw the beginnings of a Clan Donald Society USA, a Robert Burns Society, and country dance groups, largely orchestrated by Donald MacDonald, cofounder of the Grandfather Mountain Games begun in 1956.

Since Fort Bragg took over much of the original Highlander settlement in 1918, churches, graveyards, and the remains of homesteads (a chimney here and there not blown to bits in target practice) have become a focus of pilgrimage in the cognitive map of today's Scottish-American community. Longstreet Presbyterian Church (established 1758) is the home of annual church homecomings, though most of the 150–200 participants are generations removed from the weekly meetings of the congregation. The June event also serves as the annual MacFayden family reunion with a "dinner on the grounds." Infrequent or first-time participants introduce themselves and explain their genealogical connections to the church. Within the original congregation many families had close bonds through intermarriage, and first-timers are often surprised when regulars recognize them by, or comment on, their "family features." In November of 2003 the Reverend Douglas Kelly, also a genealogist and 2004 president of Scottish Heritage USA (SHUSA, a group of American supporters of the National Trust for Scotland), organized the type of reunion only genealogists can muster.[16] "The Carolina Scots' Celebration" primarily served as a Kelly family reunion commemorating the 1803 arrival of Daniel Kelly from the Isle of Skye, but also assembled descendants of all Highland Scots who came to the Upper Cape Fear Valley. Over two hundred Kellys, Blues, Buies, MacDonalds, McLendons, McIvers, McIntoshes, and MacFaydens from across the country attended a weekend of events, including seminars on genealogical records, a tartan ball, a Presbyterian worship service, and a tour of cemeteries and historic sites connected with Scottish immigrants. More Scots settled in North Carolina in the colonial period than in any other state, so that in the 1997 proclamation of a state Tartan Day (before it became a

Fig. 3. Longstreet Reunion 1966 (Courtesy of Zula Barton)

national holiday), Governor James Hunt even claimed that "North Carolina has the largest number of people of Scottish heritage of any other state or country in the world" (including Scotland)!

New York also received many Highland immigrants. James Hunter tells us that the first Highland settlers to reach colonial New York came in a group of about eighty families organized by Lachlan Campbell in the 1730s (1994, 74).[17] By the 1760s and 1770s, New York was the leading destination after North Carolina for emigrating Highlanders. Many arrived in the Mohawk Valley (between the Catskills and the Adirondacks) at the invitation of Scots-Irish Sir William Johnson. Johnson arrived in 1738, became a baronet after 1755, established relatively peaceful relations with the Six Nations of Native Americans, "whose land he and his people were invading," and fostered immigration to the area, first, by other Scots-Irish and, in the 1760s, by Highlanders (Bailyn 1986a, 577–79). The most famous ship sailing to New York was the *Pearl,* which left Fort William in 1773 and brought immigrants from Argyllshire, Invernesshire, and Morayshire, Scotland. Unlike the Protestants

Fig. 4. Longstreet Reunion 1995 (Courtesy of Zula Barton)

heading for North Carolina, many of the emigrants were Catholics from Mac-Donell lands. But as in North Carolina, the Scots-Irish fought predominantly as Patriots and the Highlanders as Loyalists, especially in Tryon County (which constituted much of upstate New York). The Mohawk Valley's Oriskany Battlefield saw one of the bloodiest battles of the Revolution in 1777. While more Patriots than Loyalists died, the state remained predominantly pro-independence, and after the war many Mohawk Highlanders fled the country, moving west beyond the Finger Lakes and across the Niagara River to Canada. While some moved to Nova Scotia and joined other refugees in the "Loyalist boom town of Shelburne," others "moved north to wilderness townships set aside for Loyalist war veterans just across the St. Lawrence boundary line," where townships were formed into counties called Stormont, Dundas, and Glengarry (after the homelands of the organizers of the emigrants who sailed on the *Pearl*) (Bailyn 1986a, 586–87; Brock 1982, 90). Descendants of the Glengarry Highlanders still live in the province of Quebec (see Iwanska 1993).

In the nineteenth century, Highlanders and other Scots settled more widely in the East, but also in the newly opening Western frontier. While contemporary hyphenated Scots in the American West could not be considered in this volume (see note 17 in the introduction), an interesting volume by James Hunter requires mention. Published as *Glencoe and the Indians* in Britain, *Scottish Highlanders, Indian Peoples: Thirty Generations of a Montana Family* (1996) is a fascinating read examining the migration of McDonalds to Montana, their intermarriage with the Nez Perce, and their continuing awareness of their heritage today.[18]

Lowland Scots

The Lowlanders, their immigration and settlement, and their influence on American culture have received far less scholarly attention than either the Highlanders or Scots-Irish. Of the three Scottish ethnic groups, the Lowlanders were less distinctive culturally and assimilated most rapidly. Generally moving into existing farming settlements and towns, Lowlanders did not as often settle in groups and moved away from Scots settlements more readily. Linguistics also played a part in their acculturation within English communities. Highlanders often retained Gaelic for several generations, while the Lowland Broad Scots gave way within a generation to more upwardly mobile speech patterns (Graham 1956, 111).[19]

J. M. Bumsted suggests that the movement of Lowland Scots "directly to America during the seventeenth century was perhaps as substantial as that to Ulster." He also notes that many Lowlander immigrants were indentured servants, transported minor criminals or homeless paupers, or were military or political prisoners (1982, 1–2). Historian William Brock remarks that "South Carolina attracted many [L]owland Scots of the landed and professional classes" and that even among these immigrants, indenture was not uncommon (1982, 25). Lowlanders also came to Georgia in the 1730s, but for economic reasons as farmers and merchants and were not recruited for strategic purposes to guard the southern frontier against the Spanish, as were the Highlanders (Dobson 2000, ii). In *Sojourners in the Sun: Scottish Migrants in Jamaica and the Chesapeake, 1740–1800*, Allan Karras has written a detailed account of Lowland Scots merchants' pre-Revolutionary presence in the Chesapeake (Virginia and Maryland) and the wages of Loyalism (1992; see also Haws 1980 and Devine 1975).

The first Lowland Scots to arrive in America in a significant group were transported Covenanters coming in 1682 to the colony at Port Royal (Charleston, South Carolina). A year later and until 1685, what Ned Landsman describes as "a series of vessels" sent by Scottish proprietors arrived in New Jersey (1985, 74). While Landsman calls New Jersey "Scotland's first American colony," he notes that "Scottish families moved back and forth within that region with such regularity that, for the eighteenth century, any meaningful description of the Scottish colony in central New Jersey must include many settlers in New York and, to a lesser extent, Philadelphia also" (10).

An important aspect of their culture, which they shared with the Scots-Irish and which became a pervasive influence among American Scots in general, was their Presbyterian faith.[20] While some Lowlanders were Episcopalians, or converted to conform with the English hegemony of colonial coastal towns, most were Presbyterians of Covenanting backgrounds. Few educated clergy traveled the frontier often, so Gaelic-speaking Highlanders often had to rely on English-speaking Lowland Scot or Scots-Irish missionaries of a Covenanting tradition.[21] Although Landsman states that the first permanent meetinghouse for a Scottish congregation in America was built in 1730 (1985, 3), Robert Leyburn has noted that by 1700 in Charleston, South Carolina, there were enough dissenters of the Reformed faith that Presbyterians, Huguenots, and Puritans founded a church to be ruled by elders (presbyters). The Reverend Archibald Stobo of the Church of Scotland ministered to them from 1700 to 1740, and from 1704 he also ministered to the Presbyterian congregation at Wilton (Colleton). Leyburn further comments that by 1710 there were five Scottish Presbyterian churches in the neighborhood of Charleston, and there were also Presbyterian churches at Cainhoy, on Edisto Island, on James Island, and on John's Island in that year (1962, 251–52).

The Great Awakening of the Middle Colonies (Pennsylvania, New Jersey, and Delaware) in the 1730s began with the work of the Presbyterian Scots-Irish Tennent family (who had been Episcopalians in Ulster).[22] Their efforts led to the creation of "the Log College" as a seminary, now known as Princeton University. Landsman claims, "By the middle years of the eighteenth century, religious life among the Scots of central New Jersey, and the society itself, had come to resemble nothing so much as that of Southwestern Scotland, especially the lower Southwest" (1985, 256). However, as New Jersey was created by proprietors belonging to Quaker or Episcopal communions who derived from the east or northeast of Scotland, this claim seems either romantic or indicative of the powerful force that Covenanting Presbyterianism had become.

As with other Scots, Lowlanders came in especially large numbers between 1763 and 1776. By mid-1775, before the ban on emigration, Lowland subscribers to the Scots American Company of Farmers began taking up lots in the Ryegate settlement in upcountry, eastern New York (now Vermont). (For a detailed account of the settlement, see Bailyn 1986a, 604–37.) Few studies focus specifically on Lowlander settlements, perhaps as they were fewer, less distinctive, more readily assimilated within colonial culture and, though significant, after the seventeenth century their numbers did not compare with those of the Scots-Irish.

Scots-Irish

From the late 1600s through the early 1800s, most emigrants from Ireland to America came from Ulster, and the largest group among these immigrants was the Scots-Irish Presbyterians. The Scots-Irish so named themselves to convey their distinctiveness from the Scots-Highlanders, whose Loyalist reputation survived long after the Revolution. Later the name served to distinguish them from "Celtic" or native Catholic Irish, who came to America in the hundreds of thousands with the famines of the 1840s and 1860s.[23] In this volume we refer to the Scots and the Scots-Irish, not the "Scotch" or "Scotch-Irish." As Ted Cowan notes, Scots have not been called "Scotch" since at least the 1920s (1999, 54), and neither should the Scots-Irish be referred to by the name for whisky.

The Scots-Irish remained a separate group in America not because of continuing cultural affinity with Ulster (where they had always been in some way marginal even among other Protestants), but through choice, religion, politics, and a tendency to settle on the frontier. They more readily relinquished cultural ties with Ulster than the Gaelic-speaking Highlanders did with their homeland. Letters sent home by Scots-Irish immigrants were riddled with homesickness, but still emphasized the freedom and independence to be found in America and encouraged others to follow (Parkhill 1997, 118–19). Historians Tyler Blethen and Curtis Wood refer to the Scots-Irish as "a people practiced in abandoning their past" (1983, 20). While they famously brought folklore, musical, and architectural traditions, the Scots-Irish did not bring a material culture as distinctly representative of their identity as the Highlander's unique fabrics and style of dress. What crossed the Atlantic and became part of their new identity related more to worldview, subsistence strategies, and farming techniques—not the artifactual material culture of the Highlanders that has become emblematic as "Scottish" in heritage celebration today, even in festivals celebrating Scots-Irish settlers.

The Scots-Irish were Lowland, Presbyterian Scots who began settling in the area of Ireland that was most problematic for British rule, the province of Ulster, during James VI's "plantation" scheme (1607/08–1618). As Maldwyn Jones notes, "more Scots settled in Ulster outside the plantation period proper than were planted during it" and the climax of Scottish immigration to Ulster came "between 1690 and 1697" due to bad harvests and famine in Scotland (Jones 1991, 288; see also Robinson 1984). The Ulster Scots, as they are known in Northern Ireland, remained distinct from the native Irish in terms of settlement, language, and religion and maintained what Rory Fitzparick (1989) has called a "frontiersman-mentality."[24] Estimates vary as to what percentage of the Ulster population the Lowland Scots composed, but Kerby Miller and his colleagues suggest that by the 1730s, "three-fifths of Ulster's inhabitants were Protestants, of whom a large majority were Presbyterians" (Miller, et al. 2003, 24). They further note that "even as the last great Scottish migrations to Ulster occurred, some of the Scots-Irish began to move to North America. Between 1680 and 1716 perhaps as many as three thousand passengers left Ulster for the New World" (24). Other authors, such as Bernard Bailyn, have set the date of 1717 as the beginning of mass migration of Ulster Scots to America, claiming that after that date and before 1760, between 100,000 and 150,000 came to the colonies, many because of repressive trade laws, famine, and a decline in the linen industry (Bailyn 1986a, 25; Ramsey 1964, 140). Blethen and Wood propose that from the 1680s until the Revolution, at least 250,000 sailed to North America (1997, 3). Suggesting that newspaper accounts of the period exaggerated the numbers, Marianne Wokeck estimates half as many (1999, 169–87). Patrick Griffin also conservatively says "more than 100,000" Ulster Scots came to the colonies between 1718 and 1775; but even with these smaller figures, Griffin notes their migration was still "the single largest movement of any group from the British Isles to British North America during the eighteenth century" (2001, 1). The figures vary, but Leonard Dinnerstein, Roger Nichols, and David Reimers note that the Scots-Irish comprised the largest number of non-English Europeans coming to the colonies during the eighteenth century. By the time of American independence, nearly a quarter of a million Scots-Irish had entered the colonies and "numbered between 7 and 10 percent of the white population." (Dinnerstein, et al. 2003, 17) Along with the Germans, the Scots-Irish were the largest ethnic group to enter America in colonial times.

The Scots-Irish settled primarily in the Chesapeake Valley before 1710. They went "next to New England, and from the late 1720s overwhelmingly to Philadelphia and the Delaware Valley, with lesser numbers landing at New York, Charleston, Savannah, and Baltimore" (Miller, et al. 2003, 24).[25] Jones writes that from the 1740s, the Scots-Irish moved south and west and by the 1750s had settled across the Georgia and South Carolina frontiers, and Bailyn notes that Scots-Irish were also in West Florida "in its earliest years as a British colony" (Jones, 1991, 294; Bailyn 1986a, 27). Those who landed in Philadelphia moved west into central Pennsylvania and either north or south following the mountain valleys into New York, Virginia, and the Carolinas. After 1735, land in the northern colonies was less readily obtainable and the Great Wagon Road became the most common route to the Carolina Piedmont and the "backcountry." The road began at the Schuylkill River in Philadelphia and continued through Virginia's Shenandoah Valley; it would eventually stretch over 735 miles to Augusta, Georgia. From Virginia and the Carolinas, the Scots-Irish pioneered settlements in Kentucky and Tennessee.[26] Scots-Irish settlements across Appalachia contrasted with those of Lowland and Highland Scots elsewhere in the Scots-Irish preference for relatively isolated, individual family homesteads and their focus on a mixed economy of animal husbandry and diversified crops. Miller has estimated that 50 percent or more of the settlers west of Appalachia by 1790 had immigrated from Ulster or were descendants of Ulster immigrants (1985, 161). In the 1990 U.S. census, 47 percent of those who claimed Scots-Irish ancestry lived in the South.

As with Scots in general, but perhaps more so than the other Scottish ethnic groups, the Scots-Irish have attracted well over a century of scholarship about their impact on American life. Historian T. G. Fraser notes that the first convention of the Scotch-Irish Congress was held in Columbia, Tennessee, in May of 1889 to commemorate the influence of the Scots-Irish on the formation of the Republic (1997, viii). James Leyburn has commented that "the Scotch-Irish Congress of 1889 . . . heard the claim that the Scotch-Irish contributed more to constitutional liberty in America than any other people" (1962, xiii). Fraser suggests that speakers invoked what has become the usual litany of Scots-Irish American heroes: Patrick Henry, John Paul Jones, Andrew Jackson, James Buchanan, Abraham Lincoln, and Ulysses S. Grant among them. The last name was included as a great Scots-Irish American despite the fact that Pulaski, Tennessee, not far from Columbia, had seen the birth of another Scots-Irish and Scottish-influenced association just over twenty years before, the Ku Klux Klan, partially in response to Grant's vision of Reconstruction.

The turn of the twentieth century saw a flurry of publications about the Scots-Irish, although most continued to provide celebratory notes on famous achievers.[27] With a few exceptions, such as Henry Ford's *The Scotch-Irish in America* (1915) and Wayland Dunnaway's *The Scotch-Irish of Colonial Pennsylvania* (1944), serious scholarship began only in 1962 with sociologist James Leyburn's *The Scotch-Irish: A Social History*. Ulster scholars R. J. Dickson and E. R. R. Green produced important works on emigration and the Scots-Irish in America respectively in 1966 and 1969. Estyn Evans considered Scots-Irish cultural adaptation and legacy in the American "Old West" in essays during the 1960s (1965; 1969). Folklorist Henry Glassie published *Patterns in the Material Folk Culture of the Eastern United States* in 1968, in which he examined the material remains of Scots-Irish settlement. William Lehmann's *Scottish and Scotch-Irish Contributions to Early American Life and Culture* (1978) considers the Scots-Irish impact on American medical history, religious developments, educational ideals, and material culture. David Hackett Fischer's much discussed *Albion's Seed: Four British Folkways in America* (1989) included some less commonly-examined accounts of Scots-Irish life on the frontier. The Ulster-American Heritage Symposium began a collaborative, interdisciplinary, and transatlantic exploration into Scots-Irish studies in the bicentennial year of 1976. Historians Tyler Blethen and Curtis Wood edited a collection of essays from over two decades of the symposium's work, published in 1997 as *Ulster and North America*. In 2001 the University of Ulster established the Institute of Ulster Scots Studies to "explore the history, heritage and legacy of Ulster Scots people," focusing on what the Institute calls the Ulster Scots Diaspora.[28]

Ethnic distinctions that were so important to Irish Catholics and Ulster Protestants in nineteenth-century America are somewhat lost on their descendants today when one hears "Scotland the Brave" as often as any other bagpipe tune in New York City's St. Patrick's Day Parade. Any enduring ethnic legacy of the Scots-Irish is probably most closely associated with Appalachian identities. Historian Henry Shapiro noted that the 1878 publication of the Reverend James Craighead's *Scotch and Irish Seeds in American Soil* established the perception of Appalachian mountaineers being Scots-Irish as an academic and popular convention (1977, 49). In the last two decades of the nineteenth century, as outside commercial interests exploited Appalachian timber and coal resources and began the tourism industry that still economically characterizes the region, "local color writers" and northern missionaries popularized images of Appalachia that endure as stereotypes of the region. Mountain people were claimed to be the most Anglo-Saxon of all Americans, and Charles Morrow Wilson even romantically suggested in 1929 that they spoke "Elizabethan English."[29] Mountain people have their own dialect (which is certainly not Elizabethan), and more recent scholarship has begun to focus on the ethnic diversity within Appalachia.[30] Along with the Germans, the Scots-Irish were the most prominent settlers in the mountains and have given America a rich legacy of vernacular architecture, musical forms, folklore, and storytelling traditions with links to Scotland and Ireland, such as Jack Tales. Their distinctive settlement and socioeconomic patterns allow scholars to more readily trace their outward migrations and communities in the nineteenth century.

More difficult is obtaining numbers for Highland or Lowland Scots immigration and settlement after the colonial period. Some communities celebrate nineteenth-century Scottish settlers—for example, on Tartan Day 2004, Sarasota, Florida, held a reenactment of the 1885 arrival of the first Scots in the area; however, much of the heritage movement and lore focuses on the colonial period. Scots continued to invest in the developing West, especially in railroads, mining, farming, and cattle ranching. In his *Scots in the North American West, 1790–1917* (2000), Ferenc Szasz traces immigrant Scots' roles as fur trappers, in the nineteenth-century cattle industry and in Western sheep herding (in the trans-Mississippi West from the Dakotas down to Texas and west to the Pacific). In terms of continued immigration nationally, there were 70,550 Scots-born living across the United States in 1850; in 1860 that number was 108,518; in 1880 this jumped to 170,136 and to 242,231 in 1890, where it remained relatively stable until 1950 (244,200). The exception is a peak decade of immigration between 1921 and 1930, when at least 159,781 immigrants from Scotland arrived in the United States, making the 1930 figure of Scots-born living in the country 354,323 (Berthoff 1953, 5–7).[31] Studies of nineteenth- and twentieth-century Scottish immigration patterns less frequently distinguish between Highlanders and Lowlanders. (Perhaps assimilation to an American culture was more rapid, or perhaps the immigrants downplayed particular Scottish ethnicities to better fit the American Anglo-Saxon mainstream and be accepted more readily than the newly arriving immigrants from southern and eastern Europe.) Immigrants in this period seemed to have arrived more commonly as individuals and single families. The communal movement so characteristic of Highland immigration in the eighteenth century shifted to Canada.

Ethnic Organization

The late Rowland Tappan Berthoff was one of the first historians to trace the development of Scottish, English, and Welsh immigration and ethnic organizations in his still much-cited book *British Immigrants in Industrial America, 1790–1950* (1953). He was updating his 1982 article "Under the Kilt: Variations on the Scottish-American Ground" for inclusion in the present text before illness intervened; he nevertheless informs any discussion of early Scottish societies in the United States. Scottish ethnic organizations in America date back to at least 1657 when a Scots Charitable Society was founded in Boston.[32] (Many of its beneficiaries were Scottish Royalists captured by Cromwell's Parliamentary Army after the Battles of Dunbar [1650] and Worcester [1651] and who were shipped to New England, Virginia, and the West Indies as indentured servants.) The first St. Andrew's societies formed in Charleston (1729); Savannah (c. 1737);[33] Philadelphia (1747);[34] New York City (1756); Alexandria, Virginia (c. 1760); Halifax, Nova Scotia (1768); St. John, New Brunswick (1798); Albany (1803); Baltimore (1806); and Buffalo (1843). St. Andrew's societies proliferated through the nineteenth and twentieth centuries to total at least seventy-two in the United States in 2003. (The largest, most highly organized is the Illinois St. Andrew's Society based in Chicago; founded in 1845, it has an open membership policy, which is unusual.)[35]

The Scottish heritage movements of the nineteenth and twentieth centuries were driven by ethnic organizations, but with different emphases. In the nineteenth century, members of Scottish societies united in a generalized celebration of all things Scottish; in the twentieth and twenty-first centuries, specific clan loyalties and tartans dominate perceptions of hyphenated-Scottish identities. Embracing Highlandist visions of Scotland, the "American Order of the Scottish Clans" formed in 1878 at St. Louis and became the first lodge of a national fraternity that spread to New England and the Middle Atlantic states and published a journal called "The Fiery Cross."[36] These "clans" were lodges that sponsored Highland games and other Scottish celebrations. About 250 "clans" existed when the fraternity was most popular in the late nineteenth century. By World War I, about 160 "clans" engaged 16,000 members.[37] These "clans" are quite different from the later twentieth-century clan societies. "Clan" members did not claim any relationship to the Highland clans whose names and tartans they adopted (Berthoff 1953, 181). Membership in these local "clans" was based on residence in the United States, not ancestral origins in Scotland. They also commemorated Scottish medieval victories like that at Largs against the Vikings and Robert the Bruce's triumph at Bannockburn, not the Jacobite defeats more commonly commemorated today with the exile and diaspora focus of heritage lore.

These were mostly male organizations, although women occasionally formed auxiliaries. The Daughters of Scotia began in 1895, and a "Grand Lodge" was organized in 1899. Membership extended to any female relative of a "Clansman of the Order of Scottish Clans," any woman born in Scotland, or a woman married to a Scottish man. As with the Order of Scottish Clans, on the death of a dues-paying member, a small sum was delivered to the family. (Today, except chapters in California and Florida, Daughters of Scotia are concentrated in northern states, with a few branches in the Midwest.[38]) These were heady times for organizing societies in the United States in general, and for women in particular (the Daughters of the American Revolution organized in

1890 and the United Daughters of the Confederacy in 1894). The Daughters of Scotia were just one of many women's ethnic organizations (Szasz 2000, 9; Berthoff 1953, 182).[39] Late-nineteenth-century Scottish, English, Welsh, and Irish associations were heavily concentrated in the Northeast and in the city of Chicago.[40] Their patterning responded to multiple factors, particularly the arrivals of new immigrants from southern and eastern Europe and the differential impacts of the Civil War. While groups such as the Daughters of Scotia had predominantly regional success, by the close of the nineteenth century, most large cities in both Canada and the United States had either a St. Andrew's Society, a Caledonian Society, a Robert Burns Club, or some other Scots-oriented social group.

Caledonian societies and St. Andrew's societies have formed around the world from Dubai to Bangkok to Hong Kong. They are autonomous organizations without an overarching authority, so their character responds to local communities. Generalizing about the type of people attracted to such societies is difficult when the profile and role of St. Andrew's societies and Caledonian societies in local communities vary greatly. In the United States they are generally at the top of an unspoken hierarchy of Scottish-American organizations, but this too varies with location. St. Andrew's societies most often (though not always) involve the local elite (bank presidents, judges, and other professionals). Where St. Andrew's societies occupy this socioeconomic strata, they often have a male-only membership policy and members may or may not have a kilt; they may or may not have an abiding interest in their Scottish ancestry and might be more interested in the cultural capital of membership than in exploring "Scottish heritage." One of the biggest annual events is the St. Andrew's Day Dinner on November 30. St. Andrew's societies tend to have formal celebrations, while local Scottish societies more often commemorate the day with a *ceilidh* or country dancing.

Next in the Scottish-American hierarchy are the Caledonian societies (in some areas of the United States these might attract more elite members than the local St. Andrew's Society). After these are Scottish societies and Burns societies. Monuments to the eighteenth-century poet Robert Burns may be found across America, from his statue in Denver, Colorado's city park to the reconstruction of his Alloway cottage in Atlanta, Georgia (built in 1910). Burns clubs are more commonly all male, which is appropriate, as the poet himself helped found a Bachelor's Club in 1780 at which he would brag to his friends about the numerous young women whom he burdened with illegitimate offspring. The most important annual event for Burns societies (and a significant event for most Scottish heritage societies also) is the anniversary of

Burns's birth on January 25. The event follows a formal order around the world and includes the ceremonial delivery of a haggis (bagpiped into the dining area and saluted with "the address to the haggis") and a speech delivered in Burns's honor always called "The Immortal Memory."[41] Burns suppers were already well established in America by 1859, the one-hundredth anniversary of his birth, when there were sixty-one suppers across the states and that in New York drew close to three thousand participants.

The most accessible and generally the largest groups in the Scottish-American community are the clan societies and local or city heritage societies. Membership in these various organizations can be overlapping, but when St. Andrew's societies are gender- and class-specific, fewer members will also be members of clan societies than when liberal membership policies prevail.

Clan Societies

The clan societies (with membership based on ancestry or perceived ancestry) have driven the Scottish heritage movement of the later twentieth century. New interpretations of Scottish heritage have led to the international rebirth of the Highland clan system as clan societies. There were a few clan societies in the United States before World War II. The MacLeans and MacBeans formed societies in the 1890s, and the MacNeills followed in 1921. But all other American clan societies have been organized since the 1950s. The Clan MacLeod Society USA was founded in 1954, the year after the U.S. visit by the clan's chief, Dame Flora MacLeod. Clan Donald was also one of the first clan societies organized in the United States. Donald MacDonald (cofounder of the Grandfather Mountain Highland Games) was the first "commissioner" for the clan society in 1954.

"Clan," from the Gaelic *clann,* means "children," but has come to mean "family," so that those sharing a surname (and hence a tartan) are considered "kin" to each other. (Actually, surnames did not become common in Scotland until the 1600s, by which time clanship was already in decline) (Devine 1994, 8–9). In heritage lore, "kinship" extends to all descendants of the clan's founding ancestor first associated with the surname centuries or even a millennium and a half ago. If we follow the ancient Greek's perception of ethnic identities as derived from eponymous ancestors, then those embracing an identity from perceived ancestors such as Gillean of the Battle-ax are embracing ethnic identities.

While people who have never met one another outside the Scottish heritage context now consider each other "kin" because of a shared surname or belief in a common apical ancestor, biological families also hold family reunions in conjunction with clan society events and maintain ties between generations through a common interest in Scottish roots. Many informants whose children have moved to other states say the only time they get to visit with their grandchildren, beyond Christmas or Thanksgiving, is when they attend Scottish Highland games together (sometimes synchronizing their vacation times to do so). Grandparents and parents often encourage children in a shared pursuit so that together they may bagpipe, country dance, weave, or simply march in a tartan parade. One Clan Henderson member had all of her children and grandchildren learn Highland dancing, another informant from Clan Campbell gave his grandchildren the choice of pipes, fiddle, or harp and paid for their lessons, a founding member of the Clan Douglas Society takes pride in having all nineteen of her grandchildren involved in Scottish athletics, expressive arts, or clan society activities.

In regional terms, southern Scottish heritage events evidence a greater emphasis on clan and kinship than do those in the North or West. At southern Highland games, the main focus is the clan tents and displays on clan heritage, whereas at some of the larger northern events like Detroit and Loon Mountain (now the New Hampshire Games), one may find between fifteen and a few dozen clan tents. The San Francisco Games (which moved to Santa Rosa in 1962 and to Pleasanton in 1994) are the oldest continuous games in the country, yet clan tents did not appear there until the 1980s.[42] At the 2003 Grandfather Mountain Games, over one hundred clan societies were represented by clan tents (not to mention the various Scottish heritage societies displaying there).

Before the Highlandism of Queen Victoria's time there were at most 40 recognized clans; today there are 140 recognized clans, with chiefs who are members of the Standing Council of Scottish Chiefs. The final and legal authority in recognizing or denying the existence of a clan, the Lyon's Court (the legal court of heraldry in Scotland), frequently receives new claims for clan status and claims to a chiefly line and position. As of 2004, the Lord Lyon recognizes 202 armigerous clans and families that have the right to bear arms but do not have a current chief. Due to the significant involvement of Americans in claims for clan status and in support of claimants to chiefly lines, the current Lord Lyon, the Rt. Hon. Robin Orr Blair, attended the Stone Mountain Highland Games in Atlanta in 2003 and made history by being the first Lord Lyon to ever visit the United States in his official capacity.

The association of clans and surnames with particular tartan patterns (what most Americans call "plaids") was largely a late eighteenth- and early nineteenth-century innovation. Though many Scottish Americans' ancestors had settled in America before this convention inspired acceptance and an industry in Scotland, the wearing of the "clan tartan" has become an important marker of identity within the Scottish-American community. Today membership in clan societies most often relies solely on surname—either having the name of the clan or having the surname of a "sept" of a clan (a group once allied with a particular clan). Though the clan system was part of Highland Gaelic culture, those with surnames of Lowland origin also form clan societies—something that, along with the wearing of tartan, would dumbfound their venerated ancestors.

Today's clan society members may choose a style of their clan tartan from an array of fabrics: dress (usually with a white background), mourning (in black and white), hunting (with less conspicuous colors for outdoor activities), district (local designs from which clan tartans probably developed and now serve as an option for those without clan affiliation), military, and chiefs'. Tartans also come in a variety of color schemes: "modern" are usually darker and more vivid than "muted" tartans; "ancient" tartans are pale, resembling the faded samples from which older designs were documented. Color distinctions follow the name of the tartan, as in "MacRae, muted" or "Dress, modern." Different American states, Highland games, bagpipe bands, and other associations also have their own tartans. Investment in Highland attire is considerable, and those who are planning to research their genealogies are cautioned about buying "too much tartan" when they first join a society. After research, some people find they might wear a "more prestigious" tartan or one "of their own" rather than that of a clan of which they had believed their ancestors to be a sept. Even if one chooses to affiliate with a clan society through the idea of septs, loyalties were flexible and any given sept might have allied with various clans, so that fledgling Scots may have an array of identity signifiers from which to choose. While they feel ethnically Scottish, the specific identity within the Scottish-American community *can* be a matter of great flexibility. The marketing of tartan has an almost two-hundred-year history—yielding well over two thousand tartan patterns today.[43] Although participants' reasons for affiliating with a particular clan society are different from those of their presumed ancestors for joining various clans, even Alastair Campbell of Airds, Unicorn Pursuivant of Arms of the Lord Lyon's Court, notes that rather than creating new clans or trying to reinvent a family as a clan, joining a group whose chief you agree to acknowledge is "entirely in the spirit of what actually happened in the past" (1994, 54).

Associating clan with kin means that tartan operates as a type of heraldry. By donning a tartan, one claims the heroic deeds of clansfolk as one's own heritage and the famous members of the clan as one's own "cousins." (Despite the survival of a Gaelic proverb in North Carolina, "all Stuarts are not kinsmen of the king" [Whiting 1949, 124]). Within the community, tartan immediately distinguishes one not only as a Scottish American but as a Graham, a MacLeod, or a Cameron. The wearer of the tartan becomes a bearer of the clan reputation. Consciousness of clan history leads to awareness of "traditional" clan enemies—also identifiable by the tartans they display. As clan feuds are researched and discussed by participants, they surface in ludic fashion on the Scottish Highland games field. Clans known for cattle thieving symbolically "return" wooden images or cardboard cutouts of cows to clans they historically offended. In 2002 the chief of Clan MacDougall and the president of the Clan Malcolm/MacCallum Society met in front of the Grandfather Mountain Memorial Cairn for a mid-afternoon ceremony designed to lift a late-fifteenth-century curse between their clans.

Most societies have a fairly open admission policy and admit members with surnames considered septs of the clan. The Clan Lindsay Society admits those with the surname Lindsay or one of the following sept names: Byer, Cobb, Crawford, Deuchar, Downie, Fotheringham, Summers, or Rhind. Clan Currie offers memberships based on surname, as well as associate memberships for those "whether Scot or not, kinsfolk or just curious." Many other clan societies officially allow "honorary memberships" for those without connections but who wish to "be a friend" to the clan (with the Clan Henderson Society, one can be a "Henderson by affection"). Annual membership dues generally range from $15 to $25 per person, with family rates available. For the truly dedicated, life memberships range from about $500 (Clan Donald) to the more economical $200 for Clan Forbes. To make sure you get your money's worth, some societies, like Clan Hamilton, step their "Life Membership" fees according to how much living you presumably have left to do (if under age forty, $350; if forty to forty-nine, fees drop to $300; and after age sixty, to $200).

Except Clan Donald, Clan Campbell, and Clan Henderson (with fluctuating memberships of over three thousand each), many larger clan societies average under two thousand members, and most others under one thousand members nationwide. In recent years, some societies overwhelmed by mounting membership rolls have begun to restrict membership to those with a demonstrable genealogical (or marital) link to specific clan lands. The Clan Donald Society, the largest clan society in the United States, now requires new members to be related to Clan Donald through demonstrated descent, by marriage, or legal adoption, and those wishing to join with a sept name must prove their ancestors came from a particular territory.[44] The official position of the

Clan Donald USA Genealogy Committee is that sept lists are invalid. Their preferred terminology relates to "Families of Clan Donald." Membership information lists 450 names that are "Families of Clan Donald," qualifying their membership by location. For example, Blues have been associated with Clan Donald, but only those Blues from Islay, Kintyre, or Arran. Scottish Blues from other areas must look to Clan MacMillan. Those of the surname MacMoris/MacMorris may join only if their ancestors are from Moidart; all others are sent to Clan Buchanan. Those of the surname "Glass" wishing to join Clan Donald must have ancestors from Islay, Kintyre, or North Uist and originally have been a MacGlashan. MacGlashans from Perth, Dingwall, or Dunblane were not a sept of Clan Donald, and their descendants are not eligible for membership. MacArthurs are accepted only if they came from Islay or Skye. MacArthurs not of Clan Donald are of Clan Arthur, which membership literature suggests had an ancient connection to Clan Campbell—a mistake about which the ancestors would not be pleased.

The Family of Bruce Society is also more selective in granting membership. One must be a Bruce or a descendant within three generations of a Bruce, which society literature specifies as those "in direct line from King Robert the Bruce, his brothers and sisters, and his Bruce forebears." Given that this king died in 1329, linking applicants to his forebears would require extensive research. Since so much research is generated by members, the society annually publishes a member roster listing their qualifying ancestors. More commonly, clan societies in the United States "adopt" those who wish to "ally" with the clan, and membership rolls include surnames such as Diaz, Roussos, Rosenberg, Lopez, Manzini, and Durand as well as Macs.

The clan societies developed in the United States and Canada since the 1950s have spurred genealogical research and heritage pilgrimage to places associated with clan history (Basu 2001; Ray 2001). Some hyphenated Scots have been active in funding the development of heritage centers in clan landscapes.[45] Places connected to clan heritage and emigration are periodically offered for sale in clan society or Scottish-American newsletters and magazines. For example, in the mid-1990s, a Clan MacGillivray newsletter advertised an offer to the clan of a Victorian stone cottage near "the presumed location . . . occupied and used by the chiefs of the Clan for perhaps 400 years" as "a possible opportunity for the Clan MacGillivray to return, in a sense, to the ancestral home of its chiefs in Scotland" (Ray 2001, 227). Square-foot parcels of land near Culloden Battlefield and at Ullapool (from where the immigrant ship *Hector* sailed for Pictou, Nova Scotia, in 1773) have also been advertised in community literature. For the ultimate "return," one's ashes can be scattered over clan lands. A company called "Return to Alba," based in East Kilbride, handles the legal aspects and advertises this service—"to strengthen and reaffirm your Scottish roots." "Return to Alba" and other heritage entrepreneurs advertise in community literature like the twenty-seven-year-old monthly newspaper *The Scottish Banner* (sold to diasporic communities in Australia, Canada, New Zealand, and the United States). Tourism supports close to 197,000 jobs in Scotland and provides at least 20 percent of the gross domestic product. The importance of specific clan heritage for hyphenated Scots is not lost on tourism promoters, kitsch marketers, or today's clan chiefs. Increasingly, clan society members organize tours of Scotland together and organize "clan reunions" at the residence of their chiefs.

Today there are over 150 Scottish clan societies and "family associations."[46] International in focus, many are the American branches of United Kingdom societies with branches also in Canada, Australia, New Zealand, and other former colonies. As with the Boyds, the Urquharts, or the Macleans/ Maclaines, sometimes two separate societies may exist for what was once a single clan—when rival chiefs or disagreements over the geographical focus of a clan exist. Large clan societies have stateside heads (variously called commissioners, deputy commissioners, lieutenants, commanders, standard bearers, and conveners), all of whom are liaisons for the chief in America. Societies may also have regional, state, and local conveners. Modeled on the Standing Council of Scottish Chiefs in 1974, the Council of Scottish Clans and Associations (COSCA) is an educational and charitable organization that offers organizational advice to clan societies and family associations. Many members of COSCA believe that membership gives "legitimacy" to a clan society or family association, but only about two-thirds of family associations and clan societies are members. COSCA is just one of the bodies that links the many national, regional, and local organizations forming the Scottish-American community.

National, Expressive Arts, and Special Interest Ethnic Organizations

COSCA is also one of nine national organizations forming "The Scottish Coalition." The others include the Association of St. Andrew Societies and the bodies listed below. In 1956 Lord and Lady Malcolm Douglas-Hamilton founded "The American-Scottish Foundation" to build bonds between Americans and Scots and to "operate as a clearing house and information center about genealogy, publications, trade contacts, music and Scottish activities." Since 1970 the foundation has given the "Wallace Award" to recognize leading Americans of Scottish birth or descent. Incorporated in 1976, the "Caledonian Foundation USA" aims "to preserve and strengthen the traditional bonds among Scotland, Canada, and the United States" and primarily supports the expressive arts. The Association of Scottish Games and Festivals was founded in 1981 to assist in "the production of Highland Games" in North America. Founded in 1965, Scottish Heritage USA supports the National Trust for Scotland. The Tartan Educational and Cultural Association (with the International Association of Tartan Studies) provides information on tartan and its history. Organized in 1981, the Scottish-American Military Society is open to any honorably discharged veteran and active duty or reserve military persons in any branch of the U.S. Armed Forces. Most recently, the "Living Legacy of Scotland" was founded in 2000 to create and present "educational displays and productions for public events, for schools, museums and libraries" and to provide academic grants and scholarships for those researching Scottish subjects.

Hyphenated Scots learning, performing, or competing in the Scottish expressive arts are also highly organized. The Alliance of North American Pipe Band Associations fosters cooperation among pipe bands in the ten regional associations across the United States and Canada. Andrew Berthoff, son of Rowland Berthoff and editor of *Piper and Drummer* magazine, estimates there are between nine hundred and one thousand competitive and noncompetitive pipe bands in North America. There are approximately two hundred Scottish Country Dance groups in the United States.[47] Teachers must pass a rigorous certification process and teach two years before taking a full certificate exam. Dancers follow regulations set by the Royal Scottish Country Dance Society (RSCDS) founded by Jane Milligan in 1923. Highland dancing competitions follow standards and judging requirements of the Scottish Official Board of Highland Dancing, formed in Scotland in 1950.[48] North American affiliates of this body are "ScotDance Canada" and "FUSTA," the Federation of United States Teachers and Adjudicators (established in 1980) and now representing approximately 260 credentialed Highland dance teachers. FUSTA president William Weaver estimates there are roughly 150 Highland dancing schools across the United States and close to 300 in Canada. Gaelic-learners most frequently join *An Comunn Gaidhealach Ameireaga* (The Gaelic Society of America), the largest Scots Gaelic organization in the United States. Based in Maryland, the society hosts Gaelic immersion workshops and holds an annual *Mòd* at the Ligonier Highland Games in Pennsylvania each September.

Additionally, the Scottish-American community includes many reenactment and living history groups with Scottish themes. I have mentioned the Oglethorpe Highlanders (circa 1742) in Georgia. The Jacobite-themed "MacFarlane's Company" makes living history presentations and teaches about Scottish diaspora topics throughout the Great Lakes region; some members have traveled to portray historical characters at properties owned by the National Trust for Scotland, including the Jacobite-associated sites of Glenfinnan, Glencoe, and Culloden. The Clan McLachlan Association of North America sponsored the formation of the United Regiment of MacLachlans and MacLeans (circa 1745) in the 250th anniversary year of Culloden. The 1745 Jacobite Society, based in Arizona, reenacts the French and Indian War and Revolutionary War period at Highland games and bivouac gatherings. The Historic Highlanders, based in New Hampshire, reenacts everyday life in Scotland from 1314 (the date of Bannockburn) to 1746 (the date of Culloden). The 78th Fraser Highlanders (an actual Scottish regiment raised in 1757 that played a role in the Seven Years War and disbanded in Quebec in 1763) now has "outposts" of living historians across North America. The 42nd Royal Highland Regiment reenacts the Black Watch (Royal Highlanders) of the late eighteenth century. The regiment was created in 1739 (renumbered "42nd" in 1749), and in 1756 was sent to New York, where half of its troops fell at the first Battle of Fort Ticonderoga in 1758. The regiment also fought in the American Revolution and is presently the most senior of all the Highland regiments. (The 6th Territorial Battalion of the Black Watch, a living history unit based in Maine, was established in 1984 to educate the public about the role of Scottish soldiers in World War I.) The 84th Regiment of Foot (Royal Highland Emigrants), with units across the United States, reenacts the first Highland regiment raised in the Americas. Raised in 1775, both battalions of the Royal Highland Emigrants were recruited mainly in North Carolina's Cape Fear Valley, in the Maritimes, and in New York's Mohawk Valley, and fought in the American Revolution.

Each type of organization forms a community within the Scottish-American community. For example, Highland dancers and reenactors describe their fellows as "extended family," sharing costumes, food, travel arrangements, and accommodation. The above summary considers only the major categories of organizations within the community, but does not begin to reveal the variety of interest groups, such as societies for fans of "Scottish Fold" cats and Border Collies, or spinning and weaving, golf and curling, or for groupies of Scottish folk bands. The venue at which the myriad Scottish interest groups gather is the Highland games.

Highland Games and Gatherings

By tradition, Highland games grew from competitions held by a king or chief for the dual purpose of amusement and the selection of fit young men as bodyguards, messengers, and laborers. One of the first recorded foot races, organized by King Malcolm Ceann Mor (Malcolm of the "big head") in the late eleventh century, was to the summit of Craig Choinnich (overlooking the Braes of Mar). Through subsequent centuries, athletic competitions combined with the periodic meetings, or "gatherings," of regional clansfolk and clan chiefs to make clan and marriage alliances and to settle disputes. In addition to these social and political roles, the Highland gatherings had economic functions. Largely self-sufficient agro-pastoral Highlanders relied principally on cattle, oats, and barley, and gatherings provided venues to trade these for other goods. In medieval times, wrestling, horse races, and foot races were familiar activities on St. Michael's Feast Day (September 29). Other sporting events took place in conjunction with *wappinshaws* (annual or periodic local musters of fighting-age men and their weapons).

The villagers of Ceres in Fife claim their Highland gathering is the oldest in Scotland and link their first event to a homecoming celebration for six hundred local bowmen returning after the Battle of Bannockburn (1314) (D. Webster 1959, 10). David Webster also notes that the first gathering organized by one of the post-Culloden Highland societies was that in Falkirk in 1781 (11). The "Northern Meeting" at Inverness has also claimed to be the oldest event in Scotland, beginning in 1788 (Livingstone 1997, 178). Most scholars also suggest that Highland games as we know them today began with the Highlandism of Sir Walter Scott's era. The first event of that period occurred in 1819 in Perthshire at St. Fillans. Another of the earliest revivals of the romantic period was an event held at Braemar, where King Malcolm's subjects had famously competed. The Braemar Highland Society (formed in 1817) first organized a gathering in 1832 and was attended by Queen Victoria for the first time in 1848. These are the events the royal family still attends. The gathering now attracts around eighteen thousand participants and observers each year; it hosts sixty-six events, and competition prize money totals over twelve thousand pounds.

In the nineteenth-century United States and Canada, Highland games were often called "Caledonian games" (from the Roman name for Scotland) (Gillespie 2000, 43). While some type of Scottish athletic competitions may have occurred among colonial Highlanders in North America, references are sketchy at best. Emily Ann Donaldson notes that the games came to the United States in 1836 when the Highland Society of New York held its first "Sportive Meeting" in Hoboken, New Jersey (1986, 12–13; Berthoff 1982, 8). Boston began an event in 1853 (Redmond 1971, 15). Two American cities claim to have the oldest, enduring Highland games: San Francisco had a games event in 1866, and Detroit in 1867 (Donaldson 1986, 24). Canada's first Highland games took place in Nova Scotia's Antigonish in 1863 (McKay 1992, 8).[49]

In the United States, the popularity of, and funding for, Highland games reveals regional patterns since the Civil War. In the South, many events founded in the nineteenth century dissipated with the Civil War and the privations of Reconstruction. Rowland Berthoff found that between 1869 and 1909 only eleven southern towns held Highland games (1982, 8).

Gerald Redmond notes that Caledonian games experienced their greatest nineteenth-century popularity in the fifteen years after the Civil War, attracting as many as twenty thousand people, except, of course, in the war-devastated South (1971, 42, 111). (Although, the Caledonian Club of Richmond, Virginia, started games in 1873.) Caledonian clubs and games flourished in the North immediately after the war. Organized in 1866, the Brooklyn Caledonian Club held its first games the following year; the St. Andrew's Society of Milwaukee held its first annual games in 1867 (43). The first annual New Haven Games began in 1871. Redmond suggests that the spread of Caledonian games was "part of the phenomenal 'rise of sport' which occurred in the United States during the latter part of the nineteenth century . . . Immigration, industrialization and urbanization, the technological revolution, the closing of the frontier, the establishment of new values, and the status that high society gave to sport were all contributing factors" in addition to an increase in school-related sporting (1971, 45, 73). Princeton University held its first Caledonian games in 1873.

During this period events were transnational (featuring athletes and judges from Scotland), international (Canadians and Americans competed together), and multiethnic (as they are today). *The Scottish-American Journal* (a weekly newspaper printed from 1857 to 1886 in New York City and continued as *The Scottish American* until about 1919) regularly published accounts of Caledonian games, noting when a particularly famous athlete from Scotland was to appear and what events would be featured. In 1867 Canadians and Americans began competing against each other in Scottish athletics, and Caledonian clubs from both countries created the North American United Caledonian Association (NAUCA) in 1870 (lasting until about 1898). In the United States, what led to the increasing popularity of the games also led to their decline as people became interested in homegrown sports such as baseball, American football, and basketball. Some scholars suggest that the Caledonian games shaped American sporting traditions.

Both Berthoff and Redmond argue that American track and field traditions evolved directly from the Caledonian games and also note that the Scottish events engaged local communities, not just those claiming Scottish descent (Redmond 1971, 140). African Americans, Irish Americans, and other "non-Scots" competed in the games. "From the first, the gatherings transcended Scottish ethnicity. Until late in the century, they were the one occasion in many towns when thousands of people of all sorts mingled indiscriminately—virtually the first mass-spectator sports in America" (Berthoff 1982, 8). In the nineteenth century, events did not have the clan loyalties or identity focus of those today. Now, Asian Americans, African Americans, as well as Hungarian Americans, German Americans, and Hispanics compete in athletic, musical, and dancing competitions, but most often as members of clan societies. Athletes competing in kilts of clan tartans are just as likely to be named Pulcinella, Gudmundsson, Vierra, or Gaenzle today as MacKenzie or Graham. In this multicultural era, not only is a hyphen desirable, but two or more are welcomed.

The games declined in the last decade of the nineteenth century and again with the onset of the Great Depression. Approximately 125 games in existence in 1920 shrunk to about two dozen by the mid-1960s before the surge of ethnic revival.[50] By 1979 that number had almost tripled, and from 1985 to 2003 it had nearly quadrupled in the United States and almost tripled in Canada. In 1982 Rowland Berthoff counted 60 games across the United States; in 2003 there were close to 230 (not including general "Celtic" festivals that would also feature Irish themes). The 26 games he identified in Canada in 1982 had grown to 70 in 2003, at a time that was supposed to see "the twilight of European ethnicities" (Alba 1985).[51] Together, Canada and the United States host three times as many Highland games as does Scotland.[52] Even so, Americans and Canadians still travel to Scotland to compete at events in "the homeland." So many North Americans were crowding the Highland dancing competitions at the Cowal Games in Dunoon that the event was expanded in 2003 to three days to accommodate a new Scottish National Highland Dancing Championship exclusively for native Scots.

Many events occur in areas with known Scottish settlers or town founders (for example, Red Springs Highland Games in North Carolina's Cape Fear Valley or the Glasgow Highland Games in Glasgow, Kentucky), but many others were created to draw tourists and boost local economies. The prestigious Grandfather Mountain Highland Games began in a Scots-Irish (not Highlander) settled area at Linville in the Blue Ridge Mountains to attract tourists. The McPherson (Kansas) Highland Games acknowledges in its promotional materials that one of its main purposes is to provide a destination event to benefit the McPherson economy. Considering the U.S. growth of Highland games *and* Celtic festivals by state, California has the most Scottish and Celtic events, followed by Texas, Pennsylvania, New York, Florida, Virginia, and North Carolina. The most rapid regional growth in post–World War II Scottish games and festivals has been in the South, where a distinctly regional style flavors events and perceptions of Scottish identity.[53]

Athletic competitions follow standards established by the Scottish Games Association, the governing body of Highland games in Scotland. In the eastern United States and Ontario, Canada, athletic events are informed by the North American Scottish Games Association (NASGA). In the western United States the information source is the Scottish American Athletic Association (SAAA), and in the Midwest the Rocky Mountain Scottish Athletic Group provides guidelines for events. (The Southeast also has a Scottish Amateur Athletics association.) Nationally, there are three classes of athletes participating in "the heavies": professionals (competing for prize money and usually participating by invitation only); amateurs (often divided further into skill levels); and masters (for athletes over forty or forty-five years of age). If the games events extend beyond one day, professional and amateur events may occur on different days. Athletes in both categories must qualify to compete and competitor numbers are limited. Even at large, multiday events like the games at Grandfather Mountain, games president and athletic judge Ross Morrison notes that participants are limited to eight professionals and ten amateurs. In the last decade women's competitions have also developed across the country.[54] The annual "North-South Challenge," which now occurs at the Highland Games of Louisiana, pits five southern athletes against five northerners and now includes women.

Native Scottish athletes tour the now-global games circuit. Athletes have been crossing the Atlantic to compete since the nineteenth century. Scottish athletic champion Donald Dinnie came across in 1871, as well as James Fleming and others, to compete with Americans for one-hundred-dollar prizes. By competing in several events, David Webster and Gerald Redmond tell us, Dinnie was able to earn over seven hundred dollars a day. Promoters also offered him passage and large sums to appear. He did not always beat the North Americans, but both Americans and Canadian athletes complained that the presence of professionals from Scotland made the games unprofitable for North American natives even to attend—something that North Americans may still be heard to grumble about on occasion. (While Americans have done well in dancing and musical competitions at Highland games in Scotland, North American athletes have not fared as well in the homeland.) Prize money for the New York Caledonian Club's sixteenth annual games in 1872 was a total of fifteen hundred dollars, of which one thousand dollars was in cash and five hundred dollars was in goods (Redmond 1971, 82; Webster 1959) At small games today the totals are not much different, with thirty to eighty dollars being common prize amounts per event. The "professional" Scottish athletes might also be preachers, insurance salesmen, construction workers, or lawyers, and the day's awards generally cover little more than participants' expenses to get to the games.

Some games have corporate sponsorship to cover the professional athletes' travel and accommodation expenses. While the Southeast has the greatest number of dancing competitions and the Northeast the greatest number of piping competitions, the biggest prizes for athletics are west of the Rockies. In the South, local businesses and clan societies generally sponsor events; in the North more corporate sponsorship flavors the events—usually beer or other companies with some regional connection (for example, Samuel Adams beer or local communications companies). In the West, in addition to clan society or local business sponsorship, international corporate sponsorship is not uncommon. For example, Glenfiddich and Guinness sponsor the games at Estes Park, Colorado, and large events, such as those at Pleasanton, California, and Estes Park appear on national television's ESPN2.[55]

Highland games shape the Scottish-American calendar. Many participants "do the games circuit," attending multiple events each year. Each event develops a distinct feel by association with a particular competition, clan gathering, public ritual, or regional flair. Most other Scottish festivals in the United States also have a Highland focus, though a few in Scots-Irish-settled areas celebrate those ancestral immigrants even if the distinction between Highland and Scots-Irish is not always clear. In 1996 Radford University in Virginia adopted the MacFarlane as its "official tartan," and began a Highlander Festival in honor of its Scots-Irish roots. In 1997 Snow Ridge, in New York's Adirondack Mountains, hosted its first annual "Scots-Irish" Festival, which locals claim has the "most authentic Scots-Irish music found anywhere in the country" (although they also have Highland dancing competitions and bagpipe bands).

Today's celebration of a singular Scottish heritage by those whose ancestors had distinct Lowland, Highland, or Scots-Irish identities is not unlike other hyphenated Americans celebrating the invented tradition of Kwanzaa with a pastiche of African language fragments, foodways, and material cultures from quite separate African cultures and ethnic groups; or celebrating an "Italian" identity when one's ancestors carefully maintained discrete identities as Tuscans, Piedmontese, Sicilians, or Umbrians. A blending of traditions that revered ancestors would find anathema is not uncommon in heritage celebrations generally. Especially in the contemporary social climate, heritage enthusiasts creatively gloss gaps in cultural knowledge by sampling a variety of related (or not-so-related) traditions that have emotional appeal.

North Americans, as do members of the Scottish diaspora worldwide, embrace a Highlandized vision of Scottish heritage. However, the contrasting immigration experience of Scots in Canada yielded a different sense of ethnicity in relation to Canadian identity and different processes of ethnic organization than those in the United States. In the next chapter, historian Michael Vance considers the role of Scots and Scottishness in Canada.

Notes

1. For works examining the formation and reformation of the Scottish national identity, see Withers 2002, 1992; Edensor 2002; Smout 1994; Pittock 1999, 2001; McArthur 2003; Broun, Finlay, and Lynch 1998; McCrone, Kendrick, and Straw 1989; McCrone, Morris, and Kiely 1995; Ferguson 1998; McCrone 2001; Nairn 2000; B. Webster 1997; Ascherson 2002; Kidd 1997, 1999; Bennett 2002; Devine and Logue 2002; S. Macdonald 1997; Harvie 1994; B. Webster 1997; Calder 2002; MacDougall 2001; Morgan 2000; Cohen 2000; Hearn 2000; Bond and Rosie 2002.

2. See T. C. Smout 1969; Neville 1979; Fischer 1989; Calder 2002, Withers 1988; Cowan 1992; Kidd 1997; Broun, 1998; and Pittock 2001. Devine claims that the convention "the Highlands and Lowlands of Scotland" dates only to the later 1300s, and at that time Gaelic was "still spoken widely in districts as far south as Fife in the east and Galloway in the west." Devine also notes that the Aberdeen chronicler John of Fordun first wrote of Scotland as a land of Highlanders and Lowlanders in 1380, describing them as differing in culture, dress, speech, and social behavior (1994, 1).

3. This is contrary to Landsman's unsubstantiable suggestion that ethnic identities of British immigrants to America did not exist in their homeland or during the seventeenth and eighteenth centuries in their new land, but were a response to "their much later followers" (1999, 463).

4. For works examining Tartanry, Highlandism/Balmoralism, see Cameron 1998; Jarvie 1991, 1989; McKay 1992, 1994; Pittock 1991, 1995; Ray 1998, 2001; Withers 1992; and Devine 1994, 2003.

5. See Macinness 1992 and 1996 and Devine (1994, 11) for arguments that the Jacobite defeat merely accelerated economic and social changes that had been leading to the demise of the clan system for over a century prior to Culloden. For the complicated loyalties entailed in the Risings, see Pittock 1998.

6. Many seemed to have worked off their indentures after seven years. For more information on Scottish bondservants, see also W. Smith 1961; Galenson 1981; and Ekirch 1987.

7. Journalist Jim Hewitson named his book *Tam Blake & Co.* (1993), describing "the story of Scots in America," after Thomas Blake.

8. I repeat these figures with caution, as Brock notes that his source (Howard

Barker's "National Stocks in the Population of the United States," *Annual Report of the American Historical Association for 1931,* vol. 1, ch. 4) estimated percentages based on surnames distinctive to the Highlands and Northeast of Scotland and may therefore underestimate the number of Scots-Irish and Lowland Scots in Virginia, Maryland, and South Carolina (which received mostly Lowland Scots immigrants). While indicative, surname studies of course belie the migration of the persons before emigration (Brock 1982, 241).

9. This survey is of course only just touching the highlights; for more on the history of Scottish immigration to North America, see Bumsted 1982; Bernard 1986; Ekrich 1987; A. Smith 1947; Aspinwall 1985; Erickson 1972; Dobson 1994, 2000; Berthoff 1953; Bailyn 1986a, 1986b; Harper 2003; and Graham 1956.

10. Eric Richards also reminds us: "It is tempting to tell the entire Highland expatriation story as a mechanical reaction to Malthusian crises and landlord oppression. Such matters unquestionably loom large in the account, but taken alone they diminish the variety and dynamism of the Highland participation in the imperial outreach" (1999, 107).

11. By the 1820s, very few representatives of the tacksman class remained to play the role they had in earlier migrations to North America (Hunter 1994, 107).

12. Landowners had "disposed" of unwanted tenants before then. As early as 1739 the Macdonalds and Macleods of Skye sold their clansfolk as indentured servants to the Carolinas. In the 1760s, sheep began to feature in the Highland economy on estates such as those of Sir John Lockhart-Ross and later Sir John Sinclair, whose Cheviot sheep were referred to by locals as "four-footed clansmen." In 1801 nearly 50 percent of the clansfolk living in the Strathglass area were cleared by William, the 24th Chisholm, and like many others, put on greatly overcrowded ships. The Sutherlands made their shepherds justices of the peace—giving them control to evict tenants. Patrick Sellar was their most infamous factor (see Richards 1999).

13. For a thorough consideration of "Gaelic Nova Scotia," see Kennedy 2002. Kennedy's 1995 PhD dissertation, "*Is leis an Tighearna an talamh agus an lan*" (The Earth and All That It Contains Belongs to God: The Scottish Gaelic Settlement History of Prince Edward Island), explores the survival of different Gaelic dialects on Prince Edward Island resulting from the immigration of neighbors from different areas of the Isle of Skye who settled together and maintained their distinctive ways of speaking even when a shared language would have seemed their greatest source of unity in a new land. See also Dunn 1953.

14. Thanks to William A. Steadley-Campbell, a descendant of Daniel Douglas Campbell and a past director of the Walton County Heritage Association, for this information.

15. In other sources "McIntosh" is the preferred spelling (see Dobson 1994).

16. The National Trust for Scotland also receives financial support from the North America Foundation in the United States, which raises a half-million dollars for the Trust in some years.

17. Campbell had previously held land in Islay, which was also the home of another *Scotus Americanus* (the pro-emigration pamphleteer) (Hunter 1994, 74).

18. The subject of underexplored relationships between Scots and Native Americans deserves a dissertation (or several). Brett Riggs (1997, 1999) has examined Cherokee-Scottish relationships in North Carolina. Considering the material condition of daily life before the "Trail of Tears," Riggs explores the documentary and archaeological records of a Removal Period (1835–1838) Cherokee household from the mountains of southwestern North Carolina. Cherokee who could demonstrate a certain percentage of Scots ancestry could avoid removal, and later photographs document Métis families holding both lacrosse sticks and fiddles in front of their homes. Tom Bryan has published a slim volume titled *Twa Tribes: Scots among the Native Americans* (Edinburgh: NMS Enterprises, 2003), which, despite unusual spellings and confused tribal histories, gives brief accounts of contacts through the fur trade and of the usually discussed figures in Métis histories (Hugo Reid, Alexander Ross, and Charles McKenzie). Grace Schwartzman and Susan K. Barnard published an article in the *Georgia Historical Quarterly* (vol. 75, no. 4 [winter 1991], 697–718) titled "A Trail of Broken Promises: Georgians and Muscogee/Creek Treaties, 1796–1826," which considers the controversial maneuvers of Chief William McIntosh (son of a Scottish father and a Creek mother). His tale is also recounted in Benjamin Griffith's *McIntosh and Weatherford: Creek Indian Leaders* (Tuscaloosa: U of Alabama P, 1988). Donald Meek considered British missionary activity among American Indians and Highlanders settled in Georgia in his 1989 essay "Scottish Highlanders, North American Indians and the SSPCK: Some Cultural Perspectives," in *Records of the Scottish Church History Society*, vol. 23, 378–96. Dorothy Downs published "British Influences on Creek and Seminole Men's Clothing, 1733–1858" in *The Florida Anthropologist* (1980, 46–65). Michael Loukinen produced and directed a 1991 documentary called *Medicine Fiddle*, examining Native American innovations on step dancing and Irish/Scots fiddle playing that spread with the fur trade (University of California Extension Center for Media and Independent Learning, Berkeley, CA). Based on the text of a Scottish Record Office exhibition (about 1990), the Record Office published *The North-American Indians: 200 Years of Scottish Contacts* by Margaret Sanderson.

19. Gaelic did not seem to be often committed to print in North America. Michael Newton has written that the "only all-Gaelic periodical published in North America was Mac-Talla, based in Cape Breton. It began in May 1892 and had a readership throughout Canada and the western and northern United States," but Newton does not comment on the size of this readership or the specific location of Gaelic-speaking communities in Canada and the western and northern United States at this time period (2001, in *Scotia* 25, 1–28.)

20. I am greatly generalizing here, but I do not go so far as to agree with Patrick Griffin (2001, 4), who follows Ned Landsman (1985) in asserting that Lowlanders and Highlanders "united around the vital piety of a Scottish Calvinist tradition" and became united in the Scottish identity. Rather, Ulster Scots, Lowland Scots, and Highland Scots did remain quite distinct socially and politically. For a detailed examination of the formation of an American Presbyterianism and the many dissenting voices and debates, see Nybakken 1982; Westerkamp 1988; and Schmidt 1989.

21. In North Carolina, only in 1758, with the simultaneous founding of Barbeque,

Longstreet, and Bluff Presbyterian Churches in North Carolina, did the first Gaelic-speaking Presbyterian arrive (Rev. James Campbell), and he was forced to leave because of his pro-independence sympathies and his Highland congregation's Loyalism. The first Presbyterian minister to visit the Highlanders in 1756 was Hugh McAden, an itinerate preacher to the Scots-Irish and Scottish settlements in North Carolina (Meyer 1957, 113).

22. The Great Awakening was really a series of revivals beginning at the end of the seventeenth century and lasting throughout the eighteenth. These occurred in different places on the frontier, outside Puritan Massachusetts and Anglican Virginia, in areas where ministers had been less available, and where religious control of society was largely absent and in fact much of the population was "unchurched." The English parish system had not crossed the water—leading to the fabulous diversity of Protestant denominations America has today.

23. Miller notes that 1.8 million people came to North America between the summer of 1845 and the early 1850s because of the Great Famine (1985, 280). Irish immigrants to America before this time were mostly Scots-Irish.

24. While such a "mentality" has often been credited for the success of the Scots-Irish in settling the American frontier, Maldwyn Jones makes a good case for rejecting this oft-repeated claim (1991, 293).

25. Maldwyn Jones remarks on the hostility that the early Scots-Irish encountered in their initial immigration to New England (1717–1718) and notes that this spurred their movement to Pennsylvania from about 1725 (for the religious freedom and economic opportunities offered in Penn's colony) (1991, 294).

26. Billy Kennedy has produced a popular series of books on the Scots-Irish in America, including *The Making of America: How the Scots-Irish Shaped a Nation* (Greenville, SC: Ambassador, 2001); *Heroes of the Scots-Irish in America* (Belfast: Ambassador, 2000); *Faith and Freedom: The Scots-Irish in America* (Belfast: Ambassador, 1999); and *The Scots-Irish in Pennsylvania and Kentucky* (1998), *The Scots-Irish in the Carolinas* (1997), *The Scots-Irish in the Shenandoah Valley (1996)*, and *The Scots-Irish in the Hills of Tennessee* (1996), all with the Causeway Press in Belfast.

27. See J. G. Craighead's 1878 account of Scots-Irish and Scottish Presbyterians in the United States; Arthur Perry's account of the Scotch-Irish in New England in volume 2 of the *Proceedings and Addresses of the Scotch-Irish Society of America* (Nashville, 1890–1900), 107–14; Charles Hanna's two-volume *The Scotch-Irish, or the Scot in North Britain, North Ireland, and North America* (1902); John Linehan's *The Irish Scots and the "Scotch-Irish"* (1902); Samuel Green's *The Scotch-Irish in America* (1895); Charles Knowles Bolton's *Scotch-Irish Pioneers in Ulster and America* (1910); John Walker Dinsmore's *The Scotch-Irish in America* (1906); Henry Jones Ford's *The Scotch-Irish in America* (1915); Robert Gartland's *The Scotch-Irish in Western Pennsylvania* (1923); Maude Glasgow's *The Scotch-Irish in Northern Ireland and in the American Colonies* (1936); and E. R. R. Green's *Essays in Scotch-Irish History* (1969). The Scotch-Irish Foundation of the U.S.A. (founded in 1889) has deposited its library and archives at the Balch Institute for Ethnic Studies in Philadelphia, Pennsylvania. As with Scots in general, celebratory publications on the Scots-Irish continue. See, for example, *Born*

Fighting: How the Scots-Irish Shaped America, by James Webb (New York: Broadway Books, 2004).

28. See *http:/www.arts.ulster.ac.uk/ulsterscots/bib_emig ration.htm* for an extensive bibliography on Ulster Scots and emigration.

29. Wilson's article "Elizabethan America" appeared in *Atlantic Monthly* 144 (August 1929), 238–44. Wilson followed a line of thinking begun by Emma Bell Miles, Horace Kephart, John Charles Campbell, and especially, Ellen Churchill Semple's 1901 article "The Anglo-Saxons of the Kentucky Mountains: A Study in Anthropogeography," *Geographical Journal* 17, no. 6: 589–93. For new scholarship on the Ulster Scots and English speech, see Michael Montgomery, *From Ulster to America: The Scotch-Irish Heritage of American English* (Belfast: Ulster Historical Foundation, forthcoming).

30. See Patricia Beaver and Helen Lewis (1998), "Uncovering the Trail of Ethnic Denial: Ethnicity in Appalachia," in *Cultural Diversity in the U.S. South,* ed. Carole E. Hill and Patricia D. Beaver (Athens: U of Georgia P), and also several essays in Ray 2003.

31. The decade of the 1880s also saw a remarkably high number of Scots immigrants (149,869 people) (Berthoff 1953, 5).

32. Berthoff noted that this society maintained a predominantly Scottish-born membership longer than any other. In the late 1970s, three-quarters of members were still Scottish-born (1982, 14).

33. David Dobson notes that this original Savannah St. Andrew's "Club" began in the 1730s, went into abeyance with the migration of influential members to South Carolina in 1740, was reestablished as a "Society" in 1764, and faded again in 1782 because of its Loyalist perspectives (Dobson 1994, 122). Some sources say the Savannah society was founded in 1750, but the society's seal uses the date 1737.

34. Records throughout the society's existence are deposited at the Balch Institute for Ethnic Studies of the Historical Society of Pennsylvania.

35. The St. Andrew's societies were the most successful and enduring benevolent societies, but there were others, one of the better known being the Scots Thistle Society founded in Philadelphia in 1796.

36. Berthoff further notes that fraction groups developed: the American Order of Scottish Clans seceded in 1889 and had a dozen lodges in Massachusetts. In the 1890s a Texas society with five lodges took the name "Universal Order of Scottish Clans," and a Canadian fraternity, the Sons of Scotland, had branches in the United States (1953, 181).

37. Berthoff notes that in 1979, seventy were still in existence (1982, 14).

38. Connecticut (4 chapters), Illinois (1), Indiana (1), Massachusetts (6), Michigan (3 lodges), Missouri (1), New Hampshire (1), New Jersey (7), New York (7), Ohio (2), Pennsylvania (10 lodges), Rhode Island (1), and Baltimore, Maryland (1 lodge)

39. The Anglo-focused Sons of St. George had two auxiliary groups, the Daughters of St. George and the Independent Daughters of St. George (with no doubt an interesting story to explain the divide). Welsh women also formed organizations, eventually developing the National Women's Welsh-American Clubs in 1915.

40. For a localized account of Welsh American organizations, see Lorraine Murray

(1990), "Unique Americans: The Welsh-American Ethnic Group in the Philadelphia Area," in *Encounters with American Ethnic Cultures,* ed. Phillip Kilbride, Jane Goodage, and Elizabeth Ameisen, 101–15.

41. One of the most unusual of the Burns's birthday celebrations I attended during fieldwork was thrown by a Scottish country dance group at Historic Old Salem in Winston-Salem, North Carolina (one of the members worked at the Moravian settlement's museum), and featured a homemade haggis in a deer stomach rather than the traditional sheep's paunch to provide for the large crowd. At the largest I attended, with almost four hundred people present, I was asked to give the Immortal Memory. Those who came to hear romantic poetry must have been disappointed by my list of women whose lives he'd ruined and the ways he was quoted as describing them. (He called one of his mother's servants, whom he impregnated, "a partridge I brought down with my gun.") After suggesting Burns should have been gelded, I do not expect a return invitation.

42. Thanks to Ross Morrison for bringing this to my attention.

43. One of the oldest known samples of tartan from the fourth century B.C. comes from a place called Molzbichl in Carinthia in Austria, where the Iron Age Celtic peoples were first identified as such. (In another interesting hybrid born of the most recent wave of fascination with the Celts, Thomas Rettl, an Austrian clothing manufacturer, is hoping to market a deer-leather kilt—a mixture of lederhosen and tartan—in Scotland.) Ancient plaid woolen twills are also found in Ürümchi, the regional capital of western China (Chinese Turkestan) with the mummies of tall, large-nosed, blond and red-haired Caucasians who settled there in the last Bronze and early Iron Age (Barber 1999).

44. This is somewhat at odds with the actual Highland clan system of demonstrated descent back four generations and stipulated descent beyond.

45. Despite multigenerational involvement in Scottish activities stateside, the prohibitive cost of three generations traveling together to Scotland means that individuals or couples joining other members of their clan societies on pilgrimages to the homeland are more common than three-generation family trips.

46. Figure thanks to Sandy Gallamore, a member of the board of trustees for COSCA. For more on clan societies, see Ray 2001.

47. Estimate again thanks to Sandy Gallamore.

48. Children may begin taking Highland dancing lessons as young as age four. With military origins, the vigorous dancing is considered a sport. While dancers often perform at heritage events and *ceilidhs,* the primary focus of dancing schools is on competition.

49. Several scholars have noted that in 1819 a group of Scots fur traders in Glengarry County, Ontario, sponsored the first Highland games in North America (Donaldson 1986; Jarvie 1991; Cowan 1992, 169), but Greg Gillespie notes that the society sponsored only solo piping contests that did not involve athletic events (2000).

50. Leading that growth was the 1956 founding of the Grandfather Mountain Highland Games in Linville, North Carolina, by Agnes MacRae Morton (who owned the mountain) and Donald Francis MacDonald (a Charlotte journalist). Known as "America's Braemar," the Grandfather Games are the most prestigious in the nation.

The events span four days with a torchlight opening ceremony on the first Thursday evening after July 4 and continue through three days of competitions to end on the Sunday evening (for more on the Grandfather Mountain Games, see Donaldson 1986 and Ray 2001). It should be noted that a few games did get their start during the "slump" of the early twentieth century: Round Hill, Connecticut, began games in 1924; Los Angeles in 1952; and Everett Washington began the Pacific Northwest Games in 1945. The Scottish Games Association was also founded in 1946 to regulate the Highland games circuit.

51. Figures on games and festivals are based on games listings annually compiled by Jim Finegan of the Clan MacLachlan Association of North America and the author's own research. Emily Anne Donaldson counted 82 games in the United States in 1985 (1986, 209). When I first began counting these events in 1992 there were just over 40 events in Canada, with the largest concentration in Ontario (17), followed by Nova Scotia with 8. In that year there were just over 150 events in the United States

52. In Scotland in 2003, there were between 98 and 101 events (depending on which are included). While Scotland has enormous events such as the Braemar and Cowal Highland Games, most are still community events. The Cowal Highland Games in Dunoon attract over 15,000 people and over 150 pipe bands; more than 3,500 people participate in dancing, piping, track and field, and "heavies"—and even shinty (*camanachd* in Gaelic), an Iron Age team sport involving a leather ball and hooked sticks like hockey without the ice, known as "hurling" in Ireland.

53. The phenomenal growth in Scottish events since the mid-1980s is not limited to North America. There are close to thirty annual Scottish heritage events in Australia; they also take place in Zaire, in Xamek Sychrov in the Czech Republic, in Lorient in France, in Tokyo, and the Netherlands (a popular destination for sixteenth- and seventeenth-century emigrant Scots) is home to three annual events. Rio de Janeiro, Brazil, hosted its first Highland games in 2001. There are also pipe band associations in New Zealand, Germany, Scandinavia, South Africa, Australia, and the Netherlands.

54. Women's divisions in Scottish heavy events currently take place at the Loch Prado Games in Chino, California, and in Costa Mesa, near Los Angeles; at the Beltane Festival at Ellis, Kansas; at Carrollton, Kentucky; in Pace, Florida; in Chatham, New York; in Richmond Hill (Savannah) and Culloden, Georgia; in Albuquerque, New Mexico; in Fort Smith, Arizona; at the Houston Highland Games in Texas; in Sterling Colorado; and in Richmond, Rhode Island.

55. Regional patterns in sponsorship, at least for large events, may be changing. In 2003, for example, the Stone Mountain Highland Games in Atlanta received sponsorship from United Distributors and Tennent's Lager.

Works Cited

Alba, Richard. 1985. "The Twilight of Ethnicity among Americans of European Ancestry: The Case of Italians." In *Ethnicity and Race in the U.S.A.: Toward the*

Twenty-first Century, ed. Richard Alba, 134–58. London: Routledge and Kegan Paul.

Ascherson, Neal. 2002. *Stone Voices: The Search for Scotland.* New York: Hill and Wang.

Aspinwall, Bernard. 1985. "The Scots in the United States." In *The Scots Abroad: Labour, Capital, Enterprise, 1750–1914,* ed. R. A. Cage, 80–110. London: Croom Helm.

Bailyn, Bernard. 1986a. *Voyagers to the West: A Passage in the Peopling of America on the Eve of the Revolution.* New York: Knopf.

———. 1986b. *The Peopling of British North America.* New York: Knopf.

Barber, Elizabeth Wayland. 1999. *The Mummies of Ürümchi.* New York: W. W. Norton.

Basu, Paul. 2001. "Hunting Down Home: Reflections on Homeland and the Search for Identity in the Scottish Diaspora." In *Contested Landscapes: Movement, Exile, and Place,* ed. Barabara Bender and Margot Winer. Oxford: Berg.

Bell, Whitfield. 1954. "Scottish Emigration to America: A Letter of Dr. Charles Nisbet to Dr. John Witherspoon, 1784." *William and Mary Quarterly,* Scotland and America, 3d ser., 11, no. 2 (April): 163–78.

Bennett, Margaret. 2002. "Being Scottish." In *Being Scottish,* ed. T. M. Devine and Paddy Logue, 18–20. Edinburgh: Polygon.

Berthoff, Rowland. 1982. "Under the Kilt: Variations on the Scottish-American Ground." *Journal of American Ethnic History* 1, no. 2 (spring): 5–34.

———. 1953. *British Immigrants in Industrial America, 1790–1950.* Cambridge: Harvard UP.

Bitterman, Rusty. 1999. "On Remembering and Forgetting: Highland Memories within the Maritime Diaspora." In *Myth, Migration, and the Making of Memory: Scotia and Nova Scotia c. 1700–1990,* ed. Marjory Harper and Michael E. Vance, 49–72. Halifax, Nova Scotia: Fernwood.

Blethen, Tyler, and Curtis Wood. 1983. *From Ulster to Carolina: The Migration of the Scots-Irish to Southwestern North Carolina.* Cullowhee, NC: Western Carolina Mountain Heritage Center.

Blethen, Tyler, and Curtis Wood, eds. 1997. *Ulster and North America: Transatlantic Perspectives on the Scotch-Irish.* Tuscaloosa: U of Alabama P.

Bond, Ross, and Michael Rosie. 2002. "National Identities in Post-Devolution Scotland." *Scottish Affairs* 40: 34–53.

Brock, William. 1982. *Scotus Americanus: A Survey of the Sources for Links between Scotland and America in the Eighteenth Century.* Edinburgh: Edinburgh UP.

Broun, Dauvit. 1998. "Defining Scotland and the Scots before the Wars of Independence." *Image and Identity: The Making and Re-making of Scotland through the Ages,* ed. Dauvit Broun, R. J. Finlay, and Michael Lynch, 4–17. Edinburgh: John Donald.

Broun, Dauvit, R. J. Finlay, and Michael Lynch, eds. 1998. *Image and Identity: The Making and Re-making of Scotland Through the Ages.* Edinburgh: John Donald.

Bumsted, J. M. 1982. *The People's Clearance: Highland Emigration to British North America, 1770–1815.* Edinburgh: Edinburgh UP.

Calder, Angus. 2002. *Scotlands of the Mind.* Edinburgh: Luath.

Cameron, Ewen. 1998. "Embracing the Past: The Highlands in Nineteenth-Century Scotland." In *Image and Identity: The Making and Re-making of Scotland through the*

Ages, ed. Dauvit Broun, R. J. Finlay, and Michael Lynch, 195–219. Edinburgh: John Donald.

Campbell, Alastair. 1994. "Names and Clans—A Closer Look, Part VI." *Highlander* 32: 54–58.

Cohen, Anthony. 2000. "Peripheral Vision: Nationalism, National Identity, and the Objective Correlative in Scotland." In *Signifying Identities: Anthropological Perspectives on Boundaries and Contested Values,* ed. Anthony Cohen, 145–69. London: Routledge.

Corbitt, David Leroy, ed. 1931. *Public Papers and Letters of Angus Wilton McLean, Governor of North Carolina, 1925–1929.* Raleigh: Presses of Edwards and Broughton Co.

Cowan, Ted. 1999. "The Myth of Scotch Canada." In *Myth, Migration, and the Making of Memory: Scotia and Nova Scotia c. 1700–1990,* ed. Marjory Harper and Michael E. Vance, 49–72. Halifax, Nova Scotia: Fernwood.

———. 1992. "Back Home and the Backcountry: David Hackett Fischer's Albion's Seed." *Appalachian Journal* 19, no. 2 (winter): 166–73.

Craighead, J. G. 1878. *Scotch and Irish Seeds in American Soil: The Early History of the Scotch and Irish Churches, and Their Relations to the Presbyterian Churches of America.* Philadelphia: Presbyterian Board of Education.

Devine, Tom. 2003. *Scotland's Empire, 1600–1815.* London: Allen Lane.

———. 1994. *Clanship to Crofter's War: The Social Transformation of the Scottish Highlands.* Manchester, Eng.: Manchester UP.

———. 1988. *The Great Highland Famine: Hunger, Emigration, and the Scottish Highlands in the Nineteenth Century.* Edinburgh: John Donald.

———. 1975. *The Tobacco Lords: A Study of the Tobacco Merchants of Glasgow and Their Trading Activities, 1740–90.* Edinburgh: John Donald.

Devine, Tom, and Paddy Logue, eds. 2002. *Being Scottish.* Edinburgh: Polygon.

Dickson, R. J. 1966. *Ulster Emigration to Colonial America, 1718–1775.* London: Routledge and Kegan Paul.

Dinnerstein, Leonard, Roger Nichols, and David Reimers. 2003. *Natives and Strangers: A Multicultural History Of Americans,* 4th ed. New York: Oxford UP.

Dobson, David. 2000. *Scots in Georgia and the Deep South, 1735–1845.* Baltimore, MD: Genealogical Publishing.

———. 1994. *Scottish Emigration to Colonial America, 1607–1785.* Athens: U of Georgia P.

Donaldson, Emily Ann. 1986. *The Scottish Highland Games in America.* Gretna, LA: Pelican.

Dunn, Charles. 1953. *Highland Settler: A Portrait of the Scottish Gael in Nova Scotia.* Toronto: U of Toronto P.

Dunnaway, Wayland. 1944. *The Scotch-Irish of Colonial Pennsylvania.* Chapel Hill: U of North Carolina P.

Edensor, Tim. 2002. *National Identity, Popular Culture, and Everyday Life.* Oxford: Berg.

Ekirch, A. Roger. 1987. *Bound for America: The Transportation of British Convicts to the Colonies, 1718–1775.* Oxford: Clarendon.

Erickson, Charlotte. 1972. *Invisible Immigrants: The Adaptation of English and Scottish Immigrants in Nineteenth-Century America.* Ithaca, NY: Cornell UP.

Evans, E. Estyn. 1965. "Cultural Relics of the Ulster Scots in the Old West of North America." *Ulster Folklife* 11: 33–38.

———. 1969. "The Scotch-Irish: Their Cultural Adaptation and Heritage in the American Old West." In *Essays in Scotch-Irish History,* ed. E. R. R. Green, 69–86. London: Routledge and Kegan Paul.

Ferguson, William. 1998. *The Identity of the Scottish Nation: An Historical Quest.* Edinburgh: Edinburgh UP.

Fischer, David Hackett. 1989. *Albion's Seed: Four British Folkways in America.* Oxford: Oxford UP.

Fitzpatrick, Rory. 1989. *God's Frontiersmen: The Scots-Irish Epic.* London: Weidenfeld and Nicolson.

Ford, Henry. 1915. *The Scotch-Irish in America.* Princeton, NJ: Princeton UP.

Fraser, T. G. 1997. "The Ulster-American Heritage Symposium: A Retrospect." In *Ulster and North America: Transatlantic Perspectives on the Scotch-Irish,* ed. Tyler Blethen and Curtis Wood, vii–x. Tuscaloosa: U of Alabama P.

Galenson, David. 1981. *White Servitude in Colonial America: An Economic Analysis.* Cambridge, Eng.: Cambridge UP.

Gillespie, Greg. 2000. "Roderick McLennan, Professionalism, and the Emergence of the Athlete in Caledonian Games." *Sport History Review* 31: 43–63.

Glassie, Henry. 1968. *Patterns in the Material Folk Culture of the Eastern United States.* Philadelphia: U of Pennsylvania P.

Graham, Ian Charles Cargill. 1956. *Colonists from Scotland: Emigration to North America, 1707–1783.* Ithaca, NY: Cornell UP.

Green, E. R. R., ed. 1969. *Essays in Scotch-Irish History.* London: Routledge and Kegan Paul.

Griffin, Patrick. 2001. *The People with No Name: Ireland's Ulster Scots, America's Scots-Irish, and the Creation of a British Atlantic World, 1689–1764.* Princeton, NJ: Princeton UP.

Harper, Marjory. 2003. *Adventurers and Exiles: The Great Scottish Exodus.* London: Profile.

Harvie, Christopher. 1994 [1977]. *Scotland and Nationalism: Scottish Society and Politics 1707 to the Present.* 2nd ed. London: Routledge.

Haws, Charles. 1980. *Scots in the Old Dominion, 1685–1800.* Edinburgh: John Dunlop.

Hearn, Jonathan. 2000. *Claiming Scotland: National Identity and Liberal Culture.* Edinburgh: Polygon.

Hewitson, Jim. 1998. *Far Off in Sunlit Places: Stories of the Scots in Australia and New Zealand.* Edinburgh: Cannongate.

———. 1993. *Tam Blake & Co.: The Story of Scots in America.* Edinburgh: Cannongate.

Hook, Andrew. 1999. *From Goosecreek to Gandercleugh: Studies in Scottish-American Literary and Cultural History.* East Linton, Scotland: Tuckwell.

———. 1975. *Scotland and America: A Study of Cultural Relations, 1750–1835.* Glasgow: Blackie.

Hunter, James. 1996. *Scottish Highlanders, Indian Peoples: Thirty Generations of a Montana Family.* Helena: Montana Historical Society Press.

———. 1994. *A Dance Called America: The Scottish Highlands, the United States, and Canada.* Edinburgh: Mainstream.

Insh, George Pratt. 1922. *Scottish Colonial Schemes, 1620–1686.* Glasgow: Maclehose, Jackson, and Co.

Ivers, Larry. 1974. *British Drums on the Southern Frontier: The Military Colonization of Georgia, 1733–1749.* Chapel Hill: U of North Carolina P.

Iwanska, Alicja. 1993. *British American Loyalists in Canada and U.S. Southern Confederates in Brazil: Exiles from the United States.* Lewiston, NY: Edwin Mellen.

Jarvie, Grant. 1991. *Highland Games: The Making of the Myth.* Edinburgh: Edinburgh UP.

———. 1989. "Culture, Social Development and the Scottish Highland Gatherings." In *The Making of Scotland: National, Culture, and Social Change,* ed. David McCrone, Stephen Kendrick, and Pat Straw, 189–206. Edinburgh: Edinburgh UP.

Jones, Maldwyn A. 1991. "The Scotch-Irish in British America." In *Strangers within the Realm: Cultural Margins of the First British Empire,* ed. Bernard Bailyn and Philip D. Morgan, 284–313. Chapel Hill: U of North Carolina P.

Karras, Allan. 1992. *Sojourners in the Sun: Scottish Migrants in Jamaica and the Chesapeake, 1740–1800.* Ithaca, NY: Cornell UP.

Kennedy, Michael. 2002. *Gaelic Nova Scotia: An Economic, Cultural, and Social Impact Study.* Curatorial Report. No. 97. Halifax: Nova Scotia Museum.

Kidd, Colin. 1999. *British Identities before Nationalism: Ethnicity and Nationhood in the Atlantic World, 1600–1800.* Cambridge, Eng.: Cambridge UP.

———. 1997. "Sentiment, race and revival: Scottish identities in the aftermath of Enlightenment." In *A Union of Multiple Identities: The British Isles, c. 1750–c. 1850,* ed. Laurence Brockliss and David Eastwood, 110–26. Manchester, Eng.: Manchester UP.

Landsman, Ned. 1999. "Nation, Migration, and the Province in the First British Empire: Scotland and the Americas, 1600–1800." *American Historical Review* 104, no. 2 (April): 463–75.

———. 1985. *Scotland and Its First American Colony, 1683–1765.* Princeton, NJ: Princeton UP.

Lehmann, William. 1978. *Scottish and Scotch-Irish Contributions to Early American Life and Culture.* Port Washington, NY: Kennikat Press.

Leyburn, James. G. 1962. *The Scotch-Irish: A Social History.* Chapel Hill: U of North Carolina P.

Livingstone, Sheila. 1997. *Scottish Festivals.* Edinburgh: Birlinn.

McArthur, Colin. 2003. *Brigadoon, Braveheart, and the Scots: Distortions of Scotland in Hollywood Cinema.* London: I. B. Tauris.

Macdonald, Sharon. 1997. *Reimagining Culture: Histories, Identities, and the Gaelic Renaissance.* New York: Berg.

MacDonald, James. 1993. "Cultural Retention and Adaptation among the Highland Scots." PhD diss., University of Edinburgh.

MacDonell, Margaret. 1982. *The Emigrant Experience: Songs of Highland Emigrants in North America.* Toronto: U of Toronto P.

MacDougall, Carl. 2001. *Painting the Forth Bridge: A Search for Scottish Identity.* London: Aurum.

Macinnes, Allan. 1996. *Clanship, Commerce, and the House of Stuart, 1603–1788.* East Linton, Scotland: Tuckwell.

———. 1992. "Scottish Gaeldom: The First Phase of Clearance." In *People and Society in Scotland, Vol. 1: 1760–1830,* ed. T. M. Devine and Rosalind Mitchison, 70–90. Edinburgh: John Donald.

McCrone, David. 2001. *Understanding Scotland: The Sociology of a Nation.* 2nd ed. London: Routledge.

McCrone, David, Angela Morris, and Richard Kiely. 1995. *Scotland the Brand: The Making of Scottish Heritage.* Edinburgh: Edinburgh UP.

McCrone, David, Stephen Kendrick, and Pat Straw, eds. 1989. *The Making of Scotland: National, Culture, and Social Change.* Edinburgh: Edinburgh UP.

McKay, Ian. 1994. *The Quest for the Folk: Antimodernism and Cultural Selection in Twentieth-Century Nova Scotia.* Montreal: McGill-Queen's UP.

———. 1992. "Tartanism Triumphant: The Construction of Scottishness in Nova Scotia, 1933–1954." *Acadiensis* 21, no. 2 (spring): 5–47.

McLean, Angus Wilton, John Edwin Purcell I, John Edwin Purcell II, and Archibald Gilchrist Singletary. 1942. *Lumber River Scots and Their Descendants.* Richmond, VA: William Byrd.

McLean, Angus Wilton. [1919] 1993. *Highland Scots in North Carolina: an unpublished manuscript,* ed. and indexed Louise Davis Curry. Dallas, TX: North Carolina Scottish Heritage Society.

Meyer, Duane. 1961. *The Highland Scots of North Carolina, 1732–1776.* Chapel Hill: U of North Carolina P.

Miller, Kerby. 1985. *Emigrants and Exiles: Ireland and the Irish Exodus to North America.* New York: Oxford UP.

Miller, Kerby, Arnold Schrier, Bruce Boling, and David Doyle. 2003. *Irish Immigrants in the Land of Canaan: Letters and Memoirs from Colonial and Revolutionary America, 1675–1815.* Oxford: Oxford UP.

Morgan, Peadar. 2000. "The Gaelic Is Dead; Long Live the Gaelic: The Changing Relationship between Native and Learner Gaelic Users." In *Myth, Migration, and the Making of Memory: Scotia and Nova Scotia c. 1700–1990,* ed. Marjory Harper and Michael E. Vance, 49–72. Halifax, Nova Scotia: Fernwood.

Nairn, Thomas. 2000. *After Britain: New Labour and the Return of Scotland.* London: Granta.

Neville, Gwen Kennedy. 1979. "Community Form and Ceremonial Life in Three Regions of Scotland." *American Ethnologist* 6, no. 1 (Feb.): 93–109.

Newton, Michael. 2003. "Becoming Cold-hearted Like the Gentiles around Them": Scottish Gaelic in the United States, 1872–1912." *E-Keltoi Journal of Interdisciplinary Celtic Studies* 2: 63–131.

Nybakken, Elizabeth. 1982. "New Light on the Old Side: Irish Influences on Colonial Presbyterianism." *Journal of American History* 68, no. 4 (March): 813–32.

Parker, Anthony. 1997. *Scottish Highlanders in Colonial Georgia: The Recruitment, Emigration, and Settlement at Darien, 1735–1748.* Athens: U of Georgia P.

Parkhill, Trevor. 1997. "Philadelphia Here I Come: A Study of the Letters of Ulster Immigrants in Pennsylvania, 1750–1875." In *Ulster and North America: Transatlantic Perspectives on the Scotch-Irish,* ed. Tyler Blethen and Curtis Wood, 118–33. Tuscaloosa: U of Alabama P.

Pittock, Murray. 2001. *Scottish Nationality.* London: Palgrave MacMillan.

———. 1999. *Celtic Identity and the British Image.* Manchester, Eng.: Manchester UP.

———. 1998. *Jacobitism.* New York: St. Martin's.

———. 1995. *The Myth of the Jacobite Clans.* Edinburgh: Edinburgh UP.

———. 1991. *The Invention of Scotland: The Stuart Myth and the Scottish Identity, 1638 to the Present.* London: Routledge.

Ramsey, Robert. 1964. *Carolina Cradle: Settlement of the Northwest Carolina Frontier, 1747–1762.* Chapel Hill: U of North Carolina P.

Ray, Celeste. 2001. *Highland Heritage: Scottish Americans in the American South.* U of North Carolina P: Chapel Hill

———. 1998. "Scottish Heritage Southern Style." *Southern Cultures* 4, no. 2: 28–45.

Ray, Celeste, ed. 2003. *Southern Heritage on Display: Public Ritual and Ethnic Diversity within Southern Regionalism.* U of Alabama P: Tuscaloosa.

Redmond, Gerald. 1971. *The Caledonian Games in Nineteenth-Century America.* Cranbury, NJ: Fairleigh Dickinson UP.

Richards, Eric. 1999. "Leaving the Highlands: Colonial Destinations in Canada and Australia." In *Myth, Migration, and the Making of Memory: Scotia and Nova Scotia c. 1700–1990,* ed. Marjory Harper and Michael Vance, 105–126. Halifax, Nova Scotia: Fernwood.

Riggs, Brett. 1999. "Removal Period Cherokee Households in Southwestern North Carolina: Material Perspectives on Ethnicity and Cultural Differentiation." PhD diss., University of Tennessee, Knoxville.

———. 1997. "The Christie Cabin Site: Historical and Archaeological Evidence of the Life and Times of a Cherokee Métis Household (1835–1838)." In *May We All Remember Well, Vol. I. A Journal of the History & Cultures of Western North Carolina,* ed. Robert S. Brunk, 228–48. Asheville, NC: Robert S. Brunk Auction Services.

Robinson, Philip. 1984. *The Plantation of Ulster: British Settlement in an Irish Landscape, 1600–1670.* New York: St. Martin's.

Schmidt, Leigh Eric. 1989. *Holy Fairs: Scottish Communions and American Revivals in the Early Modern Period.* Princeton, NJ: Princeton UP.

Shapiro, Henry D. 1977. "Appalachia and the Idea of America." In *An Appalachian Symposium: Essays Written in Honor of Cratis D. Williams,* ed. J. W. Williamson, 43–55. Boone, NC: Appalachian State UP.

Shepperson, George. 1954. "Writings in Scottish-American History: A Brief Survey." *William and Mary Quarterly,* Scotland and America, 3d ser., 11, no. 2 (April): 163–78.

Smith, Abbot Emerson. 1947. *Colonists in Bondage: White Servitude and Convict Labor in America, 1607–1776.* Chapel Hill: U of North Carolina P.

Smith, Warren. 1961. *White Servitude in Colonial South Carolina.* Columbia: U of South Carolina P.

Smout, T. C. 1994. "Perspectives on the Scottish Identity." *Scottish Affairs* 6 (winter): 101–13.

——. 1969. *History of the Scottish People, 1560–1830.* New York: Scribner.

Szasz, Ferenc. 2000. *Scots in the North American West, 1790–1917.* Norman: U of Oklahoma P.

Webster, Bruce. 1997. *Medieval Scotland: The Making of an Identity.* New York: St. Martin's.

Webster, David. 1959. *Scottish Highland Games.* Glasgow: Collins.

Wells, Miriam. 1990. "Brokerage, Economic Opportunity, and the Growth of Ethnic Movements." In *American Culture: Essays in the Familiar and Unfamiliar,* ed. Leonard Plotnicov, 179–96. Pittsburgh: U of Pittsburgh P.

Westerkamp, Marilyn. 1988. *Triumph of the Laity: Scots-Irish Piety and the Great Awakening, 1625–1760.* New York: Oxford UP.

Whiting, B. J. 1949. "Lowland Scots and Celtic Proverbs in North Carolina." *Journal of Celtic Studies* 1: 116–27. Baltimore, MD: Temple University at the Waverly Press.

Withers, Charles W. J. 2002. *Geography, Science, and National Identity: Scotland since 1520.* Cambridge, Eng.: Cambridge UP.

——. 1992. "The Historical Creation of the Scottish Highlands." In *The Manufacture of Scottish History,* ed. Ian Donnachie and Christopher Whatley, 143–56. Edinburgh: Polygon.

——. 1988. *Gaelic Scotland: A Transformation of a Culture Region.* London: Routledge.

Wokeck, Marianne. 1999. *Trade in Strangers: The Beginnings of Mass Migration to North America.* University Park, PA: Pennsylvania State UP.

3
A Brief History of
Organized Scottishness in Canada
Michael Vance

Many of the Highland games in Canada have been established only since World War II, and in the past few decades they have been joined by an increasing number of new Scottish and Celtic heritage groups. The growth of these "Scottish" events and organizations fits closely with the features of Scottish heritage celebration identified by Celeste Ray in the United States; nevertheless, if organized "Scottishness" in Canada is examined in its broader historical context, quite different features are revealed. In particular, we can see how the earliest Scottish social organizations, while promoting interest in the study of the Scots in Canada (see appendix to this chapter), were linked to class and ethnic relationships that were conditioned by Canada's British imperial connection.

In an address titled *The Mission of the Scot in Canada,* delivered to the Caledonian Society of Montreal on December 5, 1903, Alexander Fraser of Toronto, founder of the Gaelic Society of Canada, editor of *Scottish Canadian Magazine,* and grand chief of the Sons of Scotland, gave a dire warning to his audience: "We are assailed because we have organized Scottish societies in Canada . . . The position which has been taken is that our societies tend to keep alive racial divisions, that they hark back to the Old Land, and consequently are obstacles in the way of and a menace to Canadian national sentiment and national unity."[1] Fraser's address responded to these perceived assaults by arguing that the Canadian nationality was not yet formed and that the Scot in Canada had a vital role to play in shaping the emerging national character. For Fraser, "Scottish ideals" were "Broader than Scotland"; they had "inspired the thoughtful of many lands." Furthermore, the ideals held by the Scottish element in the nation were essential if Canada was to resist the corrosive influence of the individualistic materialism emanating from the United States. Indeed, it was the Scots' patriotic duty to celebrate and promote Scottish influence: "Broadly Speaking our duty as Canadians citizens, and as citizens, in full standing, of the British Empire, is clear—it is to do what in us lies to advance the common weal, to strengthen ties which bind us to the land we left and the land we live in, by every worthy means available, and in this way hold up a national ideal which our offspring can pursue . . . this is the mission of the Scot in Canada." To accomplish this goal, Fraser advocated a federation of Canadian Scottish societies to promote Scottish history, literature, and music; Scottish games; Scottish fraternal and benevolent organizations; and to preserve the records of Scottish pioneer settlers. According to Fraser, if such a federation were formed, "There would be a mighty force in the land working quietly, incessantly, and invincibly to a triumphant end. I am impressed with the need of some such power in our generation."

While Alexander Fraser was unable to accomplish his federation, his address does afford us insight into the historical role of Scottishness in Canada. Although Fraser listed dozens of Scottish organizations in the country at the dawn of the twentieth century, his address suggested that they were under threat. For Fraser, what was required was a reassertion of Scottish power and influence in the Dominion through coordinated celebrations of Scottishness. Indeed, the discussion that follows will suggest that both the nineteenth- and early twentieth-century Canadian celebrations of Scottish culture are best understood in terms of the exercise of power and influence. Aspects of Scottishness were employed to empower immigrant communities, to reinforce class power, or to exert cultural influence, but Scottishness could also have the ability to marginalize and to exclude.

One way the empowerment of immigrant communities can be seen is in Alexander Fraser's identification of the "sanctity of the family relations" as one of the central Scottish ideals: "Love for the home, respect for the family, are placed by me at the forefront here because I am convinced of their importance as virtues the exercise of which are sorely needed in this land, and which we can do a great deal to promote." As chief of the Clan Fraser in Canada, Fraser clearly had in mind clan affiliations, but his comment also reflected the importance of family connection for the Scottish immigrant communities that had developed in Canada by the turn of the twentieth century. Family connections contributed to the concentration of Lowland settlers in the Ottawa Valley and Dumfries Township of Ontario, but in general, Lowlanders, while relying on friends and relatives to facilitate their migration to Canada, tended to be widely dispersed (Cowan 1992; Brunger 1990). In the Gaelic-speaking Highland enclave communities that were established in Nova Scotia, Cape Breton,

Prince Edward Island, the Eastern Townships of Quebec, and in Ontario, personal connections appear to have had their greatest influence. Scholars have established the importance of family and friends in drawing Highland immigrants to these communities at the turn of the eighteenth and nineteenth centuries (Bumsted 1982b; Harper and Vance 1999; Hornsby 1992a, 1992b; Campey 2001; Little 1991; McLean 1992; Sheets 2000). To a lesser degree, they have also shown how kinship played a role in drawing Gaelic-speaking immigrants to the Red River settlement in Manitoba early in the nineteenth century and providing community cohesion to the crofter settlements established in the prairie provinces at the end of the nineteenth and beginning of the twentieth centuries (Bumsted 1982b; Norton 1994; Harper 2002, 1998, 1994, 1988; Campey 2003).

The negative role kinship could play in a Highland enclave settlement is exemplified in the case of "Chief" Archibald McNab, who in 1822 left Killin, Perthshire, in order to escape his creditors and attempted to set himself up as a feudal lord in McNab Township in the Ottawa Valley. McNab arranged for nearly one hundred of his Gaelic-speaking clansfolk to be transported to Montreal, where he met and escorted them directly to the township. In order to pay their passage money, McNab insisted that the emigrants hand over a portion of the crops and the timber from their lands in perpetuity. Since McNab obtained the appointment as the local justice of the peace, he was also sole arbitrator of any dispute, thus rendering him a virtual dictator of the district until the abuse was exposed in 1840 (A. Cameron and Gwyn 1985). While clan elites played a key role in organizing and directing early Highland immigration to Canada, McNab's attempt to create a feudal system in the new world was unique. Usually, preexisting clan relationships tended to positively reinforce community ties in the immigrant communities (Bumsted 1982b; McLean 1991). John Sheets's and Margaret Bennett's essays in this collection examine the legacy of the sense of community developed in these Highland enclave settlements in the present day.

A native of Kineras, Invernesshire, and an advocate for the promotion of the Gaelic language, both in Glasgow during his university student days and in Toronto, Alexander Fraser was one of several turn-of-the-century Highland immigrants who sought to promote the interests of the Gaelic community in Canada by encouraging the use of their native tongue.[2] Fraser's promotion of the language was, however, conducted in Ontario's largest urban centre rather than the rural enclaves where the majority of Gaelic-speakers were located. While it is certainly true that the Highlanders' Gaelic legacy helped to foster an intense sense of community in places like Cape Breton, the language's survival was largely a consequence of these communities' relative isolation rather than its promotion by urban groups like Fraser's Gaelic Society of Canada (Dunn 1953; MacLellan 2000, 3–54). Despite the advocacy of groups like Fraser's, Gaelic-speaking was actively discouraged by educational authorities during the nineteenth century and came under increased threat in the twentieth century from intruding technologies such as radio and television. While Gaelic still survives in Nova Scotia and the language continues to have its advocates, the revival of Gaelic-speaking has recently been represented as a potential asset for the tourism industry of the province as a whole rather than solely as a benefit to the descendants of the Cape Breton enclave community (M. Kennedy 2002).

During the nineteenth century, Scots like Fraser, who organized in the urban centres, were more likely to be in a position to exert influence on Canadian society than the Gaelic-speakers in enclave communities who were isolated and largely removed from mainstream Canadian society. In addressing the Montreal Caledonian Society, Fraser inadvertently touched on this when he noted the greater strength of "Scottish sentiment" in the city: "In the first place you are on the seaboard. The newcomer from Scotland reaches you first, and the welcome you give him is such that if he be a desirable citizen you keep him here; your shipping maintains a closer connection with the Old Land in the matter of intercourse, than can be the case with places situated inland."

Historians have also noted the intense Scottish influence on the mercantile life of Montreal. Such transatlantic links can be seen as early as 1776 when the Glasgow-trained merchant John Dunlop moved his business to Montreal from Virginia while still maintaining his commercial links with Lowland Scotland. He amassed a huge fortune in the process (Macmillan 1985). It appears that the strategies employed by Scots engaged in business elsewhere in Canada also frequently involved reliance on friends and family who remained in Scotland. For example, two Glaswegians, Peter and Isaac Buchanan, established a prosperous transatlantic dry goods business that linked their native city with Toronto in the mid-nineteenth century, while Henry O. Bell-Irving, a member of a Border gentry family, used his Scottish family connections to raise the capital that allowed him to create one of the largest salmon canning operations in British Columbia in the early twentieth century (McCalla 1979; R. Macdonald 2001–2002).

This transatlantic Scottish mercantile influence had begun in the eighteenth century in the fur trade, where Highlanders with personal connections to one another had played a predominant role. This was true of both the Northwest Company and the Hudson's Bay Company. Indeed, the latter firm made a habit of recruiting their rank-and-file workers for their trading posts from Lewis and Orkney well into the twentieth century (Goldring 1980; Cowie 1913; Szasz 2000). Many of these men married native women while "in country," and their descendants remain among First Nations populations throughout the North American West, although only a relatively small number of Highland elite company men settled in Montreal (Hunter 1996; Van Kirk 1980; Mitchell 1976). While the fur traders had been among the first to organize Scottish celebrations in the city, by the time Alexander Fraser was addressing the Caledonian society, they had been supplanted by lawyers, bankers, manufacturers, and railway developers, such as the enormously wealthy Donald A. Smith, Lord Strathcona (D. Macdonald 1996). Most of these men were from the Lowlands rather than the Highlands of Scotland, as were their counterparts in other urban centres in Canada. Although frequently in competition with one another, these Scottish elites clearly made use of both their personal and public Scottish connections to promote their economic power and influence in their adopted country.

Again, for Alexander Fraser, the extension of influence was in fact the duty of the Scots in Canada, since one "Scottish ideal which stands eminently forth among others is that of public conscience—'high honour' in public life." Certainly, there is little doubt that Scots exerted a disproportionate influence on the political life of British North America from a very early date (Evans 1976). For example, the North British Society, one of the first Scottish societies to be founded in North America, was established in Halifax in 1768 by the local Scottish professional and mercantile elite and, as a group, exerted considerable influence on local and provincial politics well into the nineteenth century. Indeed, by the end of that century, the way one would signal arrival in the local Halifax elite was through membership in the North British Society (J. Macdonald 1905; R. Kennedy 2000). Some of the Scots who engaged in trade at that time, particularly those with artisan backgrounds, rejected such elite power building and in fact challenged the establishment of institutions of privilege in Canada. This is seen most clearly in the Scots who followed William Lyon Mackenzie during the 1837 Rebellion in Upper Canada (Vance and Stephen 2001). Nevertheless, Scottishness and Scottish societies were seldom used for radical purposes but were instead mobilized for conservative ends and to reinforce elite authority.

Recent examination of the St. Andrew's Society of Montreal has revealed that it was formed in 1834 largely in response to the gains of the reformers in the 1832 election. Its membership was drawn from the city's conservative elite, who sought to promote patriotic feeling by reinforcing the connection with the mother country as a counter to the demand for radical reform. In its early days, the society was essentially an elite all-male drinking club that met once a year on St. Andrew's Day for a bacchanalian dinner. Its exclusive nature was reinforced by the fact that while the Scottish artisan population of Montreal were admitted as society members, they were not admitted to the table of the elite but were provided with a separate dinner (Leitch 2002; McNabb 1999). The conservative, elite character of St. Andrew's societies during the nineteenth century was reflected elsewhere in Canada. For example, the society that formed in Winnipeg, Manitoba, in 1871 had Donald A. Smith as its first president. The society was initially entitled the Selkirk St. Andrew's Society in honour of Lord Selkirk, the founder of the Red River settlement, and, like the Montreal society, focused its activities on the annual dinner for Scotland's patron saint. These occasions were also marked by heavy drinking and speeches from invited and local worthies, but by the end of the century the events had evolved into society balls. In the annual reports of the Toronto St. Andrew's Society, the presence of prominent guests was noted and the ladies' fashions were discussed in full. As city editor of the *Toronto Daily Mail*, Alexander Fraser made sure that accounts of these society events were published in his paper (*Constitution* 1886; *Annual Report* 1889).

A great deal was made in the society reports of the fact that these events were used to raise funds for benevolent purposes. At the 1872 annual dinner, in Winnipeg, $212 was raised to support the victims of the Chicago fire (*Constitution* 1886), while the 1888 annual report of the Toronto St. Andrew's Society reported that $250 had been donated to the Home for Incurables. These acts of charity, however, can also be viewed as reinforcing elite control. In the 1888 annual report, the managers of the Toronto society claimed that their "national spirit and social qualities are powerful incentives to liberality when countrymen are in suffering and want," but that in Toronto "the Scottish element furnishes but a very small percentage of the total number of poor." Although the lack of poverty was attributed to Scottish thriftiness and independence, the report for the following year makes it clear that the society was using its benevolent fund to discriminate between the deserving and undeserving poor. The managers assured the members that "no really deserving case has gone away unrelieved," but that the "regular dead-beat nuisance has considerably abated . . . this arises from the *fact* that your managers carefully investigate all cases before giving them relief, except in cases of immediate *need*, when our usual custom is to give them an order for a couple of meals and a night's lodging" (*Annual Report* 1890). While St. Andrew's societies did provide important relief to the poor in an era before the welfare state, their support was clearly tied to elite scrutiny and social policing. This was true in Toronto even in the heart of the depression: "Your Managers receive regular monthly reports from the Neigbourhood Worker's Association, setting out fully particulars of all cases which have been investigated and helped, with the funds from the Saint Andrews Society . . . We are often called on to supply old clothes, boots, etc., which are given as required, after proper enquiry" (*Annual Report* 1933).

The reinforcement of elite authority through the exercise of paternalistic benevolence was also paralleled by the attempt of the Scottish societies' organizers to link themselves with patriotism and the British Empire. This can be seen most clearly in the establishment of Highland games in Canada, a development that Grant Jarvie examines in his essay in this volume. The first events held in Canada, like the games at Antigonish, Nova Scotia, had largely developed in the centres of Scottish settlement, but in the second half of the nineteenth century, Scottish societies took a leading role in promoting such games in the major urban centres, from Toronto westward (Cowan 1999, 62–63). The Caledonian games held in Toronto on September 14 and 15, 1859, were organized by the Canadian Highland Society, whose rolls included several members of the legislative assembly, leading civil servants, military officers, lawyers, and physicians, as well as the mayor of Toronto, Adam Wilson. Prizes were awarded for the events, which included Scottish dancing, Highland dress, pipe music, and stone and hammer throwing. The imperial and military connections of the members, however, were celebrated by a prize for the best Gaelic poem on the theme of "The Achievements of the Highland Brigade" and performances of the Royal Canadian Rifle Band at the games and the accompanying ball. The attachment to empire was made even more explicitly the following year when the "gathering" was moved to September 10 and 11 to coincide with the visit of the Prince of Wales, who was touring in Canada in 1860 (*Fraser Papers*, Mu 1091). During the nineteenth century, a semiprofessionalized Caledonian games circuit developed in Canada, but the British imperial associations were never lost (Gillespie 2000). For example, the Winnipeg St. Andrew's Society 1881 annual games "were held in the Old Driving Park . . . in commemoration of the visit of the Marquis of Lorne. He visited the grounds, witnessed the games and replied thanks." The Winnipeg society expressed their loyalty even more dramatically during the Northwest Rebellions when "The Society built a Scottish arch at its own expense, on Main Street, as a compliment to the Scottish company of the 90th Battalion of Rifles, and joined heartily in the civic demonstration in honor of the troops under General Middleton, upon their arrival in Winnipeg, July 16th, 1885" (*Constitution* 1886).

The celebration of Scottish martial prowess at a time when settlement in the new land was resisted by the indigenous people had obvious utility in 1885 (Stonechild and Waiser 1997), but the interest in martial accomplishment and manly games had a broader significance for Scottish elites in nineteenth-century Canada. It allowed men like Alexander Fraser, a vigorous promoter of Gaelic sports, such as shinty, to tie Scottish games with the patriotic defense of empire. The first games in Toronto included a broadsword exercise competition, but the most potent symbol connecting the games with late Victorian militarism was the piping competition. As Michael MacDonald has indicated (2001–2002), organized piping can perform many contemporary social functions, but in the late nineteenth century the military associations with piping were clear. In fact, a pipe band was one of the first organizations created by the 48th Highlanders of the Canadian Militia when they were formed in Toronto in 1891, after considerable coordinated lobbying by the Scottish societies in the city. In addition to linking themselves to the potent symbol of British imperial power that the Highland regiment had become by the end of the nineteenth century, Scottish society members who formed the majority of the rank and file in the regiment were also provided with the opportunity to demonstrate prowess and loyalty in a broader imperial context. For example, Private George Stewart was the regiment's winner of the "Individual Bayonet Championship of the British Empire in 1897," and when the Boer War broke out, nineteen men from the regiment joined the Canadian contingent that went to South Africa (Fraser 1900). As a consequence of the efforts he had made in organizing the regiment, Alexander Fraser was made an honourary colonel of the 48th Highlanders, and, once bestowed, he would use his military title for the rest of his life, thus demonstrating how such connections could be viewed as enhancing one's prestige and influence.

Scottish organizations also had a role in enhancing the cultural influence that Scottishness exercised in nineteenth-century Canada. Alexander Fraser's belief that Scottish societies had a vital role in promoting knowledge of Scottish history and literature was echoed in the stated aims of the majority of the Scottish organizations in Canada (*Fraser Papers,* Mu 1091–92). According to Fraser, "The Scottish love for literature is almost as strong as that for home . . . probably no one of the nations which stand forth conspicuously in history has shown equal responsiveness to the muse, to the romantic tale, the weird legend, and the dramatic incident as has Scotland." Certainly from an early date, Scots were promoting their approach to literature in Canada. Gaelic songs continued to be produced in Highland enclave communities and began to be published in the later nineteenth century (MacDonell 1982), but it is with the Scots dialect poetry that the impact of the Scots on emerging Canadian literary culture was most marked. As early as the 1840s, newspapers were publishing poems and tales in Lowland Scottish vernacular, and by the turn of the century there was a sufficient quantity of the material for the Caledonian Society of Toronto to be able to publish a three-hundred-page anthology of Scottish Canadian poets (*Selections* 1900). Dozens of collected works by individuals were also published, and Alexander Fraser provided a biographical sketch of one such minor poet, John Imrie, for the posthumous edition of the Glasgow native's work (Imrie 1912). A passage from Imrie's "Letter Frae ower the Sea" gives the flavour of this type of poetry:

> Oh! It nearly takes my breath awa'
>   To get a letter frea home,
> An' afore I read a word or twa,
>   I can guess the sender's name!
> This ane, I ken, is frae Maggie dear,
>   The lassie I loe sae well,
> An while I'm readin' she's standin' near,
>   Her presence I seem to feel!

Such Scots dialect poetry, which was largely imitative of the work of Robert Burns, was found throughout Canada. Scots-Canadian poets published their work in the Maritimes, Quebec, and Ontario, and as far afield as the gold rush settlements of the interior of British Columbia (*Selections* 1900; Anderson 1868). Scottish societies had a hand in promoting Scottish vernacular writing. For instance, in 1859, at the first Caledonian Games in Toronto, a prize was awarded to the best "broad Scots" poem on the theme of "The Emigrant," while in 1888 the St. Andrew's Society of Toronto took over the affairs of Alexander McLachlan, "The Burns of Canada," in order to relieve the poet of his financial distress (*Fraser Papers*, Mu 1091; *Annual Report* 1889). Burns societies founded in all major Canadian centres also promoted the use of Scots vernacular in addition to their annual celebratory dinners. In fact, by the turn of the century, most Scottish societies put on a Burns supper as part of the calendar of annual social rituals.[3]

Scottish publishers, particularly newspapermen, also played a prominent role in promoting Scottish literature in Canada. Alexander Fraser, as editor of the *Scottish Canadian Magazine*, published from 1890 to 1913, was himself responsible for circulating a good deal of Scots poetry, including the occasional Gaelic piece as well as the material written in Lowland Scots. Literary scholar Elizabeth Waterston, however, has recently highlighted the vital importance of educators for ensuring that Scottish literature would have a considerable influence on the development of Canadian literature written in English. The disproportionate influence of Scots on the Canadian education system has been noted by several scholars, and as Waterston has shown, this resulted in a heavy dose of Scottish poetry and prose being a central part of Canadian English education well into this century. Recalling her own university days in Montreal in the 1930s, Waterston reflects, "The legend at McGill [was] that if you want[ed] to pass freshman English, you need[ed] to know the Ballads, Burns, and the Bible. (A variant [was] Chaucer, Burns, and Carlyle.) Clearly, at any rate, you need[ed] to respond to British (and particularly Scottish) literature, rather than Canadian" (2001, 4).

While Waterston has suggested that echoes of the Scottish literary influence can be found in several contemporary Canadian writers, it is clear that the heyday of such cultural influence was at the beginning of the twentieth century. Scottish vernacular poems are no longer found on the pages of Canadian newspapers, and Scottish literature no longer holds a prominent place in English Canadian curricula, but this should not blind us to the cultural influence that Scottishness once held in Canada. The statues of Robert Burns erected by Scottish societies in several Canadian cities at the turn of the twentieth century are physical reminders of that influence.[4]

Despite Alexander Fraser's fears that Scottish "sentiment" was declining, it is clear that the Scots in Canada exercised an influence all out of proportion to their numbers.[5] John M. Bumsted has shown that between 1815 and 1870, Scots made up only 14 percent of immigrants from the British Isles and that since 1871, Canadians claiming Scottish origin never totaled more than 15 percent of the population. When Fraser was addressing the Montreal Caledonian Society, the Scots represented 14.8 percent of the population. In the 2001 census more than four million Canadians claimed Scottish ancestry, but that still represents only 14 percent of the total population. There were certainly concentrations of Scots in particular regions at particular times, but even in the Atlantic Provinces, the area of highest concentration, they never totaled more than 28 percent of the population (Bumsted 1982a). Fraser understood that organized Scottishness, in the form of societies and celebrations, had assisted the Scots in promoting their political, economic, and cultural influence in the Dominion. He was eager to reinforce this organization as the means of maintaining the Scottish influence that he viewed as being so beneficial to his adopted country. Ultimately, though, claiming a special status for the Scots in Canada rested on a "racial" premise that has also had the ability to marginalize or exclude other groups in the country.

For Fraser, as for some of his contemporaries, each "race" had its own particular attributes and qualities. He believed that such characteristics were maintained in the immigrant population: "Oftentimes you hear a young man or woman of Scottish descent say proudly, 'I am not Scotch; I am a Canadian.' On the same principle, that of birth, a young man born in Glasgow of Russian parents could say, 'I am not Russian; I am a simon pure Scot.' So could the Chinese baby born in Vancouver, but it needs no argument to show that the young in each case is a Scot, a Russian and a Chinese." Although Fraser did not claim racial superiority for the Scots in his address, others used this perception of race to do just that. Indeed, Fraser's example of the Chinese in Vancouver is a case in point.

In July 1924 a young Scottish nursemaid, Janet Smith, was found dead in the basement of her employer's house in an upscale Vancouver neighbourhood. The Chinese houseboy, Wong Foo Sing, quickly became the object of suspicion for the Scottish community in the city. The ensuing investigations, inquests, arrests, and press reports reflected how organized Scottishness could become racist. The Council of Scottish Societies took a leading role in agitating for the prosecution of Wong despite a lack of incriminating evidence. Indeed, Scots on the local police force took matters into their own hands and captured and tortured Wong in an attempt to illicit a confession. What became known as the "Janet Smith Case," however, is more significant for reflecting how organized Scottishness could be mobilized to reinforce racism and white supremacy in British Columbia. Indeed, one of the leading figures in the Scottish community, the Reverend Duncan McDougall, used the case to promote the views of the Ku Klux Klan, and several women in the city's Scottish societies agitated for the passage of legislation banning the employment of white women and Chinese men in the same household. British Columbia Scots used the case to highlight the "dangers" posed by Chinese immigration, linking it to rising crime levels and immorality, but they also highlighted the competition such immigrants posed for immigrant Scots trying to obtain employment in the province. These agitations reinforced the anti-Asian immigration policies adopted by Canada in the interwar period (McGrath 2003; I. MacDonald and O'Keefe 2000; Ward 1978; Anderson 1991). Of course, not all Scots in British Columbia were racists. A decade after the Janet Smith controversy erupted, Scots involved in the Salmon Purse Seiners Fisherman's Union were arguing for the necessity of organizing across racial lines in order to obtain a decent living for all from the industry. Indeed, from the early nineteenth century on, Scots were involved in the promotion of democratic and universal rights for all Canadians. Nevertheless, Scots involved in these social and political reform movements seldom used organized Scottishness as a means of promoting their objectives (Vance 2003; Vance and Stephen 2001; Shackleton 1975).

Even when Scottishness was not employed in overtly racist ways, as in the Janet Smith case, elevating the Scots to privileged status could still work to marginalize other members of the community, as my essay on Nova Scotia in this volume argues. In more subtle ways, Scottishness could also work to enhance male power as a consequence of its gendered character. The emphasis on martial games not only linked organized Scottishness to the pursuit of empire, but also reflected the patriarchal nature of Scottishness itself, as seen in the all-male character of the early drinking clubs and in the celebrations of male figures like Robert Burns. Women clearly played a supportive role, and in many nineteenth-century Scottish societies they were allowed only associate memberships, full membership being reserved for the men (*Fraser Papers,* Mu 1091–92). Such divisions reflect the separate spheres ideology that predominated at the turn of the century, but were given further reinforcement by the masculine character of Scottish celebration (Ray 2001).

Henry O. Bell-Irving provides a Canadian example of a wealthy immigrant Scot whose domestic and family life, conditioned by prevailing notions of separate spheres, blended into celebrations of Scottishness. Robert Macdonald has shown that "Bella" Bell-Irving ran her Vancouver household as her private preserve, while her husband conducted the public affairs of the family. Nevertheless, trophies from his masculine pursuit of big game hunting decorated their front parlor. Henry O. Bell-Irving gloried in the vigorous physical activity of hunting, the preoccupation of Scottish gentlemen, and he frequently demonstrated his Scottish background by wearing a kilt on ceremonial occasions (R. Macdonald 2001–2002). These symbols of male Scottishness also coloured Bell-Irving's business activity. In 1914 he arranged to donate a large quantity of his company's canned salmon for the war effort, insisting that it be labeled the "Wee Scottie Brand," the appearance of which was described in the trademark application: "The right design contains a representation of a boy in highland clothes riding a salmon, and holding in his hand a tin of Wee Scottie salmon. Immediately below the image are written the words 'Mon—he's a gran' fish.'" The design thus combined stereotypical imagery of Scottish males with a product that was also associated with the sporting activity of gentlemen— salmon fishing (Vance 2003).

It would be easy to dismiss the "Wee Scottie" brand salmon as merely an early example of the Scottish kitsch that has been used to sell a variety of products found in tourist shops in both Scotland and Canada. Nevertheless, as a consequence of its wartime distribution, the "Wee Scottie" brand became associated with the troops and British patriotism, and Bell-Irving's company traded on this in the interwar period. They included a prominent display of "Wee Scottie" salmon at the British Empire Exhibition in Wembley in

1925, and in the 1930s company ads declared that "Wee Scottie" was British Empire Salmon and that the "Welsh Tin Plate Industry will live whilst Canadian Salmon is purchased."[6] All of this serves to remind us that many contemporary expressions of Scottishness found in Canada, whether organized by St. Andrew's societies, promoted by Highland games, or reflected in commercial kitsch, are embedded in a history of ethnic, class, and imperial power relations. In 1903 Alexander Fraser sought to reinforce Scottish influence through establishing a national organization to forward the "Mission of the Scot" in Canada. He did not succeed, but the power that could be mobilized this way was far from inconsequential, even as late as the 1980s, when the movement to create a nationally recognized Tartan Day was organized. The idea originated with the Federation of the Scottish Clans of Nova Scotia but gained greater acceptance when the Clans and Scottish Societies of Canada endorsed the proposal. Ontario recognized April 6 as Tartan Day in 1991, and by 1995 all other provinces except Quebec had done the same.[7] The idea to celebrate the Scottish heritage of Canada, coincidentally on the anniversary of the Declaration of Arbroath—the document most closely identified with Scottish independence—appears innocuous, but the memory of how a few Scots could use their heritage to reinforce their positions of power makes it easy to understand why the Quebec separatist government was unwilling to endorse a Tartan Day. Indeed, it took the defeat of the Parti Québécois in 2003 before Tartan Day was proclaimed in Quebec, thus illustrating that celebrations of Scottishness in Canada could still be affected by the power relations of a century ago, when Alexander Fraser gave his address to his Montreal Caledonian Society audience.

Appendix: Resources for the Study of the Scots in Canada

The following annotated bibliography provides a guide to the literature that examines the Scots in Canada. It is organized around five characteristic approaches to the subject: Celebratory and Hagiographic Volumes; Specific Group Studies; Studies in Ethnicity; The Imperial Perspective; and The Representation of Scottish Canadians.

I. Celebratory and Hagiographic Volumes

Scottish Canadians first appear in literature as the subjects of celebratory collective biographies of notable Scots and their "contributions" to the military, politics, education, the church, and business. Sir James MacPherson LeMoine (1825–1912) was an author and barrister and, despite its title, his 1881 text is one of the earliest examples of this kind of work. Like many other such texts, it took the form of an address to a local society. The Caledonian and St. Andrew's societies encouraged the production of this kind of lecture. Rattray, Bryce, and Campbell were all prominent members of Scottish societies, and their book-length studies were an extension of that activity. William Jordan Rattray (1835–1883) was a writer and journalist with the *Toronto Mail.* Wilfred Campbell [1860–1918], whose 1911 study ends with a discussion of the history and activities of Canadian Scottish societies, was a Canadian-born son of an Anglican clergyman who was a prolific literary figure in early twentieth century Canada. George Bryce [1844–1931], born in Ontario of immigrant Scottish parents, trained as a Presbyterian clergyman and became a leading figure in Manitoba. He was one of the founders of the University of Manitoba and the Manitoba Historical Society. He published several works of history focusing on the Selkirk Red River settlement.

John Murray Gibbon [1875–1952] was a writer, composer, publicist and translator. Born in Ceylon and educated in Britain, Gibbon came to Canada as a Canadian Pacific Railway publicity agent in 1913 and organized a number of festivals and celebrations for the railroad. His illustrated study of Scottish settlement (1911) was designed for the general reader and intended to celebrate the Scottish settlers' contribution to empire. James Alexander Roy's [1884–1973] study (1947) is also a celebration of the contribution of notable Scots. The genre continues with Matthew Shaw's recent volume (2003).

II. Specific Group Studies

A more focused and ultimately more scholarly approach to Scottish Canadians has come in the form of studies of specific immigrant groups, particularly those from the Highlands of Scotland. Early studies, such as Colin MacDonald's (1936), focused on the establishment of Highland communities in the Maritimes, particularly Cape Breton, but the Red River settlement in Manitoba was also the focus of early attention. Duncan Campbell and R. A. MacLean (1974), a sociologist and historian, respectively, were the first to attempt a scholarly approach to the Scots in Nova Scotia by examining the subject thematically under the headings education, culture, religion, and politics, although much of the text still reads like a "contribution" history. J. M. Bumsted (1981, 1982b, 1984, 1987) was the first to treat both the Maritime and Red River settlements together and to propose an interpretation beyond the "contribution" model. For Bumsted, the settlement of the Highlanders in Canada was the consequence of a conscious choice to emigrate in order to avoid the modernization being experienced in the Scottish homelands. In other words, emigrants attempted to preserve the Highland "way of life" in the new world. Lucille Campey's recent popular studies (2001, 2003) of the Prince Edward Island and the Selkirk settlements have reinforced Bumsted's interpretation, while Bumsted himself has changed direction from his earlier work and focused instead on the particular role of Highland Scots in the western fur trade (1999a, 2002, 2003). Marianne McLean's study (1991) of the Glengarry Highland settlement in Eastern Ontario is the most thorough historical treatment of a Scottish-Canadian Highland community to date. McLean argues for a more complex understanding of the creation of Highland Scottish-Canadian communities. She agrees that the Glengarry Highlanders were anxious to reestablish their communities in Ontario, but also argues that estate management policy had a prolonged influence on the exodus from Scotland, even for those who had accommodated the modernization occurring on the estate. J. I. Little's study (1991) of the Highland crofter settlement in Winslow County, in the Eastern Townships of Quebec, during the nineteenth century emphasizes the competition for land with French Canadian settlers, while Wayne Norton (1994) provides a detailed examination of the British and Canadian government policy that led to the establishment of crofter colonies on the Canadian prairies in the same century.

In comparison, Lowland Scottish-Canadian settlement has received little attention. Campbell and McLean (1974) touch on Lowland settlement briefly, but their primary focus is Highland. Lynda Price's (1981) study of the Scots in Quebec provided a profile of the Lowland community in Quebec City and Montreal and her work has recently been followed up by graduate theses on Montreal Scots, but to date that research remains unpublished. David Macmillan (1985) provided the most detailed published research on the Scottish-Canadian business community, which was dominated by Lowland Scots. E. J. Cowan (1992) provides one of the few examinations of Lowland migration, tracing the migration from the Scottish borders to southern Ontario. Cowan emphasizes the importance of the transformation of agricultural practice in the Borders and the networks of family and friends in the new world for encouraging migration and directing the location of settlement in Canada. Michael Vance (2001) places the urban Lowland emigration from Glasgow in the context of the early nineteenth-century artisan demand for parliamentary reform and argues for the "politicized" nature of Lowland Scottish Canadians in that century.

III. Studies in Ethnicity

It is far more difficult to find examples of scholarship that treat Scottish Canadians as an ethnic group. The most obvious exception would be the *Gaels of*

Cape Breton. Charles Dunn's (1953) study was one of the first scholarly treatments of the community in this vein, albeit from the point of view of a literary scholar. These kinds of work, of which Michael Kennedy (2002) is the most recent, emphasize the persistence of Gaelic as one of the key ethnic identifiers. The maintenance of folk belief, examined in the studies of Helen Creighton (1979), Margaret MacDonell (1982), and Margaret Bennett (1998), has also been used as an ethnic marker of the Scottish-Canadian communities in Nova Scotia, Quebec, and Ontario. To a lesser degree, religious practice, particularly Scottish Catholicism (J. Cameron 1992; Murphy and Byrne 1987) and Scottish Presbyterianism (Moir 1974), has been viewed as an ethnic feature of Scottish-Canadian society. Sporting traditions, particularly Highland games, are also seen as reflective of Scottish-Canadian ethnicity.

Historical geographers have perhaps been the most explicit in the use of ethnic categories when discussing the Scots in Canada. Rosemary Ommer (1986) tied clan allegiances to landholding practices, while Stephen Hornsby (1992b) mapped Highland and Lowland distribution patterns in early Scottish-Canadian settlement. His analysis of Cape Breton (1992a) examines the chronology and distribution of Scottish-Canadian settlement in relation to other groups. Alan Brunger (1990) has done the same for Ontario, but without distinguishing between Highlander and Lowlander. Burns societies have also been viewed as "ethnic" groups, but studies of the impact of Scottish literature on Canada have tended to focus on the role of Scottish educators disseminating knowledge of prominent Scottish authors rather than preserving an "ethnic" identity (Waterston 2001). Perhaps the most explicit connection with ethnicity has been the attempt to have the Scots considered one of the multicultural groups comprising Canadian society. This genre includes *The Scottish Tradition* (1976) in the multiculturalism series funded by the Secretary of State in the 1970s. The contents of that volume, although comprised of scholarly papers, were organized around the older Scottish "contribution" model rather than an examination of the "ethnic" characteristics of Scottish Canadians.

IV. The Imperial Perspective

Quite a large body of scholarship examines Scottish Canadians as part of British Imperial History. One older approach looks at them as empire builders and has a tendency to also take the "contribution" approach. The second places Scottish Canadians in the context of British imperial migration and tends to take the form of "from here to there" narratives.

Andrew Dewar Gibb's (1937) study was a "contribution" narrative that sought to highlight the Scottish role in building the empire. Gibb, a Glasgow law professor, was a Scottish nationalist who wished to promote home rule for

Scotland and suggested, by implication, that the Scots' ability to govern the empire demonstrated their ability to govern Scotland within the imperial framework. Gordon Donaldson's (1966) study, which was a refinement on this idea, highlighted the role of immigrant Scots in Canadian settlement and nation building. More recently Michael Fry (2001) has argued for the linked political history of Scotland and empire in the nineteenth and twentieth centuries. His study, like Gibb's, tends to focus on leading Scottish-Canadian historical figures. T. M. Devine's (2003) recent study departs from the "contribution" approach, arguing instead for a linked economic and social development between Scotland and the empire during the eighteenth century.

The imperial migration narrative has been the most common approach to Scottish Canadians. There are broad popular accounts, like Douglas Hill (1972) and most recently Jenni Calder (2003), as well as more specialized studies that focus on particular types of emigrant or specific time periods. David Macmillan (1982), Thomas Devine (1988), Marjory Harper (1994), and the essays in Catherine Kerrigan (1992) discuss merchant, Highland, juvenile, aristocratic, and clerical Scottish-Canadian migrants. J. M. Bumsted (2001) places Scottish-Canadian immigration in its eighteenth-century British Colonial context. Harper (1998) does the same for the Scottish-Canadian migration between the two World Wars, while her earlier study of migration from the Scottish northeast places the Scottish-Canadian settlement in the broader context of nineteenth-century migration from one particular region. Lucille Campey (2002) focuses on the particular role of transatlantic shipping in facilitating Scottish-Canadian migration. Alan Macinnes and his associates (2002) build on the imperial migration approach, but extend its reach to include the United States after independence as well as South America, and reproduces documents that reflect the variety of immigrant experiences in their new lands.

V. *The Representation of Scottish Canadians*

The area that has received the least amount of attention from scholars is the question of the ethnic representation of Scottish Canadians. The work that has been done has focused on Scottish-Canadian representations in Nova Scotia. John Kenneth Galbraith's (1964) memoir of growing up in a Scottish-Canadian community in Elgin County has not inspired a study of Scottish representation in Ontario. However, the public celebrations of Scottishness in Nova Scotia, particularly in Cape Breton, have attracted the attention of scholars. Norman Macdonald (1988) contrasted the "official" celebration of kilts, bagpipes, and Highland dancing in Cape Breton with the neglect of the

Gaelic language, thus suggesting a disconnect between "real" Scottish culture and the romantic stereotypes. In a recent study, Steve Murdoch (1998) countered by arguing that the stereotypical Scottish representation found in Cape Breton masks the earlier multiethnic and native history of the island. In making this argument, Murdoch follows on from Ian McKay's (1992) important essay, which argued that such "tartanism" was promoted in the interwar era by the Nova Scotia premier, Angus L. MacDonald, as part of a general antimodernist reaction in the interwar period. The elevation of a "traditional" timeless society as emblematic of the entire province had considerable political utility during the period of crisis facing industrial capitalism. Michael Boudreau (1993–1994) and B. Anne Wood (1994) have extended the argument into an earlier time period with their particular studies of the *Hector* celebration, the myth-laden Scottish emigrant vessel, and the centenary of the Pictou Academy, an early Nova Scotian educational facility founded by a prominent Scot. Marjory Harper and Michael Vance (1999) have gone further, arguing that the stereotypical Scottishness evident in Nova Scotia was a product of the romantic representations of the nineteenth century and kept alive in the present in order to support the "heritage" tourist industry. John Bumsted (1999b) sought to extend the discussion beyond Nova Scotia by identifying the elements of Scottishness found across the country during the nineteenth century and contrasting that with the development of Britishness in Canada.

Notes

1. Alexander Fraser (1860–1936) was a journalist, lecturer, and archivist with a long career in Canada. He was city editor of the *Toronto Daily Mail* from 1886 to 1898, the first Ontario archivist from 1903 to 1935, and aide-de-camp for the lieutenant governor of Ontario from 1903 to 1935. In addition to founding the Gaelic Society of Canada in 1897, Fraser served as president of the Toronto Burns Society, and was a life member of the Toronto Caledonian Society. For twenty-one years he edited the *Scottish Canadian,* and for twelve years he was Grand Chief of the Sons of Scotland, ostensibly an organization for the promotion of fraternal relations among Scots but essentially an insurance company. Fraser's many publications on Scottish subjects earned him high regard in academic circles, resulting in honourary degrees from Alfred University, St. Francis Xavier University, and the University of Toronto. His papers in the Archives of Ontario are extensive and include much of the primary material referred to in this discussion. Unless otherwise indicated, quotations are from the published version of Fraser's address (1903).

2. A later example would be Angus William Rugg Mackenzie, a Highland immi-

grant who established the Gaelic College at St. Anne, Cape Breton, in 1939. See Vance, "Powerful Pathos" in this volume.

3. The events most frequently referred to in society annual reports were the summer games, Halloween, St. Andrew's Day dinner and ball, and Burns night (*Fraser Papers*, Mu 1091–92).

4. Alexander Fraser was involved in raising funds for the statue of Robert Burns in Toronto's Allan Gardens (*Fraser Papers*, Mu 1063, 1092).

5. For British Columbia's Scottish Societies, see the online resource created at Simon Fraser University, *http://www.sfu.ca/~scotsbib*.

6. *The Grocer*, Oct. 18, 1930.

7. Accounts from two of the original Tartan Day advocates can be found at *www.electricscotland.com/canada*.

Works Cited

Anderson, James. 1868. *Sawney's Letters and Cariboo Rhymes*. Barkerville, BC: Cariboo Sentinel.

Anderson, Kay. 1991. *Vancouver's Chinatown: Racial Discourse in Canada, 1875–1989*. Montreal: McGill-Queen's UP.

Annual Report of the St. Andrew's Society of Toronto, 1887–1888. 1889. Toronto: James Murray.

Annual Report of the St. Andrew's Society of Toronto, 1888–1889. 1890. Toronto: James Murray.

Annual Report of the St. Andrew's Society of Toronto, 1931–1932. 1933. Toronto: James Murray.

Bennett, Margaret. 1998. *Oatmeal and the Catechism: Scottish Gaelic Settlers in Quebec*. Montreal: McGill-Queen's UP.

Boudreau, Michael. 1993–1994. "A 'Rare and Unusual Treat of Historical Significance': The 1923 Hector Celebration and the Political Economy of the Past." *Journal of Canadian Studies* 28, no. 4: 28–48.

Brunger, Alan G. 1990. "The Distribution of the Scots and the Irish in Upper Canada, 1851–1871." *Canadian Geographer* 34, no. 3: 250–58.

Bryce, George. 1911. *The Scotsman in Canada, Vol. II*. Toronto: Musson.

Bumsted, John M. 2003. *Trials and Tribulations: The Red River Settlement and the Emergence of Manitoba, 1811–1870*. Winnipeg: Great Plains.

———. 2002. "The Scots, Ethnicity, and the Historiography of the Fur Trade." Conference paper presented at *Character and Circumstance: The Scots in Montreal and Canada*, McCord Museum, Montreal, May 2002.

———. 2001. "The Scottish Diaspora: Emigration to British North America, 1763–1815." In Ned Landsman, ed., *Nation and Province in the First British Empire*.

———. 1999a. *Fur Trade Wars: The Founding of Western Canada*. Winnipeg: Great Plains.

———. 1999b. "Scottishness and Britishness in Canada." In Marjory Harper and Michael Vance, eds., *Myth, Migration, and the Making of Memory*. Halifax, Nova Scotia: Fernwood.

——. 1984, 1987. *The Collected Writings of Lord Selkirk. Vol. I (1799–1809). Vol. II (1810–1820)*. Winnipeg: Manitoba Record Society.

——. 1982a. *The Scots in Canada*. Ottawa: Canadian Historical Association.

——. 1982b. *The People's Clearance: Highland Emigration to British North America, 1770–1815*. Edinburgh: Edinburgh UP.

——. 1981. "Scottish Emigration to the Maritimes, 1770–1815: A New Look at an Old Theme." *Acadiensis* 10, no. 2: 65–85.

Calder, Jenni. 2003. *Scots in Canada*. Edinburgh: Luath.

Cameron, Alan, and Julian Gwyn. 1985. "Archibald McNab." In *Dictionary of Canadian Biography*. Vol. 8. Toronto: U of Toronto P. 584–89.

Cameron, James D. 1992. "Erasing Forever the Brand of Social Inferiority:" Saint Francis Xavier University and the Highland Catholics of Eastern Nova Scotia." *Historical Studies: Canadian Catholic Historical Association* 59: 49–64.

Campbell, Duncan, and R. A. MacLean. 1974. *Beyond the Atlantic Roar: A Study of the Nova Scotia Scots*. Toronto: McClelland and Stewart.

Campbell, Wilfred. 1911. *The Scotsman in Canada, Vol. I*. Toronto: Musson.

Campey, Lucille H. 2003. *The Silver Chief: Lord Selkirk and the Scottish Pioneers of Belfast, Baldoon, and Red River*. Toronto: Natural Heritage.

——. 2002. *"Fast Sailing and Copper-Bottomed": Aberdeen Sailing Ships and the Emigrant Scots They Carried to Canada, 1774–1855*. Toronto: Natural Heritage.

——. 2001. *"A Very Fine Class of Immigrants": Prince Edward Island's Scottish Pioneers, 1770–1850*. Toronto: Natural Heritage.

Cheska, Alyce Taylor. 1983. "The Antigonish Highland Games: A Community's Involvement in the Scottish Festival of Eastern Nova Scotia," *Nova Scotia Historical Review* 3, no. 1: 51–63.

Constitution of the St. Andrew's Society of Winnipeg. 1886. Winnipeg: Walker and May.

Cowan, Edward J. 1999. "The Myth of Scotch Canada." In *Myth, Migration, and the Making of Memory: Scotia and Nova Scotia c. 1700–1990*, eds. Marjory Harper and Michael E. Vance, 49–72. Halifax, Nova Scotia: Fernwood.

——. 1992. "From the Southern Uplands to Southern Ontario: Nineteenth-Century Emigration from the Scottish Borders." In *Scottish Emigration and Scottish Society*, ed. T. M. Devine. Edinburgh: John Donald.

Cowie, Isaac. 1913. *The Company of Adventurers: A Narrative of Seven Years Service in the Hudson's Bay Company, 1867–1874*. Lincoln: U of Nebraska P, 1993.

Creighton, Helen. 1979. *Gaelic Songs in Nova Scotia*. Ottawa: National Museums of Canada.

Devine, Thomas M. 2003. *Scotland's Empire, 1600–1815*. London: Allen Lane.

——. 1988. *The Great Highland Famine: Hunger, Emigration, and the Scottish Highlands in the Nineteenth Century*. Edinburgh: John Donald.

Donaldson, Gordon. 1966. *The Scots Overseas*. London: Hale.

Dunn, Charles W. 1991 [1953]. *Highland Settler: A Portrait of the Scottish Gael in Cape Breton and Eastern Nova Scotia*. Toronto: U of Toronto P, 1953. Reprint, Wreck Cove, Nova Scotia: Breton Books.

Evans, A. Margaret MacLaren. 1976. "The Scot as Politician." In *The Scottish Tradition in Canada*, ed. W. Stanford Reid, 273–301. Toronto: McClelland and Stewart.

Fraser, Alexander. 1903. *The Mission of the Scot in Canada.* Toronto: R. G. McLean.

———. 1900. *The 48th Highlanders of Toronto.* Toronto: E. L. Ruddy.

Fraser Papers. Archives of Ontario. Toronto, Ontario. F 1015.

Fry, Michael. 2001. *The Scottish Empire.* Phantassie, East Lothian: Tuckwell.

Galbraith, John Kenneth. 1964. *The Scotch.* Toronto: Macmillan.

Gibb, Andrew Dewar. 1937. *Scottish Empire.* London: A. Maclehose and Company.

Gibbon, John Murray. 1911. *Scots in Canada: A History of the Settlement of the Dominion from the Earliest Days to the Present Time.* Toronto: Musson.

Gillespie, Greg. 2000. "Roderick McLennan, Professionalism, and the Emergence of the Athlete in Caledonian Games." *Sport History Review* 31: 43–63.

Goldring, Philip. 1980. "Lewis and the Hudson's Bay Company in the Nineteenth Century." *Scottish Studies* 24: 23–42.

Harper, Marjory. 2002. "From the Prairies to the Pacific: Snapshots of the Scots in Western Canada." Conference paper presented at *Scots Heritage in British Columbia and the West.* Simon Fraser University, September 2002.

———. 1998. *Emigration from Scotland between the Wars.* Manchester, Eng.: Manchester UP.

———. 1994. "Crofter Colonists in Canada: An Experiment in Empire Settlement in the 1920s." *Northern Scotland* 14: 69–111.

———. 1988. *Emigration from North-East Scotland.* 2 vols. Aberdeen: Aberdeen UP.

Harper, Marjory, and Michael E. Vance, eds. 1999. *Myth, Migration, and the Making of Memory: Scotia and Nova Scotia, c. 1700–1990.* Halifax, Nova Scotia: Fernwood.

Hill, Douglas. 1972. *The Scots to Canada.* London: Gentry.

Hornsby, Stephen J. 1992a. *Nineteenth-Century Cape Breton.* Montreal: McGill-Queen's UP.

———. 1992b. "Patterns of Scottish Emigration to Canada, 1750–1870," *Journal of Historical Geography* 18, no. 4: 397–416.

Hunter, James. 1996. *Glencoe and the Indians.* Edinburgh: Mainstream.

Imrie, John. 1906. *Songs and Miscellaneous Poems.* Toronto: Imrie Printing Co.

Kennedy, Michael. 2002. *Gaelic Nova Scotia: An Economic, Cultural, and Social Impact Study.* Halifax: Nova Scotia Museum.

Kennedy, Rebecca. 2000. "The Scotian Legacy: Scottish Ethnicity, the Scottish Community, and the North British Society of Halifax, 1850–1914." Undergraduate honour's thesis, Saint Mary's University, Halifax, Nova Scotia.

Kerrigan, Catherine, ed., 1992. *The Immigrant Experience: Proceedings of a Conference Held at the University of Guelph.* University of Guelph.

Leitch, Gillian. 2002. "Scottish Identity and British Loyalty in Early Nineteenth Century Montreal." Conference paper presented at *Character and Circumstance: The Scots in Montreal and Canada.* McCord Museum, Montreal, May 2002.

LeMoine, James MacPherson. 1881. *The Scot in New France: An Ethnological Study . . . Read before the Literary and Historical Society of Quebec, 29th November, 1880.* Montreal: Dawson Brothers.

Little, John I. 1991. *Crofters and Habitants: Settler Society, Economy, and Culture in a Quebec Township.* Montreal: McGill-Queen's UP.

MacDonald, Colin S. 1936. "Early Highland Emigration to Nova Scotia and Prince Edward Island from 1770–1853." *Nova Scotia Historical Society Collections* 23: 41–48.

Macdonald, Donna. 1996. *Lord Strathcona: A Biography of Donald Alexander Smith.* Toronto: Dundurn Press.

MacDonald, Ian, and Betty O'Keefe. 2000. *Canadian Holy War: A Story of Clans, Tongs, Murder, and Bigotry.* Surrey, BC: Heritage House.

Macdonald, James S. 1905. *Annals of the North British Society, 1768–1903.* Halifax, Nova Scotia: McAlpine.

MacDonald, Michael. 2001–2002. "Druid in the Beer Tent: The Scottish Pipe Band in North America." Part 1, 2 & 3. *Celtic Heritage,* Sept./Oct. 2001, Nov./Dec. 2001, Jan./Feb. 2002.

Macdonald, Norman. 1988. "Putting on the Kilt: The Scottish Stereotype and Ethnic Community Survival in Cape Breton." *Canadian Ethnic Studies* 20, no. 3: 132–46.

Macdonald, Robert A. J. 2001–2002. "'He thought he was the boss of everything': Masculinity and Power in a Vancouver Family." *BC Studies,* no. 132: 5–30.

MacDonell, Margaret. 1982. *The Emigrant Experience: Songs of Highland Emigrants in North America.* Toronto: U of Toronto P.

Macinnes, Alan, Marjory Harper, and Linda G. Fryer, eds. 2002. *Scotland and the Americas, c. 1650–c. 1939: A Documentary Source Book.* Edinburgh: Scottish History Society.

MacLelland, Lauchie. 2000. *Brigh an Orain: A Story in Every Song: The Songs and Tales of Lauchie MacLelland,* trans. and ed. John Shaw. Montreal: McGill-Queen's UP.

Macmillan, David S. 1985. "Scottish Enterprise and Influences in Canada, 1620–1900." In *The Scots Abroad: Labour, Capital, Enterprise, 1750–1914,* ed. R. A. Cage, 46–79. London: Croom Helm.

———. 1982. "The Neglected Aspect of the Scottish Diaspora 1650–1850: The Role of the Entrepreneur in Promoting and Effecting Emigration." In *The Diaspora of the British: Collected Seminar Papers No. 31.* University of London: Institute of Commonwealth Studies, 20–43.

McCalla, Douglas. 1979. *The Upper Canada Trade, 1834–1872: A Study of the Buchanans' Business.* Toronto: U of Toronto P.

McGrath, Harry. 2003. "The Scottish Community in Vancouver and the Janet Smith Murder Case." Conference paper presented at *British Columbia: Rethinking Ourselves, 2003 BC Studies Conference.* University of British Columbia, May 2003.

McKay, Ian. 1992. "Tartanism Triumphant: The Construction of Scottishness in Nova Scotia, 1933–1954." *Acadiensis* 21, no. 2: 5–47.

McLean, Marianne. 1991. *The People of Glengarry: Highlanders in Transition, 1745–1820.* Montreal: McGill-Queen's UP.

McNabb, Heather. 1999. "Montreal's Scottish Community, 1835–65: A Preliminary Study." Masters thesis, Concordia University, Montreal, Quebec.

Mitchell, Elaine Allan. 1976. "The Scots in the Fur Trade." In *The Scottish Tradition in Canada,* ed. W. Stanford Reid, 27–48. Toronto: McClelland and Stewart.

Moir, John S. 1974. *Enduring Witness: A History of the Presbyterian Church in Canada.* Hamilton, Ont.: Presbyterian Church in Canada.

Murdoch, Steve. 1998. "Cape Breton: Canada's Highland Island?" *Northern Scotland* 18: 31–42.

Murphy, Terence, and Cyril J. Byrne, eds. 1987. *Religion and Identity: The Experience of Irish and Scottish Catholics in Atlantic Canada.* St. John's, Newfoundland: Jesperson.

Norton, Wayne. 1994. *Help Us to a Better Land: Crofter Colonies in the Prairie West.* Regina, Saskatchewan: Canadian Plains Research Center.

Ommer, Rosemary. 1986. "Primitive Accumulation and the Scottish Clan in the Old World and the New." *Journal of Historical Geography* 12, no.2: 121–41.

Price, Lynda. 1981. *Introduction to the Social History of Scots in Quebec, 1780–1840.* Ottawa: National Museums of Canada.

Rattray, William J. 1880–1884. *The Scot in British North America.* 3 vols. Toronto: MacLear & Company.

Ray, R. Celeste. 2001. *Highland Heritage: Scottish Americans in the American South.* Chapel Hill: U of North Carolina P.

Redmond, Gerald. 1972. *The Scots and Sport in Nineteenth-Century Canada.* Edmonton: University of Alberta.

Reid, W. Stanford, ed. 1976. *The Scottish Tradition in Canada.* Toronto: McClelland and Stewart.

Roy, James A. 1947. *The Scot and Canada.* Toronto: McClelland and Stewart.

Selections from Scottish Canadian Poets. 1900. Toronto: Caledonian Society of Toronto.

Shackleton, Doris French. 1975. *Tommy Douglas.* Toronto: McClelland and Stewart.

Shaw, Matthew. 2003. *Great Scots!: How the Scots Created Canada.* Winnipeg: Heartland Associates.

Sheets, John W. 2000. "'National Culture of Mobility': The Colonsay-Canada Connection." In *Transatlantic Studies,* eds. W. Kaufman and H. Slettedahl MacPherson, 69–83. Lanham, MD: UP of America.

Stonechild, Blair, and Bill Waiser. 1997. *Loyal Till Death: Indians and the Northwest Rebellion.* Calgary: Fifth House.

Szasz, Fernec Morton. 2000. *Scots in the North American West, 1790–1917.* Norman: U of Oklahoma P.

Vance, Michael E. 2003. "Canfisco and the Scots: Race, Labour, and Identity in the BC Salmon Canning Industry, 1900–1939." Conference paper presented at *British Columbia: Rethinking Ourselves, 2003 BC Studies Conference.* University of British Columbia, May 2003.

———. 2001. "Advancement, Moral Worth, and Freedom: The Meaning of Independence for Early Nineteenth-Century Lowland Emigrants to Upper Canada." In Ned C. Landsman, ed., *Nation and Province in the First British Empire: Scotland and the Americas, 1600–1800,* 151–82. Lewisburg: Bucknell UP.

Vance, Michael E., and Mark D. Stephen. 2001. "Grits, Rebels, and Radicals: Anti-Privilege Politics and the Pre-History of 1849 in Canada West." In *Canada 1849,* eds. D. Pollard and G. Martin, 181–208. Edinburgh: Centre of Canadian Studies.

Van Kirk, Sylvia. 1980. *Many Tender Ties: Women in Fur-Trade Society, 1670–1870.* Norman: U of Oklahoma P.

Ward, Peter. 1978. *White Canada Forever: Popular Attitudes and Public Policy toward Orientals in British Columbia.* Montreal: McGill-Queen's UP.

Waterston, Elizabeth. 2001. *Rapt in Plaid: Canadian Literature and the Scottish Tradition.* Toronto: U of Toronto P.

Wood, B. Anne. 1994. "Constructing Nova Scotia's "Scotchness": The Centenary Celebrations of Pictou Academy in 1916." *Historical Studies in Education* 6, no. 2: 281–302.

4

From the Quebec-Hebrideans to "les Écossais-Québécois"

Tracing the Evolution of a Scottish Cultural Identity in Canada's Eastern Townships

Margaret Bennett

A two-hour drive south of Montreal lie the Eastern Townships, *les Cantons de l'Est,* which border the states of Vermont and New Hampshire. All the signs for roads, gas stations, shops, post offices, restaurants, public buildings, and events are in French, the official language of Quebec. On a day-to-day basis, the general ambience is French, yet if the clock could be turned back to the time when the region was first settled, one would see an entirely different scene. The British government, claiming ownership of "Lower Canada," as it was called, sold the region to a group of Montreal and London businessmen. In 1834 the British American Land Company drew up an agreement to purchase "in the Eastern Townships of Lower Canada, a tract of country, lying inland, on the south side of the St. Lawrence, between 45° and 46½° north latitude, and 71° and 73° west longitude. This tract, containing between five and six million acres, is divided into eight counties, and these are again sub-divided into about one hundred townships" (Traill 1836, 287–89).

Three of the counties—Shefford, Stanstead, and Sherbrooke—were rich, fertile farmland, and English and Lowland Scots farmers who could afford the price quickly acquired land there. The rest, however, was a vast wilderness, with very poor prospects for land speculators. By 1839 the British American Land Company was 72,000 pounds in debt, and two years later half a million acres reverted to the Crown to cancel the debt. That same year, the Canadian government passed the Land Act of 1841, offering free grants of fifty (later one hundred) acres to be made to any British male subject willing to settle there. To the British government of the time, this scheme was to offer an almost perfect solution during the crisis and aftermath of the Irish Potato Famine.

Stories of emigration among descendants of Scottish settlers generally begin by naming a family member who was born in the Outer Hebrides. Without exception Gaelic-speaking and usually monoglots, most were from the Isle of Lewis, a few from the Isle of Harris, and fewer still from North Uist. The following account, recorded in 1990 from ninety-three year-old Christie MacKenzie (née Murray), is typical of stories about "the first of our family to settle here":

Thàinig iad à Scotland . . . rugadh m'athair ann a' Tolsta a Thuath . . . cha robh e ach ceithir là a dh'aois. Thàinig m'athair ann a' eighteen fifty-two, agus thàinig mo mhàthair ann a' 1856.

(They came from Scotland . . . My father, he was born in North Tolsta [Isle of Lewis] . . . he was only four days old [when he left]. My father came over in 1852 and my mother in 1856.)[1]

Although most families emigrated from the Outer Hebrides to Quebec in the 1850s, some surviving family memories tell of earlier arrivals. Duncan McLeod (1917–2001), a keen historian and keeper of countless newspaper articles, features, clippings, and books relevant to the history of the area, dated his family history in Quebec to the early 1840s:

Well, I had a great-grandfather, Alasdair, who came from—he came here from Ness but I believe he was a native of Back. And Murdo, another great-[grandfather], another MacLeod, not the same family, I don't think, he was a native of Back too. Angus MacDonald, my grandmother's father, was from Uig, and his father, William, was known as the builder of roads, *Uilleam a' rathad* [in Gaelic], and he built the road, and it's still visible. It runs from Miavaig ferry to the Uigan church. I have a picture of the road . . . My grandfather [Duncan L. McLeod, son of Alistair] was the youngest in the family, and he was born in Canada in 1848.

Duncan himself was the first of his family whose mother tongue was English: "The old folks figured we'd get on better in the world." Asked if he had "any idea what made the people come out," he replied:

No, I don't. It was just to better their chance for their families. There were other people coming out, and they decided [to do the same]—my great-grandfather Alasdair MacLeod was a dominie . . . a teacher. Anyway he was known as a dominie. [He came in] 1841 . . . There was Alistair,

Malcolm, and Christina in the family, and my [great-great-]grandfather, Murdo, came out with Alistair, and I believe Malcolm too, and he died that fall . . . And there's a Port Alistair on the coast of Lewis, up in the Ness area which is named after him.

Long family genealogies and the identification of the exact location of the home immigrant ancestors left in Scotland typify the kind of detail preserved through five generations of oral history. Interestingly, however, there is no mention in Duncan McLeod's account, or in that of any other descendant traced and interviewed for this study, of the hardships suffered by their kinsfolk who emigrated during the nineteenth century. From over forty hours of tape recordings and responses to letters in regional newspapers, the only remark that alludes to the circumstances of their exodus was elicited from Christie MacArthur (b. 1888), whose father, Alexander MacDonald, was one of the first settlers:

> My father was born in Scotland . . . on the Isle of Lewis . . . I think he was fifteen years [old] when he came to Canada . . . he was herding cattle, that's about all I heard. [*laughs*] Sheep or cattle, I don't know . . . [*Further prompts: Did he ever say what made him leave?*] I couldn't say, but they all came about that same time—but I think they were encouraged to leave . . . Well, they were kind of forced to leave.

An examination of records that remain in their homeland, however, leaves no doubt whatsoever that most families suffered from the effects of the potato famine of 1846–1851. Although well known in Irish history and oral tradition, both at home and abroad, the Scottish potato famine that devastated parts of the Highlands during these same years had been little documented until the late twentieth century.

The government created relief bodies to alleviate the pressure on Scottish landlords attempting to feed a starving population, but year after year crops failed and the cost became untenable. The solution for the Outer Hebrides was a new scheme offering free passage to "Lower Canada" (Quebec) with land grants from the British American Land Company in the Eastern Townships. The wealthy tea and opium merchant James Matheson (who bought the Isle of Lewis in 1844) appointed J. Munro MacKenzie as factor. MacKenzie kept a diary of events. Clearly, if grimly, MacKenzie records the eviction of those forced to comply with his harsh interpretation of the government's scheme.

Within one generation of the famine evictions, immigrants seemed to manifest (as least on the surface) mass amnesia of this gloomy period in their history. Such dismissal of this experience in folk memory might be explained, however, by the fact that in their Gaelic language the famine was known as *Bliadhna a ghais am buntata*—literally, "the year(s) the potatoes were diseased." Those who were evicted would hardly have been aware that they were part of a much larger picture, although, in the process of their emigration, they may have sensed that Highlanders, like the Irish, were the objects of shame, and their motives for leaving their homeland may have been subsequently downplayed in oral traditions. The British government official in charge of the emigration scheme, Sir John Trevelyan, was reported in *The Scotsman* of September 11, 1851, to have said:

> Ethnologically the Celtic race is an inferior one, and attempt to disguise it as we may, there is naturally no getting rid of the fact that it is destined to give way to the higher capabilities of the Anglo-Saxons. In the meantime, a part of the natural law which had already pushed the Celt from continental Europe westward, emigration to America is the only available remedy for the miseries of the race, whether squatting listlessly in filth and rags in Ireland, or dreaming in idleness and poverty in the Highlands and Islands of Scotland.

In a letter that appeared in the *Fifeshire Journal* the following year, Trevelyan informed the nation that he "contemplated with satisfaction . . . the prospects of flights of Germans settling here [in Britain] in increasing numbers—an orderly, moral, industrious and frugal people, less foreign to us than the Irish or Scottish Celt, a congenial element which will readily assimilate with our body of politic."

Although it is unlikely that impoverished migrants read newspapers, it is more than likely that the emigration agents did. There was public shame attached to being "Celtic"—Highland, Hebridean, or Irish. Setting sail with the promise of a new life, very few possessions, and a great a deal of hope, the emigrants clung to the strong faith that had brought them thus far. Without exception they were Presbyterian, and even those who could not read knew the Scriptures. Christie MacKenzie recalled her grandfather saying that all they needed in the new land was "an axe, a saw and a Bible."

> My father and mother always had family worship . . . oh boy, his father [who sailed on that boat] could read the Gaelic [Bible] and sing! He was a precentor in the church for years and years—Murdo MacKenzie,

Murchadh they used to call him. Well, they opened with a *beannachd* [blessing], the *adhrachail* [devotional], and they'd read the chapter, and sing a psalm too. And then they closed with prayer; everybody got on their knees . . . and no matter how busy they were, this was done right after breakfast, before they'd go out to work. And then, in the evening again, after supper, before going to bed.

The practice, which can still be found in a few homes in the twenty-first century, migrated with them across the Atlantic. Through the teachings of church meetings and daily family worship, they knew well what the Bible had to say about life's trials: "Blessed are ye when men shall revile you and persecute you and say all manner of evil against you falsely" (Matthew 11:5). Clearly it would be best to put it all behind them and turn their eyes on God's promises. Furthermore, unlike their Irish counterparts, the majority of whom were Roman Catholics destined for New York, the Scottish Gaels had to sever ties with the homeland completely. While the Irish financed the continued exodus of post–potato famine victims from Ireland with urban jobs, the Scottish Gaels did not have such ongoing transnational links.

For most, the story of emigration began on the point of departure, and many held on to memories of the actual voyage. There was more than enough excitement and trauma on the high seas to brighten firesides for years to come. There were even the legendary babies born on board ship, such as the one recounted by Christie MacKenzie's son-in-law, Alex MacIver, a third-generation Gaelic-speaker: "My grandfather was born on the way across . . . in 1851. And there was three born here afterwards . . . *Duine gun dùthaich*, they used to say—a man without a country." They shared experiences of the ocean crossing—six or eight weeks of cramped conditions on board, shortage of food supplies, rough seas, seasickness, the dreaded cholera, and finally, for those who survived, thankfulness of seeing land again. Listening to their stories one begins to understand why the hardships of home were no longer mentioned. The new land was full of new challenges, to say nothing of adversity, but at least most of them could realise their dream of achieving a decent living.

For a century and a half, their distant kinsfolk in the Outer Hebrides have wondered what became of the exiles.[2] A sense of loss filtered down to the late twentieth century, the age of technology, which now facilitates the current passion for genealogy and "roots" research. Aided by the ease of transatlantic communication, networks of distant relatives have suddenly reestablished family ties with long-lost relatives. Warmhearted letters, Christmas cards, and visits have suddenly become common between MacLeods, MacDonalds, MacIvers, Murrays, Morrisons, and others sharing Hebridean names. The ties "of blood" remain strong, although the language of their forebears is no longer their language of communication. There is plenty to share, including the delight that to this day the map of Quebec has place-names such as Stornoway, Tolsta, Ness, and Dell testifying to links with the homeland.

Apart from family reunions, however, can these non-Gaelic-speaking descendants of the emigrants still be identified as Gaels, or even Scottish, considering they all speak English and most also speak French? Outside of their family circles in the Isle of Lewis and in Quebec's Eastern Townships they may simply be identified as Québécois, Canadian, or North American.

Stories of emigration are an important part of Canada's past and, by extension, retain importance in the present. On a national level they attempt to explain why groups or individuals came to Canada, and, consequently, these narratives help to validate the place of the immigrant in the new land. On a regional and community level, the same stories reinforce common bonds between people who share such an experience, and they may also reach out to establish new links with other immigrant groups or individuals, regardless of their country of origin. On a local and domestic level, stories of emigration play an important part in perpetuating images of the homeland, of kinship ties, and of the lifestyle and values that laid the foundation of a new way of life in the New World.

Olav Bo of the Nordic Institute of Folklore highlights the value attached to "knowing about the past" (1988, 146). He suggests that family traditions, such as those recording "the first member of the family who actually cleared the ground for the family farm," serve to "strengthen family solidarity," and as far as the present is concerned, these traditions are "perhaps the strongest sign of identity" (148). Thus, traditions about the past become a "living force" that shapes the present and influences the future.

In the New World, descendants of immigrants keep alive images of Old World identity constructed from descriptions perpetuated in oral tradition (usually of individual characters and their specific traits); from written accounts in popular books and journals; and also from stereotypical images such as Scotland's mountain glens, heather, tartan, whisky, and oatcakes. While the picture may be incomplete and even totally inaccurate, it nevertheless serves the purpose of those who retain it. In the "Old Country" the Scots themselves may remark upon the American or Canadian more-Scottish-than-the-Scots image, often failing to consider their own perception of Scotland and Scottishness and completely overlooking the fact that they also speak English, and many have no knowledge of either Scots or Gaelic.[3] Addressing a German audience on aspects of identity, Ian Olson proposed: "In many ways Scotland, like Bohemia, ceased to exist in the earlier years of the seventeenth century, and by the eighteenth found itself part of an overwhelming empire. For like Bohemia, Scotland exists as a country of the mind, a powerful concept that has more meaning and existence than many a 'real' country in the world today" (1989, 140).

Concepts of identity cover a broad sweep of ideas viewed from many angles, operating at different levels, and stemming from a range of shared experiences. They are usually rooted in a specific place, influenced by images from previous generations, embedded in particular customs and a lifestyle that has evolved through years of sharing common bonds. Within a given group, identity is often indicated by subtle clues that act as symbols in a highly complex system best understood by those within it. Outsiders might make generalisations about the "ethnic origin," loosely applying the term that has gained currency as a label for minority groups retaining identifiable characteristics such as language or costume. In the case of Quebec's Eastern Townshippers, however, it seems inappropriate, regardless of their retention of certain items of food or dress, to apply this term to a people whose mother tongue is Canada's main language and who have been Canadian for several generations.

Göran Rosander proposes that national identity depends also on spatial or territorial identities such as native country, local region, hometown, immediate locality, family home, and land ownership. His model could be applied to the Scots of the Eastern Townships, although territory alone does not sustain identity. "Rather it is a question of fellowship, rooted above all in history." Rosander observes:

> The important thing is that people are united in a positive feeling for their local region in general, for its natural attractions and for the individual selection of cultural elements associated with it. This leads to a more active learning of local legends, local history and topography, etc. However, there usually exists a certain common core in the elements selected, a number of central themes. These are important—they have a symbolic value. In the course of conversation people defend them, up to a certain point. And it is considered desirable that they [the symbolic values] go on living, which is why it becomes important to see that they are handed on. Their content is communicated via socialization . . . daily conversation . . . celebrations . . . and by means of many different kinds of symbols. (1988, 95)

In terms of ordinary folk, these "symbols" will include items of material culture (food, drink, clothing, house décor), along with stories, songs, rhymes, and all aspects of oral tradition. Such "symbols" are grist to the mill for the folklorist who records what people have to say about their own lives—personal experiences of family, home, and community; their laughter, anguish, sorrow, joy, and fear; their travels and adventures; or any aspect of their own culture.

Central to this research into emigration and identity is a solid core of folklore recorded from the people who are the focus of investigation. The method is chosen because:

> The study of folklore is not the study of the past, though it necessarily includes it; rather it is as much the examination of the operations of tradition, from historical development of items, the stability and change they demonstrate . . . Of items, of course [songs, poems, stories, customs, and so on], but especially of their meaning, of the values they purvey, and the varying degrees of artistic or operational competence which generate not only the items themselves but also their deep content and structure. (Thomas and Widdowson 1991, xxii)

Professor Alan Dundes of Berkeley, California, speaks for the majority of professional folklorists (including myself) in his statement: "I am interested in folklore because it represents a people's image of themselves. The image may be distorted but at least the distortion comes from the people, not from some outside observer armed with a range of *a priori* premises. Folklore as a mirror of culture provides unique raw material for those eager to better understand themselves and others" (1980, viii). It is that quest for further understanding that holds the attention, prompts the questions, and motivates the continued recording of oral testimonies and traditions.

Finnish folklorist Lauri Honko also favours the study of folklore as a means to illuminating identity:

> [These] traditions may refer to language, geographical location, music, dance, costume, architecture, history, myth, ritual [legend, song, medical lore, food], etc. The selection of items may look peculiar [unrelated to one another?], but it is not to be judged by external form or by content only, because each thing and each behaviour stands for more than itself; it has symbolic meaning. The identity group is united by meaning and emotion, which pervade the symbols selected to represent its sense of cohesion and togetherness. (1988, 11; see also 1992)

Honko's recommendation that researchers should seek "the right indications of identity" might be tempered with the caution that their own identity could influence not only their perception but also their conclusions, depending on whether they observe from the point of view of the insider or outsider to the group being studied. The fact that my own identity is both Scottish and Hebridean may have had certain advantages for this study, but equally there were pitfalls to avoid. It was crucial to set aside (a) all preconceived views of Hebridean identity based on an insider's view of the lifestyle, and (b) all stereo-typical notions of Scottishness based on the widely articulated outsider's view of my culture. This approach aimed to avoid the danger of deciding on the results before examining the data, as it would have been easy to select examples of songs, stories, customs, recipes, house decoration, furniture, and so forth that could fit perfectly a "Lewis identity" of my own experience, and then observe a Quebec version of the same. Despite the existence of several such examples, these alone would have presented an entirely false image of the identity actually portrayed.

In a paper titled "Senseless Identity" (Uppsala Symposium 1982) Hermann Bausinger discusses some of the problems of accurately presenting a true representation of identity. Examining the nature of identity in a postmodern society, he argues that for most people it is a "rather shallow concept . . . something that can be played with." He analyses stages in its development, beginning with the premise that people generally sense a cultural affiliation, and discusses the role of folklore in cultural identity.

The term "cultural affiliation" might be better understood in the context of a concrete example such as: "Mother's people are Highland (as opposed to Lowland), thus our family uses the terms Highland, or Gael to present our identity." To acknowledge the role of folklore in cultural identity we might offer an example along the lines of: "going to visit friends or family, especially at Hogmanay, it's customary to bring food, such as shortbread, or drink, such as whisky. To arrive empty-handed would be unthinkable; it would instantly identify the outsider who does not share our tradition."

Bausinger continues his discussion by stating that folklore in any culture can change, and in terms of identity, he traces changes through a three-stage historical progression:

- In the first stage folklore is a ritual process in a local frame; one can speak of customs. Customs in their rather invariable, unchangeable form contribute to the firm identity of people: in general nobody has a chance to escape the obligations of custom.

- In the second stage, society is much more heterogeneous, but it is made homogeneous by ideologies. Folklore comes forth, now as a means of homogenization. Its typical appearance is what in German is called Fest, feast, less obligatory and less controlled than customs were, but good occasions for the spreading of religious or political [or nationalist] ideas.

- The third stage and latest development: folklore presented in festivals (in the more special sense of the word), an aesthetic presentation making use of particular traditions offered to a diffuse and dispersed public audience. They can identify themselves with these offer[ing]s and they often do, but this is just a contribution to a transient and floating identity. (Bausinger 1983, 9–10)

The model might operate in Quebec's Eastern Townships as follows:

- Stage 1: Membership of or affiliation to the Presbyterian Church instantly identifies the Scottishness of Eastern Townshippers in a province that is predominately Roman Catholic. Aside from religious observances, customs recognised as forming part of their Scottish identity include those surrounding birth, marriage, death; belief in supernatural phenomena such as ghosts, phantom noises, and premonitions; and traditional observance of certain calendar customs.
- Stage 2: Several celebrations that originate in shared experiences in the New World have come to be regarded as part of local tradition. They include "Old Home Week," the Scotstown Fair, the Oddfellows' Social, the Ladies' Aid tea, the Box Socials, the Leap Year Dance, the annual church picnic.[4] Though they may or may not occur in Scotland, they are all regarded as characterising the activities of a "typically Scottish" society.
- Stage 3: Festivals, such as the annual St. Andrew's Night, the Burns Supper, the Scotstown Céilidh Week culminating in the Kirking of the Tartan, and thematic events such as *Hommage aux premiers arrivants Écossais*. All highly organized and usually advertised via newspapers, such events are open to a much wider section of the population. Programmes incorporate manifestations of Scottishness, such as the wearing of tartan, the playing of bagpipes, the singing of Gaelic songs, and the singing and playing (on bagpipes) of "Amazing Grace," and saying "*Ceud Mile Failte*" (A hundred thousand welcomes).

Bausinger's statement that "in general nobody has a chance to escape the obligations of custom" does not stand either in the Eastern Townships or the Outer Hebrides. Until the second half of the twentieth century, for example, all funerals were conducted according to traditional customs, but when modern undertakers became established it became impossible to adhere to traditional customs. Furthermore, at "feasts" and "festivals" participants can temporarily assume an identity then discard it in the time it takes to change out of a national costume, remove a tartan scarf, or unpin a plastic badge.

Discussions of identity in other cultures have helped sharpen my examination of how the Eastern Townshippers perceive and present their own identity. My research, now more than a quarter of a century in duration, was initiated by the Centre for Folk Cultural Studies in 1976 as the "Quebec-Hebridean Project." The original remit was to spend six weeks recording the "Folkways and Religion of the Quebec-Hebrideans" and then produce a monograph documenting the material (Bennett-Knight 1980). It was soon apparent, however, that a quick foray with a tape recorder might preserve "items" for posterity, but there was a pressing urgency to continue while there was still a Scottish Gaelic community in this part of Quebec. A summary of field notes from my original project sets the scene:

> May 1976. Arrived in Scotstown in the Eastern Townships. Stopped at the local supermarket and immediately overheard a group of elderly shoppers in animated conversation entirely in Gaelic. Naturally, joined in. Instant introductions and invitations all round—this is the folklorist's dream. But within days, the joy of that moment is replaced by dismay— there's not a single Gaelic-speaker my own age (under 30). The gap is at least a quarter of a century; the entire Gaelic population belonging to my parents' and grandparents' generations. I'm much drawn to the company of elders, but if no children learn the language, it cannot possibly survive beyond the end of the 20th century. I've been transplanted into a world where only the elderly know what a Gaelic community is like, and there's not one young person left to sing a Gaelic song or hold a conversation.
>
> "What about a nursery or kindergarten for my little boy?" I enquire.
>
> "Certainly! They have a really good set-up at *La garderie du Ballon Rouge*. They're wonderful with children—I think one of them even speaks English . . . he'll have great fun."

I was struck that Gaelic in Quebec was headed for extinction, and if language is the vehicle that carries traditional culture from one generation to the next, then that too was doomed. At the same time, in the 1970s there was still a lively and widespread interest in all aspects of Scottish history, tradition, and folklore. As is typical anywhere, certain individuals excelled at the traditions that interested them most (emigration stories, local legends, songs, customs, or medical lore). A wealth of folkloric material was in active circulation, and "Quebec-Hebrideans" had plenty of enthusiasm to communicate it, especially in the natural setting of the house visit, or *céilidh,* as these spontaneous gatherings were called. Usually unplanned, and almost always held in the kitchen, as Bill Young described:

> Visitors were always dropping in. You never had to be invited, eh? The teapot was always on the stove. People'd just come and walk right in— there were no preliminaries . . . That was the pastime in the evening, you see. We had no TV or anything like that . . . Everyone came around and visited . . . Time meant nothing, really—quieter type of life, and us children'd sit around and the old folks'd tell these ghost stories. They didn't believe them, I suppose, but it used to scare us and we'd be afraid to go to bed, and—[*laughs*] . . . Oh, there were those that believed in the second sight.

Muriel Mayhew's childhood memories of winter evenings went back to the time "before we had stoves that were entirely closed in." Her grandparents in Lewis would gather around the peat fire, but in Quebec they all "sat in the kitchen by the stove . . . you could see the flames of the wood burning," as they shared their stories and songs.

Milan was once a busy little railway town, the highest point east of the Rocky Mountains on the Canadian Pacific Railway. Christie MacKenzie, born, brought up, and married there, had known it in its heyday. She recalled her parents telling her "it was in 1879 when work on the railway began," and soon afterwards the town boasted two hotels, a post office, and big store. You could hear Gaelic spoken in all of them. Her husband, John, born in 1892 in the nearby town of Marsboro, added that "in 1915 there were exactly four French-speaking families in Milan."

After World War II, when Muriel (MacDonald, as she was), Bill Young, and others of their generation moved away from Milan, every family knew those fireside gatherings. "Some of the French spoke Gaelic too, you know." In the mid-1970s there were a dozen homes where the custom was still a way of life. By the early 1990s, however, there was one left, that of Ruth Nicolson, as authentic a *taigh ceilidh* as any on either side of the Atlantic.

Ruth's house was a place where visitors dropped in unexpectedly, and when they did, no television took over. A warm welcome awaited, the kettle on the woodstove was brought to the boil, and her china cups and saucers were set on the table along with a generous spread of home baking. Seated round the kitchen table, the company would catch up on events then gradually move on to other favourite topics—local characters, the wise, witty, foolish, brave, or adventurous; fond memories of "the old folk"; cures or household hints; supernatural happenings or ghost stories. There were yarns about "out West," "up North," or "during the war," and when they ran out of adventures of their own they would retell stories they had read. Emotions ran the full gamut, laughter to tears and often tears of laughter, no two sessions were alike, and people never tired of hearing what they had heard many times before. The teapot could be filled and emptied several times before folk reluctantly took their leave.

When Ruth died suddenly in 1997, her death quite literally marked the end of an era for the village. Within her lifetime, she had experienced transitions that could sum up those of almost all Quebec-Hebridean families:

- grandparents: monoglot Gaelic-speakers
- parents: bilingual in Gaelic and English
- her own generation: English-speakers with a smattering of Gaelic and a little more French
- her children: bilingual in English and French
- her grandchildren: most bilingual, and some speak only French

There may be no Gaelic society on earth where the words "times have changed" can be spoken with such conviction. Every village in the Eastern Townships, every "Scotch farm" in the area, began to have its own story to tell in an attempt to explain "whatever happened?" Through the 1970s, 80s, and 90s, the ageing "Scot" population would open their discussions by personalising language issues and emphasising how strong Gaelic was in this or that village or [named] family. An article in the *Clansman News* of 1970 confirmed the past strength of the language: "At the time of the first Great War there were approximately two thousand five hundred Gaels in Marsboro alone. We were talking with a man who was born in Milan, who told us that he did not know that there was any other language in the world but Gaelic until he was seven years old." As the twentieth century drew to a close, however, that same village could claim only one Gaelic speaker, Angus Morrison (1911–2002), who was four years old at the start of the war. When he and his French wife, Marie-Claire (Mary), visited the Outer Hebrides in the 1970s, Angus was as fluent as any of his distant relatives in Harris and a better Gaelic speaker than many. At home in Quebec, however, his children and grandchildren had grown up bilingual in English and French, and all were educated in French.

In 1942 Angus and Mary began their married life in Cruvag, the farm settled by the Morrisons in 1888. When they took me there in 1992, Angus attempted to explain:

> Now, when my father went to Cruvag there was no road here . . . But the woods weren't so thick as they are now . . . bigger trees and fewer. [*We drive on.*] Now, the schoolhouse was in here . . . [*We stop, get out, but find no trace of it in the thick bush; we drive on.*] Oh, it took them a long time [to make the road]. Just imagine the people that came out here—no road, no nothing . . . there was around fifty-six all Scotch Gaelic families . . . My cousin lived up here . . . And in the winter we used to roll the road with the big roller . . . it would take four horses . . . Yeah, there was a house in there . . . five mailboxes, right here, one after the other, and that mail would come from Nantes by horse and buggy . . . I'll show you where my cousin lived . . . *An greusaiche!* Yeah, the shoemaker's house . . . [*We drive on and finally stop at the old homestead, now completely overgrown with trees.*] No, you can't see nothing.

Standing at the edge of what was once a huge hayfield, Angus gazed at the thick trees and brush that now cover the land cleared by the sweat and toil of his own people: "It breaks my heart to see this."

Analysing the dramatic shift in language and culture in the Eastern Townships and the subsequent portrayal of Scottish identity is complex and at times controversial. Expressed in general terms, forces were exerted first and foremost from within the community, and second, though eventually far more powerfully, from outside the community. It would be impossible to discuss such a process chronologically, as both factors overlapped and at times operated simultaneously.

Until the second half of the twentieth century, the Official Canadian Census classed Quebec's non-French-speakers as English-speakers. Within the mainstream population the phrase "*les anglais qui ne parlent pas l'anglais*" could occasionally be heard when referring to Gaelic-speakers. In one sense there was a ring of truth about the odd expression, for Gaelic-speakers were caught up in an education system that mirrored Scotland's policy of employing English-speaking teachers for children of Gaelic-speakers. From the outset, therefore, children learned that their culture was not highly valued, while Anglocentric culture was synonymous with progress. By the late 1800s even the Gaelic poets of the region were composing in English, partly because they were not literate in their mother tongue, and partly because English spoke louder and claimed a wider audience.

In 1918 township bard Angus Mackay, known as Oscar Dhu, published his twenty-verse composition "Guard the Gaelic: An Exhortation to the Gael." To emphasise a point in discussion about language loss, Donald Morrison sang the song in its entirety in 1976. Verses 1, 3, 6, and 7 give the gist of the song:

Is it not our bounden right
To uphold with all our might,
And with tongue and pen to fight
For our native Gaelic?

Pity the disloyal clown
Who will dwell a while in Town,
And returning wear a frown
If he hears the Gaelic.

Lads and lassies in their teens
Wearing airs of kings and queens—
Just a taste of Boston beans
Makes them lose their Gaelic!

They return with finer clothes,
Speaking "Yankee" through their nose
That's the way the Gaelic goes—
Pop! goes the Gaelic.

The son of Gaelic-speaking parents who spoke English to their children and Gaelic to each other, Donald Morrison had passionate feelings about the loss of Gaelic in his community. His parents' generation had not only deprived their own children of a birthright, but also disadvantaged them in life, for, as Donald discovered, no amount of "adult education" ever made up for the lost opportunity of childhood. Equally, it anguished Donald that most of his generation were forced to speak English to their children. Even at the age of eighty-two, Russell MacIver of Scotstown regarded himself as the victim of a similar language shift initiated by his parents: "Well, that was a mistake; a bad one too! We'd learn English, [when we went to school] I'm sure!"

Abandoning the mother tongue was, and is, the most drastic example of "undervaluing culture." It was not until it was too late, however, that an entire generation realised that the Gaelic language would slide into such decline that there would be no going back. At the same time, until the 1970s when Quebec nationalism became a major provincial issue, the Quebec-Hebrideans did not realise that it would be not English, but French, that would ultimately take over their community.

In long, complex discussions, some would cite intermarriage between Scots and French as a major factor in language shift, while others suggested that religious differences were even more influential. There was also the discovery in the second and third generation that many of the farms were not big enough, or fertile enough, to be subdivided among several sons. As a result, many of the young men "went out west," or "crossed the line" (went to the United States) for work, adventure, or both. If they found it to their liking, they simply did not return. Then came the Great War of 1914–1918, which took its toll on the young men who had answered the call to fight for the Old Country. Families and communities in the early twenties were still coming to terms with the aftermath of the war when the Ford Motor Company opened up "across the line" and lured a good many to Detroit with their promise of a five-dollar-a-day wage. Education was also cited as influencing who stayed and who left, some suggesting that the Scottish obsession with schooling might even have worked against them: "Only so many doctors and lawyers and teachers can get jobs, and they're not going to come home and work the farm."

It was not only the Gaelic population who felt the effects of changes, but also the older French families, the first of whom had been established in Stornoway since 1862 when Alphonse Legendre bought the local gristmill. He became bilingual in French and Gaelic, and his family played an essential role in the Gaelic community, where they were regarded with great affection. His daughter Ellen (b. 1897) gave her perspective of "what happened," attributing education as the major factor. At her father's insistence, she and her siblings were put through the English-speaking school system, and afterwards spent a comparatively short time at a French school. Ellen explained:

> [There was] a big difference in education . . . there certainly was. And our Bishop there in Sherbrooke—he came here when my sister died—he himself said that he thought that the good part of us, or the good spirit, came from the Scotch people . . . [They] were much better set up than the French . . . [they could afford to send their children to] places like MacDonald College in Montreal . . . [But eventually] they sold out. The

French people from Beauce started to come and buy their farms. The first thing we knew we had lost our good Scotch people.

At the time of this interview, there was only one Gaelic-speaker left in Stornoway. (There are none today.) The Legendre family had observed a shift in population of such momentum that by the 1970s most of their neighbours were second- and third-generation descendants of the incomers from Comté Beauce. And according to Ellen, most had never even heard of Scotland, much less considered its significance to the land they farmed. Eventually, the community council proposed that the town should be renamed—only a few miles away, after all, the village of Springhill had been renamed "Nantes." At the time, however, Ellen's father was the mayor of Stornoway. With pride she described how he took a firm stand and reminded the council of the hardworking Gaelic settlers who had established Stornoway and carved their farms and town out of a wilderness. He then insisted that, "as long as there is a Legendre in the town, it will remain STORNOWAY out of respect for our good Scotch neighbours."

Keeping a Gaelic presence, far less identity, in an area populated by French was never going to be easy. Left to the efforts of the Gaels themselves, it would eventually become impossible, for one by one they were dwindling away. It was heartening, however, that among the French there emerged a strong core of individuals who, though few in number, recognised the importance of retaining the Quebec-Hebridean identity in their region. Naturally, some communities fared better than others, and those who took up the challenge dealt with it in whatever manner suited their group.

In Milan, for example, the council elected to erect road signs in the 1980s and 1990s as permanent reminders to Hebridean pioneers who created their town. Rue Nicolson honours Ruth's family, Ruelle McLeod pays tribute to Duncan McLeod's people, and Chemin MacDonald remembers Muriel's family and others who shared the name. On the road out of town, there are others that acknowledge the Outer Hebrides, such as Chemin Tolsta or Rue Dell. The road signs are not only a means of introducing incomers to the local history, but they have also become an important part of the identity of an older generation of French, descendants of *les habitants*, who are also declining in numbers. Only the oldest among them can remember the neighbourliness they once shared with *les Écossais*.

A much more animated "symbol of identity" was the choice for Megantic, just a twenty-minute drive from Milan. This town boasts a hero whose fame (or notoriety) in Canada has often been compared to that of Rob Roy in

Scotland. Across the nation he became branded "the Megantic Outlaw"—there have been articles, books, documentaries, and films about him—but in the Eastern Townships he was simply known as Donald Morrison. His life story was well known to everyone in the area, Gael and French alike, his name spoken by every fireside, yet at no time during this research did I ever hear the complete account. It seemed as if the tragedy of the story weighed so heavily on every generation that even on occasions when it was discussed in the *taighean céilidh* nobody would ever retell it in its entirety. Parts would be analysed, moral issues raised, and sometimes anger and indignation expressed, such as John MacKenzie's, "You know, he was called the outlaw, but it was the ones that were after him that was the outlaw." Time and time again it was emphasised that "it wasn't only his own people who were loyal to Donald, but the French too," for not one among them, Gael nor Frenchman, would claim the price on his head.

Without a summary of Morrison's life story, it would be impossible to understand how, a century after his death, he became so significant to a new understanding of the culture of the Eastern Townships.

Donald Morrison, the youngest son of Lewis immigrants, was born in Lingwick in 1858. His father, struggling to "make a go of things," mortgaged their farm in Megantic to a moneylender, Colonel Malcolm MacAulay (from Ross-shire). In 1880 Donald went out west to earn money as a cowboy to pay off the nine-hundred-dollar debt. For seven years he sent money home to Megantic before returning to enjoy the fruits of his labours. MacAulay denied receiving a penny and had just sold the farm to a French family, *les Duquettes*. Outraged, Donald put the case into the hands of lawyers, but after three months and a fortune in fees, nothing happened. One winter night the barn burned down; Donald, the prime suspect, was charged with arson, which he denied. Not long afterwards, he was standing near the house and, in the lamp-lit room, could see Mme Duquette winding the clock. Resenting the newcomers' comfort, Donald took aim at the hand of the clock and fired a perfect shot through the window, which sheared the hand but also terrified the poor woman out of her wits. Already accused of arson, Donald was charged with attempted murder. When a warrant was issued for his arrest, Donald went on the run, and by the end of 1888 he was famous from coast to coast as the "Canadian Rob Roy." Letters of protest to newspapers earned him the sympathy of a Sherbrooke judge, who agreed to negotiate. Morrison came out of hiding but antagonised the judge by insisting he would proceed only if his parents were reinstated in the house. Furious, the judge returned to Montreal and a big-scale manhunt began, offering a reward for his capture. WANTED! posters with Donald Morrison's name in bold were everywhere, but both Gaels and French protected him, which entailed substories of, for example, the Legendres hiding him in their gristmill and Maryann Morrison bringing him food.

An American bootlegger, Lucien Warren, installed himself in the American Hotel in Megantic, determined to claim the bounty and get Donald, dead or alive. On June 22, 1888, when Warren least expected it, Morrison sauntered up the main street, unrecognised. Tipped off by a barroom companion, Warren leaped to his feet, and, with hand on hip, challenged Morrison to surrender or he'd shoot him dead. Morrison told Warren to keep his distance and put his gun away, but Warren was determined. Seconds later Warren lay dead with Morrison's bullet through his neck.

The manhunt then became serious. Despite a price of three thousand dollars on the Outlaw's head, he was protected loyally by Scots and French sympathisers for nine months. Eight of his protectors were arrested and imprisoned without bail. In April 1889 a local judge met with Morrison then declared a truce, but despite this, Morrison was shot as he visited his parents' cabin in Milan on Easter Sunday. Badly wounded in the hip, he was loaded onto a buck wagon and taken to jail in Sherbrooke, where he was tried on October 9. After listening to the jury of twelve English-speaking settlers (not a Gael among them), the judge sentenced Morrison to eighteen years in prison. Letters of protest and outrage eventually resulted in the St. Andrews Society of Montreal taking up his case. On June 19, 1894, still suffering from neglected gunshot wounds and tuberculosis contracted in jail, Morrison was released and taken to a hospital in Sherbrooke, where a few hours later he died. To this day, people say that Donald Morrison died "a free man."[5]

For nearly a century Donald Morrison had been a household name among the older people, Scotch and French alike. Most had parents and grandparents who knew him personally. It was not until 1990, however, when a French novel by Quebec writer André Mathieu titled *Donald et Marion* caught the attention of "Mills and Boone" and "Harlequin Romance" readers, that everyone in the town of Megantic wanted to know the story. Dog-eared copies of the paperback were passed around, with an eye-catching cover portraying Morrison gazing into the eyes of his sweetheart. Teenagers in high school needed no persuasion to read it, as the story is told with colour and enormous popular appeal. In no time, people in Megantic and the surrounding district were speaking about Donald Morrison as "*notre héros.*"

The sequence of events that followed came as a complete surprise to most of the Scotch, a few literary-minded among them quietly pointing out that Morrison's sweetheart was actually Augusta MacIver, *not* "Marion." If, like the classic ballad, however, it is not the historical truth of the novel that wields the power, but the emotional truth, then *Donald et Marion* had it in spades—love, honesty, integrity, trust, fairness, faithfulness, justice, devotion—values that readers think "modern" society seems to lack. Readers initially drawn to its romance, excitement, and adventure also found that the novel evoked a sense of anger and indignation as well as a strong connection to their own home territory.

As the film *Braveheart* has its worldwide devotees of Wallace and all he stood for, so Morrison attracted his followers. A local writer scripted a play about him and soon found amateur actors keen to practise the parts. Around the same time, with support from the mayor and council of Megantic, a committee was formed, "Rues Principales," to plan events intended to attract grants from government bodies set up to promote tourism throughout Quebec. "Héritage Canada" supported the proposal for a weekend festival, "*Hommage aux premiers arrivants Écossais*: A tribute to the first Scottish Settlers," to take place in 1994, the centenary of Donald Morrison's death. And central to the programme would be the play, a reenactment of part of Morrison's life, to be performed in his hometown on the opening Friday of the festival.

On the appointed evening, the crowds began to gather in the main street, scene of the opening performance. (A summary from fieldwork notes, largely in present tense, captures the atmosphere.) Duncan and Ruth are among the first to arrive, along with their adopted folklorist. Duncan chooses a prime location. We see friends who have driven from Sherbrooke, fifty miles away; they move beside us. An animated buzz of French conversation prevails. Among the spectators, we recognise and greet other groups of English-speakers, mostly the older generation. Behind us we overhear a small group who have come from Toronto—"our grandparents grew up in this area." Duncan knows who they are and welcomes them "home." A brief announcement on a loudspeaker hushes the throngs lining the street, and the play begins. The "set" is the American House Hotel, like the scene from an old movie—a barroom has been created on the open front porch. We sense, rather than see, the sawdust floor. The audience recognises Lucien Warren, beer in one hand, cigarette in the other, cowboy boots on the wooden rail. He sits boasting to the barman, then Morrison appears in the street. The atmosphere is tense, the audience breathlessly silent, as they watch the meeting. Then comes the challenge, the ultimatum, and the duel. One shot rings out and Warren falls dead. A deafening cheer goes up from the crowd. The play is over and Morrison is everybody's hero. Slowly the street empties as spectators plan to meet the next day at the fête.

"Pretty good, eh?" smiles Ruth. "Glad we came!" And all agree except the woman from Toronto on her first visit to Megantic. Apparently her group is disappointed, for they neither speak nor understand French: "Well, I think it's ridiculous to have that play in French! After all, Donald Morrison's people were *Scottish*, not French!" "His language was Gaelic," is the response. "Would that have been easier to understand?" "Oh well, I suppose—" she concludes, taking her leave.

The remaining two days of the festival were held in the Veterans' Park, by the shore of Lac Mégantic, with the scenic backdrop of Mont Mégantic in the distance. The bandstand in the centre featured Scottish music, performances interspersed with recordings, while the perimeter of the park was lined with tented stalls of local craftspeople displaying and selling quilts, woven articles, tartan (imported), needlework, wood-carving, and so on. Under a banner of "*Ceud Mile Failte*," people crowded in to taste scones with butter and jam; Ruth had baked 750 of them—500 oatmeal scones and 250 white. For many, it was their first taste of "Scotch food—the kind that Donald Morrison ate." People lingered, chatted, asked questions, and responded enthusiastically to the warm hospitality. Meanwhile, the pipe band from Montreal played, Highland dancers danced, and there was an "interpretative display" of old books and memorabilia in a nearby church. Director of Rues Principales, Danielle Tremblay, was quoted in *The Record* (Sherbrooke, July 11, 1994) as saying, "It's important to honour the founders of the city and help people learn more about their history." Her assistant, Steven Stearns, added, "I think it's important for the French Canadians in Megantic to learn what happened here many years ago. The Morrison story is a historic event, it's important for the town." Attended by more than two thousand people, the event was declared a great success, but that was only the beginning.

The reenactment of Morrison's life had a much deeper significance for the Presbyterian *Écossais* than anyone noticed on the evening of that first performance. The fact that the play ended with Warren's death, not Morrison's, does not distract from the fact that virtually the entire audience knew the heartbreaking end to the Morrison story. Had Donald Morrison lived to see justice, his life story might not have the impact that it continues to have to this day.

Thus, through death comes salvation, in that were it not for Morrison's tragic death, the Quebec-Hebridean settlers might have faded into oblivion in Quebec's history.

So successful was the 1994 festival that the committee planned a much more ambitious festival for the following year. Publicity would be spread wider, and grant applications would highlight heritage tourism and emphasise the economic impact for local businesses such as restaurants, hotels, and bed-and-breakfasts. Retaining the theme *"Hommage aux premiers arrivants Écossais,"* they were successful not only in receiving funding from Héritage Canada, but also from the British Council, which supported their application for the airfare for one of Scotland's foremost musicians. As far as possible, organisers attempted to stamp authenticity on every aspect of the festival; their project specified, for example, that the songs would be in Gaelic, not English, to represent Megantic's past.

A special building, the old railway station, was converted into a museum and tearoom, to interpret the story of *les Écossais* and to offer a taste of their hospitality—tea and scones, Gaelic songs, music on the bagpipes and fiddle—the kind of entertainment that Donald Morrison would have enjoyed. Duncan informed Rues Principales that my annual visit to Quebec would coincide with the event, so they contacted me in Edinburgh to ask for help with the proposed exhibition: to donate photos from my own collection; locate others in Scottish archives; identify objects of interest and relevance; and write a documentary text explaining the history of the migration from the Outer Hebrides. The plan was to then translate text and captions, mount the photos, collect the items on loan, and display the bilingual exhibition.

The grand opening was a splendid occasion—red carpet, speeches from the mayor and the minister of culture for Quebec, with invited dignitaries and many guests. The venue was packed, and those who could not find standing room waited outside, ready to take the first space available. People edged in to examine the displays, ask questions, and express delight at recognising faces and scenes from the past. They lingered over tea, chatted, renewed acquaintances, and collected their programmes before moving on.

By the end of the weekend, the festival had given thousands of Québécois a chance to hear the story of Megantic's first settlers, to see the reenactment of the Donald Morrison story, to enjoy Gaelic songs and music on bagpipe and fiddle. They could also taste Scotch whisky, tea, scones, oatcakes, and "genuine Scottish shortbread" (sent by Walkers of Scotland), and share time together. Nobody could doubt that the committee of Rues Principales achieved their aims, and it was deeply moving to watch the French appreciation of

Gaelic songs and music. In particular, onlookers could hardly have failed to notice a small group of Megantic's old-time French fiddlers, well into their eighties, sitting as close as they could to the stage, and jigging their feet to the music. One shouted loudly for "Beeg John MacNeil," and when he got the tune requested, he was ecstatic. At the end of the gig, they slowly approached the stage, one or two of them close to tears. Warmly they shook hands with *le jeune Écossais* and tried to communicate to him they shared a common language, *le musique du violon,* because, when they were his age, they used to play music and dance with *les Écossais.*

Festival audiences suggest many reasons why they go to a particular event: for entertainment, to meet friends, to try out new foods, just for a break, out of curiosity, for the educational value, to get away from stress. When the festival is deemed successful there is a sense of satisfaction, a "glad we went" feeling. For some, there's a reluctance to leave—"Let's just sing one more song." The Megantic festival had all of these elements, including an unexpected opportunity to have that last cup of tea, song, or tune. Before everyone headed for home, an open invitation went around the "locals" (as opposed to tourists) to stop by for tea at the newly renovated store in Gould. "We'd pass it on the way home."

The James Ross Store, as it was called, had once been a familiar landmark to the older generation, having served several communities from its crossroad location for well over a century. It had been closed many years, its faded, peeling paint, missing roof tiles, and encroaching weeds telling passersby that the elements would soon claim the building. Fate intervened, however, when two young men bought the store. Local apprehension that it would be ripped down, like so many Scotch farmhouses, and replaced by some modern creation was dispelled at the news that it was being restored and brought to life again. The cordial end-of-festival invitation came from the enthusiastic coworkers in this project, who, remarkable as it seemed, had opened the store as a restaurant that summer.

It would have been quite understandable if most of the older folk had decided to go straight home—some were already admitting "it would be good to put the feet up" after two days of punishing them. The majority, however, opted to accept, and with renewed energy, they headed for Gould. "Never turn down a cup of tea! It'll give us a chance to chat—yes, I know we haven't stopped to draw breath, but we can see what Jacques and Daniel have done to the store . . . They've done a wonderful job of the McAuley House."

Duncan went on to explain that the two young men had bought the house in 1987 when they first moved into the area:

that big, old "Scotch" house as you turn down to the Scotstown road—it's just yards from the James Ross store. It was built around 1913 by a McAuley family from Lewis, when wood was plentiful and carpenters knew what they were doing. In those days it was still popular to build in the Victorian style, but after years of being empty, it was in a sorry state. You should see it now—beautiful woodwork and ceilings, old-style glass lamps, velvet upholstery, antique lace curtains, patchwork quilts, hooked mats and all. They're opening it as a bed-and-breakfast house.

Those who had watched the restoration of Maison McAuley to its former Victorian elegance were naturally keen to see how the old store had fared. Above the door was a brand-new sign: RUÉE VERS GOULD: THE GOULD RUSH. Inside was the old, familiar, cast-iron stove, in the very same spot it had stood for years, but its metal stovepipe was new and shiny, and comfortable warmth radiated all around the store. Also still in position were the old wooden counter, smooth, well-seasoned, with brass-handled cabinets below, and the display shelves lining the wall behind it—timeless reminders of skilled carpenters from a bygone era. Tables and chairs filled the space that once stocked merchandise of all kinds, and, just as in Ruth's kitchen, the smell of home-baked scones welcomed the guests. So also did the hardworking owners, Daniel Audet and Jacques Cloutier, who had invited one and all to enjoy the traditional tastes of the old Scottish homestead—"Daniel made all the scones and the jams" we were told. Shyly, modestly, he smiled acknowledgement. The appearance of the waitresses clad in charming Victorian pinafores topped with crisp white aprons made an instant connection to the time when the store was in its heyday. All the furnishings and variations on style of dress presented "symbols" of the past—tasteful tokens of the social setting and pace of a preelectronic era. The familiar exchanges between the new owners and "old-timers" such as Duncan, Ruth, and Angus confirmed that few, if any, major decisions had been taken in the store without consulting on "how things were." Beyond that, however, there were items, carefully chosen, but that, as everyone knew, had never been part of the original ambience of the building. Above the doorway hung a Saltire Cross and a Lion Rampant (flags with two symbols of Scotland); all the tables were covered with tartan cloths; and throughout the evening, Gaelic melodies interspersed with music on bagpipes and fiddles were played softly in the background. Faced with strong symbols such as these, even if not a word were uttered, nobody could fail to make the connection with Scotland.

Undoubtedly, the folk at the old store hoped that the atmosphere and home baking would encourage people to return. Yet this was no mere marketing ploy to lure customers to a newly established inn, but a grateful dedication to a people whose kinsfolk had laid the foundations, cut the timbers, and built the place. Few who went home commenting upon the "perfect ending for the Megantic festival" may have realised that it also marked a milestone in the development of tourism in their area.

A more noticeable effect of the Megantic weekend on the dwindling Scotch population was their renewed hope that *les premiers arrivants Écossais* would be remembered, even acknowledged, by inhabitants of the Eastern Townships. The town itself has held other festivals in the years that followed, and the local council gave a permanent home to the photographic exhibition portraying the story of the Gaelic settlers. Elsewhere in the region, annual Burns Suppers, St. Andrew's Nights, and occasional *ceilidhs* struggle to promote a Scottish presence, while on a day-to-day basis a few devotees in regional museums and local history groups work to keep the Scottish flame flickering.

Several cultural projects and locally authored books interpreting the Eastern Township's history and way of life have played their part in the development of what is now recognised as heritage tourism. It is the younger French population that has made heritage tourism happen in the Eastern Townships, rather than the Quebec-Hebrideans. Newcomers to the area, initially attracted by the natural beauty and its distance from urban life, became deeply moved by the local history and culture. Had the newcomers been property developers, the fate of Gould's historic buildings would have been entirely different. Instead, French newcomers have embraced local tradition, and the philosophy behind their planning has been that while buildings may be renovated, they may only be brought back to life if the work is in tune with values of the people who originally built them. From the outset of the Gould project, therefore, it had been important to have answers to some central questions.

Who were the McAuleys and this James Ross? Where did they come from? Why did they choose Gould, or even Quebec? How did these people live? What did they eat, wear, believe in, laugh at, read, and so on? The picture was gradually built up through conversations with folk such as Duncan, Angus, or Ruth, who were only too pleased to fill in the details. Before long, word had it that Daniel and Jacques were inspired to visit Scotland, in particular the Isle of Lewis, to see for themselves, to sit by an open fire, smell the peat, taste the oatcakes and crowdie, and stand by the Atlantic. They were ready for any experience that would connect them to Gould's pioneer settlers.

Coincidentally, and in recognition of the century and a half since the potato famine, BBC Scotland produced a television documentary about the famine's effects on Scotland (Research and presentation, T. M. Devine and M. Bennett). Titled "The Great Hunger," the stark scenes, interviews, and commentary made a deep impression on viewers. Back in Quebec, having seen the Isle of Lewis and the documentary, Jacques Cloutier wrote in a note that the documentary gave him "the chance to look [at] what *really* happened in a part of your Beautiful Country. Believe me, I will never walk the cemetery [in Gould] with the same eyes and heart again."

The more attuned to the Gaels and their culture the folk at Ruée vers Gould became, the more the Scots population appreciated what they were doing. Not surprisingly, a warm sense of community prevailed in the celebration of 1995, for it had grown out of a mutual trust built up over eight years. Soon, the inn gained a reputation as a popular meeting place, the packed parking lot harking back to the days when folk used to hitch horses and wagons by the store.

The development of Ruée vers Gould seems to mirror the growth of heritage tourism in the wider area. To begin with, patrons generally belonged to one of three socioeconomic categories:

- Retired but active "seniors," who regularly came for morning or afternoon tea. Money to spare, few needs to spend it on. Plenty of time.
- Busy local families, booked for lunch every Sunday after Mass. Money stretched, but family time considered important.
- Out for dinner, a special occasion, on holiday, or after a hectic week. Money "no problem"; busy, stressful lifestyle, with too little time for leisure.

There has been no time in the history of humankind when leisure, entertainment, and travel have been so linked to the concepts of stress reduction. Stress at work is widely regarded as a fact of life, and, in some countries (Japan, for example), is also considered to be an official cause of death. This has become a key factor in marketing leisure, and the working public expects to be reminded that they "need to get away from it all."

Among those committed to finding quality leisure time are a significant number of people who are also caught up in the late-twentieth-century "roots" movement. While the idea of tracing our roots is sometimes said to have gained momentum from the television miniseries *Roots,* it is just as likely to be a response to the ever-increasing mobility of modern society. The resulting loss of contact with ancestral home territory, the fear of permanent loss of identity, or the loss of values from the past have all contributed to the need to consider the past and even to experience it through whatever means are available. An increasing number also include "visiting the Old Country" as a means to tracing family history and roots.

In the age of easy travel, transatlantic trips have become a regular feature of life. From the point of view of the Scots and the Irish, their distant American cousins appear to keep the airlines and the tourist shops in business. Gradually Quebec has been catching up with the trend, as their long association with France has inspired holiday travel to Europe. Judging by the reports from several Québécois who have made the trip, however, their experience (or perhaps perception) of their Mother Country does not compare with that of Scottish and Irish counterparts who return waxing lyrical about distant cousins, long-lost relatives, and warm hospitality. Instead, there is a sense of disappointment at finding no family connections, considerably less hospitality than at home, and even shock and anger to discover that most French people claim little in common with the Québécois. There appears to be no interest in Quebec politics, and, worst of all, some tourists feel ridiculed for the way they speak French.[6]

In general, Quebec has kept abreast with the rest of Canada and the United States with its steady increase in museum exhibitions, books, historical interpretations, reenacts, heritage trails, and so on. The heritage tourism industry in Britain depends heavily on interest generated across the Atlantic, though it is not without its critics of current trends.

In an article from the *Sunday Telegraph*, "What Is the Future of History?" (July 14, 2002), Blair Worden considered the marked increase in history-based experiences in Britain. Echoing much earlier critiques of the heritage industry by Robert Hewison (1983), there is a sense of indignation and more than a hint of contempt in his tone as he looks at what seems to be happening in the name of historical research. The subtext filtering through is that Britain, not content at becoming home to MacDonald's, now seems hell-bent on following popular American trends in education, including a fast-food equivalent of historical studies. He suggests that: "Today's popular history does not generate wisdom. It feeds the nostalgia of people bewildered by change and desperate for roots. The heritage industry, the fad for historical novels, the taste for simulated historical experiences, all cater to an instinct, not for the truthful re-creation of the past, but for kitsch. They prosper not because there is more education but—like aerobics or acupuncture—because there is more leisure and more disposable income."

There is no doubt about the dependency on disposable income, but it seems unfair and unrealistic to generalise over taste. Trends in Quebec's heritage tourism may have much in common with those in Britain and North America, yet there are other factors that are unique to the region and its history. In identifying the qualities that characterise the Scottishness and "Gaelic-ness" of their adopted community, the proprietors of Ruée vers Gould and Maison McAuley have themselves been singled out as holding the key to the success of heritage tourism in their area.

The village of Gould has a mere thirty houses and only moderate passing trade. Establishing a new inn, a bed-and-breakfast house, and, more recently, a pub, might be considered overoptimistic, or even unrealistic, especially as a pre–World War I B&B cannot conform to present-day expectations of *ensuite* facilities. Nevertheless, it was the very features antithetical to modern motels and hotels that first seized the attention of *Châtelaine*, one of Canada's foremost lifestyle magazines. A front-cover photo and double-page feature is the stuff of dreams, but it became reality for the little village of Gould when the bed-and-breakfast house Maison McAuley and the adjacent Inn were nationally acclaimed for their excellent hospitality, cuisine, and tranquil atmosphere. The reporters concluded that their 120-mile drive from Montreal was well worth the trip, for if Quebec had a better place to get away from it all, they had yet to find it (*Châtelaine*, February 1997).

The all-round appeal to the senses invites visitors to Ruée vers Gould—or the Gould Rush, as the joint establishment is now called. Some travel miles to experience *les traditions Écossaises* through the sights, sounds, tastes, and smells interpreted and presented by the authors of the project. Local folk drop by for tea and a chat and can be heard to banter with the kitchen or table staff, all French, who seem more at home in their Royal Stuart tartan aprons than most Scots. The regulars know all about scones and oatcakes, have tried out all the jams and marmalade, make a point of choosing tea rather than coffee, and, judging by the buzz at Sunday lunch, they welcome the opportunity to feast on Finnan Haddie, wild venison or rabbit pie, haggis, clootie dumpling, and *cranachan*. Quebec cuisine is also served, not just to please those who are unwilling to risk adventure, but also to reflect current traditions in the village. Occasionally, one of the local clientèle can be overheard explaining (in French) to newcomers about the food, or that the chef, Daniel, has even been to Scotland, to the Isle of Lewis, to acquire authentic recipes. The atmosphere and warm welcome more than live up to the establishment's twenty-first-century Web site advertisement with its electronic bagpipes, Lion Rampant flag fluttering in a cyber-breeze, and bilingual announcement:

Welcome to The Gould Rush!

As a tribute to the Scottish pioneers, it is with great pleasure we welcome you to Gould's first general store, in the municipality of Lingwick Township. Built around 1850, it was the center of many busy activities.

The loving restoration of The Gould Rush is a tribute to the Scots' determination to establish this village in 1837. At the beginning of the century, Lingwick Township was home to some 2000 people, both

Scots and Quebecers, in Gould and the neighbouring village of Saint-Marguerite.

After the first closing in its history, the James Ross store is alive again! The restorers, Daniel Audet and Jacques Cloutier, welcome you!

In the focus, energy, and stamina required for this venture there are clearly parallels, extending beyond the tangible and visible, to the efforts of the first settlers. A strong sense of neighbourliness and cooperation prevail, for not only are the local people valued for their clientèle, but new businesses are also encouraged. Folk at Ruée vers Gould do not regard themselves as having a monopoly on heritage tourism, but have warmly welcomed a recently established Scottish-theme pub, "Caledonia Pub," recommending it to their own customers, as "not just an ordinary place to have a drink":

> It's "Scottier" than Scotland, believe me! They work in traditional costumes—*Oui madame*, kilt and everything! They have good whiskies, beer, music from Scotland, and Jeff McCarthy even plays the bagpipes there. He is our last year's honorary president. Heather McNab, his wife, is a Highland dancer. He is completing his Pipe Major course now. He is member of the Black Watch. He composed some pipe tunes in our honour! One is "As good as Gould," the other "The McAuley House." It's very exciting! (J. Cloutier, e-mail, June 2002)

Although tartan was unlikely to have been the garb of any of the first settlers in the Eastern Townships in the mid-1800s, that is scarcely relevant today, as the process of "tartanising" Quebec began well over a hundred years ago. Highland games and gatherings in Canada had been totally won over to tartan within twenty years of the introduction of full Highland dress for pipers (1841) at the Braemar Gathering (Redmond 1971, 29–31). Canadian newspapers of the day give a flavour of the popularity among spectators, reporting that in 1869, at the Fourteenth Annual Games in Montreal, "ticket sellers were driven to despair by the demand for tickets." In 1870 at Toronto's Caledonian Gathering, "crowds of strangers poured into the city from the earliest hour by steamboat, rail and vehicles of all descriptions until with local citizens, the grounds around Crystal Palace were packed with at least 12,000 persons awaiting the Games" (Redmond 1971, 59).

Early photos from the Eastern Townships affirm that the Gaelic settlers became equally fond of their tartans, most of which did *not* come from Scotland, but "across the line" from relatives and kinsfolk. Muriel Mayhew recalled her fondness for, and childhood pride in wearing, a little tartan dress sent to her around 1920 by an aunt in Boston. In Muriel's day, just as in Scotland, such items were regarded as "Sunday best," kept for special occasions, though they also imply symbols of identity and loyalty.

What surprises today's visitors the most is how enthusiastically the French-speaking Québécois wear tartan. Daniel Audet, as keen on tracing his Quebec genealogy as any of the Gael, quietly sets the record straight by explaining that his choice of Royal Stuart is not random, but based on careful research. His own family originated in Brittany, where Daniel can trace his ancestors through several centuries to *L'Origine Doloise de la Dynastie des Stuarts* (The Doloise Origin of the Royal House of Stewart). He can claim a connection that is even older than the Auld Alliance between Scotland and France, *La Vieille Alliance Franco-Écossaise.*[7]

In the town of Dol-de-Bretagne, a parallel revival of interest in the Breton-Scottish connection adds to the Quebec association with the Stuart line:

Les Stuarts descendent d'une noble famille doloise du début de l'onzième siècle. Suite aux victoires de Guillaume le Conquérant outre-Manche, un membre de cette famille acquiert de grandes propriétés en Angleterre, puis en Écosse, où il est connu sous le nom de Alan-fitz-Flaad, "Alan fils de Flaad." Un de ses fils, Walter, devient ensuite grand intendant (High Steward) du roi d' Écosse David 1ᵉʳ. La fonction, transmise par hérédité, donne progressivement son nom à cette famille, qui, plusieurs siècles plus tard, accède au trône d'Écosse. C'est pourquoi, depuis 1967, une partie de la Grande rue de Dol-de-Bretagne porte le nom de "Rue des Stuarts."

(The Stuarts are descended from a noble Doloise family from the end of the eleventh century. Following the victories of William the Conqueror beyond the Channel, a member of this family acquired large properties in England, and then in Scotland, where he was known by the name of Alan-fitz-Flaad, "Alan son of Flaad." One of his sons, Walter, became the High Steward of King David the First of Scotland. His hereditary role gave the name to this family, who, several centuries later, succeeded to the throne of Scotland. That is why, since 1967, part of the main street of Dol-de-Bretagne carries the name "Street of the Stuarts.")[8]

Wearing his Royal Stuart kilt in the kitchen, even on a hot summer's day, Daniel takes pride in reinterpreting ties with an ancient past. In the wider picture, the Breton element completes the link to Celtic kinsfolk, particularly for

Québécois who have visited France and found little or no accord, despite claims of a common language.

It has also helped develop an understanding of "the Gael" whose language is English but whose culture is Scottish. As interpreters of culture and tradition, those involved in Gould's heritage project see that part of their role is to help visitors understand that *les Écossais* are not the same people as *les Anglais*, even though they all speak English.

Though the Eastern Townships are relative newcomers to Scottish heritage tourism, the industry has been established in North America for much of the twentieth century, albeit under other guises. Since the advent of the universally accepted label "Heritage Tourism," it has also become the focus of statistical, economic, sociological, anthropological and other studies. While most studies are based in North America, they are highly significant to Scotland in the twenty-first century, not only for their relevance to cultural understanding, but also to the impact on economics.

In her book *Highland Heritage: Scottish Americans in the American South*, Celeste Ray discusses the development of Scottish heritage tourism in the part of the United States that, arguably, invented the concept. Her study has the advantage of time, set in a region where history has been portrayed through the eyes of exiles since the mid-1700s, where nobody has spoken Gaelic for over a hundred years, and where spectacular "Highland" festivals attract thousands of people and millions of dollars in a single weekend. Ray examines the evolution of what she calls "Highlandism"—all things Scottish are portrayed through heroic images of the Highlander, regardless of historical accuracy. Nowhere is there a more spectacular example than the Grandfather Mountain Highland Games in North Carolina, where pipe bands can be heard to play "Lochaber No More" and "Dixie" in the same set, and where tartan can enhance a Confederate uniform or a new-age Druid robe. Rather than nitpick or mock the mythmaking, Ray looks constructively at the *meaning* and *function* of newly created rituals. While her focus is on grand-scale events, the issues she discusses are equally relevant to small village festivals of the Eastern Townships. Essentially the portrayal of *les Écossais* in tartan is based on the authenticity of spirit and the earnest desire to retain continuity with the past.

Tartan and bagpipes aside, in the colourful spectrum of heritage tourism spanning North America, the outstanding feature that brings people together is their collective celebration of ancient *values*—virtue, loyalty, and faith within the family and the community—features that celebrants perceive, regretfully, as declining.

In the Eastern Townships there has been no need to invent "Highlandism," as it has been rooted in the area for over a century and a half. The challenge of interpreting it for twenty-first-century Quebec has succeeded because it is inspired by the lifestyle and traditions of MacArthurs, MacDonalds, MacIvers, MacLeods, McAuleys, Morrisons, Nicolsons, Rosses, and other pioneer settlers. Jacques Cloutier continues: "For sure, you know, this is our 'energy' that helps us to get through all the work and money needs . . . James Ross and settlers . . . sounds strange but true! Believe me, many, many times, we ask for answers, pray for help . . . You should see the reaction of people when we mention this fact. They hardly believe it."

In a touching note sent to me with a photo of Gould's Chalmer's Church, Daniel Audet expressed his deep personal regard for the Scottish church built in 1891. He explained that, thanks to the intervention of one of the Presbyterian congregation, Kenneth McIver, who successfully campaigned against a government plan to demolish it, the church was relocated to the site next to Ruée vers Gould: "In my spirit, the Chalmer's Church is alone in my heart." While it is still owned by the dwindling congregation of Presbyterian *Écossais*, it has become central to the heritage experience of the region. At a cost of a modest contribution towards the upkeep, it is used for cultural events such as concerts and lectures about the lives of the Scottish pioneers. It is also the starting place for guided tours of the area, "village visits," as Jacques Cloutier explained in this interview:

> M. B.: Would you say that, apart from the attraction of the Scottish music and costume, you might be drawn to Scottish culture because the old Gaelic settlers valued nonmaterial things—the sorts of thing that modern American and western society is fast losing?

> J. C.: Yes, Margaret. You know us. But I have to say, depending on people we are talking to. We talk about the pioneers and settling in the Townships. Also, in May, Daniel and I will do a lecture on the root families of the Eastern Townships. Naturally, it will be on Scottish settlers . . . Can you explain that, two French-speaking people, sharing this heritage!

> Last year, Daniel and I did village visits. Believe it or not, we had about twenty to fifty people each time, walking in Gould! Who could even believe that it could happen one day! For those visits, *we always start in the church, taking time to explain how the Scottish settlers used to live, believe, and how they made it.* People LOVE it! *We bring them to think about these "inner" reasons of going through all they did.* (J. Cloutier, June 2002, my italics)

With the concrete aspects of Gould's heritage tourism projects successfully established, the continued challenge is to convey the importance of the spiritual dimension of the experience. The ultimate aim is that visitors should not only enjoy the good food, music and song, comfort, and a convivial atmosphere, but should also find time to reflect on and restore in their own lives some of the values that were fundamental to the pioneer settlers. The great-great-grandchildren of Quebec-Hebrideans may be speaking French, but they are talking about the heritage of the Gael and reviving transnational links between Scotland and a Scottish place in North America.

Notes

1. Fieldwork tapes from 1990 to 1996 have been deposited in the archives of the School of Scottish Studies at the University of Edinburgh; recordings from 1976 are in the Centre for Folk Culture Studies, Museum of Civilization, in Ottawa. All transcriptions are verbatim and several have already been published (Bennett 1998).

2. *Oatmeal and the Catechism: Scottish Gaelic Settlers in Quebec* (Bennett 1998) aims to answer some of the questions and to identify the influences of the Gaels on the Eastern Townships from its earliest beginnings to the present day.

3. *Being Scottish* (Divine and Logue 2002) is an anthology of a hundred essays invited from Scottish politicians, religious leaders, artists, writers, and sports personalities who express very diverse views on the subject.

4. Box socials were community fund-raising events, usually held on behalf of a family or an individual in need. Women contributed box meals that were then bid for by the men, auction style, adding fun to a community supper (see Bennett 1998, 267–69). These events were usually held in the Oddfellows' Hall, the meeting place for an all-male social and benevolent order, akin to a Masonic Lodge, Lions' Club, or Rotary Club. Oddfellows was founded in London in 1745 and by the nineteenth century was well established in North America.

5. This composite account is largely based on Oscar Dhu's epic poem *Donald Morrison, the Canadian Outlaw: A Tale of the Scottish Pioneers* (published in 1892, while Morrison was still alive), on the work of Kidd (1948), Epps (1973), and Clarke (1977), and on tape-recorded interviews (1976, 1992).

6. The general impression of a few travellers is confirmed in the wider research of Lee S. Rotherham, who monitored public reaction in France to matters concerning Quebec and the Québécois. By surveying the coverage of Quebec nationalism and separatism in France's most popular journal, *l'Esprit,* Rotherham concluded that even when tensions were at their height, among the French the general opinion was that "Quebec nationalism is a phenomenon for explanation rather than support" (1993, 191–210).

If there is little to interpret Quebec history and culture in France, happily there is considerably more in Canada, including one of the earliest and most notable centres in Ottawa's National Museum. The section known as Museum of Civilisation (formerly the Museum of Man), houses the remarkable collection of Marius Barbeau (1884–1969), founding father of Canadian folklore. Quebec is immensely proud of Barbeau's contribution to French Canadian folklore, which includes, for example, nearly seven thousand French Canadian folksongs.

7. The French town of Aubigny is known as the "Cité des Stuarts." Château des Stuarts houses a museum dedicated to *La Vieille Alliance Franco-Écossaise*.

8. Daniel Audet's research alerted me to this before I visited Dol-de-Bretagne in 2001 and was given this article by a member of the town council (my translation).

Works Cited

Bausinger, H. 1983. "Senseless Identity." In *Identity, Personal and Socio-cultural,* ed. Anita Jacobson-Widding, 337–45. Uppsala, Sweden: Academiae Upsaliensis.

Bennett, Margaret. 2002. "Being Scottish." In *Being Scottish,* ed. Tom Devine and Paddy Logue, 18–20. Edinburgh: Polygon.

———. 2001. "Calendar Customs in Scotland," "Childbirth and Infancy in Scotland," and "Courtship and Marriage in Scotland." In *The Oxford Companion to Scottish History,* ed. Michael Lynch, 60–64, 74–76, 107–10. Oxford: Oxford UP.

———. 2000. "Céilidh." In *The New Grove Dictionary of Music and Musicians.* London: MacMillan.

———. 1998. *Oatmeal and the Catechism: Scottish Gaelic Settlers in Quebec.* Edinburgh: John Donald. 2nd ed., with postscript, 2003. Edinburgh: Birlinn.

———. 1992. "Gaelic Song in Eastern Canada: Twentieth-Century Reflections." *Folksongs: Chansons: A Special Edition of the Journal of Canadian Folklore Canadien,* vol. 14, no. 2: 21–34

———. 1991. "Parlez Moi de Bretagne, d'Ireland, d'Ecosse." In *C.B.C. Journal.* Montreal: Canadian Broadcasting Corporation, 58–59.

Bennett[-Knight], Margaret. 1980. "Folkways and Religion of the Quebec-Hebridean Homes." In *Cultural Retention and Demographic Change: Studies of the Hebridean Scots in the Eastern Townships of Quebec,* ed. L. Doucette, 45–144. National Museum of Man Mercury Series, No. 34. Ottawa: National Museums of Canada.

Bø, Olav. 1988. "The Role Played by Tradition in a Local Community Today and Earlier." In *Tradition and Cultural Identity,* ed. Lauri Honko, 143–57. Turku: Nordic Institute of Folklore.

Brück, Ulla. 1988. "Identity, Local Community, and Local Identity." In *Tradition and Cultural Identity,* ed. Lauri Honko, 77–92. Turku: Nordic Institute of Folklore.

Buchanan, Joni. 1996. *The Lewis Land Struggle: Na Gaisgich.* Stornoway, Isle of Lewis: Acair.

Bumsted, John M. 1986. *Interpreting Canada's Past.* Toronto: Toronto UP.

Campbell, John L. 1990. *Songs Remembered in Exile.* Aberdeen: Aberdeen UP.

Cannadine, David, ed. 2002. *What Is History Now?* London: Palgrave.

Devine, T. M. 1988. *The Great Highland Famine: Hunger, Emigration, and the Scottish Highlands in the Nineteenth Century.* Edinburgh: John Donald.

Devine, Tom, and Paddy Logue. 2002. *Being Scottish.* Edinburgh: Polygon.

Dundes, Alan. 1980. *Interpreting Folklore.* Bloomington: Indiana UP.

Epps, Bernard. 1973. *The Outlaw of Megantic.* Toronto: McClelland and Stewart.

Ferguson, William. 1998. *The Identity of the Scottish Nation: An Historical Quest.* Edinburgh: Edinburgh UP.

Gramsci, Antonio. 1988. *Lettere dal carcere. Gramsci's Prison Letters.* A Selection Translated and Introduced by Hamish Henderson. London: Zwan Publications.

Henderson, Hamish. 1974. "A Selection of Antonio Gramsci's Prison Letters" (translations). *New Edinburgh Review* 25 and 26.

Hewison, Robert. 1983. *The Heritage Industry: Britain in a Climate of Decline.* London: Methuen.

Hobsbawn, Eric, and Terence Ranger, eds. 1983. *The Invention of Tradition.* Cambridge: Cambridge UP.

Honko, Lauri. 1992. "The Unesco Perspective on Folklore." In *Folk Fellows Network* 3:1.

Honko, Lauri, ed. 1988. *Tradition and Cultural Identity.* Turku: Nordic Institute of Folklore.

Jacobsson-Widding, Anita, ed. 1983. *Identity: Personal and Socio-Cultural.* Uppsala, Sweden: Academiae Upsaliensis.

Kidd, Henry G. 1948. *The Megantic Outlaw.* Toronto: T. H. Best.

Lawson, Bill. 1988. *A Register of Emigrant Families from the Western Isles of Scotland to the Eastern Townships of Quebec, Canada.* Compton County Historical Museum Society, Eaton Corner, Quebec.

MacDonald, Donald John. 1999. *Chi Mi: The Poetry of Donald John MacDonald,* ed. and trans. Bill Innes. Edinburgh: Birlinn.

MacKay, Angus (Oscar Dhu). 1918. *By Trench and Trail in Song and Story.* Seattle and Vancouver: MacKay.

———. 1892. *Donald Morrison, the Canadian Outlaw: A Tale of the Scottish Pioneers.* n.p. Reprint (1965, 1975), Sherbrooke. Enhanced Centennial Edition (1993), introduced by Thomas A. McKay, Arlington, VA: T. A. McKay.

Mandler, Peter. 2002. *History and National Life.* London: Profile.

Olson, Ian A. 1989. "Scottish Contemporary Music and Song: An Introduction." In *Scotland: Literature, Culture, Politics,* ed. Peter Zenzinger, 139–66. Heidelberg: Anglistik and Englischunterricht.

Oscar Dhu. *See* MacKay, Angus.

Ray, Celeste. 2001. *Highland Heritage: Scottish Americans in the American South.* Chapel Hill: U of North Carolina P.

Redmond, Gerald. 1971. *The Caledonian Games in Nineteenth-Century America.* Cranbury, NJ: Fairleigh Dickinson UP.

Rosander, Göran. 1988. "The 'Nationalisation' of Dalecarlia." In *Tradition and Cultural Identity,* ed. Lauri Honko, 93–142. Turku: Nordic Institute of Folklore.

Rotherham, Lee S. 1993. "Québec's Loudhailers: A Conflict of Nationality in the Journal *Esprit.*" *British Journal of Canadian Studies* 8, no. 2: 191–210.

Thomas, Gerald, and J. D. A. Widdowson, eds. 1991. *Studies in Newfoundland Folklore: Community and Process.* St. John's: Memorial University.

Traill, Catherine Parr. 1836. *The Backwoods of Canada, Being Letters from the Wife of an Emigrant Officer, Illustrative of the Domestic Economy of British America.* London: Charles Knight. Reprint, Toronto, 1989.

Wallace, Clarke. 1977. *Wanted—Donald Morrison: The True Story of the Megantic Outlaw.* Toronto. Doubleday Canada.

5
Powerful Pathos
The Triumph of Scottishness in Nova Scotia
Michael Vance

In the opening scenes of Sylvia Hamilton's 1993 National Film Board of Canada documentary film *Speak It! From the Heart of Black Nova Scotia,* a young man is shown walking past some of the most recognisable locations in Halifax, the province's capital. He ambles down the Spring Garden Road shopping precinct, passes the bust of Walter Scott, takes in the view at Citadel Hill, and strolls by a piper, in full Highland regalia, playing in front of the bandstand in the public gardens. While we watch these images, we hear in voice-over his indictment of the representations associated with these tourist sights.

> There has been a black community in Nova Scotia for over three hundred years, but you wouldn't know it by the history books.
> You won't find our faces on the postcards.
> You won't find our statues in the park.
> The only time white people seem to notice us is when they want to call us "niggers" or say we've got an attitude.
> Well, my name is Shingai, I'm sixteen, and my attitude is that you don't have to be from Scotland to have a history.

The context for Shingai's commentary suggests that he is reacting as much to Scottish kitsch as he is to the perceived dominance of Scots in the province's historiography.

There is no doubt that contemporary Nova Scotia is replete with stereotypical Scottish imagery—from the lone piper of the Department of Tourism's Web site to the reenacted 78th Highlanders at Citadel Hill to the Provincial Tartan. The province boasts a Ceilidh Trail highway route in Cape Breton, a renowned Highland games in Antigonish, an annual "Battle of Culloden" remembrance at Knoydart in Pictou County, a "gathering of the clans" in several parts of the province, and Tartan tour centres to help one plan a visit to these sites. Indeed, one bus tour firm advertises itself as "the company with the kilts."

This chapter will contend, with Shingai, that such apparently innocuous kitsch when linked to celebrations of the province's heritage is in fact deeply distorting. It will do so by demonstrating the tenuousness of the "Scottish" connection for much of the region's history by examining how the connection became romanticised and by demonstrating how intellectuals aided this process. Finally, by exploring the historical and intellectual factors involved in celebrating Nova Scotia's apparent "Scottishness," this chapter will ask us to consider the responsibility of scholarship in both promoting and exposing such constructions.

How Scottish Is Nova Scotia?

Despite James VI's famous seventeenth-century charter granting the territory to the Scottish baronage, the earliest Scottish connection with the area now known as Nova Scotia was limited to a short-lived colony at what has now become Annapolis Royal. Sir William Alexander's settlement was abandoned largely as a consequence of international diplomacy in 1632 (Inch 1922; Wallace Ferguson 1994; Cowan 1999, 50–53). As John Reid has demonstrated (2001), it was in fact territorially acquisitive Scots residents in New England who, with the support of the Crown, kept the name Nova Scotia alive throughout the century despite the absence of any permanent settlement in the region. Indeed, the region was populated by native Mi'kmaw and French-speaking Acadians until the early eighteenth century, when they began to be displaced by British soldiers and settlers, the Acadians through expulsion and the Mi'kmaw through dispossession.[1] At the outset, Scottish soldiers were employed to solidify British occupation of the region, but in addition to having to dispossess previous inhabitants, these small numbers of Scots also competed with large numbers of settlers from New England, England, Ireland, and Wales for both territory and advantage in the colony (Buckner and Reid 1994; Campbell and MacLean 1975, 19, 29, 38, 60). As a consequence, by the end of the eighteenth century, although the name Nova Scotia had been employed for almost two centuries, there was little that one could identify as especially Scottish about the colony.

In the iconography of the province, it is the arrival of the *Hector* at Pictou in 1773 that is often depicted as the "birth" of "New Scotland," the ship's arrival functioning as the basis for a foundation myth analogous to the role of the *Mayflower* for New England (Boudreau 1993–1994). In September 2000 such mythologising was once again apparent at Pictou in the public celebrations surrounding the launch of the *Ship Hector* replica. This was a carefully orchestrated series of events that included a reenactment of the first landing, complete with reenactors wading ashore in sodden kilts. This is a likely anachronism, since in the 1770s the wearing of the kilt was restricted almost exclusively to the elite and members of the military and was not generally popular until the later nineteenth-century development of the Highland games. Certainly, the competitive piping and Highland dancing, as well as the standardised tartans, also evident at the *Hector* relaunch, were not developed until the following century (Cowan 1999, 60; Jarvie 1991; Gibson 1998).

The amplification of the *Hector* mythology, represented in such anachronistic attachments, was developed over many years before this most recent celebration. It was preceded by an earlier public ceremony in 1923 that commemorated the 150th anniversary of the ship's arrival, an event also developed largely for tourist purposes (Boudreau 1992). More recently such ceremonies have been accompanied by the production of various items of purchasable kitsch. In June 1999 the *Ship Hector* tartan was registered with the Scottish Tartans Society in time for sale at the relaunch. According to the designer, each colour of the tartan has a significance: "white—for the whitecaps and rough seas the Ship Hector endured; royal blue—for the settler's loyalty to their homeland of Scotland; green—for the evergreen trees that grew to the waters edge when Hector arrived; black—for the lives lost on the journey, and gold—for the rising golden sun of a new day in a new land."[2] Similarly, in the mid-1990s, a local singer, Bruce Holton, produced for sale a recording of his "Ballad of the Hector," which recounted the hardships of the voyage, and encouraged his audience to remind their children of the passengers' "struggle and pain." At the same time, a local craft brewery began selling its product with the advertising claim that wood shavings from the reconstruction were used in the brewing process and encouraged those who consumed their ale to remember the hardy pioneers.[3] Ironically, the celebration of these early stalwart pioneers and indeed the craft skills necessary to construct an eighteenth-century ship, promoted by the *Ship Hector* replica project, obscures the fact that the descendants of those migrants were largely employed in Pictou's rapidly expanding industries. Indeed, one local historian has referred to the town as "Canada's Cradle of Industry." The Hector Heritage Quay, where the reconstruction took place and a visitor centre and museum are housed, was viewed by its promoters as a means to redevelop the town and its harbour as a tourist destination now that the community's once-thriving industry has virtually collapsed, with the local pulp mill being one of the few reminders of that past (Hoegg Ryan 1995; Boudreau 1992).

Despite such commercialisation and anachronistic invention, the arrival of the "first" *Hector* did indeed herald the migration of significant numbers of Gaelic-speaking Highlanders to the colony. By the 1770s, clergymen and emigration agents had begun to attract significant numbers of Highlanders to the eastern mainland of Nova Scotia and Cape Breton Island. After the American Revolution, a considerable number of Highlanders were also prominent among the Loyalists settled by the government farther west and south, but the most readily apparent areas of settlement continued to be Cape Breton Island and the adjacent mainland (Harper and Vance 1999). These migrations, however, were relatively small-scale compared to nineteenth-century transatlantic settlement.

Although the evidence is less than complete, J. S. Martell's 1942 survey of the available immigration statistics in the public archives of Nova Scotia suggests that Scots dominated immigration into the colony between 1815 and 1838. They account for 21,833 of the 39,243 known arrivals at Nova Scotian ports, among which Sydney, Pictou, and Halifax were the most prominent.[4] The depression that followed the Napoleonic War and its particularly severe impact in the Highlands and Western Isles appears to have helped encourage this migration, primarily to Cape Breton. The pressure on available land was so great that by 1837 more than half the island's population was squatting on infertile Crown backlands (Hornsby 1992a, 54). Undoubtedly, many immigrants found they had traded impoverished circumstances in Scotland for a life of rural poverty in Nova Scotia. All the same, their immigration by mid-century had indeed created pockets of Gaelic Highland culture in Cape Breton and the adjacent Guysborough, Antigonish, and Pictou Counties.

Nevertheless, focus on the remarkable growth of these communities in the early nineteenth century obscures a number of important points. First, Scots were outnumbered by those from other immigrant groups for the remainder of the nineteenth and twentieth centuries. Indeed, by the 1921 census Nova Scotians of Scottish origin represented just over 28 percent of the total population, while those of English origin constituted nearly 39 percent of the total.[5] Second, the establishment of these Highlanders detracts from the diversity of Scottish migrants entering the province. These ranged from Lowland professionals involved in medicine, law, and education to merchants and manufacturers, to colliers and stevedores (Samson 1999; Harper and Vance 1999). Finally, the rural nature of the initial Gaelic settlements detracts from the fact that they and their descendants were drawn into the industrial workforce of the Cape Breton coal and steel industries during the course of the century. These industries also drew fresh numbers of Lowland Scots to the island as well as a racially diverse, international labour force (Bitterman 1994; Migliore and DiPierro 1999; Beaton 1995; Heron 1987, 1988, 74–98).

In the elevation of the Scots to an emblematic status for the entire province, neither their minority status nor the complexity of their historical experience has been emphasised. In order to account for this oversight, we need to turn our attention to the cultural and intellectual influences that have shaped the commemoration of Scottishness in Nova Scotia.

The Romanticisation of Scottish Nova Scotia

In Nova Scotia the Highlander is employed as an icon representing the Scottishness of the province. The association of Highlandism and Scottishness is, of course, readily transparent in Scotland itself, as recent studies have demonstrated (McCrone, et al. 1995; Donnachie and Whatley 1992; Gold and Gold 1995). In the Victorian period, this identification became ritualised in celebrations of Scottishness. Edward Cowan argues convincingly that the Victorian fascination with and creation of Highland ceremony and regalia was indeed a transatlantic phenomenon. In particular, he has pointed out that the Highland games, rather than being an import to Nova Scotia, were part of a simultaneous development. Ironically, as Scottishness became more formalised with such games, the original Gaelic culture, which survived only in enclaves, began its precipitous decline (Cowan 1999; Durkacz 1983; Dembling 1997, 43–49). This points to the disconnected nature of the relationship between representations of Scottishness and actual historical experience.

One obvious explanation for this disconnection is the influence that the Romantic movement has had on our perception of Scotland and Scots. A number of scholars have pointed out that as the military threat posed by the Highlanders receded in the later half of the eighteenth century, they became rehabilitated in literary circles as tragic, sentimental heroes representing a lost cause, the exiled Stewart monarchy, and a vanishing way of life. As the Highlands were transformed to suit the needs of commercial agriculture, particularly the expanding wool industry, landlords began the systematic removal of tenants from ancestral lands. These "Clearances" and subsequent emigrations were quickly sentimentalised by Lowland authors and artists in the emerging Romantic conventions—stoic Highlanders, usually old men, grimly and heroically facing their displacement in the face of relentless rational progress (Womack 1989). This is perhaps best captured in Thomas Faed's Victorian masterworks *The Last of the Clan, The Emigrant's Farewell,* and *Oh, Why Left I My Hame?*

(Faed 1978). Certainly, landlords were set up as villains, but these sentimental depictions always implied resignation and forbearance.

As with the Highland games, these Romantic portrayals were also replicated across the Atlantic. The stoic virtues ascribed to Highlanders by the Romantics at the turn of the nineteenth century have found an echo in contemporary representation in Nova Scotia—in folk song, in museum representations, and in local history (MacDonell 1982; Boudreau 1992; Dunn 1953). In his popular Victorian account, the Reverend George Patterson celebrated the indomitability of the *Hector* settlers of Pictou both in Scotland and Nova Scotia. In particular, he highlighted the resistance of two Highland immigrants, Roderick MacKay and Alexander Fraser, to the "Saxon oppression" of impounding illicit whisky—"what Highlander's soul would not boil, even at hearing of such an outrage" (451–53)—and suggested that such treatment might have encouraged many to emigrate. In his account the Highlander's expectations of a "free farm and plenty in America" were cruelly disappointed when "the immigrants were landed without provisions and without shelter, except as with the assistance of those here before them, they erected rude camps for themselves, their wives and their little ones" (83). The reader's sympathies aroused, Patterson then proceeded to narrate the tenacity of the immigrants in the face of the dearth that accompanied the first years of the settlement, claiming that parents, if they left their children at home during this period, "trembled to enter their dwelling, lest they should find them dead, and sometimes waited at the door, listening for any sound that might indicate they were alive" (96). Such sentiments have been readily replicated in contemporary accounts such as Judith Hoegg Ryan's recent local history of Pictou: "The first year many were so desperate, they hired themselves out and bound their children to labour at Windsor, Halifax and Truro . . . Several trekked 80 miles of rough terrain to Truro and back, where they bartered their labour for potatoes and flour. These they bore home on their backs, up and down steep hills, through bogs, in deep snow and across fast-flowing streams, precariously balanced on fallen trees" (11). The official Web site for Pictou, in a "History" section that refers only to the *Hector* and the Lowland founder of Pictou Academy, the Reverend Thomas McCulloch, similarly highlights the stoicism of the Highlanders:

There were 189 passengers who boarded The Hector at Loch Broom in Scotland and dared to make the journey towards a new life in Nova Scotia. Committed to an uncertain future, this courageous band was aware of very little about their new life except that just about anything would be an improvement over conditions they were leaving behind . . . For the passengers of the Hector, a hold no more than 85 feet long and 22 feet wide would be their only home during the long arduous voyage . . . Following a three month ordeal at sea, the Hector dropped anchor in Pictou Harbour on September 15 1773 . . . These hardy Scots had survived some of the most difficult times that Scotland had endured, yet still more hardship awaited them. The ordeal that they had been through was one that suited them well as it prepared them for the challenges that would face them as they began their new lives in British North America.

Elsewhere on the Web site, direct parallels are drawn between the *Hector* emigrants and those involved in the Jacobite Rebellion, an event famously romanticised in the early nineteenth century by Walter Scott as a noble lost cause. These sentiments are clearly echoed in the following:

> Inextricable from the memory of all onboard was the image of Scottish retreat, which they were continuing 25 years after the Battle of Culloden . . . The voyage had been much longer than expected, and lives had been lost. Blown many weeks off course it seemed even fate was against their heavy-hearted decision. These families clung only to the knowledge that they were fleeing more than physical hunger, they were fleeing from a famine of spirit. To bow to a distant monarch was a reality that could be shirked in their hearts. To lose their land was a great burden to be endured. But there could be no denying the pain borne by the removal of their tartans and pipes, for these were the essence of a Highlander.

This speculative listing of priorities is probably a more accurate reflection of the current interests of contemporary Scottish heritage celebrants than these eighteenth-century migrants, but the point remains that such Romantic accounts are clearly designed to engage our sympathy.

Suffering, however, was not restricted to the *Hector* immigrants. Patterson himself reported that one David Stewart, on returning to Prince Edward Island in 1776 after a journey to Pictou, declared that it was "an awful place . . . I stayed with a man who was just eating the last of his nigger" (96). Rather than referring to an act of cannibalism, Stewart was making light of the fact that one of the first settlers to the region had recently sold a slave in Truro for some wheat. The tale, probably apocryphal, does highlight the important point that Highland Scots were not the only settlers in Pictou. They had been anticipated by immigrants from the American colonies, some of whom brought their slaves with them. All suffered from the hardships of these years, but one can imagine, given their social position, that the slaves would have fared poorly indeed. Recently, members of the African-Nova Scotian community have pointed out that these "first Black settlers arrived six years before the *Hector*" and have attempted to draw attention to this history with the construction of an Africentric Heritage Park in New Glasgow, Pictou County (Dunn 2000, 2; Best 1977, 34–35). Neither the park nor the region's black population is mentioned in the official tourist guide for the province; however, the tourist is invited to "Celebrate our rich Scottish heritage." In the more detailed ninety-four-page guide for the county there is a paragraph mentioning the "Africentric Park" and "Black Gala Homecoming" held in August, but this notice is swamped in a sea of tartan, kilts, and piper imagery. Indeed, tourists to Pictou are invited to "listen for the skirl of the pipes, haunting Gaelic verse, toe tapping fiddle tunes and uplifting Celtic rhythms. Watch for the skirl of the kilt, lilting Highland steps and spectacular Scottish pageantry."[6]

The attachment of region to Highland sentimentalism is, however, most apparent in Cape Breton. Again according to the province's official guide book:

> Scottish traditions and Gaelic folklore come alive along the Ceilidh Trail.
> Ceilidh . . . is Gaelic for party or gathering, and if you listen closely you
> might hear the heart-stirring music of bagpipes and fiddles echoing
> through the glens of this beautiful corner of Cape Breton . . . Large
> numbers of Scottish immigrants settled here between the 1780s and
> 1820s. They brought with them their Gaelic language and their passion-
> ate love of music. From these roots sprang some of Canada's top musi-
> cians . . . who bring the Celtic inspired "Cape Breton Sound" to de-
> lighted audiences worldwide.

Students of contemporary Cape Breton culture point out that while the present "Celtic" revival may partly owe its origin to the musical traditions brought by Scots in the nineteenth century, the current forms are the product of an amalgam with Irish, French, Newfoundland, and various other traditions (Mahalik 1996; O'Shea 1996). Nevertheless, as a consequence of the Romantic version of migration, the "revival" continues to be claimed as a Highland legacy. Indeed, the Romantic portrayals of this part of Cape Breton have been so powerful that in 1947 Donald S. MacIntosh, a descendant of Highland Scots immigrants, had a "lone shieling" constructed in Cape Breton along the Cabot Trail, part of the *Ceilidh* tourist route, in deference to a stanza from the *Canadian Boat Song* first published in 1829 in *Blackwood's* magazine:

From the lone shieling of the misty island
Mountains divide us, and the waste of the seas;
Yet still the blood is strong, the heart is Highland.
And we, in dreams, behold the Hebrides.

The authorship of this oft-repeated poem is not certain, but it is certain that with all the wood available in Cape Breton no Highland immigrant actually constructed a "shieling" of stone and thatch. For MacIntosh, an immigrant's grandson and university geology professor, the shieling did, however, represent the continuing importance of Scotland for Nova Scotia (Harper and Vance 1999; McKay 1992, 33–34). But clearly that importance was based on the fictional Romantic portrayal of the Highlanders rather than their actual experience in the province.

The celebration of the Highland migration to Nova Scotia as Romantic tragedy has had a distorting impact on the representation of Cape Breton's Gaelic community. Michael Kennedy's examination of the island's Gaelic oral tradition (1999), for example, has revealed as many songs celebrating emigration from Scotland as those representing feelings of homesickness and exile. He argues that the perception of emigration as a tragedy comes from a selective reading of the material in order to reinforce the Romantic tradition, a tradition itself created outside the Gaelic-speaking world. The pervasiveness of this distortion is also apparent in the creation of the Gaelic College at St. Ann's, Cape Breton. In 1939 the college was established in order to promote a revival of Gaelic on the island, but as Jonathan Dembling has pointed out (1997), its founder, Angus William Rugg Mackenzie, a Presbyterian minister originally from the Isle of Skye, clearly had a Romantic view of his task. He believed that what was required in order to have the language thrive was "a loom in operation in every rural home and more sheep on [the] Cape Breton hills"—a clear attempt to turn back the clock to pre-Clearance Scotland, save perhaps the sheep. Mackenzie's analysis completely ignored the fact that Cape Breton Gaels had supplied the labour for the island's industrialisation and had been involved in the intense labour disputes accompanying that process. Instead of solutions for declining Gaelic based on the predicament of the industrial worker, he advocated instead the teaching of pipe, Highland fling, and the production of "tartan woolen goods . . . woven on handlooms by student apprentices—yards and yards of it" (51–52).

Mackenzie was not alone in ignoring Scottish Gaels' actual experience and, instead, celebrating the Highland Scots as exemplars of preindustrial virtue. In the 1930s, desire to portray Nova Scotia as an Arcadia, where the common folk continued the ancient ways brought with them from Scotland, was particularly encouraged by Scotophile Premier Angus L. Macdonald as a way of bolstering depression-era tourism to the province. Macdonald also appears to have been at least partially motivated by political concerns. The calming influence of a sanitised past was particularly attractive to a premier who had to face demands on the left for a halt to unfettered industrial capitalism as a solution to 1930s crises (McKay 1992; Forbes and Muise 1993, 272–305). As a consequence, that decade saw the simultaneous creation of the Cape Breton Highlands National Park and the Cabot Trail Highway, named after the famous explorer Giovanni Caboto (John Cabot) who explored the Cape Breton coast for the English Crown in 1497. The trail begins in Baddeck, which boasts the family home of the famous expatriate Scot Alexander Graham Bell, winds by the Gaelic College at St. Ann's, passes "Keltic" Lodge, the government-owned resort at Ingonish, before proceeding through the Highland Park. Only when the traveller comes out of the park and enters Cheticamp, a French Acadian settlement, is it apparent that people other than Highland Scots have a claim to the region. The creation of the National "Highland" Park was similarly motivated, and parallels with the Scottish Highlands were deliberately constructed. It was expected that tourists would be enthralled by the rugged beauty of Cape Breton's mountains, but they were also encouraged to reflect on the stalwart heroism of the Gaelic immigrants who settled the region, hence the construction of MacIntosh's shieling in the park (MacEachern 2001).

The building of a road and establishment of a national park in the more remote, mountainous parts of the island was seen at the outset as a draw for tourists, particularly from the United States, who had been coming to the region to observe the "preserved" Gaelic culture since at least the 1880s. An early example is Charles Farnham, an American traveler who wrote an essay titled "Cape Breton Folk" for *Harpers* magazine in 1886 describing his grand tour of the mountainous region of the island and celebrating the simple life of its inhabitants. In outlining his object, Farnham appears to have been influenced by a desire to produce an ethnographic record as well as contemporary Romantic conventions: "It is worth while to visit a civilized people that still grinds grain by hand between two stones; for doubtless we may find among them bread of the primeval flavor, and men and women that are racy and strong. I set out for Cape Breton to see such a people" (607). Farnham, like an anthropologist, goes on to record this "primeval" community's exotic customs, their courtship rituals, their religious practices, their language, and their rites of passage:

> It is considered a marked offence not to come to a wake, and when there, not to eat and drink abundantly. Two or three funerals near together have actually ruined a family. The pious and aged in the room where the

corpse lies generally occupy their time in reading and praying, while the young, in another room, solace their grief by eating and flirting. Many are more or less drunk when the procession moves on or collects about the grave, and generally it is then that the fight occurs which seems part of every good funeral. (618)

Similarly, he takes particular note of the division of labour among this pre-industrial "folk."

The domestic life of the couple even today in most peasants' homes will be exceedingly primitive; the women will do spinning, weaving, and knitting required by the family; and the man will make nearly every-thing needed in the house and on the farm. A farm and a family will require about two hundred dollars' worth of feed food and sundries, and this amount represents the average production of the little farms of Cape Breton, together with the fishing that many do at odd times. In the spring actual want is felt by many families until fishing begins and the cows give milk once more. But the island is generally free from paupers. (616)

Poverty of course would have been all too apparent in late-nineteenth-century New York, and it is clear that in addition to an amateur ethnography, Farnham was offering his readers an escape into another, simpler world. Yet, despite such idealisation, he could not resist the attraction of the Romantic, pathetic account of the Highlander, and this is reflected in his recounting of an encounter with an inhabitant of one of the more remote parts of the island: "The life of the region seemed to be personated by a withered old man, whose ragged homespun hung on him as on a skeleton, and whose unkempt locks flew about with the wind. He bent low over his scythe, and with tragic eagerness tried to mow the few spears of wiry grass sticking up out of the barren earth" (620). This description, along with the illustration of the "old haymaker" that accompanied the article, clearly echoed the earlier artistic renderings of High-land emigration found in both Scottish literature and painting.

Ian McKay (1994) has pointed out that accounts such as Farnham's can be viewed as part of a broader "rustification" of the province that accompanied the development of the nascent tourism industry, the consequences of which are readily apparent in even the most casual perusal of recent tourist literature. Halifax, where the majority of the population resides, is rarely featured, but tourist literature abounds with rustic views of Annapolis Valley farms, South Shore fishing villages, white wooden churches, sailing ships, and heritage houses. The impression of timelessness reflected in such representations continues to be reflected in the characterisations of the "Highland" communities of Nova Scotia. In his popular account, R. A. Maclean, while rejecting aspects of the Romantic version of Scottish emigration, reinforces this tendency:

> Those who saw any hope of success would become highly competitive; this was especially true of Lowland Presbyterians. The few who were content with little, or saw little prospects of success without a lot of hard work, remained relatively static economically but they also helped to preserve the language, the folklore and the music. Content to be surrounded by kindred and friends they did not consider themselves as "exiles from their father's land." They remain brothers and sisters to those they left behind as long as two hundred years ago. Being Nova Scotian of Scottish descent is not simply to live in Nova Scotia; it is a state of mind. (MacLean 1992, 11)

Neil MacNeil's sentimental memoir, *The Highland Heart in Nova Scotia*, first published in New York in 1948 and reprinted several times since, characterised this "state of mind" in the words and actions of his Cape Breton grandfather:

> I shall always cherish the memory of the nights, long, dark, cold, Nova Scotian nights, when he would sit in front of the big, hot kitchen stove, his stockinged but shoeless feet upon it, and with one of us grandsons upon each knee he would pour forth his soul in Gaelic songs, songs of the stormy isles, songs of the glens and the lochs, songs of battle and of victory, songs of love, songs of the Clan MacNeil . . . Thus he gave us an exalted opinion of our people, but meanwhile he kept us simple and humble as individuals. (1948, 5)

MacNeil goes on to describe his Gaelic community as one that preserved not only its language but also its transported Scottish ghosts, where there was no need for money, and where the inhabitants lived in a timeless rural Arcadia: "They could fend for themselves as could the flowers in the meadow, the fox in the brakes, and the trout in the deep pools. Such people seem to have a special endowment from the God of Creation, who cares for his own. They have a calm that the people of the city can seldom acquire, a simplicity that is close to the sublime, a fortitude that belittles the adversities of life" (34).

Cape Breton's rural society, however, was far from static in either the nineteenth or twentieth centuries. Even Charles Farnham was aware of the obvious signs of the transforming effects of industrialisation on the island: "Sydney presented some fine views of a large and excellent harbor, dotted with shipping; along the shores are villages struggling with domineering coal docks and volumes of smoke from the coal mines . . . But these more commonplace and commercial features of Cape Breton were not the object of my visit" (608). Farnham could choose to ignore this economy, but recent research has shown that rural Cape Bretoners could not. Rusty Bittermann has demonstrated that far from residing in enclaves of rural self-sufficiency, from the beginning many Highland settlers of Cape Breton were drawn into the world of commercial agriculture, in the first instance supplying foodstuffs for the West Indies trade and the Newfoundland fishery, and then, as the island's mining and steel industries developed in the latter half of the nineteenth century, to the industrial communities of Cape Breton itself. Furthermore, the marginal nature of later poorer Highland "backland" settlers meant that that group was constantly balancing local farming with seasonal or temporary migration where they were employed in wage work as far afield as the "Boston States." Indeed, the ready availability of this supply of cheap labour allowed for the development of both the coal and steel industries, at times to the cost of local commercial agriculture, which could not offer competitive wages (Bittermann 1988). David Frank concurs, pointing out that by the opening decades of the twentieth century the majority of the island's population lived in industrial Cape Breton. Most of these workers were descended from the Highland immigrants, but increasingly their numbers were supplemented by African Americans and immigrants from Newfoundland, the British Isles, and Europe. Aspects of Highland culture, particularly music, remained, but these were supplemented and transformed by Lowland Scottish culture in the form of Burns societies and the music hall Scottishness of Harry Lauder. In addition, the ideology of working-class socialism, exemplified in the person of the radical Lowland Scots miner's leader J. B. McLachlan, contributed to the severe labour unrest experienced in Cape Breton in the opening decades of the century (Frank 1985, 1999). None of this experience is acknowledged in either the nineteenth-century Romantic accounts or in more recent tourist literature.

Diaspora Studies and Nova Scotia

Despite the obviously distorting effects of both the Romantic portrayal of Highland emigration and the manner in which it has been employed in Nova Scotia, this portrayal has yet to receive sustained critical analysis from scholars. It can be argued that this is a consequence of the fact that the experience has been rather too easily adapted to the interpretation of such movements as "diaspora." Viewing past migrations as "diaspora" has considerable attractions, since it allows one to examine these movements in their full complexity. Rather than a simple examination of a single sending and receiving society, by employing the concept of diaspora one is encouraged to see migration as a dispersal to many destinations, to examine the interaction between these regions and include the study of "return" migration. With the current preoccupation with questions of globalisation, diaspora studies have the added attraction of studying peoples outside of the "national" boundaries and as part of broader "global" population shifts. Indeed, there has been a phenomenal growth in diaspora literature over the last decade, including the founding of a new journal, *Diaspora: Journal of Transnational Studies;* the publication of numerous reference works; and, from the University of Washington Press, a monograph series devoted to global diasporas.

Accompanying the growth of scholarly interest has been a steady expansion in the number and type of groups identified with diaspora. In his introductory volume to the University of Washington series, Robin Cohen proposes a typology to reflect this expansion, identifying victim, labour, trade, imperial, and cultural diasporas. Although recognising the "victim" imagery of the Romantic account, Cohen (1997) classifies Scottish migration under a more general British "imperial" diaspora. In contrast, the authors of the *Penguin Atlas of Diasporas,* published in the same year as Cohen's volume, explicitly exclude the "descendants of British people in Australia, New Zealand, South Africa, Zimbabwe, Kenya, Canada, and the United States" from the diaspora category (Chaliand and Rageau 1997, xiii). The disagreement stems from a basic conflict over meaning. Cohen highlights the etymology of the word, pointing out that it derives from the Greek verb *sperio* (to sow) and the preposition *dia* (over). When the Greeks applied the concept to humans, they referred to migration and colonisation. Retrieval of the ancient meaning does indeed allow for a much broader application of the concept, but it also ignores the more contemporary connotations of the term. As the authors of the *Penguin Atlas* argue, current usage implies a dispersal of population through victimisation and persecution—the most obvious example of which is the Jewish diaspora. More recently, the term has been picked up by students of the African and Irish dispersal in order to imply an analogous experience of oppression (Akenson 1995).

That this is more than mere semantics is demonstrated by the fact that the popular Romantic account of Scottish emigration is, either consciously or unconsciously, connected with the victim perception of diaspora rather than the "imperial" category proposed by Cohen. By including Scots among the groups experiencing diaspora, we obscure the history of peoples who have suffered severe persecutions and blind ourselves to both the victimisation Scots imposed on others and the power that the Romantic image of the Highland Scot wields in contemporary Nova Scotia. For instance, the forced migration of the French-speaking Acadians in the eighteenth century was largely accomplished by a British army staffed by a large proportion of Highland Scots, while in the same century Scottish soldiers were employed to "push back" and dispossess the native Mi'kmaq. The Reverend Patterson reported that before the arrival of the *Hector*, the early settlers of Pictou tried to forestall a supposed native plot against them by warning natives that "the Highlanders were coming—the same men they had seen in petticoats at the taking of Quebec." The sight of the *Hector* men donning their "carefully preserved" Highland dress as well as a blast from the pipes, "its thrilling sounds then first startling the echoes among the silent solitudes of [the] forest" was impressive. "All the MicMacs [*sic*] fled in terror and were not seen for some time, so that trouble with the Indians was never heard of again" (82). Clearly the natives of eastern Nova Scotia would not have been at the siege of Quebec, and the fearsome quality of the pipes is an obvious stereotype, suggesting that the entire account is apocryphal. Nevertheless, demobilised Highland soldiers of the 82nd and 84th Regiments did settle in the region after the American Revolution (Patterson 1877, 114–21), and there is documented evidence that Highland soldiers were used throughout Nova Scotia, from at least 1760, to prevent native encroachments on the new settlements.[7] There is also clear evidence of Scottish settlers squatting on native land. In Cape Breton, in the early nineteenth century, several poor "backland" Highland immigrants won legal approval of such dispossession through appeals to the courts (Bittermann 1988, 43–44).

Furthermore, it is apparent that while many opposed it, some Scots participated in black slavery in the colony (Cahill 1999). Indeed, it is the black Nova Scotian experience—which in addition to slavery, included economic exploitation and marginalisation, a "repatriation" to West Africa, and the endurance of incessant racism—that would more clearly fit the common understanding of diaspora; that is, migrations undertaken as a consequence of victimisation and oppression, which produces a shared sense of community and members of which often exhibit a desire for return to a real or imagined homeland.

The forced removal of African populations to North America through the slave trade, apparent in Nova Scotia as early as the French colonisation of the seventeenth century, was extended with the arrival of African-American slaves and their white New England masters during the eighteenth century (Donovan 1995; Cahill 1994). This black population was greatly expanded by the arrival of the Loyalists following the American Revolution, the majority arriving as "free" settlers as a consequence of taking advantage of British offers of emancipation and land in return for their support in the Revolutionary War. Nevertheless, almost a third of the blacks arriving in the colony as a consequence of the war, an estimated 1,232 individuals, were brought as slaves by their Loyalist masters, and by the end of the migrations slaves still represented 25 percent of the overall black population of the colony (Pachai 1987–1991; Walker 1999, 1976, 40–42). In addition, the "free" black communities founded in this period, such as Birchtown, located beside the Loyalist town of Shelburne on the south shore, were placed on marginal land that was unable to support subsistence agriculture but sufficiently close to white communities to ensure that those settlements would have a ready supply of cheap labour (Niven and Davis; Walker 1976, 42–63). Therefore, at the outset, black Nova Scotians were settled in conditions of marginalisation and dependency.

One of the early consequences of these conditions of exclusion—exploitation and accompanying poverty—was the decision of many black Loyalists to "return" to the British West African colony of Sierra Leone. Approximately 1,196 members of the black population of the Maritimes left for West Africa in 1792. In order to qualify for the Sierra Leone scheme, applicants had to demonstrate their "free" status and be free of debt and of good character. This ensured that slaves could not depart, but neither could indentured servants or those who had been deliberately placed in debt by whites who were unwilling to see their source of cheap labour disappear. The migration involved nearly half of the "free" black population of the region, and smaller migrations followed, but the problems faced in the African colony ensured that this trend did not continue into the latter part of the nineteenth century (Walker 1976).

The black population that remained in Nova Scotia was, during the course of the century, supplemented by the arrival of refugees from the War of 1812, by escaped American slaves, and by small numbers of "free" labourers from the West Indies. Their experience encouraged them to agitate for the abolition of slavery, not only in the colony and empire, achieved in 1834, but throughout North America (Clarke 1997). African-American movements and individuals, including Booker T. Washington, Marcus Garvey, and Martin Luther King Jr., continued to influence black Nova Scotia (Hay 1997; Winks 1971), but most scholars agree that for these communities greater emphasis was placed on common ties based upon their Baptist congregations and community institutions. These bonds were further reinforced by a shared experience of resisting marginalisation, exploitation, and systemic racism in the province (Pachai 1987–1991; Hay 1997; Henry 1973).

In more recent years, the strength of these black community ties has been demonstrated in the response to the destruction of Africville. Originally known by the Scottish moniker "Campbell Road," after its main thoroughfare, Africville was, from the 1840s, the major settlement for Halifax's black population. In Halifax, blacks were employed as unskilled labourers who toiled on the docks and coal barges, hauled the city's night soil, or, if female, worked as domestic servants (Walker 1997; Morton 1993). By the middle of the twentieth century, the largely self-contained community had suffered from encroachments of white society through the construction of railway lines, slaughterhouses, a tar factory, a leather tannery, and in the 1950s, the city dump, without receiving any city services, such as sewage, lighting, or policing, in return. In addition to these physical deprecations, Africville had also attracted a petty criminal element solidifying a perception of the community as an "eyesore" and slum by the 1960s. Prominent individuals, both white and black, sought to relocate and integrate the community within the rest of the city, and as a consequence Africville was demolished, but not before several unwilling residents were expropriated and forcibly removed. It is clear in hindsight that these movements towards assimilation did not result in the elimination of racism in Halifax. Indeed they appear to have caused further economic deprivation and heightened tensions, a fact that partly accounts for the welcome extended to representatives of the radical American Black Panther movement when they arrived in the city at the end of the 1960s (Walker 1997).

The Panthers, once again, connected the black Nova Scotian community with the wider African America of which it is essentially a particular offshoot, but the destruction of Africville also resulted in a highly local sense of diaspora. In recent years, the relocation itself has come to be viewed as an act of racial oppression, and the dispersed community has sought to rebuild by documenting its genealogy and history. This in turn has generated a movement demanding the return of the Africville land from the city. Indeed there are plans for a physical return to the site through the establishment of a historical memorial and a reconstruction of the Seaview Baptist Church, reflecting the continued importance of the links of faith for the community (Walker 1997).

Halifax historian and genealogist Allen Robertson (2001) has recently described the African-Nova Scotian historical experience as a "sad legacy," but astoundingly suggests that "Scots in Nova Scotia can claim an equally multifaceted background." This "equality" is clearly not based on a shared experience of slavery, systemic racism, or community expropriation. Undoubtedly Gaelic-speaking Scots experienced hostility towards their language in the provincial schools. Scots and their descendants have also been victims of exploitation in the province's industries, and rural economic decline has compelled many to seek opportunities elsewhere, resulting in extremely high levels of out-migration from the province, but this is hardly comparable to the racial in-equality experienced by black Nova Scotians. The basis for Robertson's comparison is a shared attempt to protect and recover one's culture. However, he neatly sidesteps the fact that emblems of Scottishness, no matter how fabricated, are dominant in Nova Scotian popular culture. Despite the best efforts of remarkable artists, such as the self-styled Africadian poet George Elliott Clarke, emblems of black Nova Scotia are clearly not yet part of that dominant culture (Clarke 1991–1992, 1990, 1994, 1999). There are signs that members of Nova Scotian clan societies are themselves aware of this inequality. In an appeal to fellow clan society members to embrace the celebration of multi-culturalism in the province, A. Wayne MacKay noted that while "Scots are an important component of the multi-cultural fabric of Nova Scotia . . . the clans have sometimes regarded being Scottish as the norm in Nova Scotia and other cultural expressions as abnormal or at least on the fringes."

> In rather typical independent fashion, the Scottish clans have been so intent on developing and extending their own heritage that they have paid little attention to other cultural groups. To be blunt, they have sometimes considered themselves to be a cut above other cultural groups in Nova Scotia and have on occasions fallen prey to a kind of elitism. It is hardly surprising that clans which have spent much time demonstrating their superiority to the other clans, are less open in accepting the other cultural groups on a basis of equality (MacKay 1988).

While MacKay is clearly aware of the power relations between cultural groups in Nova Scotia, Robertson chooses to ignores them, focusing instead on the shared enterprise of recovering "roots," a task he claims is "reinforced by new ties between Scotland and Scots in the diaspora" (2001, 35). Thus, the academic usage of "diaspora" is employed in order to justify equating unequal experiences.

Conclusion

The potential for misuse of the label "diaspora" has not gone unnoticed by scholars (Akenson 1995). Anthropologist Paul Basu has recently acknowledged this problem, but still believes in the utility of the term for the study of Highland Scots: "'Diaspora' has become an anthropological 'buzzword' used to describe almost any dispersed group regardless of the circumstances of its dispersal. It is, however, an appropriate description of the Scottish Highland experience where a complex ambivalent history of emigration has generally been dominated by a moral rhetoric of involuntary exile."[8] This chapter has suggested that the rhetoric has more to do with the influence of romanticism than actual Highland experience in Nova Scotia, but it also argues that the romanticisation of the Highlander reinforces power relations in the province and that the concept of diaspora obscures those relationships.

One of the oldest Scottish Societies in North America is the North British Society, founded in Halifax by local, mostly Lowland, Scottish elites in 1768. Recently the group officially changed their name to "The Scots: The North British Society," partly because the synonyms "North Britain" and "Scotland" are no longer readily understood. The most important events in the society's calendar are the St. Andrew's Day banquet, the Burns Supper, and their annual Halifax Highland Games. Although St. Andrew's Day has been celebrated since the body's inception, the Burns event obviously arrived much later, as did the games. Indeed, the Halifax games were part of a simultaneous Victorian "invention of tradition" rather than a reflection of preserved tradition brought from Scotland. The current games now include such novel events as "The Great Halifax Haggis Hurl," along with the usual piping, dancing, and athletic competitions.[9] The society's current preoccupation with celebrating faux Scottishness masks its nineteenth-century role of providing its elite members with professional, commercial, and political advantage in the city. Until the twentieth century, local worthies in the North British Society, such as brewer Alexander Keith or mayor John Sinclair, were able to link their enthusiasm for Scottish celebration with their own personal and professional advantage. As one student of the society has stated, "To claim to be Scottish in nineteenth century [Halifax] was to publicly state one's membership in a select group" (R. Kennedy 2000). It is only in relatively more recent years that the society has aimed to be more inclusive rather than a bastion of privilege.

In his last book, *Envisioning Power: Ideologies of Dominance and Crisis*, Eric Wolf called for detailed case studies in order "to define the relations of power that are played out in social arrangement and cultural configurations, and to trace out the possible ways in which these relations of power implicate ideas" (1999, 3). Although not as ambitious as Wolf's attempt to account for these relationships among the Kwakiutl, the Aztecs, and National Socialist Germany, this chapter has attempted to demonstrate that received ideas about "Scottishness" in Nova Scotia have had important "political" consequences. They have distorted the actual experience of the Scottish minority in the province and relegated them to emblems of a bygone rustic age. The celebration of the hardy, if dejected, Highland pioneer rather than the militant Scottish steelworker has obvious conservative value. Furthermore, the pervasiveness of Scottish kitsch performs an additional role of marginalising the experience of other groups in the province, and, indeed, in the case of black Nova Scotians, aids in ethnic inequalities. The Romantic representation of the Scottish experience as that of the pathetic yet heroic Highlander has deflected attention from this history of African slavery, along with its accompanying systemic racism, and has allowed the heritage industry to portray Nova Scotia as a racially uncomplicated pre-industrial playground. Furthermore, the categorising of the Scottish presence in Nova Scotia as belonging to a diaspora aids in that image-making and not only disguises the black experience but also helps to exclude that of the original inhabitants. Clearly the Mi'kmaw cannot by any means be viewed as belonging to a diaspora, but their dispossession and marginalisation are none the less as real as that imagined or experienced by the Highland Scot in Nova Scotia.

Notes

I would like to thank Celeste Ray, Leslie Paris, and Renée Hulan, who provided valuable comments on earlier drafts of this chapter. I also wish to thank the students who, over the years, have participated in my Irish and Scottish Emigration History seminar at Saint Mary's University. In particular, I would like to acknowledge the assistance of Rosalie Robinson, Rebecca Kennedy, Don Smith, and Monica Germaná. Their various investigations helped me to flesh this paper out; nevertheless, all errors and omissions are my own.

1. Mi'kmaw is the grammatically correct adjective for things related to the Mi'k-maq and is also used as another spelling for the name. The Mi'kmaq are an indigenous people of eastern Canada (their name is also spelled Micmac, Mikmak, Mi'gmak, or Mikmaq).

2. For information about the *Ship Hector,* see *http://www.townofpictou.com/.*

3. The New Scotland Brewing Company, which opened in 1998, went out of business two years later.

4. The deficient statistics for these major ports, and nonexistent records for the outports along the Cape Breton coast and Northumberland Strait, where many migrants were landed, suggest that the number of Scots arriving in these years may be underestimated.

5. The Scots were 148,000 of 523,837 (McKay 1992, 8). See also (Hornsby 1992b).

6. *Nova Scotia: Complete Guide for Doers and Dreamers 2001,* published by the Nova Scotia Department of Tourism and Culture. *Pictou County: Visitors Guide 2000,* published by the Pictou County Tourist Association.

7. Charles Lawrence to Lords of Trade, May 11, 1760. CO 217, vol. 17, reel 13847, Public Archives of Nova Scotia.

8. Paul Basu, "Highland Homecomings Research Project," University College London. Basu's position on "diaspora" is articulated more fully in chapter 11 in this volume.

9. For a general discussion of Scottishness in Halifax, see Germaná 2003.

Works Cited

Akenson, Donald Hannan. 1995. "The Historiography of English-Speaking Canada and the Concept of Diaspora: A Sceptical Appreciation." *Canadian Historical Review* 76, no. 3 (September): 377–409.

Beaton, Elizabeth. 1995. "An African-American Community in Cape Breton, 1901–1904." *Acadiensis* 24: 65–97.

Best, Carrie M. 1977. *That Lonesome Road: The Autobiography of Carrie M. Best.* New Glasgow, Nova Scotia: Clarion.

Bittermann, Rusty. 1994. "Farm Households and Wage Labour in the Northeastern Maritimes in the Early 19th Century." In *Contested Countryside: Rural Workers and Modern Society in Atlantic Canada, 1800–1950,* ed. D. Samson, 34–69. Fredericton: Acadiensis.

———. 1988 "The Hierarchy of the Soil: Land and Labour in a Nineteenth-Century Cape Breton Community." *Acadiensis* 18, no. 1 (autumn): 33–55.

Boudreau, Michael. 1993–1994. "A 'Rare and Unusual Treat of Historical Significance': The 1923 Hector Celebration and the Political Economy of the Past," *Journal of Canadian Studies* 28, no. 4: 28–48.

———. 1992. "Ship of Dreams." *New Maritimes* (Sept./Oct.): 6–15.

Buckner, Philip A., and John G. Reid, eds. 1994. *The Atlantic Region to Confederation: A History.* Toronto: U of Toronto P.

Cahill, Barry. 1999. "Mediating a Scottish Enlightenment Ideal: The Presbyterian Dissenter Attack on Slavery in Late Eighteenth-Century Nova Scotia." In *Myth, Migration, and the Making of Memory: Scotia and Nova Scotia, c. 1700–1990,* ed. Marjory Harper and Michael Vance, 189–201. Halifax, Nova Scotia: Fernwood.

———. 1994. "Slavery and the Judges of Loyalist Nova Scotia." *UNB Law Journal* 43: 73–134.

Campbell, Donald F., and Raymond A. MacLean. 1974. *Beyond the Atlantic Roar: A Study of the Nova Scotia Scots.* Toronto: McClelland and Stewart.

Chaliand, Gérard, and Jean-Pierre Rageau. 1997. *The Penguin Atlas of Diasporas.* Harmondsworth: Penguin.

Clarke, George Elliott. 1999. *Beatrice Chancy.* Victoria, BC: Polestar.

———. 1997. "Editorial." *Dalhousie Review* 77, no. 1 (summer): 149–53.

———. 1994. *Lush Dreams, Blue Exile: Fugitive Poems, 1978–1993.* Lawrencetown Beach, Nova Scotia: Pottersfield.

———. 1990. *Whylah Falls.* Victoria, BC: Polestar.

Clarke, George Elliott, ed. 1991–1992. *Fire on the Water: An Anthology of Black Nova Scotia Writing.* 2 vols. Lawrencetown Beach, Nova Scotia: Pottersfield.

Cohen, Robin. 1997. *Global Diasporas: An Introduction.* Seattle: U of Washington P.

Cowan, Edward J. 1999 "The Myth of Scotch Canada." In *Myth, Migration, and the Making of Memory: Scotia and Nova Scotia c. 1700–1990,* ed. Marjory Harper and Michael Vance, 49–72. Halifax, Nova Scotia: Fernwood.

Dembling, Jonathan. 1997. "Joe Jimmy Alec Visits the Gaelic Mòd and Escapes Unscathed: The Nova Scotia Gaelic Revivals." MA thesis, Saint Mary's University, Halifax, Nova Scotia.

Donnachie, Ian, and Whatley, Christopher, eds. 1992. *The Manufacture of Scottish History.* Edinburgh: Polygon.

Donovan, Kenneth. 1995. "Slaves and Their Owners in Ile Royale, 1713–1760." *Acadiensis* 25: 3–32.

Dunn, Carol. 2000. "Africentric Heritage Park Unveiled: Park a 'Permanent and Visual Reminder of African Nova Scotia History.'" *Pictou Advocate* 107, no. 6 (February 6).

Dunn, Charles W. 1991. *Highland Settler: A Portrait of the Scottish Gael in Cape Breton.* Toronto: U of Toronto P, 1953. Reprint, Wreck Cove: Breton Books.

Durkacz, Victor Edward. 1983. *The Decline of the Celtic Languages: A Study of Linguistic and Cultural Conflict in Scotland, Wales, and Ireland from the Reformation to the Twentieth Century.* Edinburgh: John Donald.

Faed, Thomas. 1878. *The Faed Gallery: A Series of the Most Renowned Works of the Artist . . . with Full Descriptions and a Sketch of the Life of the Artist.* Boston: James R. Osgood.

Farnham, Charles H. 1886. "Cape Breton Folk." *Harpers* 72 (March): 607–25.

Forbes, Ernest R., and Delphin A. Muise, eds. 1993. *The Atlantic Provinces in Confederation.* Toronto: U of Toronto P.

Frank, David. 1999. *J. B. McLachlan: A Biography.* Toronto: James Lorimer.

———. 1985. "Tradition and Culture in the Cape Breton Mining Community in the Early Twentieth Century." In *Cape Breton at 200: Historical Essays in Honour of the Island's Bicentennial, 1785–1985,* ed. K. Donovan, 203–18. Sydney: University College of Cape Breton Press.

Germaná, Monica. 2003. "Historical Places of Interest, Books, Tourism and Advertising: Scottish Icons in Contemporary Halifax (Nova Scotia)." *International Review of Scottish Studies* 28: 22–46.

Gibson, John G. 1998. *Traditional Gaelic Bagpiping, 1745–1945.* Montreal: McGill-Queen's UP.

Gold, John R., and Margaret M. Gold. 1995. *Imagining Scotland: Tradition, Representation, and Promotion in Scottish Tourism since 1750.* Aldershot: Scolar.

Harper, Majory, and Michael E. Vance. 1999. "Myth, Migration, and the Making of Memory: An Introduction." In *Myth, Migration, and the Making of Memory: Scotia and Nova Scotia c. 1700–1990,* ed. Marjory Harper and Michael Vance, 14–48. Halifax, Nova Scotia: Fernwood.

Hay, Sheridan. 1997. "Black Protest Tradition in Nova Scotia, 1783–1964." MA thesis, Saint Mary's University, Halifax, Nova Scotia.

Henry, Frances. 1973. *Forgotten Canadians: The Blacks of Nova Scotia.* Don Mills, Ontario: Longman Canada.

Heron, Craig. 1988. *Working in Steel: The Early Years in Canada, 1883–1935.* Toronto: McClelland and Stewart.

———. 1987. "The Great War and Nova Scotia Steelworkers." *Acadiensis* 16, no. 2 (spring): 3–34.

Hoegg Ryan, Judith. 1995. *The Birthplace of New Scotland: An Illustrated History of Pictou County, Canada's Cradle of Industry.* Halifax, Nova Scotia: Formac.

Hornsby, Stephen J. 1992a. *Nineteenth-Century Cape Breton: A Historical Geography.* Montreal: McGill-Queen's UP.

———. 1992b. "Patterns of Scottish Emigration to Canada, 1750–1870." *Journal of Historical Geography* 18, no. 4: 397–416.

Inch, George Pratt. 1922. *Scottish Colonial Schemes, 1620–1686.* Glasgow: Maclehouse, Jackson.

Jarvie, Grant. 1991. *Highland Games: The Making of the Myth.* Edinburgh: Edinburgh UP.

Kennedy, Michael. 1999. "'Lochaber no more': A Critical Examination of Highland Emigration Mythology." In *Myth, Migration, and the Making of Memory: Scotia and Nova Scotia c. 1700–1990,* ed. Marjory Harper and Michael Vance, 267–97. Halifax, Nova Scotia: Fernwood.

Kennedy, Rebecca. 2000. "The Scotian Legacy: Scottish Ethnicity, the Scottish Community, and the North British Society of Halifax, 1850–1914." Undergraduate honour's thesis, Saint Mary's University, Halifax, Nova Scotia.

MacDonell, Margaret. 1982. *The Emigrant Experience: Songs of Highland Emigrants in North America.* Toronto: U of Toronto P.

MacEachen, Alan Andrew. 2001. *Natural Selections: National Parks in Atlantic Canada.* Montreal: McGill-Queen's UP.

MacKay, A. Wayne. 1988. "Clan MacKay and Multiculturalism." *The Clansman* [Halifax, Nova Scotia] (October).

MacLean, R. A. 1992. *A State of Mind: The Scots in Nova Scotia.* Hansport, Nova Scotia: Lancelot.

MacNeil, Neil. 1948. *The Highland Heart in Nova Scotia.* New York: Charles Scribner's.

Mahalik, David. 1996. "Music as a Living Tradition." In *The Centre of the World at the Edge of a Continent: Cultural Studies of Cape Breton Island,* ed. C. Corbin and J. A. Rolls, 101–04. Sydney: University College of Cape Breton Press.

McCrone, D., A. Morris, and R. Kiely. 1995. *Scotland—The Brand: The Making of Scottish Heritage.* Edinburgh: Edinburgh UP.

McKay, Ian. 1994. *The Quest of the Folk: Anti-Modernism and Cultural Selection in Twentieth Century Nova Scotia,* Montreal: McGill-Queen's UP.

———. 1992 "Tartanism Triumphant: The Construction of Scottishness in Nova Scotia, 1933–1954." *Acadiensis* 21, no. 2 (spring): 5–47.

Migliore, Sam, and A. Evo DiPierro. 1999. *Italian Lives, Cape Breton Memories.* Sydney: University College of Cape Breton Press.

Morton, Suzanne. 1993. "Separate Spheres in a Separate World: African-Nova Scotian

Women in Late Nineteenth-Century Halifax County." *Acadiensis* 22, no. 2 (spring): 61–83.

O'Shea, Kevin. 1996. "Cape Breton Fiddle Music as Popular Culture." In *The Centre of the World at the Edge of a Continent: Cultural Studies of Cape Breton Island, Sydney, University,* ed. C. Corbin and J. A. Rolls, 105–10. Sydney: University College of Cape Breton Press.

Pachai, Bridglal. 1987–1991. *Beneath the Clouds of the Promised Land: The Survival of Nova Scotia's Blacks.* 2 vols. Halifax: Black Educators Association of Nova Scotia.

Patterson, George. 1877. *A History of the County of Pictou, Nova Scotia.* Montreal: Dawson Brothers.

Reid, John G. 2001. "The Conquest of Nova Scotia: Cartographic Imperialism and the Echoes of the Scottish Past." In *Nation and Province in the First British Empire: Scotland and the Americas, 1600–1800,* ed. N. C. Landsman, 39–59. Lewisburg, PA: Bucknell UP.

Robertson, Allen B. 2001. "Scottish Roots: Fantasy or Reality?" *Celtic Heritage* (Jan./Feb.): 30–31, 35.

Samson, Daniel. 1999. "Industrial Colonization: The Colonial Context of the General Mining Association, Nova Scotia, 1825–1842." *Acadiensis* 24, no. 1 (autumn): 3–28.

Walker, James. 1999. "Myth, History, and Revisionism: The Black Loyalists Revisited." *Acadiensis* 29, no. 1 (autumn): 88–105.

———. 1997 "Allegories and Orientations in African-Canadian Historiography: The Spirit of Africville." *Dalhousie Review* 77, no. 1 (summer): 155–78.

———. 1976. *The Black Loyalists: The Search for a Promised Land in Nova Scotia and Sierra Leone, 1783–1870.* New York: Africana.

Wallace Ferguson, Brigitta. 1994. *The Scots Fort: A Reassessment of its Location.* Halifax: Parks Canada.

Winks, Robin W. 1971. *The Blacks in Canada: A History.* New Haven, CT: Yale UP.

Wolf, Eric R. 1999. *Envisioning Power: Ideologies of Dominance and Crisis.* Berkeley: U of California P.

Womack, Peter. 1989. *Improvement and Romance: Constructing the Myth of the Highlands.* London: Macmillan.

6

You Play It as You Would Sing It

Cape Breton, Scottishness, and the Means of Cultural Production

Jonathan Dembling

Cape Breton Island, at the eastern end of Nova Scotia in the Canadian Maritimes, occupies a unique place in the Scottish diaspora. The Gaelic language survives there—barely—on the tongues of people several generations removed from Scotland. The cultural conservatism that allowed the language to survive for more than two centuries is also credited with preserving cultural forms—in particular, music and dance—that in Scotland have either disappeared or greatly changed. In recent years, some Scottish musicians and dancers have embarked on a project to "repatriate" these traditions, arguing that they are more authentic than anything surviving in Scotland itself.

Cape Breton is hardly alone within North America in preserving archaic forms of social life and cultural expression. One may point to the Old Order Amish, the Doukhobors, Appalachian ballads, or French Canadian vocabulary. Yet none of these examples rival or displace the authenticity of the source country's culture; Parisians will not argue that speaking with a Québécois accent makes one more French. What is interesting in this case is that a small but influential segment of the traditional Scottish music and dance community is in effect arguing that Cape Breton's traditions are more authentically Scottish than their own. It is an argument for the counterflow of cultural authenticity from the diaspora to the source.

Most Scots have likely never heard of Cape Breton. The social circles in which this "Cape Breton project" takes place represent a small subset of the Scottish population, but they have a disproportionate influence on Scottish culture. They also reflect a much wider arena in which Scots are scrutinizing and renegotiating their identities. The current interest in Cape Breton music and dance thus provides one window for examining this process. The following analysis is based on fieldwork conducted in Scotland during the spring of 2003.

Background

Gaelic-speaking Scots emigrated to British North America in large numbers between 1770 and 1850. Responding to political, economic, and social upheavals in the Highlands and Islands of Scotland, tens of thousands of Gaels left (or were forced from) their homes and formed new communities from Newfoundland to Vancouver Island. When Canadian Confederation was completed in 1867, Gaelic was the third most widely spoken language in the new country (Kennedy 2002, 28). Since the late nineteenth century, Gaelic has been in decline, and today Cape Breton comprises the last living *Gàidhealtachd,* or Gaelic-speaking area, in North America. Current estimates put the number of Gaelic-speakers in the low hundreds (Statistics Canada 2001).

Despite the small numbers, Cape Breton has acquired a reputation in Canada and further afield for the strength of its living Gaelic culture, particularly its music and dance traditions. Step dancers, singers, bagpipers, and especially fiddlers have achieved national and international celebrity. But the island's musical strength is widely acknowledged as being much more than the sum of its best-known exponents such as Ashley MacIsaac and Natalie MacMaster. Although the common caricature of Cape Breton as a land of strathspeys and step dancing obscures the island's complex social and ethnic makeup, the music and dance traditions of the Gaels have flourished both within and beyond the boundaries of the island's Scottish settlements.

Although typically characterized as virtually unchanged from their eighteenth-century West Highland roots, the music and dance of Cape Breton have evolved significantly since the time of the first settlers. While the core instruments (fiddle and bagpipes), dance tunes (strathspeys and reels), and step dances remain popular, they have been augmented and influenced by other cultures and native innovations. The most obvious examples are the ubiquity of piano accompaniment for the fiddle, the importation of square dances from New England, and the popularity of jigs. But whether borrowing or innovating, Cape Breton Gaels incorporated these changes into a Gaelic aesthetic framework; they step-danced their way through the square sets, and the piano players echoed the ornamentations of both fiddle and feet (Kennedy 2002).

In Scotland traditional music and dance forms evolved along different lines. In the Highlands and Islands these traditions were severely weakened. The nineteenth century saw a surge in Highland evangelicalism, which often cast music and dance as sinful. Meanwhile, the spread of newer fashions from the south made accordion-driven country dancing the dominant form of social dance. Gaelic piping styles survived on the fringes, while step dancing was almost completely erased from the popular consciousness (Gibson 1998; M. Moore 1995).

As Gaelic society was being uprooted in the Highlands, it was increasingly romanticized and popularized in the Lowlands and England. A whole package of Gaelic traditional music, song, and dance was appropriated, wrapped in tartan, and adapted to the tastes of both the Anglophone and Gaelic-speaking urban middle class (Newton 2000; Meek 2003). Highland dances and pipe tunes were formalized and made the preserve of the military/competition circuit, replacing idiosyncratic Gaelic-based rhythms with those that could be measured and judged.

As Scottish music and dance took on an increasingly formalized and tartanist character, this new orthodoxy slowly spread across to Canada. Anglophone Scots established pipe bands, Highland games, and even the Gaelic College in St. Ann's, Nova Scotia (Kennedy 2002). The influence of Scottish-based neo-traditions came at a time when politicians and tourism officials began to aggressively market the province as a mini-Scotland, framing tourist brochures in tartan and strategically placing kilted pipers at border crossings, ferry terminals, and information centers. This development, detailed by Ian MacKay (1992), managed to erase racial, ethnic, and class diversity from the imagined provincial landscape and marginalize the living culture and traditions of the Gaels at the same time.

The combined force of tartanism and the unrelenting advances of mass communication and culture drove Gaelic music and dance to the brink even in the most conservative areas of the Maritimes. In 1971 the Canadian Broadcasting Corporation produced a documentary called *The Vanishing Cape Breton Fiddler,* drawing attention to the unique style and foretelling its imminent demise. The local response was remarkable. The Cape Breton Fiddlers' Association was formed, concerts were arranged, and dances sprung up everywhere. Older fiddlers came out of the woodwork in huge numbers, and instruction for young people took off. Within twenty years the revival was so successful that outsiders experiencing Cape Breton fiddling for the first time were incredulous that it had been in such danger so recently. The scale of the revival had immediate knock-on effects for step dancing and piano accompaniment, and more recently the Gaelic piping tradition has undergone a modest revival (Kennedy 2002, 185–87).

Given the divergent paths that music and dance forms have taken in Scotland and Cape Breton over the last two centuries, it is not surprising that many Scots who encountered Cape Breton styles were at best dubious of its Scottish origins. The home country is popularly assumed to be more culturally conservative than a diasporic community living among other groups in the North American mosaic, and this assumption was strengthened by the presumed authenticity of Victorian-era innovations. Thus Cape Breton–style fiddling and step dancing were often assumed to be Irish, or French, or at best some melting pot amalgamation (Kennedy 2002, 215–16).

Gradually, some Scots began to appreciate that Cape Breton represented another branch of the Scottish tradition. This shift was undoubtedly helped by the increased cultural confidence within Cape Breton itself, but by and large it has been Scots who have embraced Cape Breton styles as deserving pride of place in Scotland. In the 1980s two Scots, fiddler Alasdair Fraser and piper Hamish Moore, fell in love with the music of fiddlers such as Buddy MacMaster, finding in his playing a liveliness and essence they felt was missing from Scottish music (Murphy 1991; H. Moore 1994). Fraser invited MacMaster and step dancer Harvey Beaton to teach at his summer school at Sabhal Mòr Ostaig in Skye. Moore established Ceòlas, a summer school in South Uist with a heavy representation of instructors from Cape Breton. Both of these schools are very successful and have inspired many Scots to take up Cape Breton music and dance styles as their own.

Scottishness

In order to appreciate the context in which the enthusiasm for Cape Breton's traditions is taking place, it is necessary to consider the broader arena in which Scottish identities are negotiated. This is especially the case at the beginning of the twenty-first century, when devolution has granted Scots a limited right of self-determination for the first time in three hundred years. The opening of the Scottish Parliament in 1999 was the culmination of a remarkable twenty-year period in Scottish cultural politics. After the failure of the 1979 referendum on home rule, and during the ensuing eighteen years of Conservative rule at Westminster, the arts and culture in Scotland took on a more nationalist, or at least more self-consciously Scottish, form. Rock bands, novelists, painters, and intellectuals, among others, contributed to a groundswell of cultural activity that pushed an agenda of Scottishness into the political sphere (Ascherson 2002).

The coming of devolution, and the cultural activity that preceded it, spawned a great deal of thinking and discussion about what it means to be Scottish in the twenty-first century. A cottage industry in book publishing has sprung up, as author upon author tackles the meaning of post-devolution Scottish society and identity (see for example Ascherson 2002; Calder 2002; McCrone 2001;

Ferguson 1998; Devine and Logue 2002). Unsurprisingly, the quest for identity has led to a vigorous engagement with the past, leading to an even greater production of books on Scottish history (e.g., Devine 1999; Harvie 2002; Houston and Knox 2002).

There are, broadly speaking, two views of Scottish history. One sees Scotland as a broken, colonized country, culturally deformed from centuries of forced assimilation into a Greater Britain. The other presents Scotland as a willing participant in Union and Empire, industrious and plucky, maintaining its distinctive institutions while freely adopting new ideas and fashions. These views, though seemingly oppositional, are often both held in varying degrees by the same person—a manifestation, perhaps, of the "Scottish Antisyzygy"—complicating any attempt to neatly analyze Scottish identity politics.

The Lowland appropriation of Highland cultural symbols, discussed briefly above, remains an unresolved issue in contemporary Scottish identity. While bearing little resemblance to Gaelic society past or present, Highlandism has a long enough history, and has been so widely adopted, that it is difficult to argue that it is not real. Debunkers of Highlandist myths do a historical service but cannot erase the fact that many of the nineteenth-century inventions and romantic excesses have become firmly entrenched in the social fabric of the country. David McCrone (2001, 135) attributes the rise of "tartanry" to the cultural insecurities of Lowland Scots at a time when they were questioning their ability to remain distinct from the English. But the implications for Gaelic society of the whole of Scotland adopting a Highland (or pseudo-Highland) identity have received far less attention. In particular, the power and legitimacy to define what it is to be Gaelic, Highland, or Scottish must be critically examined. The Cape Breton "project" provides an opportunity for such an examination.

Debating Cape Breton

For every Scottish musician or dancer who embraces Cape Breton, there is another who is ambivalent at best. Interestingly, the style is described by fan and foe alike in similar language: *rough, aggressive, heavy, driving,* and *dirty* (more than one fiddler I interviewed spoke of the need to "put the dirt back" into their music). In contrast, Scottish styles were described as *soft, smooth, light,* and "cleaned up." Defenders of the Scottish styles describe them in terms of their pleasantness, while characterizing the Cape Breton style as harsh and abrasive. Aficionados of the latter style, on the other hand, may think of "clean" as boring and "dirty" as fun. One fan of the Cape Breton style contrasted it with Scottish styles this way: "It's not a sit-back-and-drink-your-G-and-T kind of music, it's like spill-your-beer-over-the-person-next-to-you kind of music."

At the heart of debates over Scottish history and identity is a preoccupation with authenticity. For many it is a matter of degree. This came out quite strongly among Cape Breton enthusiasts, who were all reluctant to dismiss contemporary Scottish practices as inauthentic, even when their characterizations indicated otherwise. "You know, Highland dancing is fine. We're not rubbishing it. You can't rubbish any tradition . . . It's ballet, it's Victorian, it's militarized, it's all these things that are 'bad,' you know, but it's nevertheless a development that happened in our country, and should be accepted as such."

The particular nature of Scots' interest in Cape Breton highlights some aspects of their approach to issues of authenticity and identity. Particularly revealing is the fact that they do not embrace all manifestations of the Cape Breton tradition. In choosing which pieces of the Cape Breton whole are worthy of adoption, Scottish musicians and dancers are not only deciding what they consider authentic, they are also revealing what authenticity means to them.

In Scotland the most popular of Cape Breton's cultural forms are those that existed among the emigrant Gaels *before* they left for North America. Scottish tunes are favored over those composed in Cape Breton. Strathspeys and reels are favored over jigs. Step dancing is popular but square sets are not. And the unique style of Cape Breton piano accompaniment has barely made an impact. These factors point to two possible determinants of authenticity: age and Scottishness. Yet both of these criteria are problematic.

Age is the simplest explanation for authenticity in most contexts; indeed, the two terms are often used interchangeably. As one fiddler put it: "I do think that the Cape Breton music is authentic, an old style Highland music." On the surface it would appear that age is precisely the reason why preemigration tunes are favored and postemigration innovations are avoided. But why then turn back the clock only as far as the eighteenth century? Why isn't "early music" considered the most authentic? Given the general lack of curiosity about the musical inclinations of the Picts, for example, the authenticity as age equation leaves much to be explained.

So rather than a case of the older the better, it appears that the eighteenth century is seen as a "golden age" before the impact of "all these things that are 'bad.'" Authenticity is tied to a pre-Union (or pre-Culloden or pre-Clearances) sense of Scottishness. According to this view, the Gaelic-speaking Highlanders who left for the Maritimes in the eighteenth and nineteenth centuries are the last remnant of a Scotland unaffected by modernity, English hegemony, Celtic Twilightism, twee Victorian shortbread-tin tartanism, and a host of other "-isms" that continue to bedevil contemporary Scotland.

Implicit in this view is the acceptance of earlier outside influences; thus fiddles are authentic but accordions are not. This desire to reclaim the eighteenth-century Highlands for the twenty-first-century Scotland would explain the heightened interest in the "old tunes" preserved in Cape Breton as well as the relative lack of interest in square dance sets and piano accompaniment.

Those who are not on the Cape Breton bandwagon, especially those brought up in one of Scotland's stronger regional traditions, such as Shetland or the Northeast, are often skeptical of the characterization of Cape Breton styles as "Scottish." For them, Scottishness is defined as what Scottish people do, not what they might have done in the past. They see the last two centuries of music and dance culture as an evolution, not a break, and they resent the implication that their own styles are somehow debased. They further criticize the claim that Cape Breton styles belong to the whole of Scotland:

> Even in Scotland, you only need to go about fifty miles and the landscape completely changes, the style that people play their instruments is different, you know. Go between Orkney and Shetland and we're not the same. Go between the Borders and the East Coast of Scotland, go between the East Coast of Scotland and the West Coast of Scotland, and you can see a huge difference in the styles of music. So why would you say that some music that went to Cape Breton has got to speak for the whole of Scotland?

When discussing the place of Cape Breton in Scotland, the obvious region of affinity is the West Highlands and Islands, since that is where the emigrants came from. And because the Gaelic language is widely acknowledged as being a major influence on the Cape Breton style, this connection goes beyond being a mere fact of history. In fact, one can argue that the authenticity ascribed to Cape Breton derives from its Gaelicness. The interconnectedness of the language with the music and dance is not only frequently noted but is also contrasted with the music and dance in the Gaelic-speaking areas of Scotland, where the linguistic connection is said to have been lost. This assertion is problematic, as discussed below. But the importance given to the role of Gaelic as a vital component of both instrumental music and dance indicates that the maintenance of this three-way relationship is a determinant of authenticity.

Debating Gaelicness

The assertion of a Gaelic component to the music of Cape Breton essentially boils down to a phrase I heard over and again during my fieldwork: "You play it as you would sing it." In other words, the natural rhythms of the words to a particular tune will dictate, or at least guide, how the rhythm, tempo, accent, and ornamentation of the tune will be articulated. And because Gaelic song aesthetics tend to eschew regular and predictable rhythms, the flow of syllables can sound idiosyncratic to outside ears. Composers of Gaelic songs have masterfully exploited this rhythmic potential, especially in the case of *puirt-a-beul,* or mouth music—the sung versions of dance tunes.

Some people go so far as to argue that, historically, the rhythm of these songs was more important than the melody.

> Speaker A: In the old recordings of *puirt-a-beul,* it's not the tune that matters, it's the rhythm, that's the other important thing. Like the singers might not have a note of music in their head, from what it sounds like, but they're being recorded singing obviously because they're respected in the community for singing it. But what you get is the rhythm, you don't get a tune, you get rhythm.

> Speaker B: It's Gaelic rap.

In Cape Breton a growing body of research confirms the centrality of language rhythms in the music of the older players (Shaw 1993; Gibson 1998; Kennedy 2002; Dunlay 1992). More than this, it confirms the recognition and importance of a language link to the Gaelic-speaking audience. Of course, with Gaelic in its last stages as a community language in Cape Breton, this link is now tenuous; the younger generations of players do not have the linguistic capacity to maintain the Gaelic style, and perhaps more importantly, the younger generations of audiences do not have the linguistic capacity to appreciate the difference.

Nevertheless, there are still several popular fiddlers in Cape Breton who know Gaelic and learned to play by ear. The "jigging" of tunes—singing the Gaelic words—was a primary method of learning a new tune; many older fiddlers stress that they would make no attempt to play a tune until they could properly vocalize it (Wilson and Dunlay 2002). This practice reinforced the influence of Gaelic language inflections.

The importance of the language link is often stressed by Cape Breton enthusiasts in Scotland, and this sentiment is shared generally in Gaelic-speaking Scotland. But there is a division of opinion within Scottish Gaeldom as to whether Cape Breton music sounds Gaelic at all. A few Gaelic-speaking musicians I spoke with were quite skeptical of such claims. One Hebridean fiddler said that the Cape Breton style didn't sound "remotely Gaelic" to him. He immediately qualified this statement by granting that one particular reel, "Am Muileann Dubh" (The Black Mill) was linguistically sound, but described another tune as "total chaos" because it was played for step dancing. Another fiddler from the same island described the style as "Scottish music with a French accent," no closer than bluegrass to Scottish music. Another fiddler from the Highlands, who learned Gaelic, also failed to hear any linguistic connection: "It doesn't convey any emotion to me. It's very brittle, and I don't believe that true Highlanders or West Coasters would have played like that. I think we're very soft people. I think that the way we speak is soft and flowing."

Other Gaels quite clearly and immediately heard the Gaelic *blas* (flavor) in the music. One Gaelic-speaking piper who went to Cape Breton in the late 1960s felt an instant recognition when he first heard the fiddle players there: "We were hearing stuff that wasn't being played over here, but was actually being sung over here. You know, stuff that my father would be singing, tunes like '*Caberfeidh.*' And we had been brought up playing them on the pipes in a different style, yet the fiddlers over in Cape Breton were playing them as my father would be singing them."

Several other Gaelic-speakers I interviewed gave similar reactions. One woman from the Western Isles had an epiphany when she first encountered step dancing at Ceòlas. She had seen it on television in the past and thought it was "a Canadian thing." But when she took part, her reaction changed:

When I heard about Ceòlas first of all, and I heard about people from Cape Breton coming over, I just thought, I don't know, what did I think? They're coming over to teach us something new. That's what I thought . . . But somebody said "Oh, go for one of the drop-in sessions," and I did, and I went along. And when I saw them dancing, it was just this wonderful feeling of seeing something that I wanted to do, and I just wanted to dance straightaway. And I just thought this is natural, this is not something new, it's something old, that's right in me, and it's just going to come out.

In agreeing with the language link in Cape Breton music, several Gaelic-speakers also pointed out that the same link exists in the style of accordion music played in the West Highlands and Islands. This was an interesting observation, since the biggest boosters of Cape Breton music tend to be the least interested in accordion music, and yet one of the primary rationales for promoting Cape Breton is the language link. The "Statement of Philosophy and Artistic Aims" for the Ceòlas summer school notes that "the main emphasis is placed upon traditional styles of playing, linked to rhythms associated with the Gaelic language and/or dance traditions." This would at first appear to welcome a Gaelic-style accordion component, until the next sentence, in which the meaning of a Gaelic dance tradition is defined: "This is as opposed to styles more closely related to other dance traditions (e.g., Scottish Country Dancing), other geographical areas, or a broadly classical, or military aesthetic." Since the accordion is almost exclusively employed for country dancing, its inclusion at the school is prevented.

This stance cannot be easy for the Ceòlas committee to maintain, particularly given the popularity of accordion-driven social dances in the Islands. Not only does this style have a Gaelic *blas,* which is acknowledged even by its detractors, but the feature that most clearly distinguishes it from the "East Coast" style of accordion music is the popularity of "Gaelic waltzes," which are Gaelic song melodies played in waltz time. When these waltzes are played at *ceilidhs* in the Western Isles, the dancers, as well as those sitting in their chairs, often sing along with the music. You play it as you would sing it.

For these reasons, it is no surprise that the biggest complaint I heard from local people about Ceòlas was the exclusion of the accordion. One box player spoke of feeling "left out" and implicitly acknowledged the age component of authenticity when he added: "It may be recent but it's still part of the culture."

While it might be argued that the forces behind Ceòlas are narrowly defining Gaelic authenticity to exclude postemigration traditions, there is an argument put forward by some that holds that rather than the language influencing the music, Gaelic songs have changed to suit non-Gaelic music rhythms. For example, Gaelic waltzes take songs that had irregular rhythms and force them into three-quarter waltz time, thereby evening them out. By the same process, strathspeys are now typically sung with two beats to the bar, matching the way they are played in Scotland, whereas in the days when step dancing was the norm, strathspeys would presumably have been sung as they were played then, at four beats to the bar.

I think you could get someone singing *puirt-a-beul* from say the forties, and get somebody playing the fiddle who is a Gaelic speaker who had a wide repertoire of *puirt-a-beul*—and there were some of them that were recorded I think in the forties and fifties—and look at the way they treated eighth notes in the reels, for instance. There's a certain unevenness to them. It's not da-ba da-ba da-ba da-ba. I won't try to sing for you right now, but there is something quite jagged about it, almost.

Who then gets to define what "Gaelic music and dance" is and what it isn't? The case of the accordion reveals the complex ways in which Gaelicness is defined. The mantralike "you play it as you would sing it" obscures the fact that there are different ways to sing "it," and each way has its adherents. In the absence of universally agreed-upon objective standards, the ability to define Gaelicness must turn to the question of social power and legitimacy.

Claiming Gaelicness

There are many apparent contradictions in the emphasis on language in this case. The most obvious is that most of the musicians and dancers engaged in the popularizing of Cape Breton forms do not speak the language; this includes the most vocal supporters, such as Alasdair Fraser and Hamish Moore. As one fiddler put it: "I never have heard strathspeys—Highland Gaelic strathspeys— played with such life, and such Gaelicness in them or something, it's just un- believable. Even though I don't speak the language."

The assertion of a Gaelic element by non-Gaelic-speakers can give rise to some unusual situations. At a step-dancing workshop I attended in Edinburgh, the instructor took a few minutes to explain the relationship of Gaelic song and dance, and as a demonstration she had us dance while she sang a *puirt-a-beul*. Before singing it, she apologized for her lack of fluency in the language, ex- plaining that she heard the song at a workshop and wrote down the words phonetically. One of the students told her not to worry, as "none of us would know the difference anyway." The student's response reveals how Gaelic serves an authenticating role even when it is neither assumed nor intended to be un- derstood.

Placed in a historical context, however, the claims of non-Gaelic Scots to represent Gaelicness are not unusual; it fits the long-established pattern of Lowland appropriation of Highland culture. When kilts, for example, were repackaged as a pan-Scottish badge of identity, one consequence was that all Scots were equally entitled to the symbolic ownership of the kilt. With ownership comes the legitimacy to define the meaning of that which is owned, since it is now a case of self-definition. Thus, the power to define the symbolic meaning of the kilt long ago passed from the Gaels to the Scots as a whole. And given the demographic and social dominance of non-Gaels over Gaels, this effectively means that the Gaels have long ceded, however involuntarily, control of what the kilt means.

Other emblems of Gaelic society were similarly appropriated: bagpipes, tartan, even Gaelic song. Highland history has been largely written by historians who know no Gaelic (Kennedy 1999). One only has to imagine a historian of France or Germany with no command of those languages to see the irony. Yet the irony is rarely apparent to the 98 percent of the Scottish population who do not speak Gaelic, as they are the inheritors of more than two centuries of national mythmaking that encourages the harvesting of the Highlands for cultural identity-bolstering. As a Gaelic-learner from Canada put it:

> I think it has everything to do with mainstream English-speaking Scottish identity and how they sort of mediate the problems that they face: economic problems, social problems, problems that come from being a region, essentially, in terms of the political/legal status of a very centralized nation-state. So, yeah, you see things deployed selectively for purposes that have nothing to do with the interests or the dynamics of Gaelic culture, Highland culture. But I think that's part of what's going on with step dance, you know, the fiddle traditions. There's something missing in Lowland culture, and this will help us be whole.

Thus a sense of entitlement to claim any desirable aspect of Gaelic culture, combined with social dominance, gives any Anglophone Scot the legitimacy to define Gaelicness. As a result, there is a potential danger in the Cape Breton project. The most cynical view would hold that at the end of the day, non-Gaels are using Canadian Gaels to tell Scottish Gaels how to be Gaelic. This doubly marginalizes Scottish Gaels, whose control of their own identity is further weakened at the same time they are in effect being told they have failed in their historic duty to supply the rest of Scotland with Highland authenticity.

This view would of course not go down well at all with the Anglophone boosters of Cape Breton, and there are several positions from which to critique it. First of all, not all of them are concerned with identity issues to begin with. Many musicians and dancers I interviewed were simply attracted to the aesthetics of the music and dance. It is fun, lively, exciting, different, new, and so on. And sure, the historical fact that this came from Scotland is nice, but that is hardly the primary motivating factor for them.

Others point out that all of Scotland was once Gaelic-speaking, and therefore all Scots share a Gaelic heritage. Of course one might then point out the incongruity of reaching back over a thousand years for a Gaelic identity but only two hundred years for the music to bolster it. Alternately, many of those involved do have connections with Gaelic Scotland. Of the people I interviewed, anyone who had Gaelic-speaking grandparents, or great-grandparents, was sure to highlight this fact to me. So for them one could argue that their search for roots is more personal, familial, and immediate, and therefore more "legitimate."

Finally, the view that the Gaels themselves are a powerless and put-upon minority, unified in their sense of oppression, flies in the face of both current social theory and the plain empirical evidence. Though clearly subordinate to Anglophone Scots in terms of demographic, economic, and political power, they are hardly bereft of the wherewithal to make their voices heard. In the sphere of traditional music and dance, their status as "contemporary ancestors" often engenders a degree of deference that borders on the patronizing. And for every Gael who resents the theft of their identity, there is another who wishes more Lowlanders would take up their traditions.

Nevertheless, the question of cultural power and legitimacy persists. Even without casting non-Gaels as villains and Gaels as helpless victims, the historical and current imbalance in cultural authority cannot be ignored. Those whose motives are benign must still recognize the contested ground they tread. The lack of consensus within the Gaelic-speaking community simply highlights the fact that claims of power and legitimacy *are* contested, and therefore unsettled. The short history of Ceòlas illustrates these complexities.

Hamish Moore saw the island of South Uist, a Gaelic-speaking stronghold in the Outer Hebrides, as the ideal location for his project to reintegrate the music, dance, and language traditions represented by Cape Breton. One can see straightaway the potential pitfalls; a non-Gaelic-speaker from the Lowlands, with significant cultural capital as a respected piper, sets up a school in the heart of the *Gàidhealtachd,* hiring several tutors from Cape Breton to teach a largely non-Gaelic student body music and dance styles that are touted as more Gaelic than those practiced by the locals.

By all accounts there were some local resentments, some of which remain. Many islanders I spoke with initially saw the school as an outside imposition. They found it alienating and a bit bizarre to have English monoglot Canadians brought in to teach Gaelic arts. One of my informants saw an injustice in the hiring of overseas instructors with "never a nod to the local box players." Emily McEwan-Fujita (2002) also noted grumblings about the fairness of hiring Cape Bretoners but not paying locals on the volunteer committee.

Yet to leave the picture as I have just painted it would be grossly one-sided. Moore did not found the school by himself; he was joined by a local committee, by *Proiseact nan Ealain* (The Gaelic Arts Project), and by Allan MacDonald, a Gaelic-speaking piper from the West Highlands. Control of Ceòlas has now passed to a board composed entirely of *Uibhistich,* or Uist folk, ameliorating earlier misgivings of outside impositions. Some of the Cape Bretoners brought over *do* speak Gaelic, often becoming local celebrities of a sort. And there is no shortage of islanders who agree with the Ceòlas philosophy, and who recognized the Gaelic imprint of the Cape Breton style based on their own perspectives and not any on dogma from the Lowlands.

If the place of Gaelicness in the Lowland identity is problematic, the Gaels' own sense of their Scottishness is equally so. Some Gaels claim not to feel Scottish at all, reserving the term for Lowlanders and thus implying that the Lowland and Scottish identities are the same. They may resent attempts by "Scots" to claim their identity. This was the reaction of a Gaelic singer I interviewed:

> I mean, it's difficult to define Scottish culture anyway, isn't it? But to me, it's something that happens on the mainland, you know, Scottish, Scottishness. Nothing to do with me . . . And I suspect that people who make it Scottish, it's because they're not from the islands. And instead of just admitting that, they go about saying this is Scottish. I find these inaccuracies creep up a lot when people are describing—cultural things. They sort of twist them a wee bit and bend them, to make them part of it, because they want to be part of it, you know.

This sentiment echoes an essay by Donald Meek published in the collection *Being Scottish.* Born on the island of Tiree, Meek grew up within sight of the mainland, which is where, for him, Scotland began:

> Scotland was some place far away in a big, blue schoolbook. I reasoned that those mountains on the hazy eastern skyline must belong to Scotland . . . This is a nation which wants to claim its Gaelicness when the couthy clarion call of national identity has to be sounded abroad, but it is only too happy to disavow its Gaelic roots if they need practical, and particularly financial, attention at home. (Devine and Logue 2002, 198)

Other Gaels have a much more forgiving attitude toward Lowland interest in their culture, and this extends to the interest in Cape Breton. A few Gaelic-speakers I interviewed expressed a desire to see *more* non-Gaels take up the language and culture. Referring to those who do claim a Highland identity, one said:

> *Tha mise toilichte gum biodh iad a' faireachdainn mar sin. Bhithinn na bu thoilichte nam biodh fios aca carson a tha iad 'faireachdainn mar sin.*

[quoting a Gaelic activist:] "Gaelic is the language of our country. It's ours, it's not just the Gaels'. It belongs to us." Well, *an aon cheist.* "Belongs to us." *Bhithinnsa uabhasach toilichte nan canadh iad uile sin,* aye? *Agus nan canadh iad siud ris an ceòl Cheap Breatainn.*

I'm happy that they would feel that way. I'd be happier if they would know why they feel that way.

[quoting a Gaelic activist:] "Gaelic is the language of our country. It's ours, it's not just the Gaels'. It belongs to us." Well, the same question. "Belongs to us." I'd be awfully happy if they all said that, aye? And if they said that about Cape Breton music.

Other Gaelic-speakers mentioned that in their view Gaelic is dying and the Gaels will soon disappear, so they look to fellow Scots to carry on the Gaelic tradition, even in an altered form. This view may explain why more than one Gaelic-speaker I interviewed regarded the status of kilts and bagpipes as badges of national identity to be a compliment rather than cultural theft. Lowlanders may actually serve as a buffer between Gaelicness and Englishness, a safe zone where linguistic and cultural assimilation can take place without sacrificing a Scottish identity. Consider that many Gaelic-oriented music festivals and workshops include Lowland Scots singers as a matter of course, yet representatives of the English song tradition would be unheard of. This is the flip-side of an ideology that grants the Borders fiddler a cultural claim to Cape Breton but excludes the fiddler from Northumberland (and that inflates the difference between the Borderer and the Northumbrian).

Claiming Cape Breton

Alistair MacLeod is an award-winning novelist and short story writer from Cape Breton. Setting most of his fiction in the Gaelic-speaking areas of Cape

Breton, he explores themes of kinship, community, and cultural and linguistic loss. The subject matter and his critical acclaim make many Scots eager to claim him as their own. In an article titled "Once a Scot, Always a Scot," Jim Gilchrist of *The Scotsman* quoted MacLeod's reaction to being invited to a Scottish writers conference:

> "They used to say to me, 'We're going to London, why don't you come with us—six Scottish writers,'" recalls MacLeod. "And I would say, 'But I'm not a Scottish writer, I'm Canadian,' and they'd say, 'Oh yes you are a Scottish writer; you've only been away for 200 years.'" (2002)

This sentiment is widespread in Scotland; in most major bookstores, Mac-Leod's books are placed in the Scottish Fiction section. While undoubtedly meant as a compliment, claiming MacLeod as a Scot (quite literally in this case) highlights the more general pattern of cultural appropriation evident in the traditional music and dance scene. The Cape Bretoners I spoke to were generally ambivalent about MacLeod's status. "When I found his books in the Scottish section, I was kind of, not insulted, but, for God's sakes you know, he's Canadian, he's from Cape Breton! And it's kind of, not taking credit, but there's so much more to it."

A similar ambivalence is even more evident when Cape Bretoners living in Scotland discuss their own iconic status. It often seems that they are the subject of a tug-of-war between Scots with opposing views on Cape Breton's place in Scottish culture. The same informant quoted above spoke of being pressured into playing the fiddle at a community concert, to the dismay of one local: "and he was like, 'Oh bloody bloody Cape Breton, da-da-da-da-da, this is how we'll all play.' And I was just like, great, you know, I didn't want to be here anyway . . . Sometimes I think everybody that's like 'Oh, Cape Breton this and Cape Breton that,' I just feel, okay, shut up and go spend a summer in Cape Breton, and then maybe, you know what I mean? That's how it feels sometimes."

As the fashion for Cape Breton music and dance progresses (and perhaps wanes) in Scotland, the resulting contribution to the Scottish scene will likely be quite different from its Cape Breton counterpart. The tunes, steps, and techniques may resemble each other, but the social contexts—the reasons for playing and dancing in the first place—are miles apart. Scottish step dancers, for example, rarely if ever have the opportunity to participate in social dances such as square sets, and many of them wouldn't be interested if they did. Step dancing is thus restricted to staged performances, which, according to one informant, creates a very different social dynamic among the dancers: "I thought to myself, this is very un–Cape Breton, you know. I mean, Cape Breton is 'Oh, you want to learn some steps, come on in, I'll make you some tea, and some food as well, and you can stay with me,' you know. And now you have people saying, 'hmm, we've got to keep the steps to ourselves, because I want to be asked to this event, or to that event,' or whatever. What's Cape Breton about that?"

Perhaps the greatest irony of the Cape Breton project is the almost complete absence of Cape Breton voices in the debate. In part this may be due to the disinterest of most Cape Bretoners who come to Scotland to teach and perform. Those I spoke with had no interest in gaining converts to a cultural mission to re-Gaelicize Scottish music. And the Scots I interviewed who were taught by Cape Bretoners confirmed that any rhetoric they received came from other Scots and not their instructors. Every Cape Bretoner I spoke to did admit to a strong preference for their own music and dance, but in the words of one Canadian I interviewed, their attitude to teaching or performing in Scotland tends to be more along the lines of: "'Oh, they really like our music,' and 'Certainly nice to be back in the Old Country,' you know. But there's no huge issues that have to be resolved [laughs]."

Of course, what is contested about Cape Breton has nothing whatsoever to do with Cape Bretoners themselves; it is about the utility of the island's traditions to Scotland and Scottishness. As Hamish Moore wrote in the liner notes to one of his recordings, "I am grateful that Cape Breton exists and has preserved and held our music and dance culture in trust" (1994). But the ambivalence of the Cape Bretoners I interviewed suggests that this claim of Scottish cultural ownership of Cape Breton—"our music and dance culture"—cannot be taken for granted.

Scots who pursue Cape Breton music and dance styles are taking part, wittingly or not, in a debate over what it means to be Scottish in the twenty-first century. Their embrace of Cape Breton necessarily implies a claim of ownership of that tradition. Gaels and Anglophones in both Scotland and Cape Breton all have a stake in the discussion, but their voices are not all equal. Many proponents of Cape Breton music and dance see it as a means to undo the de-Gaelicization of Scottish traditions. But if they ignore the distribution of social power—control of the means of cultural production, as it were—they could end up repeating a long history of cultural appropriation and marginalization.

Works Cited

Ascherson, Neal. 2002. *Stone Voices: The Search for Scotland.* London: Granta.
Calder, Angus. 2002. *Scotlands of the Mind.* Edinburgh: Luath.

Devine, T. M. 1999. *The Scottish Nation, 1700–2000.* London: Penguin.

Devine, Tom, and Paddy Logue. 2002. *Being Scottish.* Edinburgh: Polygon.

Dunlay, Kate. 1992. "The Playing of Traditional Scottish Dance Music: Old and New World Styles and Practices." In *Celtic Languages and Celtic Peoples: Proceedings of the Second North American Congress of Celtic Studies.* Halifax, Nova Scotia: St. Mary's University.

Ferguson, William. 1998. *The Identity of the Scottish Nation.* Edinburgh: Edinburgh UP.

Gibson, John. 1998. *Traditional Gaelic Bagpiping, 1745–1945.* Montreal: McGill-Queen's UP.

Gilchrist, Jim. 2002. "Once a Scot, Always a Scot." *The Scotsman,* August 17.

Harvie, Christopher. 2002. *Scotland: A Short History.* Oxford: Oxford UP.

Houston, Robert A., and William W. J. Knox. 2002. *The New Penguin History of Scotland.* London: Penguin.

Kennedy, Michael. 2002. *Gaelic Nova Scotia: An Economic, Cultural, and Social Impact Study.* Halifax: Nova Scotia Museum.

———. 1999. "'Lochaber No More'": A Critical Examination of Highland Emigration Mythology." In *Myth, Migration, and the Making of Memory: Scotia and Nova Scotia, c. 1700–1990,* ed. Marjory Harper and Michael Vance, 267–97. Halifax, Nova Scotia: Fernwood.

McCrone, David. 2001. *Understanding Scotland: The Sociology of a Nation.* London: Routledge.

McEwan-Fujita, Emily. 2002. "'Will No One Tell Me What She Sings?'—Language and the Aesthetics of Scottish Gaelic Song." Paper presented at American Anthropological Association Annual Meeting.

McKay, Ian. 1992. "Tartanism Triumphant: The Construction of Scottishness in Nova Scotia, 1933–1954." *Acadiensis* 21, no. 2: 5–47.

Meek, Donald E. 2003. *Caran an t-Saoghail/The Wiles of the World: Anthology of Nineteenth-Century Scottish Gaelic Verse.* Edinburgh: Birlinn.

Moore, Hamish. 1994. *Dannsa air an Drochaid/Stepping on the Bridge.* Audio CD, Greentrax Records.

Moore, Maggie. 1995. "Scottish Step Dancing." Scottish Arts Council. (Available at *http://www.tullochgorm.com/scottish.html*)

Murphy, Peter. 1991. *Buddy MacMaster: The Master of the Cape Breton Fiddle.* SeaBright Murphy Video Productions.

Newton, Michael. 2000. *A Handbook of the Scottish Gaelic World.* Dublin: Four Courts.

Shaw, John. 1993. "Language, Music, and Local Aesthetics: Views from Gaeldom and Beyond." *Scottish Language* 11: 37–61.

Statistics Canada. 2001. Census of Canada.

Wilson, Mark, and Kate Dunlay, eds. 2002. *Traditional Fiddle Music of Cape Breton Volume 1: Mabou Coal Mines.* Audio CD liner notes. Cambridge, MA: Rounder Records.

7

The North American Émigré, Highland Games, and Social Capital in International Communities

Grant Jarvie

Lord and Lady Malcolm Douglas Hamilton founded the American-Scottish Foundation in 1956 with the broad purpose of building bonds of interests and cooperation, both social and commercial, between the people of Scotland and the United States. An increasing number of Americans of Scottish descent have joined regional Scottish and clan societies, attend Highland games, and subscribe to Scottish-oriented publications. The U.S Senate conceived of Tartan Day in 1998 in recognition of the contribution made by Scots to the foundation, character, and prosperity of America. The date selected was the sixth of April, the same day when in 1320 the Declaration of Arbroath, affirming an independent Scotland, was signed and presented to the Pope. This same declaration allegedly informed the American Declaration of Independence. Enter the American-Scottish Foundation Web site, and you will be informed that there are at least thirteen million Americans claiming Scottish ancestry, according to the latest census figures, and that further research indicates the figure might be nearer thirty-five million. The American-Scottish Foundation is one of nine American-Scottish organisations forming the Scottish Coalition that also includes the Association of Scottish Games and Festivals.

Adopting as its logo the Scottish thistle and the St. Andrew's flag, the Association of Scottish Games and Festivals was founded in 1981 as a clearinghouse for information about American-Scottish Highland games and gatherings that are held in locations across the United States (see *http://www.asgf.org/*). Their listings are not exhaustive, but include only those games for which the association has given its approval. These Highland gatherings and games can be found in every month from January, with the Central Florida Highland Games, until November, with the Foothills Highland Games in North Carolina. The calendar of Highland games and gatherings in America is longer than that in Scotland. Games organisers in the United States in part aim to educate and promote an interest in traditional Scottish arts of piping, dancing, athletic achievement, and culture. Highland games schedules include traditional events such as Highland dancing, piping, and strength events such as the tug-of-war, but also more bizarre inventions of tradition such as "the bonny knees contest" (in which a blindfolded woman judges the most appealing knees from a line-up of kilted males), a "haggis toss," the kirkin' of the tartan, and golf classics.

On the one hand, the descendants of early émigrés from the Highlands of Scotland would appear to have much to celebrate in North America. The contribution made by Scots to Canada and the United States is frequently acknowledged (Hunter 1994, 1996, 2000; Jarvie 2000). Stornoway-born Alexander Mackenzie and Simon Fraser from Strathglass left their names on two of Canada's greatest rivers. Glasgow-born Sir John A. MacDonald, whose father was from Strath Oykel and his mother from Strathspey, was to become Canada's first Prime Minister. It was MacDonald, along with two other Scots, George Stephen and Donald Smith (later to become Lord Strathcona), who were to be instrumental in building the Canadian Pacific Railway. The only minister to sign the American Declaration of Independence was of Scots descent, as were the founders of many universities, such as Princeton. On the other hand, a more critical acknowledgment of the totality of the Scots émigrés' involvement in North America would also acknowledge the darker side of this émigré culture. The nineteenth-century white South was by no means wholly Scottish, let alone Highland, in origin. The "bonnie blue flag" of the breakaway and Confederate states was modelled on the Scottish national flag, or Saltire (Jarvie 2000; Ray 1998). All Confederate states were slave-holding, as were many non-Confederate states. The organisation that tried to rebuild white supremacy among the wreckage of the Confederate defeat became known, in an unwanted tribute to the Highlands, as the Klan. Scotland's influence on North America manifests itself in ways other than the continent's longstanding fondness of Highland games, pipe bands, and tartan.

Much has already been written about the significance and place of Highland games and ancient Scottish sports in the life of the migrant Scot and how popular cultural forms such as sport are absorbed, reconfigured, assimilated, transformed, or reproduced in various host communities such as America, Canada, Australia, New Zealand, England, and Ireland, to name but a few places where émigré Scots have settled, moved on, or returned from (Donaldson 1986; Gillespie 2000; Hague 2000, 2002; Jarvie 1991, 2000; MacLennan 1998). The life of the émigré Scot has been the subject of much scholarly attention in the field of Scottish history, most notably in the works of James Hunter, through contributions such as *Glencoe and the Indians* (1996) and *On the Other Side of Sorrow* (1995), but also in Jim Hewitson's *Far Off in Sunlit Places* (1998). While not dominating scholarly accounts, sporting festivals have contributed to what writers such as Tom Nairn (1981) have referred to as the subculture of the émigré.

Despite the varied perspectives of contributors to this book, all of them prove that internationality, and indeed social capital, can be sustained and developed through North American-Scottish communities' interest and involvement in Scottish sports, history, and heritage. Innocent questions about traditional games and sports can soon lead to heated debates about culture, history, the impossible search for authenticity, and the values associated with sporting practices. In *Highland Games: The Making of the Myth* (1991) and *Sport in the Making of Celtic Cultures* (1999), I rightly or wrongly argued that Scottish Highland gatherings and games and the many forms of sport within the Celtic cultures of Europe could not be properly understood without a rigorous and systematic attempt to ask how the development of these activities was influenced by the historical and social conditions of the day. It is impossible to fully explain the nature of the émigré experience or forms of ethnic culture without asking where people have come from, travelled to, and how they have adapted and/or resisted parent or host cultures. If *Highland Games: The Making of the Myth* had been written today, it would have been a far better book had the author been much more critical about America's growing obsession with its Scottish connections, which are so clearly on display during the North American Highland games season, or the extent to which different traditions of Highland games have become international and yet acquired varied meanings in different ethnic contexts. In essence, the value of recent postcolonial thinking about sport might have some value in terms of rethinking certain aspects of the way in which certain Highland games have travelled the globe (Bale and Cronin 2002).

Whatever narratives are told about the changing nature of Highland games and sports in different parts of the world, the defence of the traditional Highland gatherings and games needs to be sensitive to the bigger diagnostic pictures necessary to orientate social support and political focus for the diversity of traditional games and sport throughout the world. The current Scottish Parliament is enthusiastic about supporting internationality and Scottish-American exchange. The current Scottish Minister for tourism, culture, and sport, Frank McAveety, in almost his second day of office, attended a Highland games in the United States as part of Tartan Day celebrations. All of these and other examples serve to indicate that the study of Highland gatherings and games within the North American contexts (Canada and the United States) needs to draw upon the current political contexts that might be available. Scottish and North American Highland games do not exist in a social or political vacuum, but are part and parcel of the broader contexts in which they are situated.

The issues at the heart of this chapter are relatively straightforward: (1) the relationship between sport, ethnicity, and social capital, (2) the issue of ethnicity and America's growing obsession with Scotland, (3) the place of Highland gatherings and games in transnational American communities and (4) a defence of traditional games and sports, such as Highland gatherings and games against the power of international or global sport in the twenty-first century. In order to achieve this I have divided the chapter into the following four sections: (1) a discussion of the relationship between sport, ethnicity, and social capital; (2) a comment on American culture and society and the place of sport in terms of its social value, (3) an account of Highland gatherings and their multifaceted role in North American culture and society, and (4) an exploration of the social value of postcolonial games and sports.

While many contemporary accounts of global sport tend to emphasise the economic and cultural value of sport, the social value of sport is often forgotten. Yet, in both an intergenerational sense and a community sense, Highland gatherings and other sports have the potential to hold communities together and help generations communicate with one another. Exchange through sports even helps community members learn about how democracy works through cooperation. If the social aspects of Highland gatherings and games are prioritised in this chapter, then so too is the notion of social capital, which refers specifically here to the resources generated through the networks, norms, and trust that can be fostered through groups and communities taking on mutual obligations, such as organising a Highland gathering or games.

Sport, Ethnicity, and Social Capital

Allegedly, Britain has been actively antiracist, as well as accepting of ethnic diversity, for almost four decades now. The liberal view that has underpinned public policy during this time has tended to be that the way forward is through equal opportunities accompanied by cultural diversity in an atmosphere of mutual tolerance. The relative success of this vision depended upon promoting core values such as tolerance, mutuality, appreciation of cultural diversity, and an implicit negotiation of the cultural hegemony of the indigenous British

(Lloyd 2002). This view has been under a sustained attack from multicultural-ists and pluralists who believe that this form of liberalism is at best restricting and at worst racist. Liberalism is now attacked for combining a monocultural public realm and as contradicting the value of cultural diversity in the name of human rights (human rights now being viewed not in absolute terms but quali-fied by the logic of multiculturalism).

America and Canada have perhaps been the boldest practitioners of multi-culturalism and have relatively open immigration policies. In the United States the attack on the World Trade Center of September 11 has resulted in an im-mense boost to patriotism, a rise in social capital, and a reduction in racial conflict. The challenge for Britain and any new liberalism remains that of pro-posing a sense of inclusive identity that is capacious enough to include all who wish to live within it peacefully in an atmosphere of mutual tolerance and support. It is not necessary to omit sport from such forms of intervention, since sport per se has had close associations with both ethnicity and social capital.

It is impossible to describe modern life accurately without acknowledging the impact games and sports have worldwide. Much of the research into sport and ethnicity has tended to focus on issues of identity, multiculturalism, rac-ism, religion, and a pluralist attitude towards the tolerance of minorities where their beliefs and distinct sporting customs and practices often clash with the laws and customs of the majority (Bradley 1998, 2002; Jarvie and Burnett 2000). Struggles for recognition through sport and other forms of culture often assume the guise of identity politics. Highland gatherings and games in North America provide different ethnic groups forms of identity that are far from politically neutral. Some or all of the following arguments might apply—that North American Highland gatherings and games (1) are a form of cultural politics that helps to assert certain identities; (2) help to produce certain stereo-types, prejudices, and myths about various ethnic minority groups; (3) have some inherent property that makes a sport an instrument of integration and or conflict; (4) have been part of the colonial and imperial gaze that needs to be revisited within any postcolonial discussion of the world today; (5) may be an arena of bigotry and sectarianism; and finally (6) occur within particular ritu-alistic settings in which ethnicity contributes to a collective imagery of patri-otism, nationalism, localism, regionalism, and other forms of collective social identities. Yet perhaps the fundamental issue here is that any form of Highland gathering or games that is aimed at countering the demeaning cultural repre-sentation of subordinated groups (rather than fostering integration and the celebration of authentic collective identities) has to be careful that it does not in fact reproduce separatism, group enclaves, conformism, and intolerance.

Identity history or politics alone can be reductionistic and runs the risk of being viewed as fundamentalism.

Recently, those considering the value of sport in terms of its contribution to forms of social capital have addressed sports' role in the building of community relations, including ethnic and diaspora relations. James Coleman's (1988) concept of social capital has become popular within contemporary policy-oriented discourses about sport (Coalter 2000; Harris 1998). Coleman introduced his now well-known concept in discussing a society's capacity for educational achievement, but implicit within the notion of social capital is that the making of social capital can be active within any social sphere that involves trust. Since the late 1980s, developing social capital has been viewed as a way of renewing democracy (Hirst 1994; Hutton 1995; Marquand 1988; Putnam 1995; Schuller 1997). It refers to the network of social groups and relationships that fosters cooperative working and community well-being. It involves communities and other social groups exercising a certain degree of trust through taking on mutual obligations. Do the North American Highland gatherings and games make a contribution to this form of social understanding, or do they set communities apart from one another?

There are at least two reasons why social capital has attracted so much attention. On the one hand, civil society and communities depend upon it. Social capital contributes to social inclusion. Social groups and individuals learn more when they can draw upon the cultural resources of people around them. They learn from each other directly, but they also learn to trust that the social arrangements are in place to ensure that learning, through a multitude of mediums, including sport, will benefit themselves both culturally and for employment opportunities. They also trust that their own family or friends will grow up in a community that is intellectually stimulating. Social capital can have these effects most readily where it is embodied in the social structure—most notably, formal educational institutions and cultural organisations that have a commitment to other outcomes, such as learning.

On the other hand, democracy depends upon social capital. This is true in one very obvious sense: that democracy depends upon everyone trusting that everyone else will operate the system constructively. When that trust breaks down—for example, as a reaction to certain screening practices aimed at the control of drugs in athletes or the failure to deliver sustainable sporting and economic benefits for urban ghettos, or the adequate funding arrangements for sport in universities or local authorities—the result is cynicism about democracy in general. But the potential role of social capital is more profound than this, because citizenship requires knowledge and people who know how to work with others towards common goals. To paraphrase the words of a former Secretary-General of the Council of Europe, Daniel Tarschys, the hidden face of sport is also the tens of thousands of enthusiasts who find in their football, rowing, athletics, and rock-climbing clubs a place for meeting and exchange but above all the training ground for community life (Jarvie 2003). In this microcosm people learn to take responsibility, to follow rules, to accept one another, to look for consensus, and, indeed, seen from this angle, sport par excellence is the ideal school for democracy. The Highland games of the North American émigré cultures offer one testing ground to see if this idea can be substantiated or whether it is an ideology removed from practice. Do North American Highland games help to produce a better understanding of democracy, of respecting others, or do they create isolated group enclaves that lead to separatism and intolerance?

Sport and the Decline and Rise of Social Capital in America

In an essay titled *Bowling Alone* (1995), political scientist Robert Putnam wrote that without at first noticing it we have been pulled apart from one another and from our communities in the last third of the century. He went on to document the decline of social capital in America, which he defined as social networks, norms, and trust that enable participants to work together more effectively to pursue shared objectives. Putnam used this notion to analyse the phenomenon of what he called civic disengagement. By this he referred to the decline in participation not just in formal political activity but also in all kinds of social activities, including sport and communal physical activity. The decline of social capital allegedly included the decreasing membership in voluntary organisations, decreased participation in organised activities, and the decrease in time spent in informal socialising and visiting.

Americans were viewed as becoming less trusting of one another, with a close correlation existing between social trust and membership in civic associations. The amount of time devoted to watching television emerged as the prime suspect, although not the only suspect. In some ways, television privatised the experience of sport and replaced other activities that had created networks and trust and supported social capital and the pursuit of shared objectives. Community activities became less popular as people stayed at home for entertainment.

Following the events of September 11, 2001, Putnam returned to his survey base to track changes in U.S. social and political ideas. The former attitudes of individualism, lack of trust, and disengagement of public life had been disrupted, and Putnam now found that (1) levels of political consciousness and engagement were substantially higher than the previous year; (2) trust in government, trust in police, and interest in politics are all up; (3) Americans are more likely to have attended a political meeting or a community project; (4) more Americans trust one another than in 2000; and (5) intermarriage across racial and ethnic lines was more popular (Lloyd 2002).

It is precisely these sorts of issues that must be at the heart of any contemporary defence of social and cultural activities if the North American Scottish Highland gatherings and games are to be viewed as a valuable part of twenty-first-century American culture. In considering their relationship to current events, it may be necessary to question some of the assumptions about the Scottishness of North American Highland games. Here, I consider their social value, rather than their economic or tourist or heritage value, to be important within the current political climate.

The identities encouraged by North American Highland gatherings and games are usually multifaceted, and, like other traditional sporting pastimes, they can help to forge not only a sense of self but also a sense of place, a sense of belonging, a sense of inclusion or exclusion, and a sense of geography and history. They can contribute to a mythical or real sense of community that can often last a lifetime. North American Highland gatherings as a facet of the International Highland Games Circuit come in different forms and sizes, and collectively their defence as a forum for traditional games and sport lies not in their potential as a form of free-market or global entity but rather in their social and international importance. The following two examples are both illustrative of some of the issues associated with the Scottish North American Highland gatherings and games.

Highland Games in the Bluegrass State and a Quest for Culture

The Good people of Glasgow, Kentucky, are mighty proud of their roots, as one of the larger U.S. Highland Games proves . . . The American-Scots of Glasgow, Kentucky, are one of the many groups who attend the annual Highland Games day in many parts of the United States and Canada. Glasgow is smack in the middle of a dry county, in the crucible of the Southern United States Bible Belt. (*The Herald*, May 12, 1999: 5)

A Scot, Major John Gorin, founded the town of Glasgow, Kentucky, with a land grant he received for service as a Patriot in the American Revolutionary War. Two hundred years later, Glasgow continues to proclaim its Scottishness. The local high school band is known as the "Scotties," and they parade in tartan regalia. The town has its own monster in the water, the "Barrie of Loch Barren." Its Highland games claim to be one of the fifth or sixth largest Highland games that take place in the United States and Canada each year.

Events involve tossing the caber, country dancing contests, soccer and rugby sevens, genealogy seminars, and meetings with visiting clan chiefs. I spoke to the guest chief of the 1995 Glasgow Highland Games, Malcolm Forbes, of Castle Forbes in Aberdeenshire, whose main home was in fact in Surrey in the South of England. He sounded like he was from Surrey. Even Colin Grant Adams, the games' guest artist and writer of "The Glasgow Highland Games Song," is from Winchester, England. Many participants become involved in Scottish heritage events by chance. The Clan Kennedy tent was manned by Donald Cannaday from Cambridge, Ohio. He traced his roots in 1986 after his daughter married a Scot only to find out that Cannaday was a variant spelling of Kennedy. Now Donald is the chief of the Kennedy Society of America, presiding over 545 members.

In the MacBean tent sat Philip Bean, who came from North Carolina to spread the word about his glorious name—how Alan Bean, an astronaut aboard Apollo 11, left half a yard of McBain tartan on the moon and how L. L. Bean, the clothing giant, is one of theirs. Participants at the MacDonald tent try to reproduce the legendry hospitality of their Glencoe forebearers. David Macdonald was deputy mid-South commissioner of Clan Macdonald, with more than five thousand members and boasting to be the great-great-great-great-great-grandson of Flora Macdonald—the same Flora Macdonald who helped the Jacobite leader Charles Edward Stewart escape to mainland Scotland from the Outer Hebrides in 1746. She herself emigrated to North Carolina in 1774 with her husband, Allan Macdonald, of Kingsburgh, only to return to Scotland to die on Skye, where she was buried. The current, *American* David Macdonald—father of another Alan MacDonald—claimed to be the true sixteenth chieftain of Kingsburgh.

It is undeniable that the organisers of the Glasgow, Kentucky Highland Games are fired with a historical and cultural enthusiasm to be identified as North American Scots and that this might be interpreted as a quest for culture, a need for distinctiveness and expressive individuation. In Glasgow they know their stuff. The Highland games field in Barren River State Resort Park is crammed with clan tents and busy stalls, all proclaiming a sense of Scottishness that is loud and proud, knowledgeable and impressive. In the middle of July, the show will move on to North Carolina, where that all-consuming passion for all things Scottish is equally evident, as the Grandfather Mountain Highland Games attracts as many as thirty thousand people over the four days of events.

The programme will tell you that these ancient Highland athletic competitions can be traced to the eleventh century. It is interesting to note that in the United States as well as in Scotland, Highland/Gaelic culture is invariably cited as a potential source of that which is authentic or that which is traditional.

Identifying aspects of Scottish and Gaelic culture as traditional or authentic and dismissing others as invented or romantic is a feature of much of the revisionist history that has attempted to explain the place of Gaelic culture in both Scotland and among the wider Scottish diaspora. Linked to this has been the assertion that Scottish customs, including sporting customs, were transported with the émigré to far-off lands and flourished in contexts that were free from the pressures and turmoils that were being experienced in Scotland during the first half of the nineteenth century. The subculture of the émigré has been the focus of much ire in this revisionist history, simply because it has attempted to promote a particular vision of Scotland. Admittedly the term "authentic" is somewhat problematic, and it is perhaps more realistic to suggest that forms of culture, including sporting culture, have been promoted, marginalised, eroded, and even displaced without being drawn into a mythical debate about the authentic or traditional expression of Scottish culture.

The fact that either authentic or invented Gaelic culture has furnished so many of the worldwide symbols of Scottishness—tartan, bagpipes, whisky, pictures of scenes from Highland games, castles enshrouded in mist with monsters from Loch Ness, and golf courses—is somewhat puzzling. Let us not forget that in the nineteenth century the symbolic appropriation of Gaelic culture into mainstream culture could take place only after the substantive social barriers that the symbols of Gaelic culture stood for had receded into the past and after the Highlands had ceased to be a political threat to Britain and the Lowlands. Gaelic culture had to be reinvented before it could become a potent marker of difference and appropriated as a symbol of Scottish distinctiveness (Jarvie 1991, 54–55). Yet, paradoxically, in sporting terms, that which is celebrated in Scotland as the sport of the Gael is shinty and not "Highland athletic competitions," which in their contemporary form have become "Highland games." Did the émigré culture of the eighteenth and nineteenth centuries bring with it a Highland games culture to North America? I think not.

Scottish Highland Gatherings and Games as North American Scottish Culture

Various phases of emigration, and to a lesser extent migration from the Highlands, have often been viewed as part of a conscious protest by sections of

Highland society aimed at preserving traditional customs and a way of life. Those who emigrated to the Maritime Provinces of Canada between 1780 and 1820 took with them not only the values and close-knit texture of the local society from which they came but also the material culture and traditions that both contributed to and were constitutive of their home communities. Numerous Scottish societies, St. Andrew's clubs, Burns clubs, Thistle societies, and Caledonian societies rapidly emerged after about 1820. By 1903 the Register of Scottish Societies in the United States and the Dominion of Canada functioned to relieve the poverty of Scottish émigrés or their families; foster and encourage a love of Scotland, its history, literature, and customs (including national athletic games); and promote friendly and sociable relations among the membership. Such societies might have included those formed in Charleston in 1729; Philadelphia as early as 1747; Savannah, Georgia, by 1737 or 1750; New York City in 1756; Halifax, Nova Scotia, in 1768; St. John, New Brunswick, in 1798; Albany in 1803; Buffalo in 1843; the Burns Club of New York in 1847; and the Detroit St Andrew's Society of 1849 (which held its first Highland games in 1867). By the time the *Kingussie Record* of 1903 had reported on the efforts of the New York Highlanders' Shinty Club, traditional sporting customs had become part of the social and cultural fabric of many émigré communities. When the North American Caledonian Association was formed towards the end of the nineteenth century, Scottish Highland games and other ancient sporting traditions had become focal points of émigré reunions. The San Francisco and Glengarry Highland Games will serve as but two illustrative examples.

The Caledonian Club of San Francisco held its first Highland games in 1866. Like many other émigré societies, the objectives of the club included the encouragement and practice of Highland games; the preservation of a taste for the Gaelic language and literature; and closer binding of the social links among sons and daughters of the general descendants of émigrés. One year later Donald MacLennan addressed the club in these words:

> We are assembled here this morning to participate in the sports so dear in the memories of our native land. Though transplanted, as it were, to the shores of the Pacific many thousands of miles from bonnie Scotland, still the hearts of her children warm at the recollections of their youth and beat more strongly at the mention of her name. It has been one of the peculiarities and the pride of our people, in whatever portion of the globe we may dwell, to honour and cherish all that reminds us of our earlier

years; and in those fond recollections we harbor our national games. (Donaldson 1986, 53)

Perhaps those fond recollections of youth were akin to those from the parish of Kilchoman (Islay) who "so far are so sensible of the advantages they enjoy, and are in general so contented with the situation, that very few have emigrated" (*Old Statistical Accounts of Scotland*, Vol. 20, 394). In contrast, another MacLennan—namely Hugh MacLennan, a leading exponent of Canadian national identity—expressed more a sense of relief when he returned to Montreal from the empty glens of Kintail. Comparing the two landscapes and experiences, he wrote:

Such sweeps of emptiness I never saw in Canada before I went to the Mackenzie River. But this Highland emptiness, only a few hundred miles above the massed population of England, is a far different thing from the emptiness of our own North West Territories. Above the 60th parallel in Canada you feel like nobody but God had ever been there before you, but in these deserted Highland spaces around Kintail you feel that everyone who ever mattered is dead and gone. (Hunter 1994, 141)

Hugh MacLennan was born in Cape Breton Island, Nova Scotia. But his family origins were in Kintail. His grandfather had been one of the thousands of people expelled from Scotland as a result of the Clearances. It was inevitable that MacLennan should have mixed feelings about his trip to the place where his ancestors had lived, for he knew that the Highlands were once thickly populated, and he knew that a valuable human culture, together with a distinctive way of life, had been destroyed here. He thus returned to Montreal with a profound sense of release at having escaped from those haunted places.

Today, should you venture beyond Barrisdale into the Knoydart peninsula, now one of the most isolated localities in all of Europe, you will find within its two hundred square miles no more than two or three dozen people. So completely have many of the district's original communities been obliterated, there is among modern Knoydart's population not a single person who can claim descent from any of the hundreds of families who lived there in the period before Thomas Gillespie drove his sheep into those parts. Yet as any visitor from Scotland to Ontario's Glengarry County realises, just an ocean's breadth from Knoydart and its neighbouring localities, you can find vast numbers of folk who to some extent still think of themselves as belonging to some romanticised faraway glen or shoreline. And not without some reason the author of one 1829 publication warned prospective emigrants "Go not to Glengarry if you be not a Highlander" (McLean 1991, 125). Of the 8,500 or so people living in Upper Canada's easternmost county at that time, around three-quarters were of Scottish Highland extraction and many were still largely Gaelic-speaking. Much the same was true of the 17,500 Glengarry residents of twenty years later—when it was revealed by census data that one such resident in every six was named either MacDonnell or Macdonald.

In 1819, the same year that the St. Fillans Society of Scotland held its first Highland games, the Glengarry Highland Society was organised to promote Scottish traditional sports by means of a Highland Gathering. Although not the oldest continuous games in Canada, it is certainly often referred to as one of the original Highland games. One might add that the oldest continuous Highland games would appear to be those sponsored by the Antigonish Highland Society founded in 1816, some three years before that of St. Fillans Society.

Whether it is Glengarry County in Ontario or Cape Breton Island or somewhere else, there seems to be a self-gratifying view taken in Scotland that these people just wish their ancestors had never left in the first place. The Highland roots in these communities would seem to be enormously important, but what exactly is it that is being celebrated at the Glengarry Highland games and other similar festivals, such as those in Glasgow, Kentucky? A lost past, a romantic history, a dislocated Scottish diaspora, an authentic Highland games free from the encroachment of Anglicisation, an ancient sporting tradition that has flourished in an authentic Gaelic culture that escaped the rage of improvement? Again, I think not. Certainly the Glengarry Highland Games and the pipers, the dancers, the hammer throwers, and the heavy events give the occasion a distinct sense of being associated in some way with some part of some Highland culture that in itself is as different as it is similar and in any case almost impossible to define. Or does it owe nothing to Scotland at all—a celebration of a different sense of community whose substance has nothing to do with an émigré culture and whose customs and traditions have exorcised an early culling of nostalgic pride? Is it a Glengarry sense of identity that is as different in the twenty-first century as it was in the nineteenth century? Perhaps the celebration owes as much to the Loyalist exodus from the Mohawk Valley as to that from Scotland. The years and lifetimes not of hewing peat or kelp or coal but turning forest into farmland make Glengarry County and the Glengarry Highland Games what they are today: *something that is not Scottish or Highland* at all but that celebrates being a North American Scottish Highlander. The distinction between the two contexts—the Scottish Highland context and the North American context—is absolutely crucial for understanding the social role of Highland games.

Conclusion

Highland gatherings and games, so despised because of their association with Gaelic culture in the eighteenth century, have now become highly valued in the North American context. They have become an important symbol in the lives of many ethnic communities who in some way identify with North American Scottish culture. It is always exciting and sometimes a little confusing to live through a revival of any kind, when something long forgotten rises from oblivion and gains a fresh and potent currency in the present, or when something like the Highland gatherings and games suddenly become important in terms of their social and cultural capital beyond their original context. It serves as merely one example, of how parts of the old world are still present in the new, or that the classical, ancient, and traditional is never dead but merely residual. Residual sporting cultures, while they might never be dominant in this increasingly commercialised global and international sporting world, are ever present. They have much to say not just about the contemporary sporting worlds but also about the way we live, who we are, and where we want to go, and this may be one of the most important facets of contemporary North American Highland gatherings and games culture if carefully developed.

It seems that in the alleged era of global sport, some or all of the following arguments are just as important in the early part of the twenty-first century: that North American Highland games can (1) through their associational nature help in the production and reproduction of social capital; (2) contribute to a sense of civic pride, local pride, and boosterism; (3) play a vital role in the regeneration and sustaining of ethnic communities; (4) provide a social focus for community and consequently influence people's perceptions of locality and even nationhood and culture; (5) illustrate that the social values often associated with Highland gatherings and games are even more important today given the alleged decline in civil society and social capital; (6) provide for a strong sense of collective identification but can also be divisive; (7) cannot sustain vibrant living communities, but they can make a contribution; and finally (8) contribute to international sporting markets and patterns of consumption while at the same time influencing local sporting identity and taste. In other words, the popularity of Scottish North American culture, while internationally recognisable, may also marginalise or suppress local identity.

I should like to finish by highlighting three points. First, I have rightly or wrongly attempted to suggest that traditional games and sports in many ways may serve to provide an alternative to the readily accepted notion of global sport or more importantly the values associated with global sport. Global free-market-driven sport is often associated with commercialisation, professionalism, individualism, and profit but also corruption, drug abuse, player power, trade unionism, and in many cases a democratic deficit. Many traditional Scottish Highland gatherings and games in Scotland have their roots in the nineteenth-century notion of a friendly society that served as a form of social welfare for local communities and individuals in times of need or hardship. These values are at times worth thinking about in an alleged global world that fosters ideological notions of a free-market-driven form of global sport. The consequences seem to be civic disengagement, liberal individualism, political apathy, and lack of trust not just in forms of governance but in life itself. It might be suggested that the notion of global sport, and indeed globalisation, is in some senses flawed and that the notion of internationality might be a more reality-congruent term. With specific reference to traditional games and sport as a form of middle ground or third space between global, free-market-driven sport and state-sponsored sport, it would seem that one of the strongest defences would be that such activities help to sustain forms of social capital that are more than just educational or economic. It refers to the network of social groups and relationships that fosters cooperative working and community well-being. It involves communities and other social groups exercising a certain degree of trust through taking on mutual obligations. Traditional Highland gatherings and games have done this for centuries.

Second, community survival often requires a collective sense of identification and public spirit, which in turn often requires the survival of other kinds of organisations and associations that help to regularly renew and cement social and cultural relationships. If North American Highland gatherings and games and sports in other parts of the world are anything like the Scottish Highland gatherings and games, then such events have been part of the social glue that has held communities together. When the economic viability of life in certain community *A*, *B*, or *C* is threatened, perhaps it is unrealistic to expect such activities to make more than a symbolic significance. Clearly there are limits to what festivals, games, and sports can do in contributing to community renewal, survival, and sustainability. Nonetheless, the role of traditional games and sports in cementing new and old transnational relationships should not be underestimated either.

Finally, in an ever-changing individualised world, in which the traditional practices and forms of employment that often held communities together are increasingly under threat, the role of festivals, games, and sport in today's communities becomes increasingly important. The different groups of people, the politicians, clan societies, international tourists, locals, or representatives of "other" communities who attend Tartan Day celebrations or Highland games are in part testament to the fact that such activities are an instrument of social and cultural inclusion that can bring people of different backgrounds together. They are testament, like the enduring residual social facet of Highland games in Scotland, to the role that traditional games and sport can play in the production of social and cultural capital within and across contemporary international communities.

Works Cited

Bale, John, and Mike Cronin. 2002. *Sport and Post-Colonialism.* Oxford: Berg.

Bradley, Joseph M. 2002. "The Patriot Game: Football's Famous Tartan Army." *International Review for the Sociology of Sport* 37, no. 2: 177–98.

———. 1998. *Sport, Culture, Politics Scottish, and Scottish Society: Irish Immigrants and the Gaelic Athletic Association.* Edinburgh: John Donald.

Coalter, Fred. 2000. *Role of Sport in Re-Generating Deprived Urban Communities.* Edinburgh: Scottish Executive Publications.

Coleman, James. 1988. "Social Capital in the Creation of Human Capital." *American Journal of Sociology* 94: 95–119.

Donaldson, Emily Ann. 1986. *The Scottish Highland Games in North America.* Boston: Pelican.

Gillespie, Greg. 2000. "Roderick McLennan, Professionalism, and the Emergence of the Athlete in Caledonian Games." *Sport History Review* 31, no. 1: 43–63.

Gruneau, Richard, and David Whitson. 1993. *Hockey Night in Canada: Sport, Identities, and Cultural Politics.* Toronto: Garamond.

Hague, Euan. 2002. "National Tartan Day: Re-Writing History in the United States." *Scottish Affairs* 38 (winter): 94–124.

———. 2000. "The Emigrant Experience: The Scottish Diaspora." *Scottish Affairs* 31 (spring): 85–91.

Hague, Euan, and J. Mercer. 1998. "Geographical Memory and Urban Identity in Scotland: Raith Rovers FC and Kirkcaldy." *Geography* 83, no. 2: 105–16.

Hargreaves, Ian. 1999. *New Mutualism, In from the Cold.* London: Trafford.

Harris, Janet C. 1998. "Civil Society, Physical Activity, and the Involvement of Sport Sociologists in the Preparation of Physical Activity Professionals." *Sociology of Sport* 15: 138–53.

Hewitson, Jim. 1998. *Far Off in Sunlit Places: Stories of the Scots in Australia and New Zealand.* Edinburgh: Cannongate.

Hirst, Paul. 1994. *Associative Democracy: New Forms of Economic and Social Governance.* Cambridge: Polity.

Hunter, James. 2000. "The Atlantic North West: The Highlands and Islands as a Twenty-First Century Success Story." *Scottish Affairs* 31 (spring): 1–17.

———. 1996. *Glencoe and the Indians.* Edinburgh: Mainstream.

———. 1995. *On the Other Side of Sorrow.* Edinburgh: Mainstream.

———. 1994. *The Dance Called America: The Scottish Highlands, the United States, and Canada.* Edinburgh: Mainstream.

Hutton, William. 1994. *The State We're In: Why Britain Is in Crisis and How to Overcome It.* London: Jonathan Cape.

Jarvie, Grant. 2003. "Communitarianism, Sport, and Social Capital: A Neighbourly Insight into Scottish Sport." *International Review for the Sociology of Sport* 38, no. 1: 100–28.

———. 2000. "Sport, the Émigré, and the Dance Called America." *Sport History Review* 31: 28–42.

———. 1999. *Sport in the Making of Celtic Cultures.* Leicester: Leicester UP.

———. 1991. *Highland Games the Making of the Myth.* Edinburgh: Edinburgh UP.

Jarvie, Grant, and John Burnett. 2000. *Sport, Scotland, and the Scots.* Edinburgh: Tuckwell.

Lloyd, John. 2002. "Now the Good News for America." *New Statesman* (March): 12–15.

MacLennan, Hugh-Dan. 1998. "Shinty: Some fact and fiction in the 19th Century." *Transactions of the Gaelic Society of Inverness* 59: 148–235.

Marquand, David. 2000. "The Fall of Civic Culture." *New Statesman* (November): 27–30.

———. 1988. *The Unprincipled Society.* London: Jonathan Cape.

McLean, Marianne. 1991. *The People of Glengarry: Highlanders in Transition, 1740–1825.* Montreal: Addison-Wesley.

Nairn, Tom. 1981. *The Break-Up of Britain.* London: Verso.

Pahl, Raymond, and Lorne Spencer. 1998. "The Politics of Friendship," *Renewal* 5, no. 3: 100–07.

Pringle, Ashley. 2001. *Sport and Local Government in The New Scotland.* Edinburgh: COSLA.

Putnam, Robert. 1995. "Bowling Alone: America's Declining Social Capital." *Journal of Democracy* 6: 65–78.

Ray, Celeste. 2001. *Highland Heritage: Scottish Americans in the American South.* London: U of North Carolina P.

———. 1998. "Scottish Heritage, Southern Style." *Southern Cultures* 4, no. 2: 28–45.

Schuller, Tom. 1997. "Building Social Capital: Steps Towards a Learning Society." *Scottish Affairs* 19: 77–91.

8
Troubling Times in the Scottish-American Relationship
Andrew Hook

It is no doubt inevitable that accounts of the roles of hyphenated Americans within the national culture should prefer to emphasise their positive contributions. The stereotypical imaging of Italian Americans as the major contributors to organised crime is understandably anathema to millions of law-abiding Americans of Italian descent. But the Scottish-American example makes it abundantly clear how easy it is to fashion an account of a single ethnic group that exaggerates its positive contribution to the development of the United States, and successfully airbrushes out of existence anything in the picture that does not fit with the positive image. I have never forgotten the *Reader's Digest* article from 1955 titled "The Scots among Us," which mainly consisted of long lists of famous Americans, from presidents and generals to golfers, who could lay claim to Scottish blood somewhere in their past. In fact the kind of filiopietism that suggests that the contributions to American life and culture of the same "Scots among us" have invariably been good and positive has always been prominent in descriptions of the Scottish-American relationship. The point is well illustrated by the strange story of the title of a recent book written by Arthur Herman. In Britain Herman's book was published as *The Scottish Enlightenment: The Scots' Invention of the Modern World* (2002). One would have thought the title was making a sufficiently eye-catching claim. The American publishers, however, clearly thought not; in its American edition (2001) Herman's title was *How the Scots Invented the Modern World: The True Story of How Western Europe's Poorest Nation Created Our World and Everything in It.* In fact Herman's book lives down to its title extremely well; it is an eminently readable and judicious account of the Scottish Enlightenment and its long-term influence. But its titles—especially its extraordinary American title—situate the book very much in a filiopietistic tradition that has been characteristic of most accounts of the Scottish-American connection in particular.

The April 1954 issue of the *William and Mary Quarterly*, devoted to the topic of Scotland and America, marks the beginning of serious academic enquiry into the nature and significance of that relationship. In the subsequent half century real progress has unquestionably been made in recognising and exploring the specifically Scottish contribution to major areas of American life and culture. Many scholars now agree that from early in the eighteenth century through at least the middle of the nineteenth, American education, American science, American philosophy—including political philosophy—American economic life, American religion, American literature, indeed American culture in almost every area, all were marked by a distinct and pervasive Scottish influence. In other words, there is substantial scholarly support for Arthur Herman's suggestion that the cultural inheritance of the modern world, and of modern America in particular, does very much include the legacy of the Scottish Enlightenment. Nevertheless, there is good reason to doubt the extent to which this view of the Scottish contribution to American cultural and intellectual history has been generally accepted. In 1978 historian Garry Wills could still spark a bitter and furious debate within American academia by daring to argue in *Inventing America* that the thinkers of the Scottish Enlightenment rather than John Locke were the primary influences on Jefferson's drafting of the Declaration of Independence. Exactly two decades later, on the other hand, it is flatly asserted in Trent Lott's Senate Resolution establishing April 6 as America's National Tartan Day, celebrating the Scottish-American connection, that the Declaration of Independence was modelled on the 1320 Declaration of Arbroath, in which the then-Pope was invited by the Scots to recognise the legitimacy of Robert the Bruce's position as king of Scotland. Garry Wills's view of the Declaration of Independence is based on research and evidence that may be disputed but in no way dismissed; the Senate Resolution's view has no scholarly basis at all. So why is the resolution's assertion accorded "official" status (Scottish journalists, for example, now accept the link between the two documents as a self-evident truth) while Wills's scholarly argument is ignored? The answer is that the idea of the Declaration of Independence being based on the Declaration of Arbroath is no more than the latest manifestation of that old, filiopietistic notion of Scottish Americans that all that is positive in the American way of life somehow has Scottish origins. The Declaration of Arbroath does talk about nationality and the love of freedom and can be read as asserting the democratic rights of the Scottish people. Hence ever afterwards we are to assume that the Scots are a consciously freedom-loving and democratic people. Crossing the Atlantic some four hundred years later, the

Scots carry with them these noble principles—which are in turn assimilated by the patriotic side in the dispute between the colonies and the mother country in the 1760s and 1770s. Thus the Declaration of Independence becomes a document inspired by the ancient lessons of Scottish history. Admittedly only two native-born Scots were prepared to sign the document in Philadelphia in 1776, but then a great many of the American signatories *did* have Scottish blood somewhere in their ancestry. The only trouble with all of this is that it flies in the face of historical realities of a different kind: the actual evidence of Scottish attitudes and behaviour, both in the American colonies and at home, throughout the period of the American Revolution. Rather than freedom-loving democrats, rallying to the patriotic side, the great majority of Scots in Revolutionary America, like many of their influential compatriots at home, appear to have been more or less committed Loyalists. And this was a stance that produced in America a reaction that all the filiopietistic accounts of the Scottish-American relationship chose either to discount or ignore.

Scots Perfidy and Tyranny and Enmity to America

Some sociologists distinguish between two types of national stereotype: the stereotype endorsed by a national group is an "autostereotype"—this is the approved national self-image. The stereotype relating to another, alien national group is a "heterostereotype"—this is the way the given national group sees other nationalities inside or outside its own borders. As I demonstrated long ago in *Scotland and America* (1975), in the years immediately preceding the outbreak of the American Revolution, many Americans had developed a heterostereotype of the Scots among them. During the period of the Revolutionary War itself, that heterostereotype was powerfully reinforced. Its nature is suggested by a report in the *Virginia Gazette* in October 1774:

> *Irish influence* is of the downright, genuine and unadulterated sort. *The Scotch Influence* is of a different species. A *Scotchman,* when he first is admitted into a house, is so humble that he will sit upon the lowest step of the staircase. By degrees he gets into the kitchen, and from thence, by the most submissive behaviour, is advanced to the parlour. If he gets into the dining room, as ten to one but he will, the master of the house must take care of himself; for in all probability he will turn him out of doors, and, by the assistance of his *countrymen,* keep possession forever.

Two central points in the anti-Scots image that was developing among American Patriots are apparent here. First is the idea that the Scots were peculiarly clannish, always working together, supporting each other, and never trusting anyone who was non-Scottish. The second point is the idea that the colonies were facing a kind of Scottish takeover, especially in the area of the Atlantic colonial trade. In fact the Scots in Virginia, like their compatriots in Maryland and the Carolinas, had been outstandingly successful in coming to dominate the highly lucrative tobacco trade between the Chesapeake Bay colonies and Britain. In November 1777, Ezra Stiles, president of Yale, reported in his *Literary Diary* hearing that "the Scotch had got *Two Thirds of Virginia and Mary^{ld}* mortgaged or otherwise engaged to them or was *owned in Scotland*," and he continued, "I have had it often suggested to me by Scotch Merchants & Factors that the Scotch would in a very few years have all the Property in Virginia if not in Gen. of No. America." Exaggerations of this kind had at least some basis in the undeniable mercantile successes of the Scots—and no doubt there was no shortage of Virginians who felt mightily aggrieved at being in debt to Glasgow merchants some three thousand miles away.

American distaste for Scottish clannishness and Scottish business success, however, was soon to be overtaken by a new aspect of the American hetero-stereotype of the Scot in America: Scottish Loyalism. Once the Revolution was under way, most Americans seem to have concluded that all Scots were unpatriotic adherents of the British government. Here again the notion had at least some basis in reality. Many Scots were indeed Loyalist. For example, although it may seem paradoxical in a post-Culloden context, the Scottish Highland emigrants in North Carolina and New York State were supporters of George III's government—even if ineffectual ones. In Virginia and New England, too, there is clear evidence that many Scots sided with the friends of government. Governor Thomas Hutchinson described the Scots in Boston as "almost without exception good Subjects," while another Bostonian described the Scots as "good subjects and supporters of Government and order." Unsurprisingly, this widespread identification of the Scots as anti-Revolutionaries led to a rising torrent of abuse of Scots in general. "A free exportation to Scotchmen and Tories" became a common Revolutionary toast, while a letter from a captured officer of Frazer's Highlanders, printed in the *Scots Magazine* in 1776, reported that what upset him most was the local population's "continual slandering of our country (Scotland), on which they threw the most infamous invectives." Then Thomas Jefferson's original draft of the Declaration of Independence contained a notably anti-Scottish comment: George III had sent over "not only soldiers of our common blood, but Scotch and foreign mercenaries to invade and destroy us."[1] John Witherspoon, the Scots clergyman who had become president of the College of New Jersey, and an ardent patriot, made Congress delete this hostile reference to his fellow countrymen, but the fact that Jefferson should have made it at all is highly significant.

Clear evidence of American hostility towards Scotland and the Scots in the Revolutionary period can be found in the literature of the time. *The Patriots* is an ironically titled play by the Virginian Robert Munford, written around 1775–1776. Much of the action of the play centres on the persecution of three Scottish merchants—McFlint, McSqueeze, and McGripe—by a local, patriotic Committee of Safety; but Munford's own position is one of liberal dissent from the universal condemnation of the Scots in America. Munford's spokesman, Trueman, and his friend, Meanwell, are accused of siding with the Scots:

> Strut. Wou'd you protect our enemies, gentlemen? Would you ruin your country for the sake of Scotchmen?
> Trueman. Prove them to be enemies, shew that they plot the downfall of my country, and courtesy itself shall revolt against them.
> Brazen. There is sufficient proof that nine hundred and ninety-nine out of a thousand of them are our enemies.
> Trueman. Some may be enemies, other guiltless . . .

But the Committee of Safety remains unshaken. The three Scots are brought before it:

> McFlint. What is our offence pray?
> Strut. The nature of their offence, gentlemen, is, that they are Scotchmen; every Scotchman being an enemy, and these men being Scotchmen, they come under the ordinance which directs an oath to be tendered to all those against whom there is just cause to suspect that they are our enemies. Let it be put to the committee, Mr President, whether all Scotchmen are not enemies.

The question is finally put:

> Col. Simple. Is all Scotchmen enemies, gentlemen?
> All. Ay, ay.

Several explanations for this upsurge of anti-Scots prejudice in the Revolutionary period have already been suggested. The Loyalism of large numbers of Scots, envy of Scots business success in the American trade, and resentment of excessive Scots clannishness, were all significant contributory factors. But there is evidence that Revolutionary America's anti-Scots feeling was soon tapping into a much older and more virulent source of anti-Scots prejudice: English animosity towards the Scots. Anglo-Scottish relations had always been marked by doubts and unease. From the centuries of Border warfare in the medieval period, through the Scottish takeover of the English throne in the person of James I, and the English takeover of the Scottish Parliament in the Treaty of Union, down to significant Scottish support for the Jacobite rebellions of the eighteenth century, the Scots and English had always found reasons for mutual distrust and dislike. However, in the decade or so preceding the American Revolution, that latent Anglo-Scottish hostility had broken out with a new cultural and political potency.

George III had become king in 1760. Soon afterwards the Scottish Earl of Bute, the king's close friend and former tutor, became his head of government. Bute remained in power for a mere eleven months, but he was widely held to be the power behind the throne, and a powerful influence, in all the bitter political struggles that occurred in succeeding years. Real or not, Bute's alleged "Scotch" influence over the royal government precipitated a torrent of abuse in London against all things Scottish. Attacks identical in nature to those we have already seen in America were directed against Bute, his fellow countrymen, and Scotland in general. Scottish clannishness was now rife everywhere; the partiality of Scot for Scot was at work in the highest levels of the country's political life; and hordes of beggarly and unprincipled Scots were looting the English treasury. The leader of these attacks on the Scots was John Wilkes, editor of the ironically titled *North Briton,* an opposition paper set up to counter the propaganda of the government's own paper, *The Briton,* which just happened to be edited by another Scot: Tobias Smollett.

The Wilkesite attacks on Scotland made effective play with the idea that the Jacobite rebellions were a threat to the principles of liberty that were forever enshrined in the English constitution established in 1688. Scottish support for the Stuart kings thus identified the Scots with tyranny and reaction. In the American situation, where many Americans believed that their constitutional liberties as English subjects were equally under threat, such an identification was hugely significant. Scotland was their enemy, not England; and now in London it was the Scots who were running the British government. This was Ezra Stiles's view in 1776: "The Ministry and Parl^t have no Intention of Accommodation—The Scotch Influence blinds the Parl^t and Nation." A later *Diary* entry, made after receipt of the Declaration of Independence, reinforces the point:

And have I lived to see such an important and astonishing Revolution? Scotch Policy transfused thro' the collective Body of the Ruling Powers in Great Britain; and their violent, oppressive and haughty Measures have weaned and alienated the affections of three Millions of people.

By 1776 a great many Americans clearly believed that the oppressive policies of the government of George III towards the American colonies had specific Scottish origins. From the time of Bute on, the Scots had allegedly been undermining the Whiggish principles of the English constitution. In the persons of men like Lord Mansfield and Alexander Wedderburn, they were now successfully influencing Lord North's administration to pursue the hard line against both Wilkes and the Americans.

Once again the best evidence of this anti-Scots prejudice is provided by an American literary production of the Revolutionary period: John Leacock's 1776 play, *The Fall of British Tyranny*. The pervasive anti-Scots tone of the piece is set by the opening of its mock-dedication:

To Lord Boston (Gage, the governor of Massachusetts), . . . Lord Kidnapper (Dunmore, governor of Virginia), . . . and the innumerable and never-ending clan of Macs and Donalds upon Donalds, in America.

The theme reappears near the end of the dedication:

And ye Macs, and ye Donalds upon Donalds, go on, and may our gallows-hills and liberty poles be honour'd and advanc'd with some of your heads; Why should Tyburn and Temple-bar make a monopoly of so valuable a commodity?

A leading figure in the play is Lord Paramount, that is, the Earl of Bute. Bute's family name was Stuart, and Leacock exploits the Jacobite association. Paramount's grand design is to restore the Stuarts to the British throne:

Paramount: Now, by St Andrew! I'll strike a stroke that shall surprise all Europe, and make the boldest of the adverse party turn pale and tremble—Scotch politics, Scotch intrigues, Scotch influence, and Scotch impudence (as they have termed it) they shall see ere long shine with unheard of splendour.

War with America, explains Paramount, will be fostered; Britain will be rendered defenceless with the removal of her troops across the Atlantic; the French and Spanish fleets will appear in the Channel; and "my kinsman" will land in Scotland with thirty thousand men and march on London. Paramount will be rewarded with riches:

> I'll draw in treasure from every quarter, and, Solomon-like, wallow in riches; and Scotland, my dear Scotland, shall be the paradise of the world. Rejoice in the name of Paramount, and the sound of a bawbee shall be no more heard in the land of my nativity.

Leacock's satire is far from subtle, but the burlesque tone does not negate the strength of the anti-Scottish feeling. It is hardly surprising that John Witherspoon felt obliged to try to defend his fellow countrymen in Congress, and went on to publish a pamphlet in which he attempted to rebut the wholesale denunciations of the Scots and Scotland that he knew were echoing around all the former colonies. But nothing Witherspoon could say could silence Ezra Stiles on the subject of "Scots Perfidy and Tyranny and Enmity to America." "Let us boldly say," wrote Stiles in his *Diary*, "for History will say it, that the whole of this War is so far chargeable to the Scotch councils, and to the Scotch as a Nation (for they have nationally come into it) as that had it not been for them, this quarrel had never happened."

In his attempted defence of the Scots, titled *An Address to the Natives of Scotland Residing in America*, Witherspoon made much of the fact that many of the proponents of American liberty had seen in John Wilkes an important ally. This reliance on Wilkes, Witherspoon argued, had alienated the Scots, because for them Wilkes was known only for his "contempt and hatred of the Scots nation." There was some justice in Witherspoon's view. The Boston Sons of Liberty corresponded extensively with Wilkes and accepted his support and guidance; the South Carolina assembly even voted Wilkes a substantial sum of money to help him pay off his debts. More important in the context of the sweeping denunciations of the Scots in America, and the virulence of the attacks on the alleged "Scotch Policy" of North's administration, is the republication of the first two numbers of the *North Briton* in New York in 1769. There can be no doubt that these American reprints were part of a concerted American campaign to stir up and fuel anti-Scottish feelings—a campaign that aimed to persuade "English" Americans that the oppressive American policies of George III's government were part of a purely Scottish plan to subvert and undermine the constitutional rights and liberties of American Englishmen.

The plan did not succeed politically, in that it did not prevent the outbreak of a long and bitter war between Great Britain and the American colonies. Nor did it dissuade large numbers of Americans from remaining loyal to the British crown. But the anti-Scottish campaign in America did achieve substantial successes. It drove many Scottish colonists out of America, compelling them either to resettle in Canada or the West Indies, or to return to Great Britain; it ensured that Scottish control of the American tobacco trade was permanently broken; and it may well have persuaded, or helped to persuade, doubtful or wavering Americans to remain neutral or incline towards the patriotic side.

The Scots-Irish

American hostility towards the Scots in the Revolutionary period is well documented. But how long did this anti-Scottish attitude endure? There is evidence that elements of the English heterostereotype of the Scots survived in America well into the nineteenth century: the image of the Scot as mean, frugal, dirty, and clannish, for example. But the notion of the Scots as politically obnoxious does not appear to have been particularly long lasting. By the opening of the nineteenth century quite different images of the Scots were clearly emerging in America. These are images of a more positive kind, deriving either from growing recognition of Scottish intellectual distinction in the eighteenth century and its specific contribution to the developing intellectual and cultural life of the United States, or from the still more potent impact of Scottish romantic literature upon American readers that culminated in the immense vogue for Sir Walter Scott throughout the United States. But from the early years of the new republic, the situation was complicated by the emergence of a new stereotype—of the so-called Scotch-Irish.

The Scots-Irish, more accurately described as Ulster Scots, have to be carefully distinguished from both native-born Scots and mainstream Irish. The Scots-Irish have nothing in common with de Crèvecoeur's feckless, indolent Irish immigrants in *Letters from an American Farmer* (1782)—and only a little with his dour, industrious Andrew the Hebridean. However, the image of the Scots-Irish that developed in popular American culture in the nineteenth century was an autostereotype of a wholly positive kind: the Scots-Irish*man* is the bold, intrepid pioneer; the rough, tough, resourceful frontiersman; the natural democrat, the lover of freedom, resistant to authority. In fact, the Scots-Irish are seen as true-blue, archetypal Americans boldly expanding the United States into the south and west of a boundless continent.

Well, it may be true that the Ulster Scots were the shock troops of the frontier, but their cultural legacy to the sections of America they settled was nonetheless a mixed blessing. "'Cracker' culture," as it has been called, bears a heavy responsibility for much of the violence, intolerance, and racism that has scarred the history of the South in particular. High-sounding principles of individual or family honour readily descend into the kind of horrific mayhem Mark Twain depicted in the Shepherdson-Grangerford feud in *Huckleberry Finn;* antiauthoritarianism quickly becomes mob rule and lynch law; communal solidarity soon justifies the crudest forms of oppression and cruelty towards the ethnic or religious "other." William Faulkner's account of Beat Four in his mythical Yoknapatawpha County—most fully explored in *Intruder in the Dust,* with its people "named Gowrie and McCallum and Fraser and Ingrum that used to be Ingraham and Workitt that used to be Urquhart only the one that brought it to America and then Mississippi couldn't spell it either, who love brawling and fear God and believe in Hell"—sums up its greatest novelist's vision of the American South's Scots and Scots-Irish inheritance. What that vision is proves to be a question of unrestrained violence and lawlessness, clannishness, distrust of outsiders, rejection of authority, and a taste for home-produced whisky—all held together by a Calvinist ferocity. How terrible and how ironic it is that members of the white lynch mob confronting Lucas Beauchamp in Faulkner's novel might trace their origins to the Scots who were so viciously victimised more than a century earlier in Revolutionary America.

The Scottish Klan

Members of the contemporary Scottish-American heritage movement, constantly expanding since the 1990s, would deny that it has anything to do with intolerance and bigotry of any kind. But Scottish history and Scottish culture have indeed in the past been exploited within America to advance the cause of racial hatred and intolerance. John C. Lester, the originator of the Ku Klux Klan in Pulaski, Tennessee, in 1865, tells us that the use of the term "Klan" was felt to be appropriate because the founding members of the organisation were "all of Scotch descent." And it is entirely possible that Sir Walter Scott, the South's favourite novelist, provided at least one source for the Klan's procedures and rituals as well as, more importantly, a justification for its existence. As everyone knows, the Klan quickly became the main focus of white resistance to Reconstruction in the post–Civil War South. To achieve its aims, it employed violence and terror, elaborate rituals, and, above all, secrecy. The Klan, then, offers a powerful parallel to the Vehme or Secret Tribunal of fifteenth-century Germany as that organisation is fully described in Scott's *Anne of Geierstein* (1829). Unquestionably chapter 20 of Scott's exciting novel provides an elaborate description of a secret society that both in its methods and rituals, and in the reasons and justifications for its existence, provides an uncanny likeness to the Ku Klux Klan. Scott's character Philipson is forced to appear before the Secret Tribunal in a subterranean vault, lit only by torches borne by men muffled in black cloaks, and wearing cowls "drawn over their heads, so as to conceal their features." Set out on an altar are a coil of ropes and a naked sword, "the well-known signals and emblems of Vehmique authority." Elaborate oaths are sworn, binding adherents of the order to unquestioning loyalty and obedience. Probably most significant of all is Scott's explanation of the Secret Tribunal's rise to power: "Such an institution could only prevail at a time when ordinary means of justice were excluded by the hand of power, and when, in order to bring the guilty to punishment, it required all the influence and authority of such a confederacy." And Scott continues: "In no other country than one exposed to every species of feudal tyranny, and deprived of every ordinary mode of obtaining justice or redress, could such a system have taken root and flourished." The availability of such passages in a popular Scott novel, justifying as they appear to do extralegal action in the name of justice itself, must at the very least have contributed to the cultural context out of which the Invisible Empire of the Klan emerged. The suggestion is not that *Anne of Geierstein* is the source of the Klan. But it is difficult not to believe that a great many southern readers of the novel found in it a peculiar and reassuring relevance to their own situation.

It is in a later novel by a southern novelist, however, that the Scottish dimension of the Ku Klux Klan is explored and embroidered. Thomas Dixon's novel *The Clansman,* remembered today mainly as the source of D. W. Griffith's classic film *The Birth of a Nation,* was published in 1905. Dixon, from North Carolina, and of Scottish ancestry, was intensely proud of what he saw as the South's Scottish inheritance. His earlier novel, *The One Woman* (1903), is dedicated "to the memory of my mother to whose Scotch love of romantic literature I owe the treasure of eternal youth." A sequel to *The Birth of a Nation,* called *The Fall of a Nation* (1916), opens with a prologue exemplifying popular resistance to royal authority, and the first example is that of the Scottish Covenanting, Cameronian women martyrs, burned at the stake or drowned in the Solway Firth. In *The Clansman,* however, Dixon's Scottish preoccupations move closer to the centre of the novel's landscape.

Dixon's own sense of the story he is about to tell is made clear in an introductory note "To the Reader": "How the young South, led by the reincarnated souls of the Clansmen of Old Scotland, went forth under this cover and against overwhelming odds, daring exile, imprisonment, and a felon's death, and saved the life of a people, forms one of the most dramatic chapters in the history of the Aryan race." What follows in the novel more than lives up to what is implied here. *The Clansman* exhibits a kind of racism so crude and vicious as to make the reader of today almost unable to go on turning its pages. At the same time, there is no denying that Dixon uses a running thread of allusions to a highly romanticised version of Scottish history and traditions to support his selective view of the Reconstruction period. When Mrs. Cameron, mother of the novel's southern hero, learns that her husband is in danger, Dixon tells us that it is her Scottish inheritance that inspires her to act: "The heritage of centuries of heroic blood from the martyrs of old Scotland began to flash its inspiration from the past." When Mrs. Cameron subsequently appeals to President Johnson, the theme reappears: "Mr President, you are a native Carolinian—you are of Scotch Covenanter blood. You are of my own people of the great past, whose tears and sufferings are our common glory and birthright." Senator Ross of Kansas, whose vote saves President Johnson from impeachment, is described as "the sturdy Scotchman," and Dixon tells his readers that the Ulster Scots—settlers of the Carolinas, radicals, revolutionaries, and democrats to a man—composed the largest of all the original immigrant groups in America, and were those who contributed most to the formation of what he calls the American nationality.

But it is in Dixon's account of the Ku Klux Klan itself that the Scottish theme is most evident. He exploits to the full images associated with the Scottish heritage of clans, clansmen, clan loyalties, clan solidarity—and Presbyterianism. The Presbyterian Rev. Hugh McAlpine is chaplain to the local Klan. And it is of course Dr. Cameron who suggests the use of the Fiery Cross to summon Klan members: "A sudden inspiration flashed in Doctor Cameron's eyes," writes Dixon, and the doctor proceeds to tell the Grand Dragon: "issue your orders and despatch your courier tonight with the old Scottish rite of the Fiery Cross. It will send a thrill of inspiration to every clansman in the hills!" Walter Scott had set out the ritual of the Fiery Cross as the means by which a clan chieftain bent on war summonsed his followers in canto 3 of *The Lady of the Lake* (1810). Dixon follows Scott's description closely. In *The Lady of the Lake* the cross is set ablaze, then dowsed in the blood of a sacrificed goat. In *The Clansman* the cross is similarly set ablaze, but dowsed in the blood of the female victim of black outrage. A Klan leader declares: "In olden times when the Chieftain of our people summoned the clan on an errand of life and death, the Fiery Cross, extinguished in sacrificial blood, was sent by swift courier from village to village." Now the ritual will be repeated: the "Fiery Cross of old Scotland's hills . . . the ancient symbol of an unconquered race of men"—will bring forth the loyal members of the new world's Ku Klux Klan. Here, and in his novel as a whole, Dixon draws upon a set of images from a romanticised, heroical Scottish past to persuade his readers to accept an equally romanticised and heroical version of deeply disreputable episodes in the history of the post–Civil War South.

Braveheart Scotland and the American South

What is extraordinary is that almost a century after *The Clansman*, a romanticised and glamourised version of Scottish history is once again being manipulated and exploited in order to sustain and support American ideologies of a deeply disturbing and offensive kind. This time round, however, the stories in question are films rather than novels. Hollywood's amazingly successful and Oscar-winning *Braveheart* and *Rob Roy* both owe their existence to that romantic vision of Scottish history that enjoyed an astonishing vogue throughout Europe and America in the later eighteenth and nineteenth centuries. It was then that William Wallace emerged as an archetypal, popular representative of Scotland's grandly heroic and tragically glorious past, and the outlawed Rob Roy came to be seen as a Scottish Robin Hood. In their 1990s Hollywood incarnations, both Wallace and Rob Roy remain powerfully mythic figures; but history is being repeated in the way in which the myths they represent have once again been used to promote an extremist American political agenda.

The League of the South is a reactionary organisation campaigning for a new secessionist South. Founded at Stillman College, Alabama, by Professor Michael Hill, its membership of almost eight thousand includes historians and other academics and students from universities in the South such as Texas Christian, South Carolina, Georgia, Alabama, and Auburn. The league's immediate model is the secessionist Northern League in Italy, but its other sources of inspiration include a variety of separatist movements such as the party Québécois in Canada, Plaid Cymru in Wales, and, inevitably in the South, the Scottish National Party.

What is particularly striking about the League of the South—like other neo-Confederate groups—is the way in which in recent years it has endorsed the peculiar notion of the "Celtic" origins of southern culture and the southern way of life in general. What purports to be the intellectual justification for such an extraordinary proposition was provided by Grady McWhiney in *Cracker Culture: Celtic Ways in the Old South* (1988). McWhiney, who would become one of the founders of the League of the South, tries to show that every aspect of the behaviour of the non-English inhabitants of the United Kingdom (all subsumed under the designation "Celtic") is exactly paralleled by the behaviour of the so-called rednecks of the traditional South; thus both "Celt" and south-erner are addicted to codes of honour, violence, drink, tobacco, lack of indus-triousness, gambling, hunting, fishing, and so on. Traditional southern accounts of the American Civil War spoke of the conflict as one between southern cava-liers and northern puritans. Today's neo-Confederates see it as a clash between northern Anglo-Saxons and southern Celts. In an effort to broaden the appeal of this Celticised version of the South, efforts are now being made to include Irish American southerners within the same scenario, but it is Scotland and Scottish history that remain crucial to the South's alleged Celtic identity. Thus, according to Professor Hill, in an article titled "Extreme Traditionalism" in the 1996 *Southern Patriot,* an official publication of the League of the South, it is Scottish history in particular that should be inspirational for the league's sup-porters. The South, he suggests, needs to defend its Anglo-Celtic culture, its history, heroes, songs, symbols, and banners:

> But we should go beyond that to the task of educating our people about their ties with an honourable and inspiring past in the British Isles . . . The names and deeds of Brian Boru, William Wallace, Andrew de Moray, Robert Bruce, Sir James ("The Black") Douglas [surely he means Sir James the Good] . . . James Graham of Montrose, and Lord George Murray, among scores of others, should become commonplace. To our Anglo-Celtic cousins across the Atlantic, these names are as familiar as those of Washington, Jackson, Crockett, Davis, Lee, Forrest, and Stuart are to us.
>
> Southerners might be taught of the striking parallels between South-ern Nationalism in the 19th century and Scottish Nationalism in the 13th and 14th; between our own War for Southern Independence and the 18th-Century Scottish Jacobite uprisings; and between Reconstruc-tion and the Highland Clearances.

In such a context it comes as no surprise at all to learn that the League of the South, including its academic historians, regarded *Braveheart* as both compul-sory viewing for existing members and as a recruiting poster for new ones.

In fact, both *Rob Roy* and *Braveheart* were recruited to the neo-Confederate cause in the 1990s. In a 1995 review of *Rob Roy* in the *Southern Partisan,* the original voice of the neo-Confederate movement published since 1979 in Co-lumbia, South Carolina, an extended parallel is drawn between Rob Roy's ex-perience and that of the Confederacy. The reviewer argues that the connection between the film's concern for the acceptable "limits of government" and "the attitudes of the people of the American South to central government" was obvious; the heroic suffering of Rob Roy's wife "calls to mind the stories with which we are familiar of the great sacrifices made by women of the South for the protection and aid of the fighting men;" and the presentation of the character of Rob Roy himself "could fit any number of American Southerners at any time in our history," as for example General Robert E. Lee or General Nathan Bedford Forest (who in the period of post–Civil War Reconstruction became the first Imperial Wizard of the Ku Klux Klan).

The neo-Confederate response to *Braveheart* was still more enthusiastic. In a 1995 review in *Chronicles,* published by the Rockford Institute, and described on its Web site as a "Paleoconservative Magazine of American Culture," Michael Hill admired the film's presentation of Mel Gibson's Wallace because "he displayed all the characteristics deplored by our prevailing anti-European, anti-heterosexual-male culture;" the film celebrates "Christian devotion, populism, patriotism, home rule, self-defence, well-defined sex roles, traditional morality, and self-sacrifice for a noble cause;" the film, he asserts, "seems aimed at *Chronicles* readers;" the patriotic Scots are likened to southerners in the Confederacy—Edward II is compared to Abraham Lincoln; and the review's concluding point is that "Celtic peoples whether in 13th Century Scotland or in the 19th Century American South have been targets for subjugation and extermination." The League of the South found *Braveheart* equally praiseworthy. An editorial in the *Southern Patriot* in May–June 1995 "highly recommends Mel Gibson's movie *Braveheart*" and goes on to suggest "Unreconstructed Southerners will find it difficult to miss the parallels between the Scot and our Confederate forebears."

The League of the South, however, is far from being the only extremist American group prepared to capitalise on the *Braveheart* version of Scottish history. The old John Birch Society urged its supporters to see the film and take its freedom message to heart. Christian Identity, a racist, anti-Semitic movement, which believes in the purity of the Celtic peoples, has also exploited the film—along with the Declaration of Arbroath—for its own propaganda purposes. Finally—and here the wheel does come full circle—today's Ku Klux Klan saw Mel Gibson's film as somehow endorsing its agenda: "This movie may well become a movement pièce de resistance for Christian Patriots" is the reported comment of a Texas Klan leader.[2]

Of course no one would suggest that the various groups referred to, any more than their books, magazines, videos, Web sites, and T-shirts, are in any way representative of today's South. All of them represent no more than a tiny minority of southerners. Nor are they in any way representative of the wider Scottish heritage revival in the 1990s South so well documented in Celeste Ray's *Highland Heritage: Scottish Americans in the American South* (2001). But even within this much wider world of southern celebration of what it chooses to regard as the South's Scottish heritage, it is possible to identify troubling elements. Ray's book has a whole chapter on "Warrior Scots," and she makes abundantly clear the central role that the glorification of traditions of military prowess plays in nearly all of these burgeoning Scottish-American festivals, Highland games, and clan gatherings. The Scottish-American Military Society was founded in North Carolina. Its motto is "With Fire and Sword," and its two thousand members are past or present American soldiers who "maintain an active interest in current military affairs and politics" (2001, 160). It would be useful to know the nature of that interest. Again, what is allegedly typical traditional Scottish weaponry is regularly on display and often for sale at southern versions of Highland games. At the Grandfather Mountain Games in North Carolina the clans march past at night carrying burning torches that were originally placed on a central stand. Despite the obvious parallel with Ku Klux Klan marches, the overwhelmingly white marchers refuse to see anything sinister in such a ritual. Perhaps they should be invited to read or reread *The Clansman*. The Alabama-based Society of Southern Scots, which enthusiastically endorses and promotes Trent Lott's Tartan Day Senate Resolution, includes among its affiliates the League of the South—alongside the Scottish National Party and the Sons of Confederate Veterans. Then there is the issue of the Confederate Memorial Tartan that was officially approved by the Scottish Tartans Authority. Such approval comes as no surprise given that the Authority itself was in 1995 launched simultaneously in Aviemore, Scotland, and at the Stone Mountain Highland Games in Georgia—a location indelibly associated with both the Confederacy and the Klan. But the existence of such a tartan as a visible and material symbol of the fusion of Scotland and Scotland's identity with the Confederacy has inevitably been eagerly exploited by the neo-Confederate movement: it appears on the Web pages and publications of both the League of the South and the Council of Conservative Citizens—an organisation with a background in white supremacy and opposition to civil rights legislation. Is this the kind of Scottish-American link that the Scottish people, and all those ordinary Americans interested in things Scottish, should accept without question?

As we have seen, during the American Revolution the Scots in America were reviled. In today's America they are celebrated—but not always because they invented the modern world.

Notes

1. For these and other similar references, see Andrew Hook, *Scotland and America: A Study of Cultural Relations, 1750–1835* (Glasgow: Blackie, 1975), 47–72.

2. See Diane Roberts, "Ghosts of the Gallant South," in *The Guardian*, July 22, 1996, and Kirsty Scott, "The Fatal Attraction," in *The Herald*, August 6, 1997.

Works Cited

Dixon, Thomas. 1905. *The Clansman: An Historical Romance of the Ku Klux Klan.* New York: Doubleday, Page.

Faulkner, William. 1948. *Intruder in the Dust.* New York: Random House.

Hook, Andrew. 1999. *From Goosecreek to Gandercleugh: Studies in Scottish-American Literary and Cultural History.* East Linton, Scotland: Tuckwell.

———. 1975. *Scotland and America: A Study of Cultural Relations, 1750–1835.* Glasgow: Blackie.

[Leacock, John]. 1776. *The Fall of British Tyranny; or, American Liberty Triumphant.* Philadelphia: Printed by Styner and Cist.

McWhiney, Grady. 1988. *Cracker Culture: Celtic Ways in the Old South.* Tuscaloosa: U of Alabama P.

Munford, Robert. [1776.] *The Patriots.* First published in *A Collection of Plays and Poems.* Petersburg, VA: Printed by William Prentis, 1798.

Ray, Celeste. 2001. *Highland Heritage: Scottish Americans in the American South.* Chapel Hill: U of North Carolina P.

Scott, Walter. 1829. *Anne of Geierstein.* Edinburgh: Cadell.

Stiles, Ezra. 1901. *Literary Diary,* ed. Franklin Bowditch Dexter. New York: C. Scribner's Sons.

9

Bravehearts and Patriarchs

Masculinity on the Pedestal in Southern Scottish Heritage Celebration

Celeste Ray

Two years ago I was invited to speak to an all-male St. Andrew's Society in Birmingham, Alabama, and chose as my topic "Public Display and the Scottish-American Male." I was the only woman present throughout the evening, and in a banquet room full of kilted men, I was one of the few people in trousers. The title of my talk was a casual suggestion (anthropologists use "public display" when referring to dress, expressive culture, and ritual), but as I realized many of the society's members were in the legal profession, I also realized that "public display" has quite different connotations in their line of work. While I had meant to discuss military themes and the masculine shape of Scottish-American public rituals, I wondered what they anticipated.

I later reflected that males are "on public display" at Scottish-American heritage events, sometimes in both senses, at a time when mainstream notions of masculinity and manhood are challenged, critiqued, and redefined. Male identities, and male bodies, are celebrated in an ethnic context in ways that might otherwise be considered inappropriate or "un-PC." Gender changes and ethnic movements within American society have simultaneously displaced the white male as the normative citizen. Donna Haraway pointed out that since the 1700s, white men have had "unmarked privilege" as historical constructions of gender and race identified women, the colonized, or the enslaved as "other" (1991). However, Sally Robinson has noted: "In post-sixties American culture, white men have become marked men, not only pushed away from the symbolic centers of American iconography but recentered as malicious and jealous protectors of the status quo" (2000, 5; see also Nelson 1998). She also adds that while "making the normative visible as a category . . . can call into question the privileges of unmarkedness . . . visibility can also mean a different kind of empowerment, as the history of movements for social equality in the United

States has taught us" (2000, 1–2). If indeed identity politics may be called "visibility politics," ethnic movements with gendered imagery and motifs can chart how post-sixties changes in American conceptions of ethnic identity also relate to evolving visions of gender roles, family, and community.

In heritage dress, in ethnic organization, and in heritage events, Scottish Americans assert a non-WASP identity with predominantly male imagery. This essay examines the articulation of militarism, masculinity, and white southern identities in the southern celebration of Scottish heritage.[1] As gender roles have undergone dramatic change in the latter twentieth century, this focus within the Scottish heritage context celebrates the *un*-sensitive male: the warrior and the unchallenged authority figure. Yet, if ethnicity can be symbolic for many participants, so can such masculinity. Public rituals with exaggerated displays of masculine costume and weaponry underscore the desire to claim more than just ethnic identity. The celebration of formerly hegemonic perceptions of masculinity need not be simplistically examined as unequivocally misogynist or homophobic, but indicates that such identities are already being processed as "heritage." In the creative selection of tradition and wishful renegotiation of history that shapes heritage, the ideological significance of ancestral gender roles can be quite distinct from daily, nonfestival, lived experience.

For some participants, the Scottish heritage world is a masculinist retreat to the gender roles they were raised to expect; as one informant insists, "the Scottish patriarch was wise, just, respected and obeyed," and then added that he therefore only gets "to dress up like one for special occasions like Highland Games." Other men express displeasure with current changes in gender roles with more vinegar, and still others agree with a MacLeod informant that "dressing up like *Braveheart*, being admired by the women . . . and hanging out with your chief is just plain fun. What's not to love?" As Bravehearts or patriarchs, Scottish-American males objectify a masculinity that is assumable "in festival time" through public rituals and heritage displays. Such masculinity can be set on a pedestal for both the male and female gaze in a way that nonethnic masculinity could not. While the Scottish imagery invoked is limited and predictable, and the merger of a gendered Scottish ethnicity with southern regional identities has a long history, today's celebrations still innovatively respond to current identity politics.

Scottish-American Identity in the American South

Popularity of the Scottish heritage movement in the South is partly due to a perceived relationship between the Scottish and southern identities. Both the

Scottish and southern identities play on a sense of historical injuries and lost causes; on links between sense of place and kinship; on connections between militarism and religious faith; and on symbolic material cultures. However, southerners take to Scottish heritage so well because its present shape draws not on cultural continuities, as some historians such as Grady McWhiney (1998) and others have claimed, but on parallel mythologies that underlie the construction of *both* Scottish and southern identities.

National identities are often gendered (Enloe 1995, 25; Gutmann 1997, 399; McGregor 2003) and the Scottish national identity is masculine.[2] As I discussed in chapter 2 of this book, the Scottish identity that American celebrants embrace today is a Highland Gaelic identity, an identity claimed equally by Americans of Highland Scots, Lowland Scots, or Ulster Scots descent and engendered largely by the poet and novelist Sir Walter Scott long after the ancestors of many Scottish Americans left Scotland. Despite the history of self-segregation among the various Scottish immigrants to America, it is the kilted, Highlander image that has emerged in twenty-first-century celebrations of the "auld country" and that has also been adopted by the descendants of Lowland Scots and Scots-Irish.

How the Highlands came to represent the whole of Scotland is quite similar to the way in which plantation owners came to represent southerners generally. Highland images of a Scottish national identity evolved through romanticization of the Jacobite lost cause. The final defeat of the Jacobite Highlanders at Culloden made their region the subject, first, of military rule and legal repression and, then, as defeat in the Civil War would do for the American South, of romance and nostalgia. Once they were no longer a threat, the cultural attributes of the vanquished Highlanders eventually became symbolic of the Scottish *National* identity.

Under the influence of "Highlandism" (or "Balmoralism" of the Victorian period), non-Gaelic-speaking Lowlanders who were not part of the Highland clan system forsook the cultural divide between Highlands and Lowlands to don Highland tartans and wildly elaborated versions of the kilt. Outlawed for four decades after Culloden, tartan acquired family name associations, and after almost two centuries of marketing, more than two thousand tartan designs, or "setts," exist today. Sir Walter Scott's novels were at the heart of Highlandism and the adoption of tartan as "the Scottish habit" (Green 1993, 116). Scott's works were also extremely popular with antebellum southerners; providing them with favorable analogies in the "Camelotting" of the Old South.[3]

Southern heritage is also celebrated at southern Scottish heritage events, because participants see their southern identity as an outgrowth of their Scottish ancestry. In southern Scottish heritage celebration, "Scottish" heritage incorporates the main themes of the Old South myth, themes that were originally borrowed from Scottish Highlandism. Highlandism developed between 1780 and 1860. Drawing on antebellum origins, southern postbellum lore developed mostly between 1880 and the first quarter of the 1900s. Through legend, popular culture, and tourism, both Highlandism and the plantation legend have become systemic in southerners' and in Scots' own sense of identity and in the world's conceptions of both southernness and Scottishness. Sir Walter Scott's influence was much the same in its effect in Scotland and in the South. In Scotland it offered a Highland regional identity that appealed to the Scottish nation. In the South it flavored a regionalism that appealed to both northerner and southerner.

Kinship and Gendered Participation within the New Clan System

The Scottish heritage revival has reinvented the regional Highland clan system as international clan societies with both Highland and Lowland surnames. Descended from some of the oldest European immigrant groups to America, Scottish Americans are unusual in drawing specific links to what they call their "tribal origins" and presumed tribal traditions, at least those of Scottish Highlanders that now frame visions of hyphenated Scottishness generally.[4] Distinct in subsistence, language, and culture from the feudal lordships of the Scottish Lowlands, the agro-pastoral Highland clans were actually a chiefdom-level society. Before critiques of naming Iron Age Britons "Celts" reached their peak, Robert Dodgshon wrote:

> The Highlands and Islands of Scotland provide us with the most persistent forms of Celtic chiefdom. Only when the hopes of the 1745 Jacobite rebellion were dashed at Culloden in 1746 did central government assert its absolute authority over the region and only then can we speak of Highland chiefs finally giving way to the authority of the state. Their late survival means that the Highlands provides us with examples of Celtic chiefdoms that can actually be reconstituted, structurally and processually, through manuscript data. (1995, 99)

Because their aliterate Highland ancestors lived in close proximity to an urban, state-level society that prejudicially observed and aggrieved Highland society, Scottish Americans do have an extensive, if biased, record of what life in

Highland chiefdoms was like. Today, celebrants connect themselves to such a past through genealogical research on surnames.

Those sharing a surname (and hence a tartan) are considered "kin" to each other and to all descendants of the founding (male) ancestor first associated with the name centuries or even millennia ago.[5] Associating clan with kin means that tartan now operates as a type of heraldry: the wearer of the tartan becomes a bearer of the clan reputation. Society members research and, playfully, revive "ancient" clan feuds. Fictive kin relationships have taken on connotations of "blood kin" so that even between clan societies, members are linked in a "cousinhood." Actually, the large numbers of MacDonalds or Campbells stem not from remarkable ancestral fecundity but from the progenitors of today's MacDonalds or Campbells allying themselves with a clan chief of that name at a time when most people did not need last names.[6]

An especially southern emphasis on clan as kin is most evident at Scottish Highland games and gatherings that southern branches of clan societies advertise as "family reunions." At southern Highland games, clan societies ring the games fields with tents where they greet guests, solicit new members, discuss displays on clan history, and show images of the Scottish homelands. At the Grandfather Mountain Highland Games, the largest and most prestigious Highland games in the South, well over one hundred different clan societies and over thirty thousand people gather annually for four days of events. By tradition, Highland games grew from competitions held by a king or chief for the dual purpose of amusement and the selection of fit young men as bodyguards and laborers. Though stemming from a more ancient tradition, the earliest known competitions were those held by King Malcolm Ceann Mor on the Braes of Mar in the late eleventh century. Revived in the nineteenth century, Highland games famously feature caber tossing (flipping a 120-pound tree end over end); the hammer throw (swinging a variously weighted object in such a way as to ensure a hernia before flinging it across the field); putting the *clachneart*, "the stone of strength;" and, among other Scottish athletic events, tossing "the sheaf" (a 16-pound sack) over a goalpost with a pitchfork. Although less than in other American regions, some southern women participate in track and field events or join bagpipe bands. A handful of U.S. games, many of them in the South (Louisiana; Culloden and Savannah in Georgia; Houston, Texas; Carrollton, Kentucky; and Pace, Florida), now have women's divisions in their heavy Scottish athletic competitions. The majority of females involved in competitive events, however, are young Highland dancers.

At southern games the center of attention is visiting with one's "cousins" rather than the Scottish athletic events that form the focus of Highland games in Scotland. Few women are active beyond the organization of events and host-ing in the clan tents. Less often, they may demonstrate a household task from a chosen period, such as weaving or spinning. The emphasis on "family events" and kinship masks the exclusion of women in many events and at the organi-zational level. Women carry relatively few elected positions in nationwide clan societies. In the mid-1990s, of the 207 then-active clan societies and the 66 branches of these societies, only 19 women held a title or position of leadership. By 2004, more women were presidents of Scottish heritage societies across the country, but in clan societies, women were still more often membership chairs or secretaries than presidents, conveners, or commissioners. Married women in the Scottish-American community often give precedence to their husband's clan interests. When both partners in a marriage have Scottish ancestry, the woman may be a member of her own clan society, but still reports sitting with her husband at his clan tent and attending his society's events more often than her own. Many women with no Scottish ancestry spend a great amount of time researching that of their husbands. A button seen occasionally on retiree-age women says, "Happiness is being married to a Scot." Although it does not follow that participants' home lives are male-dominated, heritage lore and heritage play construct a male environment within celebratory venues. In Scot-tish heritage events, women play what Joseph Pleck would call masculinity-validating roles. "To experience oneself as masculine requires that women play their prescribed role of doing the things that make men feel masculine" (1995, 7).

What do Scottish-American women and men say about that? As a female fieldworker, my rather plainly stated questions about masculinity caused some amusement within clan tents. Some men answered warily, as if their individual manhood was at stake with the answer; others readily and cheerfully said they enjoyed the masculine environment of events, and still others seemed genuinely surprised by my questions. However, most all of the women I asked had al-ready given the subject some thought. Of the forty or so women I interviewed at three different Highland games, three women over the age of sixty suspi-ciously launched into a Phyllis Schlafly–esque defense of phallocentrism. The majority of the others (women between the ages of thirty-two and seventy) happily described sitting around with other women commenting on how men looked in their kilts, or laughing at those who wore them too short.

In addition to enjoying the "bonny knees contests" (in which a blindfolded woman feels the knees of several kilted contestants to pick the finest), a mem-ber of Clan Carmichael noted that Scottish events are some of the few occa-sions before which her husband does not ask her where his sox are. As she explained, "He keeps all of his Scottish gear clean and organized, like ritual paraphernalia." One Robertson woman noted, "This is the only family thing we do where I can just sit back and watch; at home all he does is grill." The consensus of women from the Hannay and Hamilton clan tents was that they enjoyed seeing their husbands "play." A Johnston woman noted that her husband's excitement over things Scottish allows her "to see the little boy in the man." While many scholars assume masculinist activities and associations are attempts by men to distinguish themselves from women or male homosexuals, Judith Kegan Gardiner suggests instead that men engaged in masculinist pursuits are really striving to appear as men rather than boys (2002, 17, 113).[7] But in whose view? Under the female gaze, Scottish-American masculine behaviors and bonding are more frequently described as "cute," "sweet," "attention-hungry," or "pompous," in terms that diminish maturity and authority rather than suggest it. While not disapproving of them, very few women describe their husbands' dress or activities, such as marching in a tartan parade or reenacting, with the words their husbands used in explaining the same, such as "warrior," "honor," "loyalty," "soldier," and "clansman." The male role model about whom men and women speak more similarly is the clan chief. As the person to whom clan society members still "pledge allegiance," he is the masculine essence of Scottishness for heritage enthusiasts, and his diction, apparel, stature, and appearance are all a source for comment.

Three-Feathered Chiefs

When I began fieldwork with other, supposedly "un-exotic" Euro-Americans, I did not expect (or hope) to be told "we want you to meet our chief." Meeting the chief of a contemporary Scottish clan turned out to be something akin to meeting minor titled persons (often one and the same). Today's clan chiefs no longer require their clansfolk to answer the call to battle, but instead ask them to answer the call to their "family" heritage and often to contribute financially to the upkeep of said heritage in the form of their personal estates. Revived interest in clan membership and veneration for clan chiefs has curiously coincided with evolving visions of gender ideals and family structures. Scottish-American interpretations and celebrations of chiefly figures and clan society honor a romanticized view of patriarchy when it has been most challenged.

Part of the appeal of clan societies abroad is that clan histories and myths situate celebrants as part of a diaspora. Stories of the clan system's demise become stories of forced immigration and ancestors' unwillingness to give up the land and traditions their descendants greatly value. In heritage lore, Hanoverian repression following the Battle of Culloden immediately dismantled Highland clan society. Actually, postbellum policies accelerated socioeconomic changes that were already at work within the Highlands, but the forty years after the last Jacobite defeat—during which tartan, firearms possession, and communal land ownership were proscribed—have become the prime motive for ancestral exile in heritage lore. Though they often encouraged and sometimes forced emigration, clan chiefs have become symbols of heritage and homeland as well as the recipients of renewed devotion and funding from internationally dispersed clansfolk.

However, like the southern plantation owner, the chiefs carried on a variety of unsavory activities that are typically excluded from discussion at heritage events. Many obtained pardon from the Crown for their part in the Jacobite Risings by turning in their own clansfolk or in return for taxes. The processes they used to gather such revenue left thousands of their "kindred" with no choice but to emigrate. Nevertheless, romanticization now exonerates the clan chiefs as paternal and benevolent "grand old men" similar to the "gallant gentlemen" of the Old South. For both, chivalry revolved around a belief in "honoring and protecting pure womanhood," yet in the Scotland of the chiefs, women could still be kidnapped and married against their will in a practice called "marriage by capture," and according to the actual behavior of "gentlemen" in the South, the designation of "pure womanhood" applied specifically to class and color. However, the shining models of masculinity in both Scottish and southern heritage are of ancient and, at least imagined, aristocratic lineage, and lore attributes their leadership abilities to their generous nature and noble characters rather than to fear or coercion.

Today, the chiefs of the hierarchically structured "revived clans" hold unquestioned authority on heritage issues, as they are presumed to have had in all matters before Culloden. As "father figures," clan chiefs travel the world making public appearances and parading with their clansfolk at heritage events wherever the Scottish diaspora has spread. (Addressed as "Madam" rather than as "chief," women account for fewer than 10 of the close to 140 recognized chiefs.[8]) Clan society members often celebrate the chief's birthday. Many comment on how unified their clan society seems after a visit from the chief, or after society members' group trips to visit the chief and clan lands.[9] New members in a clan society pledge their loyalty to the chief when one exists. Upon joining Clan Wallace, a new male member pays dues and receives a "Bond of Manrent," whereby he swears allegiance to the chief.

Originally, clansfolk demonstrated loyalty to, and received protection from, the chief through military service rather than through rents or taxation. In heritage lore the clan is then interpreted both as a "family" and as a "war machine," with the chief as military leader. When a chiefly line has died out, or a chief lacks a *tainistear* (heir), an appointed leader may take a military title as commander or lieutenant. Clan chiefs wear three eagle feathers, while commanders may wear two and armigers are entitled to display one.

A clan without a chief is considered "broken." Many of the two hundred armigerous clans and families of Scotland that lack chiefs have international clan or family societies. Driven, and often financed, by the heritage revival movement abroad, many cases to reclaim chiefships now come before the Lyon Court (the legal court of heraldry in Scotland). The Lord Lyon King of Arms decides whether a claimant may join the Standing Council of Scottish Chiefs. From several candidates for the chiefship of Clan Morrison in 1967, "the Lyon" selected a man who could trace his family thirteen generations. Morrison then became a legal clan, which required a new coat of arms, badges, crests, and, of course, a new tartan. The Lord Lyon recognized a chief of Clan Hannay only in 1983. Clan Henderson acquired a chief in 1985 after 150 years as a broken clan, and prompted by American Skenes' petitions to the Lyon Court, Clan Skene regained a chiefship in 1994 after 167 years of being "*heidless*" (headless). Both Clan Moffat and Clan Shaw waited four centuries for the restoration of their chiefs, in 1983 and 1970, respectively. In 2002 the Lord Lyon granted new Arms to Edward Stewart Dugald MacTavish of Dunardry, who in 1997 had been named chief of Clan MacTavish—after two centuries of dormancy in the chiefship.

Reporting on the Highlands in 1724, General George Wade remarked that though clansmen paid a "servile and Abject Obedience to the Commands of their Chieftains . . . they are treated by their Chiefs with great Familiarity, they partake with them in their Diversions, and shake them by the Hand whenever they meet them" (Grant and Cheape 1987, 46). A chief's activities were at the center of Highland life, and they continue to be a major focus in Scottish heritage celebration. In speeches at heritage events, clan chiefs remind their clanspeople of their traditional relationship from generations past and affirm current "bonds of kinship, trust and respect." In his remarks as honored guest at the first annual Culloden Games in Georgia (1995), Lord MacDonald—High Chief of Clan MacDonald—said he felt "the special bond of clanship, stronger than even twenty or thirty years ago" and that he had "the feeling of being a father looking down on my children."

Public ritual at Scottish heritage celebrations is ceremoniously focused on chiefly figures but also emphasizes egalitarian male bonding. Such ritual has as much fratriarchal as patriarchal emphasis and meaning.[10] Public patriarchy, as Jeff Hearn notes, can be characterized by public domain processes that are simultaneously patriarchal (hierarchical domination by men) and fratriarchal (collective domination by men) (1992, 67). While Americans show deference that chiefs might not receive in Scotland, they are also just as likely to talk with chiefs who are dukes and earls, or lesser lordlings, as old friends. I have seen one or two chiefs jocularly slapped on the back by a delighted and kilted American "kinsman"—something a Scot with a similar surname might not do!

Heritage Dress: Kilting the Cavalier

Just prior to attending a St. Andrew's Day dinner in 2003, I had shown my introductory anthropology class a film about the Wodaabe (Fulbe-speaking, Fulani nomads of west Africa). The Wodaabe hold an annual festival called the *Geerewol,* in which men make up their faces, ornament their hair, dress in colorful costumes, and compete with one another in "Yakke" dances to be judged the most beautiful and graceful. In the film, one of the Wodaabe men asked, "Isn't it the same with the birds, the female always chooses the most beautiful male?" At the St. Andrew's Dinner, a female informant and I discussed the men's obvious delight in their colorful apparel, compared with the women's relatively plain outfits. I was surprised to hear her echo the film I'd shown the day before by remarking, "Isn't that the way it is with the birds? The males are supposed to dress up for us." Certainly it is the men who are "on display" at Scottish gatherings.

Heritage dress has a variety of expressions for males, but not for females. Though one sees fairly few kilts at Highland games in Scotland, worn mostly by judges and organizers, kilts are actually required for men at many Scottish-American events and are omnipresent at Highland games. Women might wear shorts or jeans with a simple sash or a ribbon of their tartan, while men wear kilts with accessories and Highland weaponry. Tartan is now a marker of "familial" affiliation, but, being worn in greatest abundance by males, it also signifies the traditional male role in "perpetuating" the family name and being the "chief" of his own family.

It is the men who are "bonny" in heritage dress. A man's acquisition of "Scottish" attire and accoutrements entails community rituals: a new dirk may be "blessed," a new kilt will be christened with whisky or Scottish spring water, and the wearer may be marched around a Highland games field behind a standard-bearer with a banner of his clan tartan. Selecting the style of kilt and an "ancient," "dress," or "hunting" tartan is just the beginning. Men also wear kilt pins, jackets, and belts in day and evening varieties (brass buckles for day, silver for evenings). They may wear a plaid: a length of tartan secured on one shoulder with an ornamental brooch. The sporran, a purse that wraps about the waist and hangs in front of the pelvic region, will be of leather for daywear, or more expensive sealskin with horsehair and silver trim for evening. An "animal mask sporran," in which an animal's head is the opening flap, may be worn day or night. (A man's choice of animal and the condition of its fur—some men wear old and molting sporrans—is a source of jokes among women.) In footwear, men choose from brogues, wing tips, or dancing shoes that lace several times about the ankle. Headgear is usually in the Balmoral style of wool, possibly with a white cockade (bow) to show Jacobite sympathies, or in the Glengarry style worn with badges by military men and pipers. To transport the various day and evening collections, many men carry individual cases for their accessories and allow a significant amount of time between events for dressing. Multiday Scottish heritage events are the only gatherings I've attended in America where men excuse themselves early from an afternoon activity to dress for the evening. These are also some of the only venues where one will regularly see heterosexual men freely adjust one another's apparel and endlessly discuss fashion.

While "Scottish dress" has precise rules—down to the number of pleats in a kilt (29)—some men create a personal style they become known by (for example, wearing cowboy boots or suspenders with a kilt, a fringed jacket, or a unique piece of decorative weaponry). Men under age forty-five are less likely to "follow the rules" and may wear their kilts with T-shirts and trainers. A recent trend is the "Utility Kilt." The Utilikilts Company, established in 2000 in Seattle, Washington, designs kilts for "working men" with side-mount saddle pockets, loops for tools, and a modesty snap. With the slogan "we sell Freedom," the company claims twenty thousand customers and markets its garment in green camouflage and black or tan twill ($125) or leather ($700), all available in a "beer-gut cut."

As important as what men wear is what they do *not* wear. *Nothing* is worn under the kilt. This is called "going regimental." Surprisingly, among people who would otherwise be conservative about displaying the male body, accidentally revealing underwear beneath the kilt draws more laughter and ridicule than accidentally demonstrating one's adherence to regimental standards. While it doesn't happen often, having the word circulate in good fun that one "dresses correctly" is reason for pride rather than embarrassment. Howard Eilberg-Schwartz proposed that in Judaeo-Christian cultures male bodies, especially male genitals, are covered for fear of homoeroticism (1996, 43). In this case, an occasional glimpse of "the family jewels" makes the revealer a respected figure of fun, while the concealer is "unmanly." Although Americans remain timid about the male body, this is one arena in which a certain amount of exhibitionism is allowed. One Scottish man who attended American events regularly amused friends and passersby by performing a kilted handstand. When occasionally the kilt failed to stand, cameras were poised and ready.

Because true kilts are off-limits to women (unless in bagpipe bands), they have fewer options for exhibiting tartan in the Scottish style. Reenactors may wear the eighteenth-century *arisaid,* three yards of tartan gathered at the waist over a skirt, which can be used as a cape simultaneously. From 2001 to 2004, more women dressed in Victorian-style tartan dresses (popularly called "wench dresses") than had done so in the 1990s, but the types of heritage dress for women remain lackluster compared with the variety of day and evening apparel for men. Southern women get around this by blending traditions in heritage dress. Some women wear the hoop skirt of a southern belle (often in their clan tartan) to Highland games, to symbolize perceived links between their southern and Scottish ancestry.

The interweaving of Scottish and southern heritage found both literal and symbolic expression in 1997 with the introduction of a Confederate Memorial Tartan by Georgian Mike Bowen and Pennsylvanian Phil Smith. Texan John Wilson says the design of the Confederate Memorial Tartan was actually the work of at least ten people on both sides of the Atlantic, also including Patrick Griffin of Maryland (a past Commander in Chief of the Sons of Confederate Veterans) and Trudi Mann (a retired archivist from Wick, Scotland). The tartan features a Confederate gray background with stripes of infantry blue, cavalry yellow, and battle flag, or artillery, red. Through costume and imagery, the simplified, unproblematized visions of Scottish and southern masculinity are easily comparable and blended by those reared on the latter.

A Highlander and a Gentleman

Heritage lore of Scots abroad gives prominence to legendary Jacobite events as the point from which later Scottish history must be seen through the eyes of exiles. Lore fixes Highland, and by extension Scottish, culture at Culloden. Perceived as the reason for ancestral migration, the dramatic and military nature of this event continues to color conceptions about the way of life it is deemed to have ended. Focused initially on the romance of Jacobitism, Highlandism evolved with the needs of the British Empire. The seemingly antithetical defeat of Prince Charles and loyal service in the Hanoverian imperial cause came to identify not only Highlanders but Scots in general during the Balmoralism of Victoria's time. By the late nineteenth century, the British military required all Scottish regiments, Highland and Lowland alike, to wear tartan. Once emblematic of treason, the "Highland habit"—as revived in the military context—became not only "the national dress of Scotland," but symbolic of "Scottish military prowess." Kilted Scottish soldiers became known as "the ladies from hell." When British military tacticians needed a strong front line (or a disposable one), they cried, "Bring forrit the tartan." Military recruitment strategies, period literature, and popular media drew upon visions of a Gaelic Highland warrior heritage and helped to Highlandize Scotland as a warrior nation. The glorification of war and empire in nineteenth-century Highlandism remains prevalent in the Scottish national imagery perpetuated through the tourism industry and in that adopted by twentieth-century heritage movements throughout the Scottish diaspora.

Military themes are, not surprisingly, prevalent at southern Scottish heritage events. Heritage lore and celebration employ ubiquitous military themes and rituals distilled by Highlandism suggesting that Scots are "natural soldiers," despite the Highlanders' defeat at Culloden. Military metonyms tied to images of Scottish culture easily merge with those of the American South. While the Scottish warrior, "wilder" and "closer to nature," finds parallels with the frontier Scots and Scots-Irish Patriots and Carolina "Overmountain Men" of the Revolutionary period, the stereotypical image of a disciplined Scot as a bagpiping, kilted soldier finds masculine parallels in the "gentlemen gallants" and "colonel" characters of later southern myth. In the battle-driven histories of both Scotland and the South, military defeats become "lost causes" and symbolic of the loss of distinctive rural ways of life. The romancing of the Highlands and of the South was a relief from the tragic consequences of both civil conflicts. It provided a means for reacceptance of the defeated as representatives of past, but idyllic, lifeways—a past quite removed from either's actual historical experience. By emphasizing the military prowess of the defeated, Highlandism and the lore of the Old South also redeemed the masculinity of the vanquished.

Highland and southern men have somehow become both heroic in defeat and famed for loyal military service to their former enemies following defeat. In fact they have contributed disproportionately to their national militaries since their respective disasters, and military imagery has become a part of both regional stereotypes and regional self-images. Southern men seem, in Nina Silber's words, forever enshrined in their Lost Cause (1993, 173). Likewise, the Highlander, once defeated, is perpetually dressed for battle, with claymore in hand. Soldierly male icons, prominent in both southern and Scottish defeat-generated mythologies, are isomorphic in southern Scottish heritage celebration. The southern cavalier is important in southern visions of Scottish heritage as a descendant, literally and spiritually, of the Highland clansmen.[11] Today, cadets at Virginia Military Institute, bastion of southern military tradition, now man their own tent among the clan tents at Highland games and as of 1997 have their own tartan. The bagpipe band of South Carolina's Citadel, the Citadel Pipes and Drums (organized in 1955), wears kilts of the school's own tartan (registered in 1981).

Expressions of a Warrior Culture

Community members describe the most basic aspects of clan, religious, and artifactual Scottish heritage with consistent reference to a "warrior culture" and its ethics. For many informants, admiration for the ideal soldier's strength of resolve, loyalty to kin, and sense of honor add a powerful, emotional dimension to their vision of ancestral warriors. Joe Dolce writes: "[T]here is a romantic notion of the honorable warrior, the gentle defender (always male) with ethics who only fights when provoked . . . only defends when attacked . . . defends only country and family" (1993, 7). As Walter Scott romanticized Scotland and influenced Old South mythology, he likewise glamorized war. In his works (as in Highlandism and the southern cavalier legend), soldiers "fell" rather than died, horses were "steeds," the enemy was "the foe," the dead never became corpses or carrion, but "ashes and dust" (De Pauw 1998, 209). Much of community discourse about Scottish and Scottish-American military exploits idealizes the actions of warriors and "genteel soldiers" by channeling their bellicosity to lost causes; though the causes themselves remain undeliberated in celebration. And for some, the appeal of Scottish military history lies in a different type of romanticization that is roughly parallel with today's professional wrestling. From either perspective, military interests predominate in both heritage literature and event conversation, in which any military endeavor engaging Scots becomes evidence of the innate military talents of "Scotia's sons."

Those aspects of Highland material culture forbidden by the 1746 Disarming Act and the 1747 Act of Proscription (targes, dirks, claymores, and tartan) have become central artifacts of "Scottish" heritage today. While historian John Gibson argues that bagpipes were not included in either of the two acts, he does note that pipes were considered "instruments of war" and that popular and academic perceptions of bagpipes as outlawed after Culloden contributed significantly to their inclusion in stereotyped images of Highland, and Scottish,

Fig. 5. Lieutenant Colonel David Cone in period dress
of a Scottish soldier (Photo by Celeste Ray)

identity (1998, 28–33). Likewise, William Donaldson notes, "The Highland
pipe has become a potent icon, instantly evoking Scotland and the Scots both
to themselves and to the wider world" (2000, 3). The bagpiping, kilted soldier,
so well known in the British colonies, is omnipresent at heritage events.

Scottish weaponry accessorizes varying styles of male attire. Nineteenth-
century Highlandism restricted the use of the claymore to full-dress formal occasions, but today a variety of weapons may accompany both casual and
formal, day and evening apparel. The plain day "*scian dubh*" (black knife)
tucked in their knee-high socks may be replaced with an ornamental one for
evenings. Day or evening ensembles may also incorporate broadswords, dirks,
and targes.[12] In tartan parades at Highland games, men also carry reproduction
Lochaber axes, halberds, and broadswords, which they lower as they pass the

Fig. 6. "Mad Max" in one of his unusual ensembles
(Photo by Celeste Ray)

"review stand" of honored guests. Attached to clan tartan banners are pendants noting the battles in which the clan has participated. While other ethnic groups might decorate an assembly area with murals, saints' statues, flags, or crafts, weaponry (now symbolic of a warrior culture, Jacobitism, and exile) forms an integral part of event decorations, providing a "Scottish feel" to rented assembly rooms and dining halls. Heather and leather targe centerpieces ornament dining tables and clan tent information booths. Claymores and basket-hilted broadswords cross above entranceways to dances and *ceilidhs* (social gatherings for dancing, singing, and story-telling).

In clan tent or campfire discussions of the American Civil War or any subsequent war, heritage group members are quick to point out how someone was motivated by "his Scottish courage," though his ancestors may have been

Americans for well over a century. Identifying the clan's founding apical ancestor as a great warrior, many societies use the clan war cry for banners, in clan tent displays, and to title their newsletters. Recognition of clan military prowess is a recurrent theme in society literature, events, and organizational purposes. Among the Clan Fraser Society's listed goals is "to mark with plaques and statuary, historic battle sites in Scotland and North America where members of the clan have gained undying fame" (1994, 2).[13] Because of exposure to military heritage within the community, even Scottish Americans who claim not to be particularly interested in military history can detail their clans' military exploits and stress the role of "the Scottish impulse to battle" in stories of the clan system's demise.

Clan histories focus overwhelmingly on military episodes, in descriptions of both early and recent history. Community members' self-published booklets on Scottish traditions record beliefs in a biological propensity for soldiering that also surface in toasts, commemorative speeches, and clan tent discussions. In his *Scottish Character and Lifestyle,* Christian McKee writes: "The Scots have always been known as great warriors. The value they placed on deeds of valor, heroism and prowess in war certainly played a part in forming their distinguishing characteristics. The early Highlanders were always dressed and ready for war, even when going to church. Their primary weapons were knives, which were almost an integral part of their bodies" (1989, 28). Clan Henderson's promotional literature notes that though "a small clan, we have been involved in the mainstream of history, from clan battles in the Highlands to the Jacobite uprisings, and the Massacre at Glencoe" (1994, 1).

That "each clan was both a family and an army" has become a pivotal tenet of community lore, as it was a central theme of Highlandism. While all history is the product of selective recording of events, the southern Scottish-American community largely interprets the marked focus on warfare in Scottish history not as the survival of the most dramatic events in oral tradition, or in terms of the interests of the literate, but as the very driving force that made Scots Scots—their "love of the fray."

Scottish-American Military Professionals and the Warrior Inheritance

In his book *Soldiers of Scotland,* John Baynes defines a Scottish soldier as "having been born in Scotland or born of Scottish parents, or else by descent, having a Scots name and belonging to a family retaining its original, national traditions even if living in another country" (1988, xv). Such a liberal definition is popular among Scottish Americans with military careers who are, accordingly, also "Scottish" soldiers. Scottish heritage events in the American South are popular with military career people whose military identities and branches are immediately recognizable by their attire. They combine military shirts, badges, and medals with kilts of clan tartans to express a blended pride in career, American patriotism, and Scottish "family" heritage. Military members tend to be not just the rank and file, but members of the Army's Special Forces, the Navy Seals, and officers from the various branches. They often credit their career paths and success to their Scottish *and* southern ancestry, which, in heritage lore, both feature a "martial spirit."[14]

Community members within and outside the armed forces similarly explain the appeal of Scottish heritage for military career people with regard to the martial traditions, music, and history of Scotland. Those with military backgrounds discuss presumed parallels between "ancestral" Highland life and their own military culture as a primary reason for their affinity with things Scottish. The military has some analogues with the clan system. The hierarchy of Gaelic Highland society translated into rank in any clan military endeavor, as distinctions between officers and enlisted personnel flow over into the social lives of military personnel today. Providing distinct identities, today's various military branches and regiments or units also construct a further set of loyalties and a sense of "family" within the military. While united against common enemies, military groupings hold "traditional" animosities and competitive relationships, as did the clans.

A particular attraction of the community is the clan chief's celebration as military leader and the hierarchy present in clan societies, reminiscent of military rank. Informants Dan Matheson and Mitchell Mclean (retired and active military, respectively) specifically compared clan society rankings with those of an eighteenth-century chief's bodyguard. Older military members also comment on the predominance of pre-boomer-aged participants in the community with whom they share worldviews shaped by the experience of World War II and the Cold War. In practical terms, military men additionally suggested that Scottish interest groups are easier and more affordable to join than are golf or country clubs. Though perhaps an after-the-fact rationalization, retired military men explained that despite the initial costs of outfitting oneself in "Scottish" attire, heritage activities are an affordable "hobby."

Scottish activities engage military career people, battle reenactors, and military bands across the country, but a military emphasis and presence is especially strong in the South. By invitation, war veterans may join the national Scottish-American Military Society (SAMS), which has a very strong presence in public rituals, often providing honor guards and pipers for parades, festivals, and Scottish-American weddings and funerals. SAMS was organized at the Grandfather Mountain Highland Games in North Carolina in 1981 to celebrate the patriotic activities of the Scots/Scots-Irish during the Revolutionary War and beyond. Highlanders were known for their initial lack of pro-American sentiment during that war, but the imagery of Highlandism and that of the Scots-Irish as warrior frontiersmen easily merge. SAMS members from local and regional "posts" set up information (often called "recruitment") tents next to the clan tents at Highland games.

North Carolina's Fort Bragg, one of the world's largest military complexes and home to the U.S. Army's Airborne Corps and the Special Forces, is located in Fayetteville and occupies 160,000 acres of the Cape Fear Valley, settled by Scottish Highlanders in the eighteenth century. Most of the military professionals whom I met did not have a direct connection to the colonial Cape Fear Scots, but became involved in the area's Scottish activities through other military friends, often knowing very little about their own Scottish ancestry at the time of their initial involvement. Many of those posted at Fort Bragg remain in the Fayetteville area on retirement and become involved in local Scottish activities through membership in military bands and honor guards, or through interest in Scottish military or local history. Active military join for many of the same reasons.

Informants Steve Johnstone and Dale McCain also note that the Scottish heritage community provides an extended family environment that they feel is positive for their children—especially being stationed far from relatives. For both active and retired military coming to the area through Fort Bragg, genealogical interests were not a prime motive for joining the Scottish community. Participants may have known their names were Scottish, but generally an interest in researching their Scottish ancestry developed after becoming involved with Scottish heritage activities. To quote one North Carolina participant, Thomas Grant, "Scots come from a warrior culture . . . we [military men] are naturally drawn to military careers and Scottish events to begin with and find out why (because we're Scots) later on."

Weekend Warriors: Reenacting the Experiences of Soldier Ancestors

In the context of Scottish Highland games and other heritage events, military-themed reenactment and living history has become a popular form of acting out perceptions of ancestral lifestyles and communicating to newcomers and

Fig. 7. Tim and Timmy Morris (Photo by Celeste Ray)

children the core tenets of heritage lore. Heritage drawn from a history framed by military events transforms all such events into ancestral experiences. Re-enactments and living history displays interpret ancestral Scots primarily through scenes of war in which reenactors seek both intersubjectivity with forebears and comradeship within a community of their descendants.[15] Basing their activities most commonly on the Jacobite period or on a particular colonial war effort in which post-Jacobite Scots were involved (but also the Confederate period), reenactors and living historians provide a military presence at heritage events and are never absent from southern Highland games where they demonstrate the use of "traditional" weapons.[16]

Reenactment and living history groups associated with Scottish events are often ceremonial military units participating in parades and presenting battle vignettes or short reenactments of a famous charge. Their activities revolve around military encampments. While reenactors generally claim they truly "reenact" because they camp out at a site, attempt to cook with period implements, and leave the stereos, ibuprofen, and other contemporary amenities at home, they say living historians "stay at the Holiday Inn." Both varieties of costumed interpreters play an important role in communicating a militaristic vision of "the heritage." Numerous groups frequent the Highland games circuit in the South, reenacting Celtic, Viking, or Jacobite periods of Scottish history and colonial history of Scottish Americans. Jim Finegan explains the rationale behind his reenactment group, the United Regiment of MacLachlans and MacLeans, Circa 1745:

> Why would we want to do this? The only answer we can give you is that it will be fun! It's an opportunity for us to get dressed up in silly costumes, listen to a musical instrument that has been declared a weapon of war . . . and serve our community as teachers in one of the lost cultures of the past. . . . to present a living memorial to those Highlanders who fought for a cause that ultimately led to a devastating defeat that irrevocably changed the Highlands forever.

Finegan's ideas echo what I was repeatedly told by informants and challenge Richard Handler and William Saxton's dismissal of reenactments as a search for an alternate reality to one's "unauthentic existence" (1988, 243). Rather, reenactors in the Scottish heritage movement celebrate perceived continuity of their heritage from ancestral immigrants. They say that researching and performing ancestral moments is an enjoyable hobby and sociable activity that provides a sense of community and brotherhood in the present. Rather than "escape," reenactors seek connections with what they perceive to be the lived experience of their forefathers and with a vision of masculinity no longer in fashion.

Reenactors also supply a military presence at religious services such as local church "Scottish Heritage" days and "Kirkin's of the Tartan," symbolically uniting the Presbyterian and military heritage of Scots. "Kirk" means "church" in Scotland. Peter Marshall, chaplain of the U.S. Senate, a Presbyterian and native Scot, designed the "kirkin'" as a service of prayer for all Britons during World War II. The ritual spread rapidly through the Scottish heritage movement in the 1980s and 1990s and has acquired emotive stories suggesting eighteenth-century Jacobite origins. The kirkin' concludes with a "blessing of the tartan," though endorsing the blessing and iconization of a material product is unusual for Presbyterians. The kirkin's have a quite militaristic format as formal parades led by a piper alternating hymns with martial airs. Participants carry large tartan banners (now seen as symbols of clan loyalty), which are held up much like flags, evoking clan patriotism and rivalries. The kirkin' is said to be a rededication of tartan to God's service. Members of the Scottish community have argued that tartan was worn by men marching off to battle and the kirkin' suggestively links "God's service" with battle.[17]

Arguments about tartan as a soldier's garb maintained sex segregation at many kirkin's into the 1990s and at the South's most prestigious tartan parade, that at the Grandfather Mountain Scottish Highland Games. Though young boys could lead the parade holding swords, women were barred from participation for the parade's first three decades. In 1980 the ritual's inventor, Murvan Maxwell, defended the exclusion of women "due to space limitations" (1980, 55). Through the eighties, the stated reason for an all-male parade was that only men marched off to battle wearing the "clan tartan." By 1989, Maxwell argued more creatively for women's passive spectatorship in the Grandfather Mountain Games program:

> In the old country, Scots liked to march to the sound of pipes and drums—in true military fashion. Scots are born soldiers and off to the wars they would go, ever parading, with wives and loved ones watching and cheering. So why not a GMHG event to arouse their male martial spirit, to knit together their clanship and to provide a format for their ladies to cheer them on, arouse their clan pride and excite their old-country interest? A semi-military type of parade, the males stepping along to the cadence of pipes and drums, marching in individual clan groups with their own tartan fluttering in the breeze while the lassies cheered and applauded from the sidelines, seemed to be made to order for the natural outleting [*sic*] of the Scottish spirit. (Maxwell 1989, 31)

First marching at the Grandfather Mountain parade in 1994, many women claimed they had been more amused than bothered by the exclusion. Informants Jean Ross and Annie Montgomery concluded that although the men did not know it, they did have a point about males wearing tartan in battle, since the classical sources explicitly note that Celtic women joined in battle naked in order to terrify the opponent.

While drawing on the idea of a "Celtic" warrior inheritance, the celebrated warrior culture remains essentially a male culture, although both history and legend provide us with female Iron Age warriors. Historically, Tacitus and Cassius Dio document the examples of Boudicca, who led the Iceni tribe against the Romans in 61 A.D., and of Cartimandua, who led the neighboring Brigantes. Diodorus and Ammiamus Marcellinus, among others, describe women in warfare on the continent. Quite short of being safe and secure and cheering on the sidelines, women of slave status in Iron Age Britain and Ireland were forced to fight in battle either as frontline soldiers or as servants of other male or female warriors (Rankin 1987, 254).

In the early Welsh tales from the *Mabinogion* we see heroes seeking martial education from groups of women. In the Ulster Cycle of Irish sagas, we learn of women warriors such as the Scottish Dordmair, Scatach, and Scatach's daughter Ualtach "the very terrible," who taught the formidable Ulsterian hero Cu Chulainn the martial arts. We also learn of women like Nes, the mother of King Conchobar, who led bands of warriors and Queen Medb's undisputed authority over her warriors and her famous *creach* (cattle raid), the *Tain Bo Cuailnge*. While diasporic Scots claim a "Celtic" heritage, such Iron Age heroines are forgotten in the focus on the Highland soldier of the British Imperial period.

Contemporary celebrations neglect even the heroines of the better-known Jacobite period (a period when the English and Lowland Scots complained of women's power within the clans). On horseback, Jenny Cameron led her clansfolk from Glen Dessary to join Prince Charles at Glenfinnan and for her active patriotism was vilified as Charlie's harlot by the Hanoverians (Craig 1997, 44). While her Mackintosh husband served as a Hanoverian officer, "Colonel Anne" (a Farquharson) raised her husband's clansfolk for the Jacobite cause. Staunch Jacobite Lady Nithsdale secured her place in history after the Jacobite Rising of 1715 by rescuing her condemned husband (a Maxwell) from the Tower of London on the eve of his execution. Yet, when women appear in living history scenarios, they appear as camp followers. While women now march in tartan parades across the country, the most stereotyped aspect of the Gaelic clan system retains Highlandism's masculine focus in reenactments of ancestral experience.

Military Origins of "the Scottish Arts"

In Robert Bly's best seller *Iron John,* which kicked off the mythopoetic men's movement, Bly quotes what he calls "an old Celtic motto: 'Never give a sword to a man who can't dance'" (1990, 146). Many aspects of heritage celebration that may seem quite unmilitaristic to non-Scots in fact have military origins. The dancing and piping traditions featured at nearly every heritage event continue to play a part in the Scottish military traditions from which they derived. In the twentieth-century evolution of games traditions, Highland dancing has become the only event in which females are now the predominant participants.[18] Historically, men performed the Highland dances in honor of a chief or a new marriage, or to celebrate victory in battle.[19] Men still perform the oldest military dances, the "Highland fling" and the "Sword Dance," at games in Scotland and on Scottish regimental pipe bands' international tours. Originally performed around a spiked targe, the Highland fling celebrated performance in combat. By tradition a divining ritual to predict the outcome of a battle, the Sword Dance was performed over two crossed swords or a sword crossed with its scabbard. If the dancer did not touch the swords while executing the steps, victory was assured; if he did, defeat was at hand and he braced himself to glory in a hero's death. Several informants relayed varied but consistently gory tales of the dance's eleventh-century origin. The most popular version suggested that MacBeth first performed the dance over his bloodied claymore and the head of a man loyal to his archrival for the throne, Malcolm Canmore (of Highland games fame). More moderate accounts replace the severed head with the vanquished's sword, and still others suggest links to the ancient Celts.

Of Lowland origins, Scottish Country Dancing also carries military themes. Country dancing is somewhat akin to square dancing, but is gentrified as "Scottish ballroom dancing" in Scotland and abroad with standardized Highland apparel. Dances such as "Dashing White Sergeant," "White Cockade" (the emblem of a Jacobite), and "O'er the Border to Charlie" draw upon Jacobite themes. According to Scottish country dance instructor Alex Gallamore, new country dances with more recent military origins have also become popular with transnational Scots. Choreographed in 1984 for the 350th year of Britain's oldest infantry regiment, the "Reel of the Royal Scots" is now a familiar exhibition dance for country dance groups. Internationally, during the anniversaries of World War II events, all-male dance ensembles performed the "Reel of the 51st," conceived during World War II by Scottish soldiers in German prisoner-of-war camps. Less militaristic fiddles and accordions now provide the steady tempos of today's country dance music, while bagpipes always accompany Highland dancing.

In heritage lore, bagpipes were outlawed as weapons of war after Culloden. As Gibson notes, however, non-*ceòl mór* piping ("great music," including marches, battle tunes, salutes, and laments) *within* the British Army was not suppressed and remained popular throughout the Disarming Act years (1998, 63). Bagpipe music has many varied expressions in Highland culture, but with Highlandism it came to internationally symbolize loyal and dependable (and expendable) Scottish soldiers. Even Lowland regiments such as the Royal Scots, Scotland's national senior regiment, acquired bagpipe bands in the nineteenth century. Pipe bands now evoke the days of the empire, especially in former colonies. Today, local pipe bands based on the Scottish model play in full Highland dress from Vancouver, British Columbia, to Hong Kong. As military bands from the United Arab Emirates go to Scotland for training, members wear a tartan sash over their uniforms. Scottish military bands travel worldwide to perform, and several of my informants linked their early interests in Scottish heritage to attending a concert by one of the many regimental bands.

Deftly integrating Highland and military themes (now a traditional association) through costume, narration, and music, the performances of touring bands play on clan rivalries, historical incidents, and patriotism tied to current events. Displaying full Highland dress with military badges and medals, and a specific tartan linked to the regiment, band members wear decorative Highland weaponry and some drum majors carry claymores. The Scottish regimental bands are the "original" model for heritage and military pipe and drum bands around the globe.[20] Pipe band competitions and "massed" pipe band performances are an arresting part of larger Highland games. Many games give their name, and increasingly their own tartans, to their host bands, which carry local and regional pride into national and international competitions. Just as Scottish bands tour the globe, many civilian and military pipe bands begun in the former colonies now come to Britain to perform and compete in Highland games, but all emulate bands like that of the senior Highland regiment, the Argyll and Sutherland Highlanders.[21]

Much of the pipe music heard at heritage events focuses on clan feuds, battles, massacres, or other like incidents in the history of "Scotland the Brave." Some of the best-known Scottish tunes originated as military marches or have developed around military themes. Scottish regiments have their own martial airs (or marches), and many clan societies, perceiving clans as small armies, have adopted their own military tunes. As I became more familiar with popular *ceilidh* songs and campfire recitations of martial poetry, I was less surprised at the numbers of event participants with military backgrounds. Heritage events that celebrate the stereotyped Scot of the late eighteenth and early nineteenth centuries, by extension, celebrate the career path and something of the worldview of military career people and overtly masculine identities.

Conclusion

As I've noted elsewhere (2001, 206–08), the Scottish heritage movement in the southern United States may be seen as a revitalization movement—as an intentional and organized attempt to create a more satisfying state of existence by recovering or re-creating traditions and selecting and claiming "roots." But here Anthony Wallace's classic distinction between a revitalization movement and revivalism proves relevant. He defines the aim of the latter to be the "return to a former era of happiness, to restore a golden age, to revive a previous condition of social virtue" (1985, 320). Celebrating the past and wanting to be in the past are vastly different phenomena. Scottish heritage celebration calls for a return only to some ancestral values and the security that predecessors are presumed to have had in their identity—the type of security born in moments of societal drama. Today's drama comes from within and plays out in culture change rather than in lost causes.

In some ways, aspects of southern Scottish heritage events could be seen as part of male revitalization movements. Public rituals, speeches, songs, and celebratory costume relate to the ultra-masculine identities challenged in the critique and reinvention of masculinity since the 1960s. As Michael Kimmel notes, "The 'old man,' as opposed to the 'new man,' is still around, not exactly enjoying a renaissance, but far from slipping quietly into oblivion" (1996, 300). Unlike other American male revitalization movements (by this I mean attempts to reassert what participating males believe to be their traditional and natural, if not divinely ordained, roles and positions), such as the antifeminist "Promise Keepers" or secretive male-bonding drumming retreats, Scottish-American males assert warrior themes and parade patriarchy within particular public arenas: celebratory events and Scottish social organizations. Celebration does not advocate these roles "at home." Public oration, ritual, and song do not relate to the "good provider role," nor do they emphasize any expected roles for women, other than that they enjoy the show.

Scottish-American males' "deep play" as weekend warriors links them in fraternal societies that cross class and educational boundaries. The clan chief is hailed as a hierarchical leader, but also the first among brothers. However, male Scottish heritage activities are not quite the mythopoetic return "to an idealized tribal mythology of male homosociality" (Messner 1997, 2; see also Kimmel and Kaufman 1994). Scottish-American men are exploring the "plurality of masculinities" modeled by forefathers and from which to draw a sense of male identity (Conway-Long 1994, 61). They are also submitting themselves, in ritual and in dress, as objects to the gaze of women and other men. When we speak of the southern belle "on the pedestal," we assume she was limited to certain roles and that she was there in place of having real power. If patriarchy and masculinity are now put on the pedestal, perhaps this reflects very real changes in the power of gender identities. Although it may in some instances seem a ritual response to recent social changes, the masculine and military focus of Scottish-American heritage lore and celebration is much more complex than a simple backlash to feminism and evolving "family values." Several centuries of transnational cultural links coupled with the selective integration of battle-driven Highlandist and southern motifs have produced a unique regional vision and celebration of identity.

Notes

1. Some portions of this essay have variously appeared in a 1998 article titled "Scottish Heritage, Southern Style," in *Southern Cultures* 4, no.2: 28–45, and in Ray 2001 and 2003.

2. However, see Pittock (1999) for interesting arguments that the Scottish identity was feminized as Celtic. For more on masculinity and national identities, see McGregor (2003) and Hooper (2001).

3. Southerners named their homes, pets, and children after characters and places in Scott's novels (for more information, see Ray 2003, 259–60). Not only did southerners blend the St. Andrew's cross into the Confederate battle flag and call a national flag "the Bonny Blue flag," but the Scottish "belt and buckle" that encircles a clan chief's crest appeared on Confederate bills. Thanks to John Wages for pointing out that the five-hundred-dollar bill featuring Stonewall Jackson also used the belt-and-buckle motif.

4. While informants employ the word "tribal," scholars refer to the Highland clan system as a "chiefdom-level" society. The Highland clans straddled classic anthropological definitions of tribes (pastoralist-based, with leaders selected by prestige) and chiefdoms (more agriculturally based, with leaders inheriting their positions). While a chief could nominate an heir in his lifetime (his *tainistear*), Highland chiefs were generally selected, or elected, from a family group, so descent *and* prestige were important in the clan system. Their subsistence strategy might best be described as agropastoral with some semi-feudal aspects such as landholding tenures and association with localities.

5. Few clans claim female apical ancestors. Clan MacFie claims descent from a *selkie* (seal-woman). Clan MacDuff claims Queen Gruoch, married to Macbeth, to be the earliest known ancestor in its Scoto-Pictish line. The Marjoribanks took their name from the lands of the only daughter of Robert the Bruce, Princess Marjorie.

6. However, for community members, *communitas* (which I use here to mean united community spirit) arises from perceived kinship, and this familial dimension distinguishes Scottish Americans as an ethnic group from what Benedict Anderson has called "imagined communities." Though often a reclaimed identity, Scottish Americans consider their ethnic identity involuntary because of their interpretation of clan.

7. "Historicizing masculinity," her age-inflected theory of gender examines how it evolves over the course of an individual's life as well as in relation to social changes like the erosion of the breadwinner model of masculinity in the United States.

8. Historically, when a woman succeeded to the chiefship, a male relative would also be appointed as a *ceann-cath*, or commander, to lead the clan militarily.

9. Older members of Clan Mackintosh relate how two disputatious Clan Mackintosh societies united through the 1973 American visit of "Mackintosh of Mackintosh."

10. Male members of Scottish heritage organizations are often members of other male associations such as the Masons, and especially those connected with the military. Despite an assertion to the contrary in the *Oxford American* (Roberts 1999), few participants are also members of the six-thousand- to nine-thousand-strong League of the South, which advocates devolution for the southern region. Men I have interviewed may be a part of reenactment militias but express great concern over what they consider the "bastardization" of Scottish and southern imagery by nonrecreational militia groups, especially white supremacist groups in the northwestern states.

11. Scottish Highlanders were far from aristocracy in the period since romanticized. Similarly, most southerners were pioneers with little of the extravagance now portrayed as antebellum standard. David Hackett Fischer notes that in Virginia many of the first settlers "were truly cavaliers . . . younger sons of proud armigerous families," but that the majority of Virginia's white population were indentured servants (1989, 786–87). Those who provided the cavalier model were also overwhelmingly English, not Scottish.

12. Targes are wooden shields made of hide or made of wood and covered in hide, sometimes with a ten-inch spike in the center.

13. Informants and the literature also note the fame of the *Galloglas* (Scottish mercenaries employed across Europe from the late Middle Ages to the time of Napoleon) and the Scottish reputation for valor within the British Army. Certainly it is their battlefield exploits that are mentioned, not the off-field activities for which mercenaries are more infamous.

14. For speculations on the "martial spirit" in the South, see Higginbotham (1992).

15. For more on the meaning of comradeship, see J. Glenn Gray (1996).

16. Since 2001 there have been fewer reenactors at Scottish events. It is tempting to link this to a period of actual war, however defined.

17. See Wood (1990) on Protestantism and the Scottish military tradition.

18. Unlike the Irish dancing style, Highland dancers perform in soft shoes making no sound and traveling very little on stage.

19. Competition dances now often include jigs and hornpipes known as "national dances," as well as the more balletic "Village Maid," "Earl of Errol," or "Blue Bonnets over the Border," which often have Jacobite themes.

20. Many American military units have pipe and drum bands that also wear specially designed tartans like those that now exist for the U.S. Navy and the Marines in addition to a general U.S. Forces tartan.

21. Perhaps ironically with the Jacobite focus of Highlandism, Sutherland and Argyll were territories with pro-Hanoverian chiefs.

Works Cited

Baynes, John. 1988. *Soldiers of Scotland.* Elmsford, New York: Pergamon.
Bly, Robert. 1990. *Iron John: A Book about Men.* Reading, MA: Addison-Wesley.
Clan Fraser Society. 1994. Information Leaflet.

Clan Henderson Society. 1994. Information Leaflet.

Conway-Long, Don. 1994. "Ethnographies and Masculinities." In *Theorizing Masculinities*, ed. Harry Brod and Michael Kaufman, 61–81. London: Sage.

Craig, Maggie. 1997. *Damn' Rebel Bitches: The Women of the '45.* Edinburgh: Mainstream.

De Pauw, Linda. 1998. *Battle Cries and Lullabies: Women in War from Prehistory to the Present.* Norman: U of Oklahoma P.

Dodgshon, Robert. 1995. "Modelling Chiefdoms in the Scottish Highlands and Islands Prior to the '45." In *Celtic Chiefdom, Celtic State: The Evolution of Complex Social Systems in Prehistoric Europe,* ed. Bettina Arnold and D. Blair Gibson, 99–109. Cambridge, Eng.: Cambridge UP.

Dolce, Joe. 1993. "The Warrior, the Wound, and Woman-Hate: The Politics of Soft-fear." *Changing Men* 26 (summer/fall): 6–12.

Donaldson, William. 2000. *The Highland Pipe and Scottish Society, 1750–1950.* Edinburgh: Tuckwell.

Eilberg-Schwartz, Howard. 1996. "God's Phallus and the Dilemmas of Masculinity." In *Redeeming Men: Religion and Masculinities,* ed. Stephen Boyd, Merle Longwood, and Mark Muesse, 36–47. Louisville, KY: Westminster John Knox.

Enloe, Cynthia. 1995. "Feminism, Nationalism, and Militarism: Wariness without Paralysis?" In *Feminism, Nationalism, and Militarism,* ed. Constance R. Sutton, 13–34. Association for Feminist Anthropology/American Anthropological Association.

Fischer, David Hackett. 1989. *Albion's Seed: Four British Folkways in America.* New York: Oxford UP.

Gardiner, Judith Kegan. 2002. *Masculinity Studies and Feminist Theory: New Directions.* New York: Columbia UP.

Gibson, John. 1998. *Traditional Gaelic Bagpiping, 1745–1945.* Montreal: McGill-Queen's UP.

Grant, I. F., and Hugh Cheape. 1987. *Periods in Highland History.* London: Shepheard-Walwyn.

Gray, J. Glenn. 1996. "The Enduring Appeal of Battle." In *Rethinking Masculinity: Philosophical Explorations in Light of Feminism,* ed. Larry May, Robert Strikwerda and Patrick D. Hopkins, 45–62. Lanham, MD: Rowman and Littlefield.

Green, Martin. 1993. *The Adventurous Male: Chapters in the History of the White Male Mind.* University Park: Pennsylvania State UP.

Gutmann, Matthew. 1997. "Trafficking in Men: The Anthropology of Masculinity." *Annual Review of Anthropology* 26: 385–409.

Handler, Richard, and William Saxton. 1988. "Dyssimulation: Reflexivity, Narrative, and the Quest for Authenticity in 'Living History.'" *Current Anthropology* 3: 242–60.

Haraway, Donna J. 1991. *Simians, Cyborgs, and Women: The Reinvention of Nature.* New York: Routledge.

Hearn, Jeff. 1992. *Men in the Public Eye: The Construction and Deconstruction of Public Men and Public Patriarchies.* London: Routledge.

Higginbotham, R. Don. 1992. "The Martial Spirit in the Antebellum South: Some

Further Speculations in a National Context." *Journal of Southern History* 58, no. 1 (Feb.): 3–26.

Hooper, Charlotte. 2001. *Manly States: Masculinities, International Relations, and Gender Politics.* New York: Columbia UP.

Huddleston, Joe. 1998. "The Highlander: Definition and Description," *The Highlander* 36, no. 1: 56–61.

Kimmel, Michael. 1996. *Manhood in America: A Cultural History.* New York: Free Press.

Kimmel, Michael, and Michael Kaufamn. 1994. "Weekend Warriors: The New Men's Movement." In *Theorizing Masculinities,* ed. Harry Brod and Michael Kaufman, 259–88. Thousand Oaks, CA: Sage.

McGregor, Robert. 2003. "The Popular Press and the Creation of Military Masculinities in Georgia Britain." In *Military Masculinities: Identity and the State,* ed. Paul Higate, 143–56. Westport, CT: Praeger.

McKee, Christian. 1989. *Scottish Character and Lifestyle.* Landisville, PA: Self-published.

McWhiney, Grady. 1988. *Cracker Culture: Celtic Ways in the Old South.* Tuscaloosa: U of Alabama P.

Maxwell, Murvan. 1989. "The History of Parade of Tartans," *Grandfather Mountain Highland Games Program:* 31. West End, NC: Harris Printing Co.

———. 1980. "The Parade of Tartans." *Grandfather Mountain Highland Games Program:* 55. West End, NC: Harris Printing Co.

Messner, Michael. 1997. *Politics of Masculinities: Men in Movements.* Thousand Oaks, CA: Sage.

Nelson, Dana. 1998. *National Manhood: Capitalist Citizenship and the Imagined Fraternity of White Men.* Durham, NC: Duke UP.

Pittock, Murray. 1999. *Celtic Identity and the British Image.* Manchester, Eng.: Manchester UP.

Pleck, Joseph H. 1995. "Men's Power with Women, Other Men, and Society: A Men's Movement Analysis." In *Men's Lives,* ed. Michael Kimmel and Michael Messner, 5–12. Boston: Allyn and Bacon.

Rankin, David. 1996. *The Celts and the Classical World.* London: Routledge.

Ray, Celeste. 2003. "'Thigibh!' Means 'Y'all Come!'" Renegotiating Regional Memories through Scottish Heritage Celebration." In *Southern Heritage on Display: Public Ritual and Ethnic Diversity within Southern Regionalism,* ed. Celeste Ray, 251–82. Tuscaloosa: U of Alabama P.

———. 2001. *Highland Heritage: Scottish Americans in the American South.* Chapel Hill: U of North Carolina P.

Roberts, Diane. 1999. "Your Clan or Ours?" *Oxford American* (Sept./Oct.): 24–30.

Robinson, Sally. 2000. *Marked Men: White Masculinity in Crisis.* New York: Columbia UP.

Silber, Nina. 1993. *The Romance of Reunion: Northerners and the South, 1865–1900.* Chapel Hill: U of North Carolina P.

Szechi, Daniel. 1994. *The Jacobites: Britain and Europe, 1688–1788.* Manchester, Eng.: Manchester UP.

Wallace, Anthony. 1985. "Nativism and Revivalism." In *Magic, Witchcraft, and Religion,* ed. Arthur Clehmann and James E. Myers, 319–24. London: Mayfield.

Wood, Ian. 1990. "Protestantism and Scottish Military Tradition." In *Sermons and Battle Hymns: Protestant Popular Culture in Modern Scotland,* ed. Graham Walker and Tom Gallagher, 112–36. Edinburgh: Edinburgh UP.

10
Finding Colonsay's Emigrants and a "Heritage of Place"

John W. Sheets

Today, literally hundreds of thousands of Americans and Canadians claim Scottish descent, join clan societies, participate in Highland games, and celebrate a Celtic nostalgia. This burgeoning heritage industry creates a flexible past and unites countless imagined kin. Heritage events often renegotiate clan defeats, family evictions, and forced emigrations into transatlantic success stories that reference tartan dress, Gaelic sport, bagpipes, and the Highlands. Privileging such symbols is a potent retreat into myths and memories with vague boundaries and a fragile authenticity (Crane 2000; Ray 2001).

More subtle, more restricted, but equally intense is the "heritage of place," a "lost locus" abandoned by specific ancestors where contours and stories have echoed through the generations. Membership here designates an ancestor or two whose record of marriage, baptism, burial, or appearance in a census count (or in a printed text) forever binds one to a precise piece of Scottish geography. Just a name and date can trigger relentless, sometimes expensive, searches for more family facts. The reward is a genealogical spot to grasp, envision, share, and ultimately visit. It can become a personal quest with other relatives, proximal and distant, all of whom discover, then deal with, a potpourri of place-names, conflicting sources, differing descriptions, previous searchers, and the many pasts offered by today's place. The newest searchers seize and depend upon virtually any information for their creation of identity and connection. Given the ubiquity of e-mail and Web sites, this construction of Scottish identity in North America is perhaps not as flamboyant as a tartan parade, but is instantly, quietly, and creatively contagious over the Internet of our twenty-first century. And the objects of desire can be some of the tiniest places in Gaelic Scotland's Highlands and Islands.

The Colonsay Diaspora

The remote island of Colonsay lies off Scotland's Argyll coast, a part of the Inner Hebrides sandwiched between much larger Mull, Islay, and Jura. Its twenty or more square miles were the medieval home of Clan Macfie (earlier McFee or McDufee), whose chief found himself between the powerful McLeans of Mull and the even more powerful McDonalds of Islay, the legendary Lords of the Isles (Byrne 1997).[1] Traditionally, Macfie of Colonsay kept the records, weights, and measures for the lordship. A mid-sixteenth-century description claimed "ane fertill ile guid for quhte fishing . . . This ile is bruikit [owned] be ane gentle capitane, callit McDuffyhe." Soon the Campbells of Argyll had toppled Islay's McDonalds and displaced the last Macfie chief in Colonsay—Malcolm. James VI of Scotland (I of England), "for services rendered to him and his forefathers, and for sums of money received," sold Colonsay to the 7th Earl of Argyll in 1610. Near the end of the century, Martin Martin included Colonsay in his *Description of the Western Isles of Scotland*, not quite so favorably: "the middle is rocky and heathy . . . bred here are cows, horses, and sheep all of a low size. The inhabitants are generally well proportioned, and of a black complexion; they speak only the Irish [Gaelic] tongue . . . they are all protestants, and observe the festivals of Christmas, Easter, and Good-Friday." In 1701 Malcolm McNeill of Crear (in Argyll) purchased Colonsay from the 10th Earl of Argyll, specifically its "houses, biggings, yards, orchards, mills, multures, mosses, muirs, meadows, woods, fishings, grazings, pasturages, annexis, connexis, outsetts, insetts, parts, pendicles and their universal pertinents whatsoever lying in the Parish" (Loder 1935, 212, 219–20, 236–37, 261–62). Thus began in Colonsay two centuries of McNeill lairds and McNeill tenants. Their entirely separate ancestry originated in Barra of the Outer Hebrides, but is now a perennial point of confusion for Colonsay descendants in search of their McNeill roots.

Across the Atlantic, the colony of North Carolina flourished under its second (and longest serving) royal governor, Gabriel Johnston (1699–1752), who arrived at Port Brunswick on October 27, 1734. According to his English investors and colonial critics, the St. Andrews–educated Scotsman shamelessly recruited fellow Highlanders to settle throughout the Cape Fear Valley. Apparently they came, since Johnston moved inland during March 1739 and a large group from Argyll followed him. Under "Black Neil" McNeill, the "Thistle" departed Campbeltown at the tip of Argyll's Kintyre peninsula in July. Among its 350 passengers were McAllisters and McNeills from the Argyll coast, and possibly Colonsay, plus many named Buie, Campbell,

McCranie, and McDougal, probably from Jura; McNeill of Colonsay owned Jura's northern district of Ardlussa, where a number of Colonsay people lived and worked. They reached Port Brunswick in September and quickly established their "Argyll Colony" one hundred miles up the Cape Fear River. In Colonsay, Angus McNeill had petitioned the sheriff-substitute of Argyll in June 1739 about his father's brother Archibald, "Tacksman of *Garvard*." The uncle had granted his nephew a bond in 1730 for one hundred pounds, but young Angus now sought any tangibles, since "the said Archibald McNeill has lately sold off his effects in order to go to America" (Cunningham 1944, 1–14; Fowler 1986, 20–24; Budge 1960, 69–70; Meyer 1961, 54–59; National Archives of Scotland, Edinburgh, SC54/2/53/1739).[2]

The *Scots Magazine* then reported "fifty-four vessels full of emigrants from the Western Islands and other parts of the Highlands sailed for North Carolina between April and June 1770, conveying twelve hundred emigrants." Five hundred more from "Islay and the adjacent islands" prepared to leave in the summer of 1771 (MacLean 1900, 419). A popular Gaelic song promoted "*Dol a dh'iarruidh an fhortain do North Carolina* (Going to seek one's fortune in North Carolina)" (ibid., 108).[3] Only the American Revolution stemmed this transatlantic tide of Hebrideans, including *Colbhasaich*, or "People from Colonsay."

Why did so many Gaelic-speakers in North Carolina remain loyal to the king? When General Donald McDonald raised the Royal Standard in Cross Creek's public square on February 1, 1776, former clansmen joined the regiment, perhaps painfully yet with good reasons. After Culloden, the English had forcefully applied both "the stick and the carrot." Prisoners were executed, lands confiscated, people banished, and Gaelic culture outlawed; Highlanders coming to North Carolina feared and never forgot the reprisals. But the king and William Pitt also formed the Highland regiments, who fought gallantly against the French on the Continent and in North America. In fact, many regiment officers retired to North Carolina and its profitable land. One of the first to volunteer at Cross Creek was Allan MacDonald, husband of Flora MacDonald, who famously assisted the escape of "Bonnie Prince Charlie" from Skye in the Outer Hebrides! For these Highlanders, any advantage of Loyalism disappeared on February 27, within the space of a few minutes at Moores Creek Bridge, just north of Wilmington. The rebels (or Patriots, based on perspective) disabled the bridge, then waited in elevated positions for McDonald's regiment. In place of a sick McDonald, Colonel Donald McLeod foolishly charged the bridge. The rifle and artillery retort cleared the field with nearly nine hundred Highlanders captured. The rebels jailed them, raided their farms, and scattered their families; many of them later fled by ship to Nova Scotia. The skirmish at Moores Creek permanently compromised the British strategy in North Carolina and thoroughly diluted sympathy among the Highlanders; they did not respond in any similar fashion when Cornwallis arrived in 1781 (Meyer 1961, 146–61).

America's independence from the British Empire carried irreversible consequences for transplanted Gaels from Argyll and their descendants. The new nation generated new documents and often ignored, or destroyed, those from its colonial past. A search for one's Argyll ancestors in pre-Revolutionary North Carolina can end with bits and pieces, or sometimes a surprise ripe for speculation and story. One of the oldest gravestones in Fayetteville's "Cross Creek Cemetery Number One" records Jura's Colin Shaw: "native of Scotland came to Cross Creek in 1744, twice commissioned in King's Army . . . Loyal in word and deed" (Sherman and Lepine 1988, 1).

As a prelude to war, the British had terminated emigrations to the American colonies by September 1775. Afterward, the 1783 Treaty of Paris coincided with poor harvests and widespread famine in Scotland. In 1784 Benjamin Franklin warned "those who would remove to America" that "the Government does not at present, whatever it may have done in former times, hire people to become settlers by paying their passages [or] giving land" (Cooper 1795, 231–32). The renewed transatlantic emigrations merely revived the drain on rural populations; this time the passengers were more destitute and often without plans or leaders. So severe was the depopulation in Colonsay that the parish minister complained in the *First Statistical Account of Scotland* (1791–1796, Vol. 12: 329 and 332): "in the summer [of] 1791, a considerable proportion of the inhabitants crossed the Atlantic . . . Instead of trying the effects of industry at home, they foster the notion of getting at once into a state of ease and opulence, with their relations beyond the Atlantic." In May, June, and July of 1806, no less than five ships collected almost five hundred people in "the West Highlands & Islands—esp. Mull and Colonsay" bound for Prince Edward Island. To obey the new Ship's Passenger Act, each ship maintained its register code and a passenger list; and in one case, they offer vivid witness to the exodus from Colonsay now shifted toward Canada.[4]

Important to Colonsay's emigration history (and to descendants' collective memory) is the *Spencer* of Newcastle. It was a 330-ton, three-masted, fully rigged vessel of "E1" code, meaning "Second Class, Perfect Repairs [in 1803], with Satisfactory Equipment." Constructed in 1778, it measured 100 feet long, 25 feet wide, 17 to 18 feet deep, with four "4-Pounder" guns. A "deck with beams" allowed planking for an extra level to accommodate the emigrants; the planks were removed to carry timber and other cargo on the return. The *Spencer* left Oban, on the Argyll coast, in late July for Colonsay's harbor at Scalasaig, where over a hundred islanders waited. And they were not a random sample of the local population. Many came from the isolated north of Colonsay at Balnahard; they were mostly McMillans, McNeills, and Munns tied into a Gordian knot of kinship. Their common property and shared provisions for the forty to fifty days at sea consisted of "72 chests, 4 trunks, 35 barrels, 8 boxes, 1 hogshead, 1 kettle, 40 parcels, wearing apparel/bedding." The current laird, John McNeill (1767–1846), was busy draining, enclosing, improving, and populating the interior of Colonsay, Kilchattan, around Loch Fada; these tenants chose relocation across the Atlantic, not elsewhere on their native island. The *Spencer* reached Pinette Harbor in the southeast of Prince Edward Island on September 22, 1806. The collector of customs carefully enumerated its 115 surviving passengers: 64 males and 51 females, with 43 "under 16," 68 "from 16 to 60," and only 4 "above 60." They spent the winter in quarters and with provisions provided by an agent. The next spring these Colonsay settlers moved to the nearby Wood Islands area (on "Lot 62") to begin their new lives in a New World (Campey 2001, 135, 140–42; Sheets 2004).

More islanders boarded the ships for seemingly more free land along the new frontier of "Upper Canada"—also called *An Talamh Fhuar* (The Cold Land). From the Maritimes, Colonsay people ventured into the wilderness north of Ontario's "York" (later Toronto), where "by 1815 [Highland Scots] had made Gaelic the third most common European language in British North America [after English and French]" (Bumsted 1991, 388). Like the "pioneers" to Prince Edward Island, they too left a recoverable record in property surveys, parish registers, and rural cemeteries. For example, in the 1820s, Catherine, Donald, Duncan, John, Lachlan, and Sarah McKinnon (with their elderly parents) moved to Kilchattan from Mull. Except Duncan, the brothers and sisters migrated to Erin Township of Wellington County, Ontario, in 1831, where their large families established contiguous one-hundred-acre farms. They were soon followed by others from Colonsay, like Angus Bell and Margaret McCalder, who were married at the Scalasaig church on October 30, 1835, and settled in nearby East Gwillimbury Township the next year. Donald, John, Lachlan, and Sarah McKinnon are buried in Erin's Coningsby Cemetery, "together in death as they always were in life" (Sheets 2000, 81; Old Parish Register of Colonsay).

In Colonsay the first household census, of 1841, recorded 979 residents, or nearly 50 per square mile. For those staying, John McNeill was forever the affectionate "Old Laird" of paternal instincts, Gaelic speech, and staunch Presbyterianism. His favorite district of Kilchattan boasted 255 in forty-three households, while Balnahard struggled with 32 in just six houses. An image of success continued in print. An 1841 "Emigrant's Guide to North America" (in Gaelic) remarked that the best variety of cattle to take to Canada "came from Colonsay" (Thompson 1998, 102; Kidd 2002). Scotland's *Second Statistical Account* (1845, Vol. 7: 546) applauded him: "Mr. McNeill has thus, by judicious, persevering and well-directed efforts, not only brought his estate in a high condition of cultivation and productiveness, but he has likewise much improved the condition of the small crofters, and afforded constant occupation to a numerous and comfortable population." Actually, he had witnessed a decade or more of falling prices for Colonsay's exports and mercifully died on February 24, 1846, the eve of the potato famine. That year the islanders received a shipment of American corn, and the next year young men and women went to find seasonal work in mainland towns and cities. Rather ominously, the parochial death register for Colonsay starts in 1848. By the 1851 census, the population had declined by 15 percent to 837, signaling more decades of emigration and 150 years of depopulation (Loder 1935, 179; Sheets 1984).

The influx of famished Irish and Scots around Lake Ontario forced the provincial government to survey Bruce and Grey Counties near Lake Huron. In 1852 the Crown Lands Department opened "Canada West" for "Ten shillings per Acre . . . occupation to be immediate and continuous." Among the earliest to settle in Elderslie Township of Bruce County were Galbraiths, McLugashes, and McNeills from Kilchattan in Colonsay. They would stop at Wood Islands, Prince Edward Island, or Wellington County, Ontario, to meet previous settlers from Colonsay, perhaps stay awhile, and learn the ways of life in Canada. This "Chain of Migration" ensured the arrival of other Colonsay people to Elderslie, and way beyond the Great Lakes (Sheets 2000).

A Witness and a Scribe

Born in 1839, seventh of seven children, raised during the lean years, and witnessing the departures was Domhnall MacFhionaghain, or Donald Mackinnon. His father was Duncan McKinnon, whose brothers and sisters had gone to Ontario in 1831; his mother, Mary Currie, remained in Colonsay close to her parents and her married sisters. Like the emigrants, those staying tended to cluster in kin groups around the island; young Donald was surrounded by maternal grandparents, aunts, uncles, and cousins. His father was an "agricultural labourer" for the McNeill lairds, while the family lived on a croft of "4 Acres arable." Their stone cottage on the west coast lay behind the cemetery at Kilchattan, anglicized from *Cille Chattan* (Catan's Church). Catan was a disciple of Columba, Argyll's patron saint from Ireland, and the medieval ruins of a church cell at the cemetery attest to Colonsay's ecclesiastical status. Also in view is *Dun Meadhonach* (Middle Fort), where ancient clans and Macfies sought safety and comfort. Not far down the coast, one encounters *Traigh an Tobair Fhuar* (Cold Well Strand). Its shore, and bones rumored to lie beneath it, mark *Latha Cath na Sguab air taobh tuath Dun Ghallain* (The Day of the Battle of the Sheaves on the north side of Galan's Fort), or the time a thousand years ago when islanders repelled the Norse armed only with birch spears.

Around cottage hearths at night, the Colonsay children learned their Gaelic language and local lore through such vivid legend and metaphor. *Cuidh Catan* (Catan's Heel-mark) designates a round depression in a large Kilchattan rock, "specially in charge of the M'Vurichs of the locality," who gauged wind and weather from that spot. By repute, the "M'Vurichs" descended from a select class of ancient Irish scholars; the surname mutated several times to McMhui-rich, to McCurrich, to McCurry, and finally to Currie, young Mackinnon's mother's name (Loder 1935, 15–16, 32–33; Sheets 1999).

Local Gaelic place-names told of danger as well as sustenance. *Eilean Ban Scalasaig* (Island of the Scalasaig Women) was visible off the west coast; long ago women from the east side of Colonsay waded over the sand at low tide to gather shellfish, misjudged the currents, and drowned. With infinitely more care, Donald Mackinnon and his friends learned to "fish and trap" from small craft anchored near their cottages at *Port Mor* (Big Harbor). The preferred catch were *sgadan* (herring), *trosg* (cod), *langa* (ling), *giomach* (lobster), *cruban* (crab), and *easgann* (eel). Should they encounter strangers, Mackinnon knew how to judge them based upon easy comparisons: "A Mullman, an Islayman, and the Devil; the Mullman is worse than the Islayman; the Islayman is worse than the Devil." Above all, trust those closest to you, instructed one of the many Gaelic proverbs: *Is math an sgathan suil caraide* (The eye of a friend makes a good mirror). For its men, women, and children, Colonsay seemed a self-contained world of mutually supportive family, friends, and McNeill lairds. Mackinnon certainly needed them the month after his twelfth birthday, when his father died in May 1851, which was followed by the death of a twin sister in November; the other twin sister died in May of the next year. More and more people were leaving the impoverished island. Mackinnon painfully noticed it and soon joined them—but not across the Atlantic. He followed a path of academic excellence and public service, forever tempered by a devotion to Colonsay, its dwindling population, and his published memories of it.

Donald Mackinnon attended the nearby *Sean Sgoil* (The Old School) staffed by teachers fluent in Gaelic; they used the language and translated Bible to instruct the students in arithmetic, composition, prayer, and English. For any teacher in any subject, he displayed a prodigious skill; he could read a printed page, English or Gaelic, then recite the contents from memory. In 1857 this "Lad o' Pairts" ("very clever boy") earned admission to the Church of Scotland's Training College for teachers in Edinburgh. Upon certification, he ventured far north to Lochinver, Sutherland, for three years as the parish schoolmaster and his first exposure to a much different dialect than Argyll's Gaelic. In 1863 he enrolled at Edinburgh University, where he excelled as an arts student, receiving First-Class Honors and the prestigious Hamilton Fellowship. The *Oban Times* (December 4, 1869) wanted its Argyll readers to share in the triumph: "It is very gratifying to think that one coming from a distant island in the county should have been selected from among some of the ablest students in the University." Donald Mackinnon also belonged to the university's Celtic Society. Every other week the Gaelic-speaking students gathered to debate and discuss issues of the day. He served as a president, secretary, and treasurer and was a frequent presenter to the membership. Among his topics were "Highland Emigration" and "Life in Canada" based upon letters from family and friends no longer in Colonsay. One of the best and most poignant sources for his speeches was his surviving sister, Janet. In 1862, after their mother's death and with her husband and four children, she had followed other Colonsay families to Elderslie, never to return.

The island registered only 456 people for the 1871 census, less than half its 1841 size. Donald Mackinnon lived in Edinburgh, where he was deeply involved in the Celtic revival. After graduating, he agreed to serve on Edinburgh University's committee seeking "a Chair of Celtic Literature and Antiquities." In March 1873 the city's new school board hired him as its secretary and treasurer. In November he married a Colonsay girl, Catherine McPhee, in the parish church at Scalasaig; their first child was born in Kilchattan the following August. What free time this civil servant and family man could spare, he devoted to a Gaelic-English journal, *An Gaidheal* (The Gael). Contributing virtually every month, he offered essays, book reviews, and multipart series about Gaelic proverbs and literature. In a March 1875 review he lamented the cost of Gaelic emigrations: "Abroad, as is well known, Highlanders are and have been among our foremost colonists [but] our Highland peasantry, in order to find a fair field in which they may be able to benefit themselves and their fellow men, must seek other lands." The next month, in an essay about "National Prejudice," he identified a cause: "The English taunt the Scotch; the Saxon ridicules the

Gael . . . it is the outcome of a prejudice which is neither healthy nor instructive" (Sheets 1999; Mackinnon 1875a, 1875b).

In an unpredictable and delayed fashion, Donald Mackinnon was elected to Edinburgh's Celtic chair at the end of 1882, a position he kept for thirty-two years. A few months later Prime Minister William Gladstone appointed him to the Napier Commission, charged to tour the Highlands and investigate its current unrest. Mackinnon was the youngest member (of six) and one of two Gaelic-speakers. Although the commission bypassed Colonsay, it convened in a Mull church close to the birthplace of Mackinnon's father. The *Oban Times* (August 11, 1883) hid nothing from its readers: "The crofters here are very poor, and during last spring some of them were only saved from actual destitution by assistance received from their sons and daughters who had gone south for employment." For the commission's *Report and Evidence* to Parliament, Donald Mackinnon, the "fisher boy" from Colonsay, composed the section about "Fisheries and Communications." In plain English, he presented an initial cure for Gaeldom's malaise: "Improved communication by post, telegraph, roads, steam vessels, and railways is of great significance to all classes and interests in the Highlands and islands." Such an investment was years away and never comprehensive (Sheets 1999).

Four years later Mackinnon disguised an impatience with the government inside Edinburgh's leading newspaper, *The Scotsman*. The Mackinnons and their four children annually spent a long summer holiday in Colonsay. After communion at the Scalasaig church on July 17, 1887, Donald left the island, fearful for its future. He published "Lonely Colonsay" in *The Scotsman* of August 23; its title came from a phrase of poetry by Sir Walter Scott. In a lengthy piece, the Celtic professor unabashedly promoted a place needing assistance ("The lonely island is becoming yearly better appreciated as a health resort and retreat for a quiet holiday. With improved communication, it is likely to become more so"), cited landmarks of his youth ("St Catan's church still stands in ruins at Kilchattan"), and pleaded to newcomers ("few places are better fitted to maintain a rural population than the island of Colonsay"). But the prospects were dim: "The interesting island fondly remembered by visitors, inexpressibly dear to those brought up in it, looks as if doomed to a solitude not due to its geographical position alone." Then, from early November through January 1888, *The Scotsman* presented Mackinnon's "Place Names and Personal Names in Argyll" in no less than eighteen parts. The series endures as a cornucopia of Gaelic words, phrases, stories, emendations, and stunning erudition about pre-Celtic and Celtic roots, archaic words, Norse elements, saints, hunting and fishing, land, boundaries, and personal names. The conclusion of the series, "Family Names. XVIII," carried no pretense as to why Colonsay examples permeate the series. And he fully intended to focus on the island through one final, unusually personal marker: "The lonely isle of Colonsay has furnished so many illustrations for these papers . . . Thirty years afterwards, in 1881, there were only 395 inhabitants, considerably less than half, and in the current decade the outflow continues . . . Currie, the leading name ninety years ago, has entirely disappeared." Never again, in his many lectures, manuscripts, and publications, would his native place appear so often.

Transatlantic Visitors, Memories, and Images

If the government would not come to the rescue, at least Donald Mackinnon tried. Colonsay's first Parish Council under the Local Government Act was reported in the *Oban Times* of March 30, 1895. Among the four men serving, with the Presbyterian minister, was "Professor Donald Mackinnon of the Celtic Chair, Edinburgh, and Balnahard, Colonsay." The Mackinnon family now split their home and residency between city and island, committing considerable time, money, and effort to the farm, equipment, and livestock at Colonsay's north end. The following month the council elected Mackinnon chair and representative to the County Council. For the last twenty years of his life, Donald Mackinnon faithfully, and more frequently, traveled to Colonsay and the nearby isles to attend meetings, resolve disputes, solve problems, and, above all, support the local school. His tireless work quickly showed results; Colonsay's first resident physician arrived in 1897. Nevertheless, a weak economy and government's neglect forced more people to leave; the 1901 census was only 313. In August 1902 the laird and everyone in Colonsay hurried to prepare for the royal family; Edward VII had suddenly ordered an overnight anchorage for the royal yacht at Scalasaig. Donald Mackinnon, though, took time to answer a letter from Guelph, Ontario. Robert Lachlan McKinnon was a young attorney there and the son of one of Donald Mackinnon's many paternal cousins in Ontario. Thirty-year-old Robert wished to know about any relatives not in Canada, so the older "cousin," whose father had stayed behind in the 1830s, gave him a blunt summation: "I knew Janet who went to Mexico . . . John and Cormick and Angus were married and lived latterly in Glasgow. They are all dead."

The last McNeill laird of Colonsay, a close friend of the king, died in 1904. When no one in the family bid on the indebted estate, it was purchased by one of Canada's wealthiest men (also an emigrant), Donald "Labrador" Smith, also

Canada's High Commissioner and "Baron Strathcona and Mount Royal." Other visitors from Canada noticed the conditions in Colonsay, Argyll, and throughout Scotland. "Lachie" McNeill from Fort William, Ontario, spent Christmas 1904 in Colonsay ("birthplace of his parents," where "the old Gaelic language is still spoken") and later met Donald Mackinnon in Edinburgh ("one of the most noted scholars of the British Isles"). Once at home, he wrote to the Paisley *Advocate* (March 9, 1905), candidly comparing the transatlantic life to that in Scotland: "The conditions this side of the Atlantic are better than there, especially among the working class. At present a great many are out of employment." Another Colonsay descendant from Canada followed and, like some others a generation or two removed, had jumped onto the road of professional success. The Reverend John J. McNeill came to Colonsay in August 1905 to see the vacant cottages of *Druim Clach* (Stone Ridge) at Kilchattan, home of his grandfather, Lachlin, buried in Rusk's Cemetery, Elderslie (with over one hundred *Colbhasaich*). He had served the First Baptist Church in Winnipeg since 1899, just attended a church convention in London, and would soon start his next ministry to a large congregation in Toronto. He gazed over the few acres on which Lachlan McNeill had toiled and at the Kilchattan cemetery with other ancestors, such as Lachlan's wife. For this extended family, going from Colonsay to Canada and back again entailed both continuity and change, always part of the emigration story. A few years later in cosmopolitan Edinburgh, an aging Celtic professor still suffering the pains of youthful memory sometimes shared with a special audience. Donald Mackinnon usually addressed Edinburgh's Gaelic parish of St. Oran's during the New Year's *ceilidh.* On January 9, 1908, he tried to describe and explain "The Melancholy of the Gael" only to relive the "emigration from his native parish upon a somewhat larger scale—friends, neighbours, relatives parting in this world forever. No one who has witnessed the heart-breaking scene is likely to forget it" (Mackinnon 1908; Loder 1935, 187–99; MacKay 2001–2003; Sheets 1999).

Mackinnon died early Christmas morning, 1914, inside the farmhouse at Balnahard, from where so many people left for Prince Edward Island in 1806. Now, with the rest of Britain, Colonsay plunged into the "war to end all wars." Within months, the islanders buried the remains of seamen from the HMS *Viknor,* sunk off the west coast by a German submarine. Colonsay men on both sides of the Atlantic served with distinction and at great loss. The Reverend McNeill took leave from his Toronto church to minister to Canadian troops in England and France; he received the Military Cross for saving wounded soldiers on the battlefield. Dr. Malcolm McKechnie from Paisley, Ontario (and of emigrant great-grandparents from Colonsay), served with the

179th Cameron Highlanders. His second cousin in Edinburgh, Dr. Duncan Mackinnon, youngest child of Donald Mackinnon and a recently widowed father, served with the Glasgow Highlanders. In 1918 both men were killed near the front line, with their respective ambulance and hospital units, and buried in a French military cemetery. At the Scalasaig harbor stands a slender, granite Celtic cross in recognition of "Colonsay men lost in World War I, 1914–1918." The sixteen names attest to the decimation of Colonsay men struck down in the prime of life—a demographic blow from which the island's population never recovered. In 1921 the population was 284—in 1981, only 137.

Catherine and Mary Mackinnon raised their brother Duncan's daughter in family fashion; Catherine lived in Edinburgh, while Mary stayed at Balnahard. Young Elise thought every child spent the school year in a city, then the summer on a beautiful island being spoiled by unmarried aunts. The Mackinnon sisters wrote to their cousins and friends in Ontario where the Reverend McNeill garnered national attention. In 1928 he began a term as president of the Baptist World Alliance, numbering over ten million members; in 1930 he was appointed principal of the faculty of theology at his alma mater, McMaster University; beforehand he would tour India, Burma, China, and Japan for the Alliance. Another distinguished Canadian branch of the Colonsay tree was Robert McKinnon, the Mackinnon sisters' second cousin who had queried their father about family history. By royal appointment in 1928, he became judge of Ontario's Wellington County Court; in 1935 he received the King George V and Queen Mary Medal for illustrious service. By 1936, though, he desperately wanted to fulfill a lifelong dream of going to Colonsay.

Catherine, Mary, and Elise Mackinnon invited "Judge McKinnon" (and his wife, Annie) to visit their summer residence in the Hebrides. On August 13, 1936, after London and Edinburgh, they boarded a Glasgow steamer in Oban that stopped at Scalasaig—from where his grandfather Lachlan and others departed in 1831. Like the islanders for centuries, a mile from the Colonsay shore they unloaded into a small boat "with big waves dashing it up and down" for a rough ride to the quay and a newly found family. Robert, Annie, and the Mackinnons toured the island "in a two-wheeled cart with a pony," met more relatives, attended church, and walked among the empty cottages of Kilchattan. By chance, at the Oronsay Priory they met John de Vere Loder (Lord Wakehurst and a renowned diplomat), author the previous year of the definitive book *Colonsay and Oronsay*. Loder, also brother-in-law to the then-current Lord Strathcona, had put into orderly print the long story of Colonsay's history in periods including the Age of Columba, the Norse invasions, the Lords of the

Isles, the Campbells, the "Last of the Macfies," and what he deemed "Recent Times." He quoted a little-known recollection by Donald Mackinnon about his childhood, when potatoes, fish, eggs, and milk were the staples; children wore shoes of tanned hides; and "Little money passed" (Loder 1936, 184–87). The copious appendixes offered genealogies, transcribed documents, historical descriptions, and lists of common plants and animals. But the epitome must be its last one of local "Gaelic Place-Names." Working with a friend of the late professor, Loder amassed over thirteen hundred entries of priceless reference material already fading from the social memory of Colonsay's older, fewer Gaelic-speakers.[5]

Today's Searchers and the Many Pasts

As Donald Mackinnon had urged, better communications mean survival for any island in Gaelic Scotland. A telephone line came through Islay to Colonsay after World War II. However, the island remained isolated until the County Council built the Scalasaig pier in 1965. Now, more visitors and tourists arrived aboard the more frequent ferries, and among them was an American journalist (and future Pulitzer prizewinner), John McPhee. He later wrote, "Not long ago, it occurred to me that although all my clansmen in America had talked for so long about Colonsay, as far as I knew none of them had ever been there . . . As soon as I could, I took my wife and our four daughters and went to live for awhile in Colonsay" (1970, 10). In a nascent way, McPhee fancied himself the keen observer who joins his subjects for a mutual dose of reality.

The American McPhees moved to Kilchattan for a few months. Their girls attended the local school, while John befriended the McNeill couple next door. He encouraged them to explain Colonsay, its landmarks, history, legends, and especially their lifelong friends around the island. "Yanks" staying with children in school was quite a novelty in a place where news spreads fast. McPhee's neighbor (and "landlord") took him lobster fishing, walking about, and to the hotel's pub, where American generosity kept glasses full and tongues wagging. John McPhee seemed a "likeable chap" just wanting to know about his ancestors. He was no "innocent abroad," but a magazine writer after a story, not about ancient clansmen but the very people entertaining him. Back home in America he published a series of articles in the *New Yorker* that eventually became *The Crofter and the Laird* (1970). McPhee's book makes use of Loder's work (1935).[6] It also "named names" and repeated conversations within the literal confines of quotation marks. According to McPhee, "There is apparently a point at which gossip can become so intensely commonplace that it is not only beyond hurting anyone but is, in fact, a release" (99). This statement is certainly true for the spoken word, which evaporates—but not for the printed version, which persists. The work made public exchanges about drinking, personal problems, even personal hygiene, or the laird's alleged avarice. For example, "'I think, between ourselves, that _____ married money . . . when he's in his cups he makes no bones about it'" (62). Or, "'I think they're all mentally ill'" (100). The literati of Long Island may enjoy it, along with a Central Park agent or editor, but Colonsay people were not amused. In 1973 regular ferry service commenced from Oban; more than a few passengers carried *The Crofter and the Laird.* McPhee's caricature of private lives and personal talk hurt deeply. At least one reviewer thought, "Some readers have found McPhee's past choice of subjects eclectic to the point of anarchy" (*Time,* December 5, 1977). In Colonsay the quiet chaos lingered long after he left.

I first arrived at Scalasaig on a "ferry-boat" in late June 1977, another American staying awhile to befriend and quiz the few people on a small island. Unlike McPhee, I worked through the local doctor, with whom I had corresponded the year before and who told the community about me. With printed forms and home interviews, I would gather facts of birth, death, marriage, genealogy, and health to compare with Jura's population; a release form given to every household guaranteed confidentiality. Still, the doctor's next sentence after "Welcome to Colonsay" was "Do you know of McPhee?" And my hosts, a local family running the hotel, posed the same question. After walking anywhere the first week, marveling at the scenery, and waving to anyone (including the English tourists), I borrowed a copy of *The Crofter and the Laird.* Here was the antithesis of a researcher in the field. No wonder the islanders suspected I was "another McPhee." I talked to the hotel staff about the book, their feelings, and my shock; I also considered a quick exit to Jura. Luckily, word of mouth from the hotel detached me from my American nemesis. The data collection started slowly, then reached a workable rate of return. When I departed from Scalasaig harbor in a tiny lobster boat for Jura, I promised to return. My new friends scoffed, "We've heard that before from so many of you [visitors]." But I did, and have for over twenty-five years.

The return trips to Colonsay were shorter additions to much longer times in Edinburgh. With support from Colonsay's doctor and minister, I gained access to the historical registers dating from the eighteenth century. This allowed me to reconstruct the complicated family histories over seven to eight generations and measure the impacts of emigration. For example, in the 1881 census, Colonsay registered virtually no men twenty to twenty-nine years old. Now I knew why Professor Mackinnon said, "A marriage is a rarer event than a Parliamentary election" in "Lonely Colonsay" of 1887. In 1988 the research took a wonderfully unexpected turn. At the hotel's pub one night, a friend and influential islander asked me to pursue a topic with deep ties to the island's heritage—to tell the story of Professor Mackinnon, born and buried in Kilchattan, the "fisher boy" who rose to such prominence in Victorian Scotland. I said that I was not a biographer, not remotely acquainted with his language of Gaelic, and not sure if I could gain any funding. Yet, I also recalled a day at the cemetery in July 1977, with the specter of McPhee over me, seeing Mackinnon's Celtic-cross gravestone and musing, "How did a lad from here achieve so much?" Suddenly, I saw an opportunity to give something back to a place that gives me so much (Sheets 1994).

I had already consulted some of Mackinnon's papers at Edinburgh University and encountered his family's facts at the National Archives of Scotland. With the advice (and endearing friendship) of Scotland's premier genealogist (Cory 1997), I located the lone family of descendants (through the son killed in World War I) then living in rural Wales. They shared pictures, antiques, and stories, especially one of a transatlantic fortune somehow lost; most amazing was a typed family history by "Judge Robert McKinnon" from his 1936 visit to Colonsay. Where in Canada were "Erin" and "Elderslie" with more Colonsay descendants keeping more pictures and papers? I later located one of Robert's grandsons, who volunteered a box of letters and other memorabilia. Its contents reconstructed the incredible story of Donald Mackinnon's maternal grandaunt from Mull, Catriona Bheag (Little Catherine), going to St. Petersburg around 1800 with an English diplomat's family. She eventually served the Romanovs as a nursery governess to the future Alexander II. So devoted was this czar to his "old Scotch nurse" that he sang a Gaelic lullaby at her funeral in 1858. While traveling with a Romanov princess and settling in Florence, she often wrote to her extended family in Colonsay, Mull, and Ontario, promising to share her wealth (Sheets 1993). Beyond this fascinating side of Donald Mackinnon (of great interest in Colonsay), I also discovered many more Canadians with deep roots to, and a deep longing for, the island of Colonsay. These Colonsay years unfolded an unwitting conspiracy of people, publications, and passions that form their heritage of place, at many levels, from various sources, but on paths of convergence.

About the time John McPhee left Colonsay for New York, Dr. Earle Douglas MacPhee (at the University of British Columbia) revived today's version of Clan Macfie. His efforts began societies first in Canada, Australia, and New Zealand. He then contacted the MacDuffie Clan of America and

Fig. 8. Dr. Earle D. Macphee, Clan Commander, with
Jennie M. Macphee, Clan Patron, "tying on the Macfie
tartan" to Macfie's Standing Stone, June 1981 (Courtesy of Sylvia M. McPhee)

even Macfies in Sweden. On May 10, 1977 (a month before my arrival), Ulf
Hagman (from Sweden), Earle and Jennie MacPhee, Lord Strathcona, and
local men dedicated a repaired *Carragh Mhic a Phi* (Macfie's Standing Stone)
in southeast Colonsay in honor of the clan's one-thousand-year history on the
island. (In 1623 enemies had bound the clan's last chief, Malcolm, to the ver-
tical slab and executed him.[7]) On May 27, 1981, Scotland's Lord Lyon, King
of Arms, officially reactivated "Clan Macfie" and later installed Dr. MacPhee
as its first commander. The doctor died in 1982, and in June 1985, clan members erected a plaque commemorating him next to *Carragh Mhic a' Phi*.

By the Canadian Clan Society's brochure, "membership is open to all persons male or female having the name 'MacDhubhsithe [Black One of Peace],' however spelled, and all persons connected by marriage with or descended from or adopted by such persons." It lists the motto ("Pro Rege" [for the King]), the badge ("Darag [oak] or Dearca Fithich [crowberry]"), the Clan Day ("May 27 each year"), and, of course, "Our Homeland . . . Isle of Colonsay, Argyll." The clan parliament meets every fourth year in Scotland, and in 1993 the sixth such meeting took place in Colonsay, the first formal meeting of Macfies in Colonsay in 370 years. Clan Macfie returned there in September 2001 following the eighth parliament, in Oban. Members were welcomed and informed of the island's history at the village hall, the site of an evening *ceilidh*. On the following day, clan members traveled together to visit *Carragh Mhic a Phi*. Islanders gathered at the pier to say farewell to each departing group of clansfolk. Informants and clan society publications frequently reflect on the meaning and significance of the event for a reunited clan.

Beginning in the late 1970s, improvements in communications and transportation paved the way for greater guest traffic to the island. Kevin and Christa Byrne came from Ireland with their young children in 1978, purchased the island's hotel, and began to promote local heritage to guests. The island's connection to the main electrical grid (in 1985) made providing services for guests easier, and the reconfiguring of a hinged ramp at the Scalasaig pier for "roll on—roll off" traffic in 1988 meant the larger ferries could then approach with heavy equipment and shipments regardless of tide or weather.

By the early 1990s, Colonsay had become an attractive destination for tourists, returning Macfies, other expatriates, and potential residents. Guidebooks on Colonsay and Oronsay's history became available (Newton 1990), and a good portion of Colonsay House and several cottages on the laird's estate were modified to accommodate seasonal tourists—many who return year after year. Despite the accompanying arrival of external influences, one devotee of two decades testified in a manner sure to have eased Mackinnon's worry about change on the island: "Arriving in Colonsay is like walking off the world. It's so unspoiled that you forget all your problems." In 1995 Lord Strathcona's Colonsay Press reprinted Loder's book with the laird's introduction, "Sixty Years On." He summarized the years after World War II and noted that despite just a hundred residents, "Colonsay looks better placed than most other small islands off Scotland's west coast to take on the twenty-first century."

I visited a snowy Colonsay in March 1995 after six weeks in Edinburgh gathering more material about Donald Mackinnon. Over dinner at the hotel, the Byrnes said they were selling it and entering the publishing business. They had support from Argyll and the Islands Enterprise and the convenience of

Colonsay's new digital telephone exchange (for computer-based orders). By early May, the thrice-weekly ferry brought "13 tonnes of books" to the House of Lochar warehouse, and the Byrnes had established the first business on the island that was not dependent on agriculture or tourism. House of Lochar publishes volumes that preserve and promote the local heritage. *Colkitto!* (Byrne 1997) details the life and times of Colla Ciotach (Left-handed Coll), who shot the last Macfie chief in 1623. *Moch is Anmoch* (Earlier and Later) (Scouller 1998) presents the translated Gaelic poetry of Donald A. MacNeill and other "Colonsay bards."

Meanwhile, in April I went to Bruce County, Ontario, where the museum and archives at Southampton organized, publicized, and sponsored an entire Saturday there for me to meet Colonsay descendants. In the morning I compared family information with individuals and small groups; in the afternoon I extended "greetings" from the people in Colonsay, then presented a slide lecture (in three parts) to more than fifty potential Colonsay pilgrims. The next day I arranged for Bruce and Colonsay children to correspond and, with the genealogical society's president, to collaborate in the study of Rusk's Cemetery.

Interest in clan lands among Colonsay descendants has grown tremendously through the 1990s. Colonsay's Web site, *www.colonsay.org.uk,* opened on the Internet in 1999, featuring information about the island's landscape, flora and fauna, weather, and amenities, as well as information about how to "get there" and on accommodation and genealogy. Kevin Byrne started a linked e-newsletter called "The Corncrake" that reports on island topics such as Colonsay whisky, churches, and recent events, and provides ferry and tide schedules. The newsletter lets anyone follow a *ceilidh* at the new village hall or "Quiz Night" at the hotel, or see pictures of the school's play, or know the serving hours of "The Pantry" at the pier, in addition to considering social issues such as health care and housing. Especially interesting to Colonsay descendants is the editorial policy encouraging "brief genealogical and related queries . . . from *Colbhasachs* overseas." Family traditions relating to Colonsay emigrants are a regular feature, contributed from North America, South Africa, New Zealand, Australia, and the rest of the United Kingdom.

Since late 1999, external users of the Web site seek Colonsay and its heritage of place through the "inscriptive process" of local connections. They consult and absorb layer upon layer of historical sources for a sense of mutual identity. Using surnames (like Macfie/McFee/McPhee and McNeill), pictures, letters, diaries, or prior research from Prince Edward Island, Ontario, or Edinburgh, hopeful descendants seek a real, *not* imagined, link to a Colonsay spot, a Colonsay record, a Colonsay person, past or present. Now readily accessible are more than a century of publications of differing images of Colonsay by a Celtic professor, an antiquarian, a laird's brother-in-law, a journalist, an anthropologist, a linguist, a local publisher, and now a growing body of anecdotes and folk memories from *Colbhasachs* overseas. I now put manuscripts on-line (e.g., *www.islandregister.com/colonsay_selkirk.html*) or wherever a descendant can read them, respond, and join the emerging network of today's *Colbhasaich* (Sheets 1994, 2004; *The Torch*, September 2002). The past president of the Bruce County Genealogical Society recently visited Colonsay to follow her interest in the one-hundred-plus emigrants buried in Rusk's Cemetery. From family histories and Bruce newspapers, she publishes short narratives about the emigrants; their sales in Canada and in Colonsay support the cemetery's renovation and preservation (MacKay 2001–2003). "The Corncrake" offers a search engine, while Kevin Byrne and the current editor keep a "Colonsay Register of Emigrants" ("Your e-mail address can be placed alongside the individual in question, so that like-minded folk can get in touch with you directly"); he proposes a "Colonsay Biographical Dictionary" and, in 2006, a transatlantic voyage to Prince Edward Island, commemorating the Colonsay emigrants who sailed on the *Spencer* of 1806.

While heritage research is now easier, even those seekers who come to Colonsay may be challenged in a search for roots. Looking for a particular past often means scouring gravesites and being outdoors, and the Atlantic weather does not always cooperate. Finding relatives or precious facts in today's population of a hundred does not always happen; fewer than twenty-five people (out of 313) carried the "McPhee" surname or immediate ancestry in the census of 1901! As they did a century ago, the islanders welcome all visitors and will share a ride, a boat, a fishing line and a story, or dry clothing and a warm room. One trip may provoke another, occasionally leading to relocation on the island. The welcome of newcomers belies economic and social changes occurring on the island that are leading some "old timers" to depart. High freight rates, contentious ferry scheduling, limited housing and shopping, and the general isolation (so attractive to tourists) all lead islanders to think of the mainland. Angus McPhee, a council chairman, came to Colonsay because he is a McPhee and his grandfather was born there, but he says the island is too expensive and distant from his children and grandchildren in England. Perhaps it is that "living on Colonsay is quite different from remembering life in Colonsay." One might add that visiting the island to "experience" the place of transgenerational stories is another thing altogether.

By plane, train, bus, and ferry, or by the touch of a keyboard, Colonsay's global offspring have entered another dimension of shared cultural space. Though they follow previous searchers, their heritage of place and construction of identity supersede the literal topography, recent history, and local customs of the island (Hirsch 1995). Their need for authentic places and written materials deviates in some ways from Romantic Highlandism.[8] Clan Macfie's Internet home page is an international kinship of names, addresses, sources, and data electronically accessed, globally explored, and still evolving. Just as there are "many Scotlands of the imagination," so there are many "Colonsays" of the keyboard. Such constructions of heritage and identity spring from "the meetings of local historical societies, their e-mail addresses, and their Internet websites" (Strathern and Stewart 2001, 191, 279). The electronic mantra for today's countless descendants from Colonsay might be the opposite of that Gaelic song from the eighteenth century: *Dol a dh'iarruidh an fhortain do Colobhsa* (Going to seek one's fortune in Colonsay). Their fascination, contacts, visits, and computer communication provide support for a small community in a changing economy.

The Macfie Clan Society of America hosted the 14th International Clan Gathering at the Gatlinburg, Tennessee, Scottish Highland Games in May 2003. The current commander, Sandy McPhie from Australia, was a "Special Guest of the Games." Did North American Macfies, pushed from a homeland, and North Carolina McNeills, pulled to a new land, discover a shared, constructed identity from a common point of origin? Clan Macfie will hold its 15th International Gathering and 9th Clan Parliament in Inverness, Scotland, during September 6–11, 2005; the clan will visit Colonsay on the 11–14th. Colonsay's "Corncrake" of January 18–31, 2004, observed and cited, "Approximately 50 million people of Scots descent are scattered around the world—many with island roots—representing a significant market for business." And another North American contingent, the Clan Currie Society of New Jersey, may promote Colonsay on its Web site, *www.clancurrie.com.* Can other islands profit from this explosion in ancestral tourism? By coincidence, I recently sent data and publications to the new Feolin Information and Research Centre on the Isle of Jura that will serve genealogical researchers and heritage tourists. Can other island communities profit from developing transatlantic links with descendants of émigrés while at the same time still losing their populations to emigration? The *Glasgow Herald* of November 29, 2003, editorialized that "We must act now to turn the population tide in our island communities," while an accompanying article featured the emigration of a family that can trace its history on Colonsay for 250 years. Will the island survive as a community or as a memory, or both?[9]

Notes

1. I use the spelling "Macfie" at the request of my informants.

2. Not every Argyll "tacksman" led his kin to North Carolina in 1739. For example, Captain Lachlan Campbell and forty families left Islay in August 1739 to join previous settlers in upstate New York, but the governor there did not honor the land claims (MacLean 1900, 176–78).

3. Not everyone shared this vision. In 1766 a traveling Anglican missionary, Charles Woodmason, wrote: "The Manners of the North Carolinians in General are Vile and Corrupt—The Whole Country is in a State of Debauchery, Dissoluteness and Corruption—And how can it be otherwise? The people are composed of the Out Casts of all the other Colonies who take Refuge there" (Hooker 1953, 80–81).

4. Unfortunately for all searchers and researchers, only eleven of the early passenger lists to Prince Edward Island have survived (Campey 2001, Appendix I, 105–34).

5. Mackinnon in Loder (1935, 184–87) from Macalister (1910, 2–6); Loder's *Colonsay and Oronsay* supplanted the two-volume, error-prone *Book of Colonsay and Oronsay* (1923) by the antiquarian Symington Grieve.

6. He parenthetically and unspecifically calls Loder's volume "a book compiled by the [current] laird's uncle" (54).

7. So elusive was Malcolm that at least six or seven Gaelic places in Colonsay claim *Leab' Fhalaich Mhic a Phi* (Macfie's Hiding Place) (Loder 1935, 131–32). At that time, the stone actually "stood some yards to the east of its present location, upon a low knoll"; it later broke, "having been used by generations of cattle as a scratching post" (Byrne 1997, 98).

8. Past and present champions of Highland Scotland as merely "Invented Tradition" (e.g., Samuel Johnson and Hugh Trevor-Roper) find themselves under suspicion (Ferguson 1998).

9. Selected sources are reproduced with the kind permission of the Registrar General for Scotland, Edinburgh. Scotland's tourist office, "VisitScotland," now offers a Web site "to ensure that you get the most out of your visit to the birthplace of your ancestors"; *www.ancestralscotland.com* buries Colonsay's paragraph within a section about the Inner Hebrides and Argyll.

Works Cited

Budge, (Rev.) Donald. 1960. *Jura: An Island of Argyll*. Glasgow: John Smith.

Bumsted, John M. 1991. "The Cultural Landscape of Early Canada." In *Strangers within the Realm: Cultural Margins of the First British Empire*, ed. Bernard Bailyn and P. D. Morgan, 363–92. Chapel Hill: U of North Carolina P.

Byrne, Kevin. 1997. *Colkitto!* Colonsay, Scotland: House of Lochar.

Campey, Lucille H. 2001. *"A Very Fine Class of Immigrants": Prince Edward Island's Scottish Pioneers, 1770–1850*. Toronto: Natural Heritage.

Cooper, Thomas. 1795. *Some Information Respecting America Collected by Thomas Cooper*, 2nd ed. London: Printed for J. Johnson in St. Paul's Churchyard, 1794.

Cory, Kathleen B. 1997. *Tracing Your Scottish Ancestry*, 2nd ed. Edinburgh: Polygon.

Crane, Tara Christopher. 2000. "Scottish Folk Costume in Ethnic Identity." *Missouri Folklore Society Journal* 22: 75–90.

Cunningham, Mary. 1944. "Gabriel Johnston: Governor of North Carolina, 1734–1752." MA thesis. Chapel Hill, University of North Carolina.

Ferguson, William. 1998. "Samuel Johnson's Views on Scottish Gaelic Culture." *Scottish Historical Review* 77, no. 2: 183–98.

First Statistical Account for Scotland, 1791–96, Vol. 12.

Fowler, Malcolm. 1986. *Valley of the Scots*, privately published by Wynona Fowler.

Grieve, Symington. 1923. *The Book of Colonsay and Oronsay, Volumes I and II.* Edinburgh: Oliver and Boyd.

Hirsch, Eric. 1995. "Introduction to The Anthropology of Landscape." In *The Anthropology of Landscape: Perspectives on Place and Space,* ed. Eric Hirsch and Michael O'Hanlon, 1–30. Oxford: Clarendon.

Hooker, Richard J. 1953. *The Carolina Backcountry on the Eve of the Revolution.* Chapel Hill: U of North Carolina P.

Kidd, Sheila M. 2002. "*Caraid nan Gaidheal* and 'Friend of Emigration': Gaelic Emigration Literature of the 1840s." *Scottish Historical Review* 81, no. 1: 52–69.

Loder, John de Vere. 1935 [1995]. *Colonsay and Oronsay.* Edinburgh: Oliver and Boyd.

Macalister, Francis. 1910. *Memoir of the Right Honourable Sir John McNeill.* London: John Murray.

MacKay, Mary. 2001–2003. "Lauchlan's Legacy . . . We Must All Stay Together . . . Tatters in My Life . . . I Think We'll Go Too . . . The Scooptown Diary." Privately published, Ontario: Paisley.

Mackinnon, Donald. 1908. *The Melancholy of the Gael.* Mackinnon Collection B1(7), Special Collections, Edinburgh University Library.

——. 1887. "Lonely Colonsay." *The Scotsman*, August 23.

——. 1875a. "Olim Marte, Nunc Arte." *An Gaidheal* 4: 87–89.

——. 1875b. "National prejudice." *An Gaidheal* 4: 121–23.

MacLean, J. P. 1900. *Settlements of Scotch Highlanders in America prior to the Peace of 1783.* Glasgow: John MacKay.

McPhee, John. 1970. *The Crofter and the Laird.* New York: Farrar, Straus, and Giroux.

Meyer, Duane. 1957 [1961]. *The Highland Scots of North Carolina, 1732–1776.* Chapel Hill: U of North Carolina P.

Newton, Norman. 1990. *Colonsay and Oronsay.* London: David and Charles.

Old Parish Register of Colonsay, 1796–1854, 539/2, New Register House, Edinburgh.

Ray, Celeste. 2001. *Highland Heritage: Scottish Americans in the American South.* Chapel Hill: U of North Carolina P.

Scouller, Alastair McNeill, ed. 1998. *Moch Is Anmoch.* Colonsay, Scotland: House of Lochar.

Second Statistical Account for Scotland, 1841–46, Vol. 7.

Sheets, John W. 2004. "The Americans, the Earl of Selkirk, and Colonsay's 1806 emigrants to Prince Edward Island." *Scottish Local History* 61: 11–21.

———. 2000. "National Culture of Mobility": The Colonsay-Canada Connection." In *Transatlantic Studies,* ed. Will Kaufman and Heidi S. Macpherson, 69–83. New York: UP of America.

———. 1999. "Professor Donald Mackinnon and Doctor Roger McNeill: Gaelic 'Lads o' Pairts' from Colonsay," unpublished manuscript.

———. 1994. "Fieldwork as Reverse Information for Local Tradition." *Folklore in Use* 2: 79–88.

———. 1993. "Miss Catherine McKinnon's 'Russian Fortune.'" *Scottish Studies* 31: 88–100.

———. 1984. "Economic and Demographic Consequences of Population Decline: Colonsay and Jura during 1841–1891." *Northern Scotland* 6: 13–32.

Sherman, Anna Sutton, and Kate James Lepine. 1988. *Cross Creek Cemetery Number One: Cumberland County.* Fayetteville, NC: Katana.

Strathern, Andrew, and Pamela J Stewart. 2001. *Minorities and Memories: Survivals and Extinctions in Scotland and Western Europe.* Durham, NC: Carolina Academic Press.

Thompson, Elizabeth, ed. 1998. *The Emigrant's Guide to North America by Robert Mac-Dougall* [1841]. Toronto: Natural Heritage.

11
Pilgrims to the Far Country
North-American "roots-tourists" in the Scottish Highlands and Islands
Paul Basu

Early morning, Morag looks out the train window. Small rocky hill-sides
are sliding past, and fir trees, and white birches. Brown creeks (here called
burns?) tumble along over stony riverbeds. A station flashes by. The train
does not stop, but Morag reads the sign:

CULLODEN

There is such a place. It really exists, in the external world. Morag feels
like crying.

—Margaret Laurence, *The Diviners*, 1974

[H]e gazed away towards the moors and crests that for so long had been
names with the remoteness about them of names in Judea but far more
intimate and thrilling because they were used by grown men he knew.
This far country was the country that he had hoped one day to see. And
the day had come.

—Neil M. Gunn, *Highland River*, 1937

I am clearly one of those who are fond of using literary quotations to preface
academic essays. Perhaps it has become an overused convention. But especially
when one is dealing with an entity as elusive—and arguably as fictive—as an
ancestral homeland, there is sometimes a particular aptness, an insight offered, that is hard to resist. Besides, we have learnt in anthropology, history,
folklore—the disciplines that this collection embraces—that literary reflection
can be as valuable a resource as the lauded "eyewitness."

Thus I begin with not one, but two quotes: one from a Canadian novelist of Scots-Irish descent, Margaret Laurence, the other from a Scottish author, a native of Caithness, Neil M. Gunn. Both *The Diviners* and *Highland River* deal with quests to places that had been imagined long before even the possibility of visiting them could be conceived of. Thus the "old country," the Scottish Highlands once inhabited by Laurence's and her heroine's ancestors, and the "far country," at the higher reaches of Gunn's beloved river, are both notional realities before becoming material manifestations. The shock of discovering that Culloden actually exists, "in the external world," outside Morag's personal imaginings, or the cultural narratives that give rise to them, is a profound one; equivalent, perhaps, to that "peak experience" described by Alex Haley in *Roots* after journeying to his ancestral home in "the back country of black West Africa"—"that which emotionally, nothing in your life ever transcends" (Haley 1991, 676).[1]

Similarly, for Gunn's young hero, Kenn, to glimpse the storied world of the once populous and now deserted Dunbeath Strath, even a mile or two from his home, is in some senses like the medieval pilgrim's first sight of Jerusalem: to have glimpsed heaven on earth, the sacred in the mundane. No matter how ardently imagined, the experience cannot be anticipated, hence the shock of revelation and the rush of unexpected emotion. It is a moment I have been privileged to witness myself during fieldwork with people of Scottish descent from the United States, Canada, Australia, New Zealand—even England and the Scottish Lowlands—making journeys to the homelands of their ancestors in the Scottish Highlands and Islands.

Much could be written on the quests evoked in Gunn's and Laurence's literature, but I shall not even begin to summarise the contexts of the above quotations. I cite them merely to introduce and illuminate an essential aspect of the nature of the Scottish homeland for people of Scottish descent dispersed throughout the world. Scotland is at once a notional and a material reality, an imagined place as much as a geographic territory, a symbol—even a sacred one—that may yet be seen, touched, photographed, driven across, walked upon. But neither is there any unitary "Scotland." For many diasporic Scots, Scotland is rather a complex of names of places—some, like Culloden, known from the grand historical narratives, others from intimate family stories—but names that, like those in Judea, might one day be glimpsed over the crest of a distant ridge.

"Diaspora" has become an anthropological buzzword used to characterise almost any dispersed population regardless of the circumstances of its dispersal (Clifford 1997). It is, however, an appropriate category with which to describe the Scottish Highland experience, where a complex and ambivalent history of emigration has generally been dominated by a moral rhetoric of involuntary exile. The narrative of Scottish emigration to North America, Australia, and New Zealand from the mid-eighteenth century onwards is thus replete with motifs of defeat, betrayal, eviction, and loss of homeland. And in spite of two centuries of migration and assimilation, a sense of belonging to a distinctively Scottish community is maintained, or has been "recovered," in the diaspora: witness the remarkable popularity of Scottish clan societies and Highland games in the United States and Canada and the recent establishment of a "Tartan Day" (Ray 2001).

Safran (1991) and Cohen (1997), two revisionists of the term, both emphasise the centrality of "homeland" in the constitution of "diaspora": homeland, literally, as the "centre" from which a dispersed population was originally displaced; as the locus around which a collective remembering and mythologising is constructed and enacted; as the destination of an eventual return movement; as the common bond between member communities regardless of other social or cultural differences. My approach to studying Scottish diasporic identity has therefore been to position myself in the Scottish homeland and to join people of Scottish descent, wherever their place of ordinary residence, on their journeys to places associated with their ancestors. These are journeys that constitute a genre of diasporic travel—"roots-tourism," I suggest—which may be considered as a kind of "return movement" in itself (see Basu 2005).

Indeed, so popular has roots-tourism become that the Scottish Executive has recently identified it as an important niche market and, considering the vital importance of tourism for the Scottish economy, has commissioned the Scottish Tourist Board to develop a strategy with which to encourage it further (Scottish Executive 2000). But these bodies, equipped with rather cumbersome visitor profiles and market research statistics, are, I believe, in danger of missing the point entirely—even of dissuading potential visitors—because they fail to ask the most obvious questions: Why do people make these journeys? What is it that such visitors hope to find among the ruins and graveyards of their family histories? They fail to ask why it is that "roots-tourists" do not consider themselves to be tourists at all (Basu 2000b, 2001).

In this chapter, drawing on North American case examples, I explore the nature of these journeys and suggest that they provide an opportunity for self-discovery—and this through a process of self-narration. They are performative acts—in which actor is often also audience—in which the story of the self is (re)located in the story of the family, the community, the nation, and ultimately within the transnational category of the diaspora. Implicit in such a perspective is the suggestion that in our mobile, transient consumerist society the self is somehow dislocated, unanchored . . . homeless (Berger, et al. 1973; cf. Rapport and Dawson 1998). In fact the self is schizophrenic, both "at home" in a world of movement and "at sea": celebrating the fluidity and creativity of self-determination on the one hand, while on the other craving a "return" to the certainties of an externally determined essential identity. Here the disaporic self is not alone, and indeed "heritage" is valued just as highly (though differently) within the old country. But when the past is quite literally "another country," an oppositional mode of thinking, pivoting around the trauma of displacement, is irresistible. Thus, the pristine, "authentic" state is projected onto the homeland of "before," whereas the disintegration and decline into "inauthentic" living is restricted to the here and now of "after." Such a distinction raises the peculiar thought that the past, with its wholesome values, might somehow be revisited at the reasonable cost of a transatlantic airfare.

In his influential work *After Virtue,* the moral philosopher Alasdair MacIntyre, himself an émigré Scot, explores the idea that modern identity can be understood as a "quest," that life itself can be defined in the process of self-discovery (1981, 203–04). MacIntyre invokes the medieval conception of a quest, because it postulates a goal while accepting that the goal remains abstruse. Thus, the nature of "a quest is not at all that of a search for something already adequately characterised," but rather it "is always an education both as to the character of that which is being sought and in self-knowledge" (204). A quest, like a pilgrimage, is also at once "an outward physical journey through concrete space" *and* an inward cognitive progression (Snelling 1990, 393). Borrowing a phrase from the Bengali poet Rabindranath Tagore, we might say that the quest for self-identity resembles a journey to an unknown destination (Tagore 1984, 28).

The notions of "quest" and "pilgrimage" are not merely convenient and, indeed, poetic metaphors for the anthropological analysis of modern, in this case, Scottish diasporic identity, but they are also commonly used by diasporic roots-tourists themselves in their descriptions of what they are undertaking in their journeys. Thus, Sarida, a Texan correspondent, describes the homecoming experience as follows:

> A Diasporan Scot returning to the ancestral lands is more of a traveler or pilgrim [i.e., than a tourist]. He or she is not necessarily going to the major tourist centers or popular destinations of Scotland. Usually there is a quest involved here, a quest for ancestors or the lands where the family originated. A quest for lost memories and traditions, a hunger for identity

and belonging, a reaching for connections from something severed long ago. Like the quest for the Grail itself, it is a complex, convoluted and perilous journey and perhaps the Grail of our selves is unobtainable.

Another correspondent, Frank, from Colorado, also finds resonance in the Grail myth and explains that in his experience the quest is not simply a cognitive one, but involves journeying to a very particular, physical landscape.

> In the old Grail myths there is a sense that the holy object can simultaneously heal the king of his wound, as well as the land itself . . . Like many other instances of Celtic sovereignty, in the old Grail tales the king is connected to the land. What happens to the king happens to the land. So, in this context, the Arthurian tales speak of the land falling into a wounded state because of the wounded king.
>
> The knights are sent out on a quest for the only object that can restore the king and the land: the Grail . . . In the tales there is a guiding question that if answered truly will result in the seeker finding the true Grail. The question? What ails thee?
>
> So, not to discount the line of inquiry re: are we tourists?, but whether one is a Homeland or a Diaspora Scot I think another question to ask alongside this is: what ails thee?
>
> How does participating in the dynamism of the Scottish landscape assist you in that ailment? What was wounded in the first place, and is that wound related to the Scottish landscape itself?
>
> In my own participation with the Scottish landscape, and my own family's relationship to our place of origin (Argyll, the Isles and the Orkneys), the premise of the Arthurian and other Celtic tales seems to suggest a formula of sorts.
>
> There is an old saying, "The healing of the wound must come from the blood of the wound itself." This denotes the biological reality that it is largely the blood of the wound that cleanses the wound. If the blood is our ancestry and cultural heritage as well as the landscape and the wound is a ripping up of foundation, a severing of connectedness, the formula suggests that it is precisely by revisiting the landscape that we begin to participate "in the quest" for our healing and reconnection.

Some may find the New Age tone unpalatable, but Frank articulates what remains implicit or at best vaguely intuited in many such journeys. Although rarely apprehended as such, for many the homecoming journey *is* a therapeutic act. And if, as this informant suggests, the journey is the cure, then it is left for us to extrapolate the ailment: "a ripping up of foundation," "a severing of connectedness"?

The wasteland motif, with its association between the health of the person and the health of the land, is also significant in the context of the Scottish diaspora. Wandering around those areas of the Scottish Highlands affected by the notorious "Clearances" of the late eighteenth and nineteenth centuries—landscapes of ruins and deserted townships—one is left with the impression that the "land" has indeed fared ill. Gunn describes one of those areas, the Sutherland clan lands of his own ancestors, in a 1935 essay: "In Kildonan there is today a shadow, a chill, of which any sensitive mind would, I am convinced, be vaguely aware, though possessing no knowledge of the clearances. We are affected strangely by any place from which the tide of life has ebbed" (1987, 32).

The "struggle" for and with the land is a key narrative of contemporary Highland identity in both homeland and diaspora. The Clearances, in particular, provide the cultural trauma characteristic of the classic "victim diaspora": its origin myth, a "folk memory of the great historic injustice that binds the group together" and that was responsible for its dispersal (Cohen 1997, 23). Many Scottish Americans are in no doubt that their ancestors were *pushed* from the (home)land, torn away from their foundations, rather than *pulled* by the prospect of opportunity in the "New World," severers of their own roots.[2]

Regardless of whether, in the majority of cases, this claim of being an exiled people, separated from the land that confers their identity, withstands serious scrutiny, the narrative is internalised and central to many individuals' senses of what it means to be descended from Highland Scots. The "memory/myth" is transmogrified over the generations, incited by periodic jingoism and mobilised in the arena of a global identity politics. Little wonder, then, that at an individual level the "exile's return" is often a poignant and even restorative experience.

I should now like to explore in a little more depth examples of these quests or pilgrimages to the "far country." When making journeys with informants I usually offer to drive: we stay in the same bed-and-breakfast accommodation, eat together, visit places and people together, and, in between, spend a good deal of time talking. At some stage, I usually conduct a more structured, recorded interview. Here, then, I switch register and, making extensive use of this interview material, tell three stories of three journeys.

Sounding the Stones: Bonnie and Pat—Uig, Lewis

Bonnie, fifty-six, and Pat, fifty-four, are sisters. Both live in the state of Washington in the United States. Bonnie is an education outreach manager, Pat an environmental project manager. Their great-grandparents, Malcolm Matheson and Margaret Buchanan, emigrated from the Isle of Lewis in Scotland's Outer Hebrides to Canada in 1870. This would be Bonnie's second visit to Lewis, Pat's third, but their first journey to the island together. Indeed both felt it was very important for them to make this trip "as sisters." In addition to five days on Lewis, Bonnie was also enjoying a walking holiday in the Highlands with her partner, while Pat had spent three days on Iona, a place sacred to both the early church and the contemporary "Celtic spirituality" movement.

Pat's first visit to Lewis, in 1996, was very much a "first pass," without the time or sufficient information to make much progress establishing family connections with either people or places. It was, however, a powerful experience with memorable visits to Callanish stones and to places associated with the broader Clan Matheson: "I was the first of our family to actually go to Scotland. It changed my life and connected me with that part of my heritage."

On returning home, Pat compiled a book about the trip, including an account of where she and her husband had visited, photographs they had taken, notes on Matheson clan history, copies of tourist leaflets, and excerpts from a Canadian local history that included a biographical section about her pioneer great-grandfather. These she copied and distributed to family members as Christmas presents, encouraging them to make the journey too and to add their own discoveries to the book. What especially surprised Pat in that first visit was a feeling of connectedness to her *female* ancestors: "As the boat approached Lewis, I could almost 'see' years of Scottish women on the shores and bogs. I got my first real sense of the female side of the Scots (it had been a very male based, bagpipe playing, Scotch drinking part of my U.S. upbringing) and I suddenly felt like I acquired a lineage of strong Scots women that was not available to me in our male clan family mythology." This is a significant observation, not least for the study of Scottish North America, which also inevitably focuses on that most visible aspect of "Highland" identity: the masculine myth of clanship, with its parades, games, and gatherings, its banners, badges, and tartans (see Ray 2001 and chapter 9 of the present volume). Thus, rather than the specificities of a particular family's story, Bonnie and Pat had been raised with a more generic sense of "Scottishness":

Bonnie: What we were brought up on was what a "true Scot" was.

Pat: "The clan."

Bonnie: The clan, the family, the sense of honour, the integrity, the loyalty . . . that you stuck together and took care of your own, that you were honourable and honest and hard-working . . . hard-drinking probably too!

Pat: It was very male.

Considering this bias, I asked whether their father had any interest in visiting Lewis himself.

Bonnie: I think Dad is one of those Scots who would never come back, regardless of what his health was or circumstances, because he would not have wanted the reality to be any different from the dream. He's been the quintessential Scot all my life, I mean we've had the tartans up in the house, and he's taught himself to play the pipes, and most of his closest friends are Scots . . . of Scottish heritage, and he's kept alive in his heart and in his mind his image of what Lewis and the Highlands were. And I don't think he would ever have wanted that to have been challenged.

Pat: I certainly encouraged him to go—before I'd been here—and I think other people had, you know, it was "Why don't you go?" The direct answer always was, "Oh no, it's just a bunch of big cities now . . . it's not like Scotland was." He sort of ended up taking the easy way out.

Here the fascinating, and familiar, complexity of diasporic identity is apparent: the binary opposition between the urban/inauthentic/uprooted present of the diaspora and the rural/authentic/rooted past of the homeland. But there is also a reflexive awareness that such a view *is* a myth, or likely to be so, and Bonnie and Pat's father engages in a willing suspension of disbelief. He prefers to live with the myth rather than to risk exploding it by discovering that Scotland, too, has entered the twenty-first century. The sisters were disappointed that he couldn't be persuaded, especially after they themselves had taken the chance. Bonnie explained that when Pat returned from her first trip, "the image that she brought back wasn't just as good as what the dream was, it was better."

As we visited places associated with the family history—burial grounds, the sites of deserted townships, the beach near the village where their great-grandfather was born and lived before emigrating—I wondered whether Bonnie and Pat also had a sense of travelling back in time, of visiting the past in this Other country.

> Pat: I think part of the excitement has been that when we got to come and see these places, we know that they look relatively like they did at the time of the ancestors that we're finding out about. There hasn't been a lot of change, and so you get to see it with those eyes and go, "My God! This is what it looked like 150 years ago! . . . this is what the beach at Aird looked like when our great-grandfather decided to leave . . . " I don't think you get that chance too often.

Of course such an opportunity does not exist—not, at least, to the same extent—for those roots-tourists who trace their ancestors to Scotland's cities or those areas that have been more heavily developed. But, nevertheless, rural Lewis *has* entered the twenty-first century. I asked Bonnie and Pat whether they were slightly disappointed that their old country "cousins" were living with all the comforts and conveniences of any modern North American suburban home.

> Bonnie: No, I don't think I expected everyone to still live in blackhouses. I think what amazes me is that, as difficult as it must be to make a living in this area, the people are affluent enough to almost take for granted double-glass windows, heating systems in separate rooms, not just mod cons, but high-quality, very modern, state-of-the-art conveniences.

There are, of course, others for whom the idea of a dishwasher and watching CNN on satellite television does not accord with their image of the homeland, and we found advertising leaflets for the nearby "Gearrannan Blackhouse Village" appealing to this market. Here was "a cluster of thatched, drystone buildings overlook[ing] the Atlantic Ocean"; self-catering cottages, where you can "immerse yourself in the ancient culture of the West Side of Lewis" and find "a haven of peace and tranquillity" in the "traditional setting." Needless to say, the "traditional setting" does not extend to the inconvenience of sleeping on lice-infested straw mattresses, cooking over a smoky peat fire, or surviving a week without running water and a flush toilet.

After Pat's original visit, Bonnie took over the role of family historian and made contact with a respected Western Isles genealogist, Bill Lawson. Lawson was able to produce a basic family tree chart and sufficient information for Bonnie to plan an "ancestor hunting" trip more precisely. Thus, when Bonnie made her first visit to Lewis in 1998, she had some knowledge of the region her ancestors had lived in. Serendipity played its part too, however, when Bonnie found herself staying at a hostel, "which turns out to have been the manse just above the old cemetery where all our people had been buried for hundreds of years." The hostel manager, not a Lewisman himself, suggested Bonnie contact a member of the local historical society: "once I'd made contact with her, it was just like doors opening."

> Up until that point I had had no personal conversation really with any-body in the area . . . would not have known . . . probably would not have knocked on her door cold . . . but I no more than called [the representa-tive] of this historical society, and she read me a list of people who were related.

Bonnie soon found herself being invited to tea at the house of ninety-year-old Malcolm Og and his sister, Peggy Ann, with whom, she was told, she shared a nineteenth-century ancestor. This was to be a very significant meeting for Bonnie.

> Malcolm was special to me because he was the first person who could tell me what life had been like, and he was the first person who could say to me, "Well, yes, I'm directly related to you"—you know, "We have the same blood, the same genes, and this is where your family was from. This is your home country. This is your home soil, and, yes, where you are is where your ancestors have been buried." It was very much like being at the nexus of all my questions at that time, and it was like suddenly having discovered this phenomenal resource.

Malcolm was well known locally for his great knowledge of genealogy, and he had many stories to tell Bonnie of their common ancestors. Alas, he could throw no light on why Bonnie's great-grandfather was the only one of nine siblings to leave Lewis for Canada. Bonnie had hoped to introduce Pat to Malcolm Og during their current visit, but it was with great sadness that she learnt of his death a few months before they were due to leave.

What had begun in Pat's visit only two years previously as a general interest in the Matheson clan, its history and lands, had now become a very particular

Fig. 9. Bonnie and Pat with four generations of their Mackay family cousins in Carishader, Lewis (Photo by Paul Basu)

quest. The generic clan identity, so important in the sisters' "Scottish upbringing," seemed to have become almost irrelevant in the context of new more personally relevant intrigues: Why did Bonnie and Pat's great-grandparents leave Lewis? Why did Malcolm say that their great-great-grandfather, born in the early nineteenth century, was not a "true" Matheson? He seems to have been "adopted" into the family, but what were the circumstances? And what about the story of their Buchanan ancestor who had to be carried across Uig Sands when the family home was "cleared"? These were some of the questions the sisters had in mind as they visited and enjoyed the hospitality of other sets of "cousins" Bonnie had subsequently discovered—Mathesons, Buchanans, MacAulays, Mackays, all still living in close proximity to one another, very much an extended family.

The contrast between the communities the sisters found on Lewis and those among which they lived in the United States was marked; "I mean, I barely know my neighbours on both sides," remarked Bonnie. The experience was sufficient to alter the way she perceived herself:

I feel "webbed" for the first time . . . I tend to be a pretty visual person, and if I were to have drawn my family before, we would have looked at a circle, and then there would have been five dots or whatever inside the circle. After having been here, if I were to draw my family again, we are then looking at a central circle, but [with] all sorts of overlapping designs and arms shooting out with circles on them in each area based on which family connection we happen to be investigating at a time . . . It just expands, not only my vision of who those individual people are, and that knowing them enriches my life, but it expands in some way my perception of who I am myself, because it connects me to all these other people.

But if this homecoming was more "people-centred" than many such journeys, Bonnie and Pat's hosts were also keen to show their "American cousins" the land. Here, then, were the remains of the blackhouse that the sisters' great-great-great-great-aunt once occupied at Bostadh on Bernera. The village had been abandoned in the 1870s, but the MacAulays who guided them knew exactly which of its several ruins had been the family home. They were told that stones from the houses had been used to build the nearby cemetery walls. They were also shown the remains of a recently excavated Iron Age settlement: "this could have been the home of an ancient MacAulay," someone joked. But the joke was only partial. Spread before Bonnie and Pat was at least two thousand years of Bostadh's history—culminating in the still-used cemetery and a reconstruction of an Iron Age house—and they were part of that history.

Journeying from the impersonal clan myth evoked in castles and feuds, tartans and tales of clan chiefs, Bonnie and Pat had found their own personal heritage in the intricacies of their genealogical charts, in the stories of Malcolm Og and other newfound relatives, in an outline of turf-covered stones that mark the place of an abandoned home. But ultimately the process is not one of extracting the individual family story from a broader social or cultural history. On the contrary, it is through the family narrative, made tangible in the homecoming journey, that the grand narratives of history may be understood in their true human dimensions.

The "history" in which Bonnie and Pat's own story could now be placed was not about clans and tartans, but about the struggle of a rural community undergoing structural change. We were taken to see a cairn erected to commemorate the "Bernera Riot" of 1874 (see figure 10). The "riot," a demonstration of resistance and solidarity among the small tenant farmers against the unrestrained power of their landlords, represents for many a turning point in the Highland "land war," the beginning of a process that eventually led to far-reaching agrarian reform (Buchanan 1996, 25).[3] It was in the context of this struggle that Bonnie and Pat's great-grandparents left Lewis.

Fig. 10. Bonnie and Pat visiting the Bernera Riot Cairn
(Photo by Paul Basu)

Neither is the struggle over; it continues in more insidious form. "This is a dying place," one elderly relation told us. "I could take you to the place where my grandfather's house was, but it's been taken away. Its walls were up when I was a boy . . . The gravel was more important than the house, so the house lost out." While accepting the inevitability of change, there is still an understated resistance to the notion that the economic benefits of a quarry, for instance, should necessarily take precedence over the rich store of memory and personal significance associated with the crumbling ruins of a house.

This same relative described how his great-grandfather (Bonnie and Pat's great-great-great-great-grandfather) had been "cleared" from the township of Carnish to marginal land at Aird in 1849. He explained that until recently there were ten houses at Aird, "now there are six, and of the six three are occupied . . . and not a young soul among them." Thus the struggle for the land continues, the irony observed in many regions of the Highlands and Islands being that once the battle against rampant landlordism was won, there was a far greater adversary to contend with: the desire of the young to leave the region and seek opportunities elsewhere.

Both Bonnie and Pat felt a particular affinity for Uig Sands. This was the bay across which, according to Malcolm Og's story, their Buchanan ancestor had to be carried when he, too, was cleared from the family home at Carnish, this time to Crowlista on the opposite side; this was also the location of the ancient burial ground at Balnakeil that Bonnie discovered on her first trip.

> I'm tied to Uig Sands. I don't know why . . . Balnakeil just represents sort of the centre of the historical universe for me, and it is a particularly beautiful setting, and for me, if I were to picture my historic home, then it's going to be someplace on Uig Sands, whether its Carnish that sits on one side or Crowlista on the other side. That bay is sort of "ground zero" for me. It's strange that it didn't turn out to be Aird, but Aird to me is always a sort of removal place, someplace that we went after we left the homeland.

"Homeland," then, which once may have been defined by Bonnie and Pat as Scotland as a whole, and only later as Lewis, was now identified not even as the parish of Uig or as Aird, the village of ten houses where their great-grandfather (who emigrated to Canada) was born, but to what they understand to be their great-grandfather's own ancestral home two or three miles away.

For Bonnie, especially, the connection to place extended to the people of that place: descendants of those same ancestors, the ones who have stayed in the area.

> Whereas our ancestors were cleared off Carnish and moved from their ancestral home into a multitude of other small villages, there was always a remnant that [stayed] in the area, and their being in this area made it currently relevant to me. That I intellectually like knowing that they'd been here for hundreds of years, but it was important to me emotionally that they were still here. I think Americans, and particularly someone whose life history has been as nomadic as mine has been, suffer from that

lack of sense of place, and for me it wasn't just the natural surroundings, but my sense of place includes the people.

Bonnie and Pat were welcomed into the homes of strangers as cousins. "So you're a Matheson *and* a Buchanan?—Yes, I can see it now," said one distant relation. "We're two of a kind," said another. Bonnie was conscious of an irony that after just two visits to Uig, totalling perhaps no more than seven days, she somehow belonged to the place and its people in a way that incomers who may have lived in the area for decades could not. She referred to the owner of the hostel she had stayed at on her first visit.

> As Richard at the inn there says, he will never be an insider in this culture. It doesn't matter that he's lived here for twenty years and he's raised his kids here, he will never have the same status in the community as I do. And I haven't lived here at all! But the connections, that unseen Scottish chemistry, the blood and sinew and bone, whatever, that somehow is shared in some respect, however dilute, between the people who live here and those of us who come back looking for our roots separate us from the English people who come to the island, from the Germans who come to the island.

The issue is not whether Bonnie is correct in her assessment of the local politics of belonging, but rather that she perceives her relationship to Uig, its people, places, and culture, in these terms. Here, at "ground zero," Bonnie found herself to be part of a web that extended beyond herself both spatially and temporally.

Such a search for connections as incontrovertible as those conferred by the "blood, sinew and bone" of kinship was not always a part of Bonnie's self-conception, but rather an aspect of maturity, an evaluation of her "true nature" after the self-forging ambitions of youth had subsided.

> Bonnie: I think part of it is maturity. We didn't think seriously about coming here when we were much younger. I think you reach a certain age and you begin to want to place yourself in the stream. Instead of the young person's approach to life, which is kind of adventuresome and "do everything" and "no boundaries," I think maturity is beginning to understand that there are limits on experience and there are limits on life, and there's a structure and a pattern in your life, and that you can see where you fit . . . and, for want of anything else, this visit is a matter of "fit" for me.

It takes me back to the Scottish Soldier song—do you [Pat] remember listening to that over and over?—I think there's a line in it somewhere that "they aren't the hills of home" . . . you know, it's being supposedly sung by a fellow who's somewhere else, he's off fighting somewhere else, and "the hills are beautiful and the hills are green, but they aren't the hills of home."[4] And what it makes me think of is that you can understand why Scots have been adventuresome and travellers for hundreds of years, but there tends to be a need to come back and refuel, to refresh . . . and go out again. It doesn't mean that after you've been gone for a while, that you're somehow empty and you go home and you go home to stay, but that you can refresh yourself spiritually or emotionally or however it is that you need to tap into that energy that comes from the place you belong . . . and then you go again.

Pat: I keep thinking of the phrase you [Bonnie] and I talked about a long time ago. It doesn't have anything to do with Scotland—but it does to me now . . . It was something that had resonated literally with each of us, this process of a sculptor, how he sounds a stone. He sounds it, and it's by sounding it that he kind of figures out internally where it's dense and what resonates and what shape he could pull out of that. And Bonnie and I have done some talking about that, that we feel like a lot of our life has been about sounding stone and figuring out what rings true, what resonates internally.

Bonnie: Where the cracks are and what slabs chip off under pressure . . . and it's finding the shape underneath.

Pat: Part of this [journey] is a tap on that rock and we know whether it's true and real . . .

Bonnie: We're sounding the stone . . . we're sounding the stone.

For Bonnie and Pat, then, the journey to their ancestral homeland—Scotland, Lewis, Uig, the burial ground at Balnakeil—is about searching for their own "shape," it is about self-knowledge. But, importantly, the shape is not determined (not, at least, *perceived* to be determined) by the self itself, but by a "pattern" external to the self. The sisters needed to travel to a place outside their routine experience, a symbolic "home from home," a far country into which they somehow "fitted" and that represents the opportunity for personal renewal. Bonnie and Pat had "sounded the stone" of their homeland and discovered in its web of intermingled histories, landscapes, and genealogies something of themselves.

The Last of the Clan: Don—Strathnaver, Sutherland

Don is seventy-four, a retired serviceman and carpenter from Ohio. He has harboured an ambition to visit Scotland since childhood. At last the dream has come true, thanks to his wife, Gladys, who has encouraged him to make the trip and who bought their air tickets as a fiftieth wedding anniversary present. After a week in the Highlands, visiting the "Mackay Country" of Strathnaver in Sutherland, Don and Gladys intend to spend a week in Edinburgh.

Don explained to me that he had been brought up to be proud of his Scottish heritage: "I was raised a *proud* Mackay, and as a proud Scotsman. And my father used to say, 'Ahm a Heelan' Scot an' damned proud of it!' and I was raised that way. Oh, yes, I've gotten into some pretty good fist fights over the fact that I was a Scotsman . . . *and I won 'em all!*" Yet, despite this bravado, he actually knows very little about his Scottish family history. Don had been very close to his grandfather, but "Granddad didn't talk much. I really didn't know enough then to ask him. Didn't have sense enough to ask him about all that stuff. So as far as his people and where they came from, I got very little of it. They did say something about one of them being born in Edinburgh, now I'm not sure about whether they were talking about my great-grandmother or great-grandfather or somebody totally unrelated." Indeed, Don's grandfather had led a colourful life. According to an old obituary Don showed me, he was born in England in 1860 and was brought to the United States at the age of eight when his parents emigrated. He was orphaned soon after and went to sea as a cabin boy working on the "square riggers" plying between Liverpool and New York. He then jumped ship in New Orleans and worked his way up to Canada driving ox carts in lumber camps; he became a Pony Express rider carrying mail through Death Valley between Las Vegas and Fresno; and in 1876 he became an Indian scout in Custer's Seventh Cavalry. It is hardly surprising, then, that as a child Don was more than satisfied to hear about his grandfather's all-American adventures and wasn't particularly interested in the more distant past.

Don appeared to be used to narrating his own life adventures too. He had a repertoire of stories that he retold frequently, often repeating the exact phrasing. Many of these were quite brutal stories concerning the acquisition of what he identified as Scottish values and traits: loyalty, pride, and self-reliance. For instance, there is one story of his grandfather telling Don he had no intention of leaving him any inheritance, "firstly, because I don't suppose I'll have anything to leave you, secondly, because if I did you'd only piss it away." "Instead," his grandfather explained, "I'm going to leave you a trade, because, with a trade, a man will never go hungry." Then there is the story of his father threatening to beat him if he caught him running away from the neighbourhood bullies. He made Don confront them, and "from that day on I have never run from a man, I don't care how big he is: I'm seventy-four and I'll still stand and fight." It was through such "lessons" and the masculine posturing of his father and grandfather that Don learnt what it was to be a Scot in his neighbourhood in the 1930s:

> When I was a boy there were three Scottish families in a German and Italian neighbourhood: the McIntyres, the McLeods and the Mackays. Aside from being looked on as foreigners, my grandfather didn't help much by playing the pipes every night at nine o'clock. In the summer you could hear doors slamming for blocks around . . . He would pipe three pieces, one of which was the "White Banner of Mackay," then he would go to bed and things would return to normal. Sometimes when I am sitting alone I can still hear him pipe.

Since his childhood, Don has pursued a casual interest in Scottish culture— "I've been pickin' up a little here, pickin' up a little there, a little Scots history, a little clan history"—but it was only when he damaged his back and was temporarily bed-bound a few years ago that the opportunity presented itself for him to look into his heritage more seriously. "I decided to do what I had never had time to do before, find out who I was and where I came from."

Don's research has mainly been conducted via the Internet and has been focused on the Clan Mackay. Thus Don has read voraciously all he can find on Mackay genealogy: a genealogy of kings, chiefs, and warriors spanning the centuries. Don's objective has been to connect his own family history to this exalted clan history: "My great-grandfather is the missing link . . . If I can connect my great-grandfather to what I've got now, then I'm done. I've got it all . . . all the way back to Macbeth . . . Otherwise, I'm back to the 1830s, as far as I can go back." Alas, he has been unable to locate any further information concerning his great-grandparents beyond their names on their son's death certificate, that vague reference to Edinburgh, an assumption that they were born in the 1830s, and a belief that the family were Mackays from Strathnaver in Sutherland. Don had hoped that a meeting with the Highland Council's genealogist, Alistair Macleod, during the trip would help, but there were too few clues to go on. I asked Don whether he was disappointed at not being able to establish this link: "Well, no, not really. Naturally I was expecting to find some definite, solid proof of my great-grandfather, but it's really evident that I'm not going to, not right now anyway. And I didn't come over here with the idea that I was absolutely going to find him, I came over with the idea that I was going to look."

To be honest, Don was expecting rather a lot of his elusive great-grandfather: a blood link with the characters of this clan mytho-history in which Don had steeped himself. He would have to contend himself with a working-class man and woman who appear to have lived in the north of England in the 1860s, emigrating with their child to North America before disappearing from the records and leaving Don's grandfather an orphan with a Highland surname and a sense of Scottish pride. And like so many nineteenth-century immigrants, Don's grandfather epitomised the self-made-man ideal of the American dream: a wanderer without roots, an opportunist and a survivor.

Despite having failed to establish this link, Don still styles himself as "the last of the clan"[5]: "I realised that I was the oldest living member of my branch of the Mackay clan. Then it hit me like a brick, when I go there will be no one old enough to remember." And thus he set himself the task of writing a book for the benefit of later generations of his family—particularly the male line. The volume, somewhat grandly titled *The Book of Mackay*, is to have three parts: "History of the House of Mackay," "The House of Mackay," and "Bits and Pieces from My Life." The first two sections, which concern the clan, its history, and genealogy, are comprised more or less entirely of printouts from various Scottish-interest Web sites. The final part is autobiographical. Don hopes that this book will form a kind of family chronicle that his son, grandson, and great-grandson will take forward after him. "It ought to, when they get it, give 'em a pretty good insight of the clan from the beginning, all the way through, right up to their day—you know what I mean—to right now: immediately. Then [my son] will add to it, then, when he goes, his son will add his bit to it, then my great-grandson will read that and he'll add his little bit to it."

It struck me that Don wanted to bequeath to his great-grandson what his own great-grandfather had not been able to bequeath to him: a past. I asked Don what "bits and pieces" of his life he was including in the autobiographical section. "I'll tell them the story that I just told you about Dad teaching me not to run. About my grandfather and what he said about ever leaving me anything other than a trade, stories like that that they have no other way of knowing, and I know they'd be interested in . . . I know I would, if I was a kid and I was sitting at somebody's knee and they were telling me stories like that, I'd be

Fig. 11. Don overlooking the Kyle of Tongue, Sutherland (Photo by Paul Basu)

interested in them." Don's book seemed to compensate for a regret for stories untold.

As we drove through the Highlands to Northwest Sutherland, the Strath-naver homeland of the Mackays, Don advised me that he was not inclined to get emotional or indulge in daydreams and speculation, and that he believed there was more to Scotland than "piles of stones and old graveyards." He was responding to the messages frequently posted to an e-mail discussion list I had established for the research in which "homecomers" described profound, even supernatural, experiences at ruins and burial grounds associated with their ancestors. Given his desire to play down the personal significance of such places, I asked Don why he felt compelled to make this journey to the clan homeland himself.

Because this is where I'm from. Not physically. I didn't physically come from here . . . I wasn't physically born here, but this is where I'm from, if you can understand that. Before, I was proud of being a Scot, because my father was a Scot, my grandfather was a Scot, my aunts, uncles, all of them were Scots. I was a Scot. I was proud of that. But this gives all that meaning, actually . . . so that not only am I proud of being a Scot because of my family, but I'm proud of being a Scot because of this. This is where they lived. Because of the battles and that kind of thing that the clan had fought. I'm part of that clan. That's who I am.

That the experience of visiting a deserted township site near Bettyhill, or the Strathnaver Museum, housed in the old parish church at Farr and surrounded by its graveyard, did affect Don was evident despite his resistance to the idea. He counted fifteen or twenty gravestones that bore his own name or those of known relatives and marvelled that he might be standing among kin. Indeed, he seemed to forget that he hadn't actually substantiated any direct family connection to the area and that his great-grandfather apparently died (or, at least, disappeared) after emigrating to the United States: "I looked at those stones and I thought now, by golly, that could be my great-grandfather buried there, because I know he came from this area, the Strathnaver area. That's where I was, and being in that area gave me the feeling like, well, hey, my great-granddad used to run around here. Now here I am standing where he at one time stood."

In effect, Don's "history" began when his eight-year-old grandfather was brought to the United States in 1868. Don was unable to find the missing link that connected him incontrovertibly with the more ancient cultural heritage represented by the "far country" of Strathnaver. While denying any inclination to speculate, it appeared, however, that Don had unconsciously "forged" that link. This extended to internalising the Clearance narrative and using it to explain his own family's plight. In a posting to the project e-mail discussion list, Don claimed that he came "from a family that at one time was cleared from Strathnaver," and even that his grandfather was shamefully aware of repeating history in his own actions, implicated as he was in the "clearance" of native Americans from their lands to make way for European settlers: "My grandfather was an Indian scout for General Armstrong Custer's Seventh Cavalry. In later years he made mention of the fact that he was not too proud of the fact that he had been a part of the same actions that had brought his family to [the United States]. His father was a child when they were forced from their home, and he felt he was betraying the family by being a part of yet another eviction." This despite admitting in another e-mail, "to be true about the whole issue of the Clearances all I really know about it is from writings by Ian Grimble and John Prebble."[6] But identity is not contingent on the "facts" of history or the family tree, and, as such, the "fact" that Don has been unable to ascertain that his family came from Strathnaver, let alone that they were affected by the infamous Sutherland Clearances of the early nineteenth century, is of secondary importance. Of primary importance is that, consciously or not,

Don chooses to identify with the tragedy myth of a once noble people reduced to exile.

In the Strathnaver Museum, Don was struck by the fact that the clan armorials and insignia that decorated the "Mackay Room" were, indeed, the same as those he had made in his workshop and hung on what he called his "heritage wall" at home in Ohio: "I'm saying to myself, hey, I've got those! And since they're in the museum here, they've got to be authentic." The images in the museum display validated Don's sense of membership: he bore the appropriate badge.

But Don was insistent that he was not just interested in the past or seeing places associated with clan history, he also wanted to know what the people of Scotland were like today. There was little opportunity of acquiring such knowledge within the few days of the trip, but he and Gladys particularly enjoyed meeting and talking with some acquaintances of mine in the locality when we stopped in for a cup of tea. "They live different than we do, yet they live the same. By that I mean you don't find everybody running around in kilts and tootin' on pipes. The people live basically the same as we do, day-to-day: normal household duties, normal work duties, but that's the thing I'm interested in as opposed to all the gift shops and all the tourist attractions and all that kind of stuff."

Don distanced himself from both the "average tourists," whom he characterised as enjoying rather superficial experiences, and from other homecomers, whom he felt had rather overactive imaginations and were obsessively interested in those piles of stones and old graveyards. No, in this respect Don was keen to make connection at a decidedly domestic level: home(land) at its most humdrum. When he was sure my tape recorder was switched off, he quietly confided in me, "I feel right at home here. I don't feel out of place at all."

"Two worlds, two minds, I live them both": Brenda—Strathaird, Skye

Brenda, forty-one, is a youth counsellor. She was born in Halifax, Nova Scotia, but has lived most of her life in Ontario. When Brenda made her first trip to Scotland in 1998, she vowed to herself that she would return every other year for the rest of her life. I began corresponding with Brenda a few months before her second visit, in 2000, after she completed an online questionnaire that was featured on my research Web site. Brenda's answers were particularly full, amounting to several thousand words of comment about her "Scotland feelings," and they deserve more thorough discussion than space allows here. I should, however, like to mention just one or two aspects of Brenda's experiences.

As with many other informants, Brenda's journey had long been anticipated: "My love and sense of belonging to Scotland has always been intense since childhood. I knew (no wondering, but knew) at the age of 14 that I would be there someday. It wasn't a promise to myself nor a dreamed commitment—it was just the way it was. I would be in Scotland someday." Although her parents had moved to Ontario when she was just two, Brenda was aware of an undercurrent of Scottishness in her upbringing, especially during summer holidays back in Cape Breton: "We'd stop and see all the relatives and we'd spend weeks there . . . I can remember Sydney Forks, you know, was Uncle George, Uncle Charlie and Grandma's house, right next door to each other . . . You were just all together, all of us all together . . . that kind of closeness." The family was musical, and Brenda remembers family gatherings "with the combinations of fiddles, spoons, guitars and whisky." At the time, Brenda thought of this simply as a "down east" style, "but now knowing some Scottish music," she realises "it's the same thing."

The destination of Brenda's initial quest was very much Scotland as a whole. It was a "place" she had inhabited in her imagination for many years based on her avid consumption of Scottish books, Web sites, music, and so forth, a place of "powerful beauty in nature, misty rains, remote kirkyards, miles of walking in solitude." When Brenda finally visited, it would appear that she projected her imagined Scotland onto the actual Scottish landscape. Unsurprisingly, she derived some satisfaction from apparently discovering what she had hoped to find.

> Each moment, each experience, each mile of travel I felt and saw what I had anticipated. I truly felt at home, and never once felt lost. It continually amazed and comforted me. To simply awaken with the dawn, walk or hop on a train not knowing where I would lay my head that night and feeling comfort in that. I felt continually humbled and comforted by all around me. Each kirkyard wandered was remote and beautiful . . . Each evening I found water that flowed the same as it always did throughout any turbulent history it saw. That was always emotional—to walk in my bare feet alone . . . waiting for the setting sun, my footsteps washed away forever when I left but merged with thousands of others who walked there before me.

In her choice of language and imagery, Brenda expresses a desire to relinquish control, to give herself up to "Scotland," to merge with her homeland and with the generations that had gone before, to be part of a timeless landscape—a desire that is expressed most literally in her wish to eventually have her ashes scattered there.

Elsewhere in her questionnaire Brenda described the violent emotions she experienced during a kind of catharsis when first encountering the grandeur of Glencoe. Regaining some composure as the episode abated, she found herself standing beside a mountain stream.

> I stepped into the pool knowing what I had to do. Both feet in the freezing water I let go of my dress letting it soak up the water. I reached down and placed my hands into the water . . . I washed that water over my face with my hands. Oh it was so fresh! Then, compelled, without even a thought, I cupped the water again and drank from it. I felt inside the cool and I felt settled. Scotland was now in me, coursing through me, filling me.

The incident suggests a baptism: Brenda's rebirth as a Scot, with "Scotland" entering her as some kind of holy spirit. Indeed there is no doubt that Brenda felt this to be a spiritual experience: "I realise that I have never, ever felt this whole in my life. I feel as if a part of my soul is filled and I am content, I am whole finally."

The objective of Brenda's second journey to Scotland was to visit those areas associated with her MacKinnon clan: regions of the isles of Mull, Skye, South Uist, and Barra. I joined Brenda for part of this two-week trip, exploring with her the MacKinnon strongholds of Castle Moil and Dun Ringill, along with numerous other sites in the Strathaird region of Skye. Brenda remarked at the "power" she sensed at the dun and castle, but it was an old burial ground at Kilmarie that left the greatest impression on her. She placed pebbles on the MacKinnon graves and lingered over a row of older uninscribed stones, one in particular that she felt seemed "small and all alone."

Many roots-tourists collect stones and other souvenirs from ancestral sites to take home. They function as relics acquired at religious shrines, fragments of the sacred introduced into the mundane: in this case fragments of the ancestral homeland introduced into the domestic home-space where the "roots-tourist" ordinarily resides. Brenda had many such stones that, along with her books and CDs, she used to transport herself to Scotland when she was in Canada. But Brenda was also keen to leave something of herself behind in Scotland. Thus I observed her depositing a ring in the massive walls of the ancient Dun Ringill. She wrote to me later, explaining why she did this: "By putting my cheap ring inside the walls, I felt I was giving a humble offering,

Fig. 12. Brenda at Castle Moil, Kyleakin, Skye (Photo by
Paul Basu)

asking, almost begging to be part of it forever . . . I wanted to leave a part of
'me' there. I did not know this before that moment, nor had I planned to do so.
But when I did it, I felt extremely good, extremely relieved." Again, obvious parallels may be drawn with the practice of pilgrims leaving ex-votos at
shrines. Such objects represent metonymically those who have travelled to seek
a cure, perhaps, and are left at the shrine after they have departed to suggest a
continued presence.

Brenda had not yet discovered the identity of her MacKinnon ancestor who
emigrated to Canada, and therefore didn't know where the old family home
had actually been. She had not pursued her family history rigorously but was

confident that the facts would emerge at the appropriate time.[7] For now she was content to let fate guide her and enjoy this "communion" with MacKinnon lands. Indeed, Brenda identified herself strongly as a MacKinnon, but she seemed not to be referring here to a clan or family identity so much as a sense of personal integrity. She was conscious of losing this integrity as she grew older, married, became a mother, and took on other responsibilities. Part of her journey to Scotland and to these MacKinnon lands was an attempt to recover for herself this primary identity aside from subsequent roles.

Brenda: Over in Canada, I don't feel that world right now. I haven't thought of [my daughter] all morning. And that's so bizarre for me. I'm here, I'm me. I'm alone, I'm me.

Paul: Do you mean, in some senses you're not "you" when you're back home in Canada?

Brenda: Yeah, yeah. I'm not. I don't have all those hats on my head. All those different people. I'm just me right here.

Paul: So what are those "hats" that stop you being you?

Brenda: Oh, well . . . motherhood, responsibility. You know when you're a wife you think of others, and I'm working with high risk [children], you're on the outside always relaxed, but on the inside always thinking and formulating things for other people to get through their problems and that . . .
    I just feel so lucky to be here. And this is the real me. At home, I mean of course that's the real me—don't get me wrong—and I love my family and my life and I'm very proud of my life at home. But this is where . . . I don't want to say this is where my heart is. It goes deeper. My heart is with my child and my husband and my MacKinnons at home. My soul's here. It's deeper. It's like no one can take that away. When I'm at home you can't feel it, but when you're here, the skies give you permission to feel it. It's beautiful.

Returning to the far country of the MacKinnons, Brenda was also able to return to the secure identity of her youth, an identity lost with the acquisition of responsibilities and her husband's surname. It was important for Brenda to make the journey alone to find her "real" self—not as wife, mother, professional child counsellor, or other possible identity, but as "Brenda MacKinnon," her essential self, her "soul."

But there was clearly a tension here. I sensed Brenda felt guilty that the reality of her Canadian home seemed to diminish as she became immersed in this alternative reality represented by Scotland, that she had to leave behind her husband and child in order to feel "whole." She described her mixed emotions when, returning from her first trip, her husband met her at the airport. "When I arrived in Canada and saw my husband and he said, 'Well, what was it like?' as he hugged me, I cried immediately and said that I have to go back, and then I told him to let me cry and I couldn't talk yet. I think returning to Canada caused me to suddenly realise that in my soul, I had actually left my true country (Scotland) and I wasn't feeling happiness to be home in Canada."

Brenda sent me a poem that she believed expressed her feelings. She didn't know who had written it but explained, "it's the closest I have ever seen in print of how I feel each day of my life here in Canada."[8]

> Of days winter and cold, I watch from sunbleached sands
> And look beyond the sky's edge toward this other land.
> Pride flows hot in this eager blood born unto this place,
> But to the past I would follow away from this time and space.
> Thoughts create reflection of thistle and tartan splendour
> Old worlds renewed like the lover's kiss, I crave the rampant tender.
> One foot leading to the future, the other in yesteryear.
> Many generations have left her shores, yet still I must travel there.
> And born far away I hear the call, my feelings forever roam.
> Two worlds, two minds, I live them both, this new land
> and Scotland . . . my homes. . . .

Conclusions

Brenda stated in her questionnaire, "I am not and never will be a tourist in Scotland." In the above narratives, I hope I have been able to demonstrate that in this instance "pilgrimage" is not merely an anthropological analogy, but a genre of travel invoked by certain visitors to Scotland—and, no doubt, to a greater or lesser extent, certain visitors to other "old countries" too—to distinguish and define the purpose and meaning of their visits (Basu 2005). Pat had been given a book by her daughter to read during her journey to Lewis, a personal development manual titled *The Art of Pilgrimage: The Seeker's Guide to*

Making Travel Sacred (Cousineau 1998). Pat had copied some quotes from the text into the back of the volume. For example, she wrote:

"Personal answers to ultimate questions. That is what we seek."—Alexander Eliot.
"Footprints of the Ancestors."
"Songlines"—Bruce Chatwin.
"Our lives are woven from a melody of calls that draw us out and help us to define ourselves"—David Spangler.
"We must find our touchstones where we can."—John Bunyan.

These few excerpts, divorced from their original contexts, delineate the nature of these homecoming journeys with some precision. These quests are, without doubt, personal responses to the insistent questions of our narcissistic late modern age: "Who am I?" "Where do I belong?" (Giddens 1991). They are also characterised by attitudes of devotion, respect, and mystical reverence towards place informed, perhaps, by a growing awareness of native American and Australian conceptions of ancestral landscapes. As the Australian anthropologist W. E. H. Stanner suggests, "White Man Got No Dreaming" (1979, 24), but might we not find in these "Celtic odysseys" some parallel to the Aboriginal "Songlines," a modern, urban, Western quest for the "Aborigine within" (Rolls 1998)?

Spangler's "melody of calls" reminds us, however, that modern identity, even self-defined, is plural and dynamic: some roots-tourists select discriminatingly which of their several possible ancestral heritages to pursue, others combine elements from each in strange and creative ways. Finally, in the quote from Bunyan, is the acknowledgment that identity *is* a constructive project of the self in which the self is also at liberty to act as arbitrator: it may "sound the stones" until it finds one that rings, not "true," but according to its wishes.

Homeland Scots sometimes respond to the sentiments expressed by their diasporic cousins with embarrassed incredulity. One informant, from British Columbia, found their attitude "disparaging" and offensive: "With the Scottish people it seems that you are some sort of emotional cripple if you are trying to make a link to the old country." Yet, indeed, one of the key motivations for setting out on pilgrimage is to seek a cure. I did not directly ask my informants "what ails thee?" as my correspondent from Colorado suggested, but I did attempt to understand what "salvation" each of them found in the Scottish homelands they encountered. The senses of connection, depth, resonance, "fit," authenticity, belonging, and being "in place" that Scotland seemed to confer have, ultimately, little to do with Scotland itself. The homeland, rather, is a product of the diasporic imagination, a far country onto which, as with the bones of saints, a capacity for working miracles is projected—even a salve for the ills of modernity. But who is to deny the transformative power of the moment, like Morag's first glimpse of Culloden, Kenn's first glimpse of the Dunbeath hinterland, when *homeland* becomes manifest in *Scotland*? Daniel, a North American Scot from New Mexico, articulates it so well:

> Being disenfranchised, unattached to my heritage, going to Scotland was becoming connected to an origin that had never before existed. Whether the Scots themselves or anyone else acknowledged it or not, it was my connection. It was sacred to me because it was something of my soul, that part that you don't share with anyone, can't share with anyone. My "self" has changed since that pilgrimage, whether anyone believes, acknowledges, validates or confirms it or not. Yes, to me it was sacred. I now know that my ancestors came from somewhere, and I've been there, I've breathed the same air and touched the same ground as they did. Perhaps a little esoteric? I guess you have to be an American and "generic" all your life to understand.

Notes

1. The authenticity of Haley's depiction of his ancestral homeland in *Roots* has been debated by several critics. See Shoumatoff (1995, 219–24) and Lowenthal (1985, 228) for discussion.

2. For a discussion of the Clearance narrative and the mnemonic power of the Highland landscape, see Basu 1997, 2000a; also Gourievidis 1993; Richards 2000; and Withers 1996.

3. The full inscription on the Bernera Riot Cairn reads as follows: "THIS CAIRN WAS ERECTED BY THE PEOPLE OF BERNERA AND TIR MOR IN 1992 TO COMMEMORATE THE PARTICIPANTS IN THE BERNERA RIOT OF 1874. This event was the first successful confrontation with authority leading eventually to the passing of the Crofters Act which gave Security of Tenure to all crofters. Stones from every croft in Bernera and Tir Mor are incorporated in the Cairn. The coping stones are taken from the houses of the three men who stood trial." Note the explicit narration of local identity contra centralised authority in this "intentional monument," also the symbolic incorporation of the stones from the crofting lands themselves and the "unintentional monuments" represented by the rioters' houses (see discussion of Riegl 1982 and the Scottish Highland landscape in Basu 1997, 2000a).

4. "Scottish Soldier," the popular folksinger Andy Stewart's version of "The Green Hills of Tyrol":

Because these green hills are not my highland hills
Or the island hills, they're not my land hills
And fair though these green foreign hills may be
They are not the hills of home

5. Along with J. W. Nichol's "Lochaber No More" and his later "Oh Why Left I My Hame," Thomas Faed's painting "The Last of the Clan" has become something of an icon of Highland defeat, clearance, and exile. When first displayed at the Royal Academy in London in 1865, the painting was accompanied by the following extract from an apocryphal "Letter to a Kinsman in America": "When the steamer had slowly backed out, and John MacAlpine had thrown off the hawser, we began to feel that our once powerful clan was now represented by a feeble old man and his granddaughter; who, together with some out-lying kith-an-kin, myself among the number, owned not a single blade of grass in the glen that was once all our own" (Royal Academy Catalogue 1865).

6. He is referring to Ian Grimble's *The Trial of Patrick Sellar* (1962) and John Prebble's *The Highland Clearances* (1963).

7. Soon after returning to Canada, Brenda was to discover that it was her great-great-great-grandfather, Niall Alasdair MacKinnon from Allasdale, Barra, who emigrated to Canada in 1821. Brenda intends to locate and visit Allasdale on her next visit to Scotland.

8. The poem "Loch Lomond" is credited to Paul Watson on various diasporic Scots' Web sites.

Works Cited

Basu, Paul. 2005. "Roots-Tourism as Return Movement: Semantics and the Scottish Diaspora." In *Emigrant Homecomings,* ed. Marjory Harper, 131–50. Manchester, Eng.: Manchester UP.

———. 2004. "Route Metaphors of 'Roots-Tourism' in the Scottish Highland Diaspora." In *Reframing Pilgrimage: Cultures in Motion,* ed. Simon Coleman and John Eade, 150–75. London: Routledge.

———. 2001. "Hunting Down Home: Reflections on Homeland and the Search for Identity in the Scottish Diaspora." In *Contested Landscapes: Movement, Exile, and Place,* ed. Barbara Bender and Margot Winer, 333–48. Oxford, Eng.: Berg.

———. 2000a. "Sites of Memory—Sources of Identity: Landscape-Narratives of the Sutherland Clearances." In *Townships to Farmsteads: Rural Settlement Studies in Scotland, England and Wales,* ed. John Atkinson, Iain Banks, and Gavin MacGregor, 225–36. Oxford, Eng.: BAR British series 293.

———. 2000b. *Genealogy and Heritage-Tourism in the Scottish Highlands and Islands.*

Report commissioned by Highlands and Islands Enterprise and Moray, Badenoch, and Strathspey Enterprise.

———. 1997. "Narratives in a Landscape: Monuments and Memories of the Sutherland Clearances," unpublished MSc thesis, University College London.

Buchanan, Joni. 1996. *The Lewis Land Struggle—Na Gaisgich.* Stornoway, UK: Acair.

Berger, Peter L., Brigitte Berger, and Hansfried Kellner. 1973. *The Homeless Mind.* New York: Random House.

Clifford, James. 1997. *Routes: Travel and Translation in the Late Twentieth Century.* Cambridge, MA: Harvard UP.

Cohen, Robin. 1997. *Global Diasporas: An Introduction.* London: UCL Press.

Cousineau, Phil. 1998. *The Art of Pilgrimage: The Seeker's Guide to Making Travel Sacred.* Shaftesbury, UK: Element.

Giddens, Anthony. 1991. *Modernity and Self-Identity: Self and Society in the Late Modern Age.* Cambridge, Eng.: Polity Press.

Gourievidis, Laurence. 1993. "The Image of the Highland Clearances, c.1880–1990," unpublished PhD thesis, University of St. Andrews.

Grimble, Ian. 1962. *The Trial of Patrick Sellar.* London: Routledge and Kegan Paul.

Gunn, Neil Miller. 1987 [1935]. "Caithness and Sutherland." In *Landscape and Light: Essays by Neil M. Gunn,* ed. A. McCleery. Aberdeen, UK: Aberdeen UP.

———. 1937. *Highland River.* London: Porpoise Press.

Haley, Alex. 1976. *Roots.* London: Vintage.

Laurence, Margaret. 1974. *The Diviners.* London: Macmillan.

Lowenthal, David. 1985. *The Past Is a Foreign Country.* Cambridge, Eng.: Cambridge UP.

MacIntyre, Alasdair. 1984. *After Virtue: A Study in Moral Theory.* Notre Dame, IN: U of Notre Dame P.

MacLean, Malcolm, and Christopher Carrell, eds. 1986. *As an Fhearann/From the Land: Clearance, Conflict, and Crofting.* Edinburgh: Mainstream.

Prebble, John. 1963. *The Highland Clearances.* London: Martin Secker and Warburg.

Rapport, Nigel, and Andrew Dawson, eds. 1998. *Migrants of Identity: Perceptions of Home in a World of Movement.* Oxford: Berg.

Ray, Celeste. 2001. *Highland Heritage: Scottish Americans in the American South.* Chapel Hill: U of North Carolina P.

Richards, Eric. 2000. *The Highland Clearances: People, Landlords, and Rural Turmoil.* Edinburgh: Birlinn.

Riegl, Alois. 1982 [1928]. "The Modern Cult of Monuments: Its Character and its Origin." *Oppositions* 25: 20–51.

Rolls, Mitchell. 1998. "The Jungian Quest for the Aborigine Within: A Close Reading of David Tacey's *Edge of the Sacred: Transformation in Australia.*" *Melbourne Journal of Politics* 25: 171–87.

Safran, William. 1991. "Diasporas in Modern Societies: Myths of Homeland and Return." *Diaspora* 1, no. 1.

Scottish Executive. 2000. *A New Strategy for Scottish Tourism.* Edinburgh: Scottish Executive.

Shoumatoff, Alex. 1995. *The Mountain of Names: A History of the Human Family.* New York: Kodansha.

Snelling, John. 1990 [1983]. *The Sacred Mountain.* London: East-West Publications.

Stanner, W. E. H. 1979. *White Man Got No Dreaming: Essays, 1938–1973.* Canberra: Australian National UP.

Tagore, Rabindranath. 1984. *Some Songs and Poems from Rabindranath Tagore.* Trans. P. Bose. London: East-West Publications.

Withers, Charles. 1996. "Place, Memory, Monument: Memorializing the Past in Contemporary Highland Scotland." *Ecumene* 3, no. 3: 325–44.

12
Tartan Day in America
Edward J. Cowan

When John Witherspoon left Paisley in 1768 to assume the presidency of Princeton University, he reckoned it took him a mere three months to become American. Recently, increasing numbers of Americans have chosen to declare themselves Scots, instantly, without ever having set foot on the Old Sod. Some of them, together with others possessed of less contentious credentials, annually celebrate Tartan Day on April 6, the anniversary of the Declaration of Arbroath in 1320—the inspirational document, according to U.S. Senate Resolution 155, 1998, upon which the American Declaration of Independence was modeled. In a remarkably short space of time the influence of the one declaration upon the other has become a truth that many sincere folk hold to be self-evident on both sides of the Atlantic. But how could a seemingly obscure parchment from medieval Scotland possibly have had any impact upon a bunch of disenchanted colonists who, in 1776, appeared to be about to face annihilation at the hands of one of the world's major military powers? And, furthermore, why should some Americans suddenly wish to commemorate this eight-hundred-year-old document some two and a quarter centuries after the momentous birth of their nation—226 years in which Arbroath had never even been mentioned as a possible contributor to American constitutionalism, let alone an inspiration to American ideology?

The Arbroath Declaration was actually a letter sent to Pope John XXII by forty-four individually named nobles, barons, freeholders, and the "Community of the Realm of Scotland." Robert I, King of Scots—or Robert Bruce, as he was known until he made his bid for the kingship in 1306—had fought long and hard to secure the independence of his kingdom. Scotland's and America's independence heritage differ in one crucial respect, namely that while Americans fought to achieve independence, the Scots battled to preserve it. As the

Declaration of Arbroath stated, the Scottish nation, since time immemorial, had held its possessions "free of all servitude" under the protection of 113 kings, "the line unbroken by a single foreigner." The missive was highly propagandist, for its intention was to persuade Pope John to bring pressure to bear upon Edward II of England to recognize the legitimacy of Robert's kingship. A colossal victory over the English at Bannockburn in 1314 had failed to persuade Edward of the righteousness of the Scottish cause. Furthermore, King Robert was under sentence of excommunication for earlier misdemeanours, an invitation to any lunatic or grudge holder to take a pot shot at him without fear of papal or ecclesiastical retribution. The document stated that though the Scots dwelled "at the uttermost ends of the earth," God had selected them among the first for salvation under the auspices of St. Andrew, their future patron saint, but after centuries of peace they had been invaded by the treacherous, tyrannical English in the guise of friendship. Robert Bruce had arisen like another Joshua or Maccabeus to liberate his country. Manipulating pure bluff for rhetorical effect, the document goes on to state that if Robert should ever give up what he had begun, seeking to make the Scots, or their kingdom, subject to the king of England and the English (at this juncture an utterly inconceivable eventuality), then they would drive him out as a subverter of their rights and make another person, who was better able to defend them, their king, declaring in ringing tones that "For so long as a hundred of us remain alive, we will never on any conditions be subjected to the lordship of the English. For we fight not for glory nor riches nor honours, but for freedom alone, which no good man gives up except with his life" (Cowan 2003a, 1–4).

I have already attempted to explain something of this remarkable document, exploring the relevance of the deposition clause, hitherto largely doubted or ignored by academic criticism, and have sought to investigate the inspirational roots of the celebrated freedom passage, nowadays so often quoted if imperfectly understood.[1] It is something of an irony, if appropriately reciprocal, that Resolution 155 should assert that the American Declaration of Independence is modeled upon the papal letter of 1320, since that missive was dubbed the Scottish Declaration of Independence, very early in the twentieth century, in due homage to the emotive document of 1776. Such identification owed nothing to professional historians but was advanced by local champions of the east coast burgh of Arbroath, mainly famous today for its delicious smokies (haddocks cured over oak chips).

J. M. M'Bain, writing in 1897, believed that the declaration "asserted for all time the independent nationality of the Scottish people," considering it one of the most remarkable documents in Scottish national history, and praising "its stalwart assertion of national independence and the democratic spirit which inspires it." In his opinion the document was redolent of an unconquerable spirit, and it established for all time the nationality and independence of the Scottish kingdom. He was followed by another parish chauvinist, J. Brodie, who produced a pamphlet proclaiming Arbroath as the birthplace of the Declaration of Scottish Independence. Brodie was in no doubt that the man who defeated "English pretensions to the suzerainty of Scotland," and who effectively foiled papal diplomacy, was Abbot Bernard of Arbroath, who certainly had something of a hand in the declaration.[2] Academic historians, however, remained curiously uninterested in the document's sentiments and antecedents until the approach of its 650th anniversary in 1970. To mark the occasion, the Scottish Record Office issued a facsimile of the 1320 missive and, indeed, the then-Keeper of the Records published a book about it (Fergusson 1970). The government agency, however, had been anticipated by the Burns Federation in 1949 when it issued a reproduction to every secondary school and teachers' training college in the land. Interest in the Arbroath Declaration, at least since the later nineteenth century, can truly be said to have been democratically driven. But even in 1970 the Scottish establishment, fearful of the implications of its nation's history and almost paralyzed by the Scottish National Party's recent electoral surge, was obsessed with commemoration rather than celebration. On the other hand, there has been no serious research to bolster American claims either, though there can be little doubt that Resolution 155 was supported by the Senate's right wing, more inspired by *Braveheart,* the movie, than by Bruce the king, and seeking some sort of mystical reaffirmation of the Celtic South, libertarianism, and the ethos of militarism, for which modern Scots can hardly be held responsible. While senates may make history, they have been known to have a poor understanding of the past.

The uniqueness of the Arbroath letter is such that it does not require the reinforcement of American accolades. It preserves the first articulation of the contractual theory of monarchy in European history, of the elective kingship, of the notion that just as a king is elected by his subjects, so he may be deposed by them if he fails to act in their best interests, ideas that are fundamental to all concepts of modern constitutionalism. In addition, it offers one of the earliest paeans to freedom, equating the liberty of the nation with the liberty of the individual, that most precious of commodities that no person will ever lose but with life itself. Such are the twin pillars of liberty, which few would deny are well worthy of celebration. And this is true despite the political plaything that we all know the word "freedom" all too often to be, a concept of variable and frequently doubtful interpretation. In Scotland, too many special pleaders have invoked the word as meaning "freedom for me but not necessarily for you," a problem that persists wherever it is used; suffice it to say that my personal freedom does not permit me to infringe on the liberty of anyone else.

Although the establishment of National Tartan Day in the United States has been welcomed by Americans from a wide range of backgrounds that are not exclusively Scottish, it has, predictably, but from an American point of view disappointingly, proved highly controversial among the chattering classes (mainly journalists and academics) in the Auld Country. While the campaign to observe a "Scottish Day" originated in Canada, with Jean Watson of Nova Scotia, and has now had an impact upon Australia and New Zealand as well (albeit on a different date), it would appear to be the alleged American usurpation of the occasion that has particularly stuck in Scottish critical throats. It thus seems appropriate, in a book devoted to the investigation of transatlantic scots, to investigate something of the origins of Tartan Day and the remarkable blossoming of interest in what many of the celebrants worldwide would regard as an obscure document emanating from an unfamiliar period and a country that only a minority of people have ever visited. It must be stressed that although a flock of Scottish politicians and businesspeople descend upon New York and Washington each year in early April, Tartan Day is an American, not a Scottish, occasion. It is Americans, not Scots, who have decided that Arbroath influenced Philadelphia. They are understandably impressed by the earlier document's celebration of freedom and its invocation of elective kingship, the inspirational notion that monarchs (especially those of a tyrannical disposition) are answerable to their subjects by whom they may be deposed.

Scottish influence on America remains a somewhat under-researched topic apart from a number of studies on the Enlightenment in both countries, yet it was real enough. But just as in the case of Tartan Day the interest seems to be in Scotia's remote past, would it be true to suggest that so far as Scotland is concerned the American gaze has always tended to be backwards? It may be worthwhile to briefly survey some of the broad Scottish fields that may be deemed to have inspired Americans as a sort of precedent to the adoption of Tartan Day. Inspirational areas might be summarized as religion, rhetoric (in the sense of learning or education, as well as literature), recreation, roots, and reinvention—not to mention, let it be admitted, the ridiculous and the risible, two counts on which the Scots in Scotland are themselves far from guiltless.

Presbyterians, notably of the Covenanting or dissenting variety, emigrating in the seventeenth and eighteenth centuries, arrived ready programmed for revolt against monarchical despotism, having inherited the heroic legacy of resistance to Stewart absolutism, in defence of their religious beliefs (Schmidt

1989; Lambert 1999; Cowan 2002). Nor should the Ulster Scots, or Scots-Irish, who were, after all, Scottish in origin, be ignored in this regard. Indeed one of the few parallels to the American phenomenon of claiming Scottish roots, with or without entitlement, is the current government-inspired scheme to foster a sense of Scottishness among Ulster protestants, through the promotion of literature in the medium of Ullans, the language of Ulster Scots, now actually, and bizarrely, being used for legislation (Erskine and Lucy 1997, 113–45). Another area of undoubted potentiality is Freemasonry. Both George Washington and Thomas Jefferson were committed Masons who wove the brotherhood's iconography and ideology into the creation of the republic, but the order was virtually invented in Scotland, which can boast the oldest genuinely historical Masonic records in the world, in the shape of lodge minutes (Stevenson 1988a, 1988b).

Rhetoric was understood to be the art of using language, either written or spoken, correctly, effectively, and eloquently, a subject essentially pioneered by Scots and now returning to a number of American college curricula. The legacy of the classical world, rhetoric experienced a spectacular revival in schools and universities during the Scottish Enlightenment (Hook 1999, 44–57) and was easily exported in the wake of religion to America and Canada, whose schoolrooms were often entrusted to Scottish teachers, while, as is well known, Scottish ideas also made an impact on the establishment of transatlantic colleges and universities. It has been asserted that a majority of the revolutionary generation of Americans had been educated by dominies, as the Scots dubbed their schoolmasters. Nor were the sciences forgotten. Many a Scots emigrant did well because he was not only literate but numerate as well. This is one area where contemporary Scottish ideas had a contemporaneous impact. Despite the skepticism and uproar (Hook 1999, 8–24) that greeted the publication of Garry Wills's challenging book *Inventing America*, few scholars would now doubt the significant contribution to American thought made by such individuals as Frances Hutcheson, Adam Ferguson, David Hume, Adam Smith, Thomas Reid, Lord Kames, and a host of other Scots intellectuals.

Scottish literature was also popular. Although a Scot living in New Jersey wrote home in 1769 explaining that books were scarce in America, it is known that a number of Scottish publications did in fact cross the Atlantic, at least two imprints of Allan Ramsay's *The Gentle Shepherd* appearing before 1773. More common were theological works and a scattering of texts by Enlightenment writers. John Home's play, *Douglas*, was performed in Philadelphia in 1759 and many times thereafter. James Macpherson's *Ossian* was also phenomenally popular, his English translations of what purported to be Gaelic originals lauding the deeds of the great dead and the passing of a warrior culture, finding a resonance in American attitudes towards the native peoples (Macpherson 1996). An interest in Scottish ballad and song was reinforced through the works of Robert Burns, particularly, it seems, in the South. But the greatest contribution was that made by Walter Scott; to cite a much-quoted statistic, five million volumes of the *Waverley Novels* series were printed in America between 1813 and 1823. Heinrich Heine distinguished their appeal as "the mighty sorrow for the loss of national peculiarities, swallowed up in the universality of the newer culture." Most noteworthy was the reception of Scott in the South, where his poems and novels perfectly gelled with southern self-perceptions to the point that items of the Scott vocabulary were appropriated, such as "The Chivalry" and "aristocratical," while the term "Saxon," used by the Gaels to designate the English (*sassenach* in Gaelic), was adapted for application to Yankees. Even more surprisingly, Scott's word "Southron"—meaning a southerner or Englishman, and thus not exactly a term of endearment—was eagerly adopted by southerners as a descriptor for themselves (Osterweis 1949, 42–48; Hook 1975, 145–67; Hook 1999, 94–115). Even if Mark Twain exaggerated Scott's influence in crediting him with contributing to the Civil War, his legacy was incontrovertibly enormous in terms of aristocratic and chivalric pretension, Ivanhoe on the Mississippi. But Scott, who has much to answer for, should not be blamed for the reception of his own works, just as in his native country it is unfair to blame him for the "invention" of the tartan mania. In both cases he could have had little idea of the genie he was releasing from the whisky decanter. It is high time that serious scholarly attention was directed to explaining why the Scott phenomenon was so eagerly welcomed, why people chose to live in the fantasy worlds that he so brilliantly created, populating them with figures from the past but never in his wildest imaginings anticipating that he was providing habitations for the future. Herein is a partial explanation of his popularity in America, for just as Macpherson, Burns, and Scott were unwittingly engaged upon the greatest re-branding of their native country in its entire history, so they were constructing a template for a new young country desperate to escape the literary and terminological shackles of the former colonial power, namely England. *Ossian, Waverley,* and *Rob Roy* were about human struggle and epochal transition acted out in vast landscapes, while it was the genius of Burns and Scott to depict and explain the role of the humblest citizens in the great drama of the historical process. In short, their searching in the past for a way forward was very American. Yet Rollin Osterweis makes a telling point, namely that so far as southerners, dazzled by tales of knights and chivalry, were concerned, "Scott happened to offer models which appealed to them the most. If it hadn't been Scott it might well have been Malory, Froissart, Byron [incidentally, another Scot], Bulwer, Dumas, or someone else" (1949, 52). In short, the interest in Scotland per se was secondary, which may in a sense be diagnostic and may offer suggestive parallels to the later adoption of Tartan Day.

There was a further dimension, for the wilderness was the host of liberty. When David Ramsay observed in his *The History of the American Revolution* (1789) that "The natural seat of freedom is among high mountains, and pathless deserts, such as abound in the wilds of America" (Kelsall 1999, 53), he echoed William Robertson's assertion (1759) that Scotland's "mountains, fens and rivers, set bounds to despotic power and amidst these, is the natural seat of freedom and independence" (Cowan and Gifford 1999, 12). Robert Burns rejoiced that the "Tree of Liberty" had been planted in America and France, but in his view it had first taken root in Scotland in the days of Wallace and Bruce; he explicitly compared George Washington to both of these Scottish national heroes, the highest accolade that could ever have been conferred upon any non-Scot (Cowan 2003a, 113–14).

Another massive Scottish contribution to the Canadian and American experience was in the field of recreation, particularly in sports, such as golf and hockey (still referred to in some parts of Canada as "shinnie" from the Gaelic game, shinty). The greatest spectacle of the Scots at play, however, was to be found in the Highland or Caledonian games (Cowan 1999, 62–64). If Tartan Day is symptomatic of heritage revival, or more accurately, perhaps, of heritage invention, then the games should surely be considered some sort of an indicator, though their history cannot be easily separated from that of Scottish organizations such as the St. Andrews societies, the oldest of which was founded in Charleston, South Carolina, in 1729. Such societies, and there were others, existed not only to provide relief to indigent Scots and their families but also "to foster and encourage a love of Scotland, its history, literature and customs," the promotion of comradeship among members, and, in some cases though not all, the "encouragement of national athletic games." The progress, or otherwise, of such games, which seems to have risen and fallen with the bewildering rapidity of mountain rivers in flood, has been lovingly chronicled (Donaldson). What is of interest is that there were only four games in existence before the Civil War—in Boston, New York, Philadelphia, and Newark, New Jersey. As Celeste Ray notes in chapter 2, as many as 125 games were held in the generation following the war, reduced to 82 by 1986. Such meetings started to pick up again in the 1960s when 13 revivals or creations appeared, followed by 26 during the "seventies explosion" and some 24 between 1980 and 1986

(Donaldson 47–48). The daddy of them all was, of course, Grandfather Mountain, founded in 1956 and expertly investigated by Ray (2001). Although their revival predated the "Roots phenomenon" and the craze for genealogy and clan societies, there can be no doubt that the coincidence of clan connections and caber-tossing generated a novel type of event that was American in origin and developed largely independently of Auld Caledonia, rather like Tartan Day. Those who first attended the Grandfather Mountain Highland Games camped out and labeled their tents with their surnames, hoping thereby to attract kinsfolk (Donaldson 1986, 203). From such humble beginnings there developed the invasion of the pedigree snatchers, the legions of the ancestor worshippers, who erected the tented townships of clan pavilions, coincidentally reminiscent of medieval tourneys that now surround American meetings and, increasingly, Scottish events in the United States at which no games necessarily take place, such as Tartan Day on the Washington Mall. The emphasis upon, and reinforcement of, notions of family and clan on these occasions inescapably recall Jefferson's First Inaugural, when he praised the "chosen country, with room enough for our descendants to the thousandth and thousandth generation" and the idea of the nation as family under the "Great Father" (Kelsall 1999, 30–31). While those seeking clan roots remain emphatically American, their quest may indicate something of a disjuncture, some sort of alienation, or a reaction against crass materialism. Those are matters for American commentators, upon which an outsider should not presume, but it could be argued in any case that one day, or a few, per year, does not a Scottish American make. On a daily basis, the average Scot is exposed to far more American culture than the corresponding American receives of any other. In Scotland there are some five million hyphenated Scots, most of whom are not in the least aware of their predicament.

There are now numerous ceremonies associated with games in America and Canada that have never been heard of in Scotland, as there have been flourishes added to Burns suppers, and novel reenactments commemorating events that never actually happened, such as the "Kirkin' of the Tartan." Yet it may be allowed that despite all the carping and criticism back home in the Motherland,[3] American Scots or Scottish Americans, like their counterparts in Canada, Australia, New Zealand, or on Planet Zog, are perfectly at liberty to develop their own traditions and ceremonials as they wish. And develop them they do! A trawl of Tartan Day Web sites nets numerous Bonnie Knees contests. The Dallas/Fort Worth site refers to the Arbroath Declaration as a "treaty," which, Webbies are assured, will sound very familiar to Americans, since much of their declaration comes from that document. One place offers a display by the

Wicker Clan Kilted Balloon Team; another distributes tartan bows to all visitors during Tartan Week, yet another holds a Kilt and Celt Golf Tournament. On the more positive side there are numerous educational programmes for schools, and any other interested parties, on history, music, culture, and literature, even on modern Scotland and the Scottish Parliament. Some organizations raise money for university scholarships and distribute information sheets about Scotland. Not all activities, therefore, are to be summarily dismissed by the media miseries back home. Just as they liberally invent, so have Americans freely borrowed from Scottish culture at different times in their history—notably in such fields as religion, learning, literature, music and song, Scottish games and sports, and genealogy, not to mention such pursuits as medicine, science, natural history, architecture, and technology, to name but a few. Obviously America draws upon the entire world, and the Scottish dimension has to be seen in perspective, but what should have emerged from the foregoing remarks is that Americans were not always totally fixated on the Scottish past, for many were often influenced by the Scottish present. Furthermore, there is plenty of precedent for innovation and creationism of the type currently associated with Tartan Day.

I have previously provided a rough sketch of how Tartan Day developed, from its origins in the 1980s, as an occasion on which to celebrate the Scottish contribution to the early history of Canada (Cowan 2003b). It was then adopted by the Clans and Scottish Societies of Canada (CASSOC), which, with energetic input from the Scottish Studies Foundation, brought Ontario on board. Today all of the Canadian provinces, excepting Newfoundland, celebrate Tartan Day (Quebec having first celebrated the event in 2004); but it should be noted, in view of claims that the anniversary in the United States was usurped by the American right, that there was emphatically no political agenda in the Canadian campaign. The country never had a declaration of independence, and as one heavily involved in the proceedings I can categorically state that no one's political credentials were ever scrutinized, and neither were their birth certificates. There was definitely no conspiracy; all were united, of whatever persuasion, by a desire to promote Scotland, its culture, and its history.

The situation in the United States, not surprisingly, was somewhat different. In March 1996, representatives of the Caledonian Foundation met with Neil Fraser, past chairman of CASSOC, at a meeting in Sarasota, Florida, of what would shortly become "The Coalition of U.S. Scottish Organizations," an organization that actively promotes Scottish celebration. There the Americans became enamoured of Tartan Day. Reports of discussions suggest that there was some question about dates, Fraser apparently having to explain that July 1 would not be suitable to Canadians, since it was Canada Day and thus no more of an option than July 4.[4] The point is of interest because if the Americans had attempted to change the date, a possibility to which the Canadians would never have agreed, the link with Arbroath and its declaration would have been lost, and the whole debate about the relationship between the two declarations would never have transpired. Neither would National Tartan Day, because without the Scots' "momentous document" it is difficult to see how the American Senate, which was known to be rather reluctant to adopt any more "national days" would, or could, have legislated April 6 as a date of "special significance for all Americans."

The Scottish Coalition is made up of nine organizations, all of which subscribe to its shared vision, namely, "that fruitful and mutually supportive relationships can be forged between individuals and organizations in the United States and in Scotland, in order to assure that the unique Scottish identity and heritage shall become better known and more widely celebrated for the benefit of peoples throughout the world" (*www.scottish-coalition.org*). As noted in chapter 2 of the present volume, the partners represent a wide range of interests and include the American-Scottish Foundation, the Caledonian Foundation, the Association of Scottish Games and Festivals, the Living Legacy of Scotland, the Tartan Educational and Cultural Association, Scottish Heritage USA, Council of Scottish Clans and Societies, the Association of St. Andrew's Societies, and the Scottish-American Military Society (SAMS). As Ray has noted (2001, 164–66), SAMS is dedicated to the "preservation and promotion of Scottish and American Armed Forces customs, traditions and heritage" (*www.s-a-m-s.com*). Members I have personally encountered have almost universally been fiercely patriotic military veterans with only the vaguest notions of Scotland, save for the conviction that they somehow belong to bloodlines of genetically engineered psychopathological warriors dating from time immemorial. Even in the Auld Country the relentless military associations of kilts and ceremonial dress, with overtones of army uniforms, accompanied by bristling weaponry, repel as many people as are attracted.

However, a suitable corrective to the overwhelming impression that all American societies concerned with Scotland are hopelessly fixated on the past is supplied by the American-Scottish Foundation, founded in 1956, which is "dedicated to advancing contemporary Scottish interests and meeting contemporary Scottish needs," regardless of heritage, lineage, or gender. It recognizes that the American Scottish community is made up of "ancestral Scots" and "contemporary Scots," the former nostalgic, distanced from "present-day reality" and a country that many have never visited, the latter focusing on current Scottish issues, opportunities, and requirements. For example, the organization promotes business, cultural, and travel links as well as fund-raising and education (*www.americanscottishfoundation.com.highlights.htm*). It is probably not well known in the land of Calvin, Oatcakes, and Sulphur that the Council of Scottish Clans and Societies actually sponsors workshops on "Exploding Tartan Myths" and "The Kilt, Fact and Fiction" (*www.cosca.net/workshops.html*).

In 1997 Senator Trent Lott made an announcement from the floor of the U.S. Senate to the effect that Tartan Day was about to be observed throughout the country, the arrangements being made by members of "The Coalition," a point they are somewhat proud of because "they took action on an issue important to them and did not wait for the government to specify the date." The event was apparently a great success, reported in one source with almost, we might think, a frisson of 1776:

> Around the country, a true grass-roots effort took place. Thousands of Scots-Americans found ways to observe the first tartan day: in churches, on village greens, at Scottish festivals, at social gatherings, and in the home. It would seem that at last the Scots in America had found a cause around which all could rally. Tartan Day was observed on April 6, 1997, for the first time in U.S. History. And it is a day that will be observed so long as there are Scots who care about their heritage. (Cowan 2003b, 20)

A year later, on March 20, 1998, Lott rose in the Senate to present his resolution, which stated that April 6 "has a special significance for all Americans, and especially those of Scottish descent, because the Declaration of Arbroath, the Scottish Declaration of Independence," was signed on that day and the American declaration was modeled upon that inspirational document. The resolution celebrates the role that Scottish Americans played in the founding of the nation, in that "almost half of the signers of the Declaration" were of Scottish descent. Duncan Bruce's assessment is that of the fifty-six signers, twenty-one "or almost 38 per cent, have been identified as having Scottish ancestry." The Senate acknowledged Scottish Americans as having "helped shape this country in its formative years and guide this nation through its most troubled times." They have made "monumental achievements and invaluable contributions" across most fields of human endeavour, contributions recognised by more than two hundred organisations such as "clans, societies, clubs, and fraternal organizations." In conclusion, the Senate designated 6 April as National Tartan Day. Thus it came to pass that the Arbroath letter of 1320 wound up on Capitol

Hill, and literally thousands of Americans are clamouring to find out what it is all about.

Having ignored the Arbroath Declaration for over six and a half centuries it may be thought that the Americans, once they made up their minds, almost overcompensated by establishing Tartan Day with indecent haste. The comments of Euan Hague in this regard have proved profoundly upsetting in certain Scottish-American quarters. The occasion, in his view, represents the spurious invention of a totally bogus tradition. His interesting investigation actually reveals more about the opinions of the recently disgraced Senator Trent Lott than it does about the myriads of well-intentioned and curious folk who wish to indulge in a day excursion into Scottish culture. American politicians are well practiced in using rhetoric as a cloak for ignorance. Presidents in particular always seem to spit out their remarks as if they were already inscribed in marble. The revolutionary generation of the 1770s and 1780s were truly confident that they were embarking on a monumental and earth-shaking enterprise, and they produced the rhetoric to match, since that time feebly echoed not only by political speechwriters but frequently also by American historians of their revolution. Thus the Declaration of Independence was regarded as "the initiatory act from which the liberation of the nations of Europe (and then the entire world) would proceed" (Kelsall 1999, 6), and it is still so revered by the American political classes, if denied by multitudes of their contemporaries across the planet. Lott repeated the familiar saga of the heroic formation of the United States, reinforced by a "genealogical appeal to Scottish origins," which is in the main questionable. Further reinforcement was sought in assertions that the one declaration was modeled on the other, and that a sort of continuum in declarations is somehow reflected in Scottish bloodlines running in the signers of 1776. Hague also challenges the assumption that privileges European males at the very heart of American history and society to the detriment of women, not to mention other ethnic groups and native peoples (2002, 94–124).

There is no doubt whatsoever that much of Lott's history is sheer invention and that he is guilty of totally unsubstantiated claims, making unqualified assertions that others would wish to challenge or modify. The senator made it known, when accepting the Wallace Prize in Washington in 2000, that a major influence in his thinking was Mel Gibson's *Braveheart* movie. Indeed, he confided to his audience on the steps of the Capitol that having seen the film he wished to pass on the inspirational news to fellow senators from the South. In their absence he intoned the word "freedom" into their answering machines. Derisible though this may be, we should recall that in Scotland, where the same film was accepted quite uncritically throughout the nation, a certain political parry attempted to sell memberships to patrons emerging from the cinema, thus presumably predicating a Scottish future upon a bogus past. In the United States countless enthusiastic supporters of Tartan Day state that they have no time whatsoever for the Trent Lotts of this world, but that they were happy to exploit his interest in order to have the event officially recognised. A point that all too many Scottish critics seem oblivious to is that "Tartan Day has been specifically developed outside of Scotland to serve a diaspora community" (Hague 2002, 95). Despite the Scottish politicians, businesspeople, performers, and academics who troop across the pond each April, the celebration is not, in a crucial sense, a Scottish event at all. Indeed, some Americans have been heard to mutter darkly about a Scottish monopolization or takeover. In 2004 Scottish newshounds made much of a public spat between Sir Sean Connery and Scotland's First Minister Jack McConnell, who courageously appeared in a designer kilt by Howie Nicholsby, which outraged traditionalists back home.

Tartan Day had barely been created before the girning started. Skeptics of the Scottish variety, we are told, have voiced their belief that the event is of marginal significance compared to St. Patrick's Day. Once again American optimism is confronted, bafflingly, by Caledonian pessimism. This is true despite the fact that Tartan Day in America has made more headway in five years than St. Patrick's did in a thousand. Washington and New York are not alone. Tartan Day events are already held in Chicago and in Tidewater, Virginia, from Florida to New Hampshire, Alabama to Minnesota, and Kentucky to California. It is planned that before long April 6 will be observed in every major American city. Yet there has been no shortage of non-diasporeans more than willing to disburden themselves of their opinions about "Brigadoon on the Potomac," to preach that "the 12 million U.S. citizens who claim Scottish ancestry lack profile, political clout and any real sense of coherent identity," arguing that they "should be trying to reconnect with modern Scotland," and suggesting by way of encouragement that Tartan Day is invented and spurious (Cowan 2003b, 21–22). Neal Ascherson writes that Tartan Day is a "heavenly junket" for Scots in the United States, "but it is also a test of integrity; behind the day is a web of nonsense about the past of Scotland. Do Scots have to accept these fibs, in case we hurt our big host's feelings?" (2002b). The immediate response is to ask if there is no such web of nonsense, nothing of the spurious and invented, associated with the likes of January 25 or St. Andrew's Day then. The second is to state that in over twenty years of lecturing in America, on virtually an annual basis, on numerous different subjects, I have never once felt constrained by audience expectations any more or less than I have been in Scotland or Canada, Australia, or New Zealand. Americans, for some reason, are educable in a way that too many Scots are often not; if told that their views are erroneous, their attitude is to ask why and weigh the evidence accordingly. Most of them exist in a culture of debate. People have seen *Braveheart,* are well aware that it is a movie designed for entertainment, and are happy to reject it as history, while employing it as a starting point for consideration of the deeper issues involved in the Scottish Wars of Independence. Recently, Ascherson, who actually writes much more soberly and sensibly on this topic in his *Stone Voices,* has found an ally, in the shape of Michael Fry, who delights in ridiculing the Reverend John Ogilvie, chaplain to the Senate, in 2001, leading the assembled multitude on the steps of the Capitol, in rousing shouts of "Tartan" and "Freedom" (Fry 2003, 224–25). I was present and I was not shouting; to my knowledge Michael was not, and now he is!

The crucial question is whether there is any evidence that the letter sent by the community of the realm of Scotland to the pope in 1320 asking him to pressure Edward II of England into recognizing Robert Bruce as legitimate king of Scots could have influenced the declaration drawn up at Philadelphia in 1776. There are some remarkable, if superficial and coincidental rather than substantive, parallels between the two documents. Both, for example, utilize the rhetoric of tyranny against the brutal and illegal actions of Edward I and George III, respectively; both rehearse the miseries these kings inflicted upon different peoples almost half a millennium apart. In both cases there are problems about exact dates, about how the documents were physically sealed or signed, and about how they were largely forgotten before they later emerged into a climate as much informed by mythos as by history. There has hitherto been no certainty about why the Arbroath missive is dated April 6; American independence was actually declared on July 2, but only through a series of accidents did July 4 come to be regarded as Independence Day. The problem of how and when all of the seals were affixed to the Arbroath letter is matched by similar doubts about when individuals actually signed the 1776 declaration, a process that began on August 2 and lasted for some six months. Both documents were fully reproduced for the first time in 1812–1813.

It is now possible to resolve the problem of the dating of the Declaration of Arbroath, April 6. In 1320 Easter Sunday was observed on March 30. This means that April 6 fell on Quasimodo, the Sunday exactly one week after Easter Sunday, sometimes known as "Low Sunday" or in Ireland as "Little Easter." The name arises from the introit at Mass, *Quasi modo geniti,* "as newborn babes" (1 Peter 2:2), which celebrated "Sunday in taking off white robes," that is, the robes shed by those who had been baptized at Easter a week earlier. The wording of the second chapter of Peter is apposite, for it is much concerned with obedience and subservience: "Ye are a chosen generation, a royal priesthood, an holy nation, a peculiar people; that ye should shew forth praises of him who hath called you out of darkness into his marvellous light: Which in time past were not a people, but are now the people of God: which had not obtained mercy, but have now obtained mercy," particularly appropriate sentiments for a king and those subjects loyal to him who were seeking the raising of a papal ban that had been in place for some fourteen years. Equally suggestive are the texts that follow: "For so is the will of God, that with well doing ye may put to silence the ignorance of foolish men: As free, and not using your liberty for a cloak of maliciousness, but as the servants of God . . . For ye were as sheep going astray; but are now returned unto the Shepherd and bishop of your souls." Thus errant Scottish sheep are returning to their shepherd and master, the pope. The medieval mind, especially of the clerical variety, was attuned to code employing a discourse brimming with symbology and analogy. By dating the declaration to April 6 the Scots were signifying that they were cleansed and penitent, in preparation for regaining the good graces of the pope (Cowan 2003b, 29). Celebrants of Tartan Day should thus be aware that they are also commemorating the feast of Quasimodo, a name that, in another context altogether, rings a familiar bell!

In making its resolution the Senate adduced no evidence. Can such a glaring deficiency be remedied? A major sticking point is the assertion that the American declaration is "modeled" upon the Arbroath letter. Duncan Bruce's book *The Mark of The Scots* proved hugely influential in this regard, furnishing the most detailed case for such dependency through a comparison of the two documents. His assessment is that almost 38 percent, rather than half, of those signing the American declaration had pure Scotch flowing in their veins—my words, not his (Bruce 1996, 38–41). Although the idea is not new, and Bruce's examples may be thought to be superficially persuasive, the American historical establishment is unlikely to be moved. Yet he makes a more convincing prima facie case than exists, for example, for the influence of Magna Carta, which scholars have been more or less happy to accept for very many years. The skeptics, however, this writer included, will demand more evidence before the case is totally convincing, though it is far from closed; for us the jury is still out.

James Wilson and John Witherspoon were the only Scots-born, and two of the best educated, among the fifty-six signatories of the American declaration, graduates respectively of St. Andrews and Edinburgh. Both consciously chose the cause of independence, adopted it as their own and worked toward the final goal. They were converts to America, so to speak, devoted through commitment and conviction.

Witherspoon was to invent the term "Americanism," "exactly similar in its formation and signification to the word Scotticism," by which he meant any word, grammatical form, expression, or pronunciation peculiar to Scotland. Like many Scots who emigrated during the eighteenth and nineteenth centuries, Witherspoon used his own sense of nationality to inform the identity of a new nation: "There are many instances in which the Scotch way is as good, and some in which every person who has the least taste as to the propriety or purity of language in general, must confess that it is better than that of England." He believed that through time the American contribution would be as great, or greater, than that of the Scots. "Being entirely separated from Britain, we shall find some centre or standard of our own, and not be subject to the inhabitants of that island, either in new ways of speaking, or rejecting the old." He was thus intent upon transmitting to his newly adopted country Scottish ideas that might be described as "Americable," concepts that potentially inspired and enabled Americans, in the formation of nation and identity. Some such notions, we are now told, were transmitted by the 1320 declaration to that of 1776. There remains, however, the small but pertinent question of whether it can be demonstrated that Wilson and Witherspoon had ever encountered the Arbroath Declaration.

According to a recent authority, James Wilson (1742–1798), one of only six men to sign both the Declaration of Independence and the Constitution, remains "perhaps the most underrated founder," and yet, "the American constitutional system is closer to his vision than to that of any other." James of Caledonia, as he was known, described liberty as "a sacred gift descended to us from our ancestors. We cannot dispose of it: We are bound by the strongest ties to transmit it, as we have received it, pure and inviolate to our posterity." Through time he would leave three great legacies. He is acknowledged as the main architect of the U.S. Supreme Court. He is also credited with suggesting the one-man executive office that is the presidency of the United States. Even more significant in the present context is that it was Wilson who convinced Congress that "all power was originally in the People and that all the Powers of Government are derived from them—that all Power, which they have not disposed of, still continues theirs." This was "the Revolution Principle." As he wrote, "this truth, so simple and natural, and yet so neglected or despised, may be appreciated as the first and fundamental principle in the science of government. The sovereignty of the people was a principle to which he unwaveringly adhered, and it is, of course, an idea that is implicit in the Arbroath Declaration. A further echo can be detected in Wilson's acknowledgement of the existence of a compact or covenant between a king and his subjects. More promising is a passage in which he refers to "essential Liberty, which . . . we are determined not to lose, but with our lives." This might be thought to provide fairly compelling evidence, since it chimes with and indeed replicates the Arbroath Declaration's "for freedom alone, which no good man gives up except with his life." However, in both cases, the emotive and stirring quotation is drawn from the Roman writer Sallust, who was studied by generations of Scottish schoolchildren, Wilson included, in Latin class. Consequently, the citation does not afford proof that he had seen the Arbroath letter, but the possibility nevertheless exists.

Wilson never specifically mentioned the document of 1320, but neither did he refer to the undoubted Scottish antecedents that certainly informed his radical political ideas. It is quite likely that from his St. Andrews University days he knew the works of George Mackenzie, Gilbert Burnet, and James Anderson, all of whom had helped to popularise knowledge of the Arbroath letter. On such topics as the relationship between law and liberty, on divine right kingship, the social contract, and the inalienability of the sovereignty of the people, Wilson's thought irresistibly recalls John Knox, George Buchanan, and various Covenanting theorists, none of whom mentioned the Arbroath Declaration although they would have lauded its sentiments, particularly on resistance theory (Cowan 2003, 124–27).

Much better known is John Witherspoon (1723–1794), a high-flyer, or evangelical, who belonged to the same church party as Burns's Holy Willie. Witherspoon was intensely proud of his birthright: "I am certain I feel the attachment of native country as far as it is a virtuous or laudable principle . . . I have never seen cause to be ashamed of my birth." He believed that his nationality was an advantage, reflecting that had he been born and educated in America far fewer people would have paid attention to his ideas and opinions.

As early as 1771 Witherspoon was eloquently rejecting the charge that he was an enemy to Scotland because he encouraged emigration to Nova Scotia. He anticipated some of the arguments at the heart of the emigration process that later became known as the "Clearances" when the landlords dispossessed their tenants in favour of sheep. The British establishment frowned upon emigration until persuaded otherwise by the economic depression consequent upon the ending of the Napoleonic wars. Witherspoon's voice was thus one of the first to be raised in criticism of the landlords and their attitudes. He could never admit that the happiness of one man should depend upon the misery of another. It was laudable, he thought, to assist people to escape the tyranny of the landlords. People would be more disposed to move, he mischievously added, when "they found their landlords anxious that they should stay." In his philosophy lectures Witherspoon taught Francis Hutcheson's doctrine on the right of resistance, ideas also informed by Covenanting precedents. He was the only cleric to sign the Declaration of Independence.

There is no specific mention of "Arbroath" in his writings, though much that chimes with its sentiments. However, Ezra Stiles, no lover of Scotsmen, observed that Witherspoon and Wilson were the only two in Congress who were "Both strongly national & can't bear any thing in Congress which reflects badly on Scotland. The Dr. says that Scotland has manifested the greatest Spirit for Liberty as a nation, in that their History is full of their calling kings to account & dethroning them when arbitrary and tyrannical." Thus, while Witherspoon did not actually quote the Arbroath letter, he drew upon a body of ideas that the document so brilliantly represented. We can suggest with some confidence that he, like Wilson, almost certainly knew of the Arbroath Declaration, for it had been printed at least fourteen times before 1776 (Cowan 2003, 26–27). It is possible that Witherspoon and Wilson suggested the value of Scottish ideas and the noble sentiments of the Arbroath Declaration, as they did the Scottish management of bad kings, to their congressional colleagues, thus ensuring that a hefty dose of Scottish political assumption affected the final American product. More evidence may well emerge in the future; the quest, after all, has barely begun. In the present state of our knowledge there can be little doubt that if the Scottish declaration did influence the American Declaration of Independence in any way, then it should have left more of a trace. On the other hand, there were over a quarter of a million Scots in America in 1776. It is not beyond the bounds of possibility that some of them had read and digested the Declaration of Arbroath (Cowan 2003, 127–35).

The Tartan Day story is still unfolding. In 2004 the event was celebrated not only in Quebec but also in France. The first Scottish event was also staged by a promotional campaign group known as Angus Ahead, representing the Angus District Council, with events mounted at Arbroath and Carnoustie. On two separate days there were reenactments of the medieval pageant at Arbroath Abbey commemorating the drawing up of the declaration in 1320. A memorable dinner at Carnoustie on April 6 was followed by a round of golf the next morning on the world-famous open links course. Billed as a homecoming for Canadians, Americans, and others, the event was shunned by the Scottish Executive, which did not find the east coast of Scotland as appealing or trendy as the eastern seaboard of the United States. Yet perhaps in the future, descendants of Scots abroad will replicate the pilgrimages of the Middle Ages as they return to the shrine of freedom by the grey North Sea, to the burgh that taught Scottish kings that they were the servants of their people, by whom they were elected and to whom they were answerable. Angus offers numerous distractions from such inspirational sentiments in its mountain landscape and glens, its abundance of bird and animal wildlife, its unsurpassed historical heritage, and its delicious, mouth-watering Arbroath smokies.

The Canadians invented Tartan Day, and however much some Scots may deplore the label, it must be respected as a piece of uniquely North American Scottish heritage. Heritage, as we know all too well in Scotland, is not the same as history, and the past is often pressed into the service of the present. But Tartan Day provides an opportunity, which must be welcomed, to celebrate Scotland's influence on America, the shared concept of the sovereignty of the people, and the universal appeal of freedom, while permitting the pleasing speculation, at this stage it be no more, that the pungent reek, or smoke, of Arbroath infected the inspirational rhetoric of Philadelphia's Liberty Hall.

Notes

1. A fuller version of what follows will be found in the two items listed under Cowan 2003 in the bibliography.

2. Abbot Bernard of Arbroath, as I think, the most likely author, or editor, of the declaration has long been identified, traditionally and erroneously, with Bernard de Linton, though it is now known that the two Bernards were different people (Duncan 1998, 198–203). Abbot Bernard is still identified as de Linton in many popular books and in the Arbroath Pageant that takes place every five years. The wrong Bernard received the accolade of commemoration in the name of a local pub, Bernard de Linton's, which was subsequently upgraded to Bernard's Bistro. In April 2004 "Bernard" had totally disappeared, and the establishment was renamed Liquid Anticipation. Yet another bar has opened, however, that rejoices in the name The Declaration.

3. Scots, as the descendants of Scota, the daughter of Pharaoh, unusually inhabit a *matria* rather than a fatherland, thus explaining perhaps why their men wear skirts! The latter phenomenon, however, has had little impact upon the gendering of the nation, whose image remains overwhelmingly male. Tartan, it seems, is heavily infused with testosterone.

4. Personal comment.

Works Cited

Ascherson, Neal. 2002a. *Stone Voices: The Search for Scotland.* New York: Hill and Wang.
———. 2002b. "Nothing to Declare," *Sunday Herald,* June 30.

Barrow, Geoffrey, ed. 2003. *The Declaration of Arbroath History, Significance, and Setting.* Edinburgh: Society of Antiquaries of Scotland.

Bruce, Duncan, A. 1996. *The Mark of the Scots: Their Astonishing Contributions to History, Science, Democracy, Literature, and the Arts.* New York: Citadel.

Brodie, J. 1904. *About Arbroath: (Fairport of Scott's "Antiquary") The Birthplace of the Declaration of Scottish Independence, 1320.* Arbroath: No publisher.

Cowan, Edward J. 2003a. *"For Freedom Alone": The Declaration of Arbroath, 1320.* East Linton: Tuckwell.

———. 2003b. "Declaring Arbroath." In *Declaration of Arbroath*, ed. Geoffrey Barrow, 13–31. Edinburgh: Society of Antiquaries of Scotland.

———. 2002. "The Covenanting Tradition in Scottish History." In *Scottish History: The Power of the Past*, ed. Edward J. Cowan and R. J. Finlay, 121–45. Edinburgh: Edinburgh UP.

———. 1999. "The Myth of Scotch Canada." In *Myth, Migration, and the Making of Memory: Scotia and Nova Scotia c. 1700–1990*, ed. Marjory Harper and Michael E. Vance, 49–72. Halifax, Nova Scotia: Fernwood.

Cowan, Edward J., and Douglas Gifford, eds. 1999. *The Polar Twins: Scottish History and Scottish Literature.* Edinburgh: John Donald.

Donaldson, Emily Ann. 1986. *The Scottish Highland Games in America.* Gretna, LA: Pelican.

Duncan, A. A. M., ed. 1988. *Regesta Regum Scottorum: The Acts of Robert I.* Edinburgh: Edinburgh UP.

Erskine, John, and Gordon Lucy, eds. 1997. *Cultural Traditions in Northern Ireland Varieties of Scottishness: Exploring the Ulster-Scottish Connection.* Belfast: Queen's University of Belfast.

Fry, Michael. 2003. *"Bold, Independent, Unconquer'd, and Free": How the Scots Made America Safe for Liberty, Democracy, and Capitalism.* Ayr, Scotland: Fort Publishing.

Hague, Euan. 2002. "National Tartan Day: Rewriting History in the United States." *Scottish Affairs* 38: 94–124.

Hook, Andrew. 1999. *From Goosecreek to Gandercleugh: Studies in Scottish-American Literary and Cultural History.* East Linton: Tuckwell.

———. 1975. *Scotland and America: A Study of Cultural Relations, 1750–1835.* Glasgow: Blackie.

Kelsall, Malcolm. 1999. *Jefferson and the Iconography of Romanticism: Folk, Land, Culture, and the Romantic Nation.* Basingstoke: St. Martin's.

Lambert, Frank. 1999. *Inventing the "Great Awakening."* Princeton, NJ: Princeton UP.

M'Bain, J. M. 1897. *Eminent Arbroathians: Being Sketches Historical, Genealogical, and Biographical, 1178–1894.* Arbroath: No publisher.

Macpherson, James. 1996. *The Poems of Ossian and Related Works*, ed. Howard Gaskill. Edinburgh: Edinburgh UP.

Osterweis, Rollin G. 1949. *Romanticism and Nationalism in the Old South.* New Haven, CT: Yale UP.

Ray, Celeste. 2001. *Highland Heritage: Scottish Americans in the American South.* Chapel Hill: U of North Carolina P.

Schmidt, Leigh Eric. 1989. *Holy Fairs: Scottish Communions and American Revivals in the Early Modern Period.* Princeton, NJ: Princeton UP.

Sloan, Douglas. 1971. *The Scottish Enlightenment and the American College Ideal.* New York: Columbia UP.

Stevenson, David. 1988a. *The Origins of Freemasonry, Scotland's Century, 1590–1710.* Cambridge, Eng.: Cambridge UP.

———. 1988b. *The First Freemasons: Scotland's Early Lodges and Their Members.* Aberdeen, UK: Aberdeen UP.

Stringer, Keith. 2003. "Arbroath Abbey in Context, 1178–1320." In *Declaration of Arbroath*, ed. Geoffrey Barrow, 116–41. Edinburgh: Society of Antiquaries of Scotland.

Wills, Garry. 1978. *Inventing America: Jefferson's Declaration of Independence.* New York: Doubleday.

13
Transatlantic Scots, Their Interlocutors, and the Scottish Discursive Unconscious
Colin McArthur

[Cultural] identities are the names we give to the different ways we are positioned by, and position ourselves within, the narratives of the past.

—Stuart Hall

Consider the following quotations:

From the green saucer of Glenaladale, dipping down to Loch Shiel, Alexander Macdonald had taken one hundred and fifty men to serve in Clanranald's regiment. Within a century there was nothing there but the lone shieling of the song. (Prebble 1961, 315)

[T]his is Glencoe, the village at the foot of that most dramatic of glens, where the waters run down the precipitous black rock-faces like tears of pain and shame at what happened 300 years ago. (Pendreigh 1992)

In Kildonan there is today a shadow, a chill, of which any sensitive mind would, I am convinced, be vaguely aware, though possessing knowledge of the clearances. We are affected strangely by any place from which the tide of life has ebbed. (Gunn 1987, 32)

I'm tied to Uig Sands. I don't know why . . . Balnakiel just represents sort of the centre of the historical universe for me, and it is a particularly beautiful setting, and for me, if I were to picture my historic home then it's going to be someplace on Uig Sands, whether it's Carnish that sits on one side or Crowlista on the other side. That bay is a sort of "ground zero" for me. It's strange that it didn't turn out to be Aird, but Aird to me is always a sort of removal place, someplace that we went after we left the homeland. (Cited in Basu, ch. 11 in this volume)

The first quotation is from the deracinated Canadian writer John Prebble's *Culloden* (1961); the second from indigenous Scots journalist Brian Pendreigh's 1992 newspaper account of the three-hundredth anniversary of the massacre of Glencoe; the third is from a 1935 essay by the Scots novelist Neil Munro; and the fourth is a statement by a transatlantic Scot on her recent return to Scotland. The latter two are cited in Paul Basu's essay in this volume (ch. 11). A factor worthy of investigation is the extent to which all four, despite being produced at diverse moments and by both indigenous Scots and North Americans, sound the same elegiac note or display the same rhetorical trope of running the names of people and places, mantralike, off the tongue. Basu alludes to this trope in one of the quotations he uses as the rubric to his essay: "[H]e gazed towards the moors and crests that for so long had been names with the remoteness about them of names in Judea, but far more intimate and thrilling."

Wherever one looks within discourse relating to Scotland—whether produced by Scots or non-Scots is irrelevant—one is confronted by the same restricted range of images, tones, rhetorical tropes, and ideological tendencies, often within utterances promulgated decades (sometimes even a century or more) apart.

Another example: In 1953 the film *The Maggie* was made in Scotland by the London-based Ealing Films. That it was directed by Alexander Mackendrick, born of Scots parents in the United States but brought up in Scotland, is interesting but, as is suggested above, not crucially relevant. In *The Maggie* an American executive (Paul Douglas), through a misunderstanding, has his valuable cargo of domestic effects, en route for his Hebridean holiday home, transferred to a beat-up Clyde "puffer," the kind of small, usually coal-hauling, boat that plied the Clyde estuary. He engages in a duel of wits with the vessel's cunning captain to retrieve his cargo, but when the boat lands on the rocks, the American, having been transformed through his encounter with Scotland and the Scots, orders his valuable effects to be jettisoned in order to save the puffer. Exposed to Scotland, he has learned to let his heart rule his head (McArthur 2003a). Almost three decades later the London-based Enigma Productions made *Local Hero* (1983) in Scotland, written and directed by indigenous Scot Bill Forsyth. In this film an American oil tycoon (Burt Lancaster) sends his aide to Scotland to close a deal for an oil refinery in the Highlands. He comes to Scotland himself to iron out difficulties, and both he and his aide, transformed through their encounter with Scotland and the Scots, abandon their plan for an oil refinery, opting instead for an observatory and a sanctuary for marine life. Like the executive in *The Maggie*, they too have learned to let their hearts rule their heads. The American in *The Maggie* meets an ethereally beautiful Scots woman who, faced with the choice of marrying an ambitious businessman or a fisherman, opts for the latter; and the two Scots women in *Local Hero* are called Stella and Marina, the stars and the sea, Scotland as Nature. By all accounts Forsyth had not seen *The Maggie* before he came to make *Local Hero*. How should it be, therefore, that his film should land on precisely the same ideological mark as the earlier film?

The writings of Stuart Hall, among others, on ideology and cultural identity have consistently struggled with the contradiction between individual human agency and transindividual influence if not determination. The quotation from his work (1990, 225) that opens this essay leans both ways in relation to "the narratives of the past," implying individual agency by suggesting that we position ourselves within them but recognising the possibility of determination by suggesting that we are also positioned by them. As the above concrete examples of discursive repetition imply, when it comes to discourse relating to Scotland, I bend toward determination (albeit complex *over*determination) rather than agency. Having been preoccupied with this question for over two decades, I have sought to fashion and elaborate a theoretical concept that will help explain the limited, repetitive repertoire of images and utterances relating to Scotland (McArthur 1993, 1996, 2003a, 2003b). That concept is the Scottish Discursive Unconscious, the suggestion being that anyone setting out to describe, comment on, or make images of Scotland and the Scots, rather than producing a novel and "personal" take on the subject, switches on to automatic pilot, so to speak, slots into a preexisting and hegemonic bricolage of images, narratives, subnarratives, tones, and turns of phrase suspended in the aspic of the Scottish Discursive Unconscious (SDU). The metaphors of "suspended" and "aspic" perhaps imply too high a level of fixity in the SDU. The metaphor of the kaleidoscope—with its infinite capacity to disassemble and reconfigure its contents—might be more appropriate. Angela McRobbie, describing the rise, under the sign principally of Foucault, of antiessentialism within feminism, talks of "gender discourses rush[ing] in to fill over the cracks of fragile, unstable sexual identities" (1999, 78). We might here talk of the Scottish Discursive Unconscious rushing to fill the cracks in (transatlantic) Scots' cultural identities. Clearly the idea of the SDU relates to Foucault's general emphasis on discourse, has some affinities with Edward Said's idea of Orientalism (1978) wherein the West *constructs* rather than describes the Orient, and connects with the process anatomised by Frantz Fanon (1952) wherein blacks in a white world adopt masks fashioned by their exploiters. The SDU also shares with Orientalism the fact that much of its elaboration has taken place outside the land that is its focus, for example, the European vogue for things Scottish in the late eighteenth and nineteenth centuries and the construction of cinematic images of Scotland in London and Hollywood.

The Scottish Discursive Unconscious has been a long time in the making. It was precisely the vogue for things Scottish in nineteenth-century Europe that pushed Robert Louis Stevenson, with some element of awareness of what he was doing, to slot into a version of the SDU when pressed by German friends for an account of his native land. In a letter of 1882 to his mother, he writes: "[A]nd thence, as I find is always the case, to the most ghastly romancing about the Scottish scenery and manners, the Highland dress and everything national or local that I could lay my hands upon . . . There is one thing that burthens me a good deal in my patriotic garrulage, and that is the black ignorance in which I grope about everything . . . I am generally glad enough to fall back again . . . upon Burns, toddy and the Highlands" (cited in Noble 1981, 72).

There is some measure of consensus regarding the key personnel "responsible" for the articulation of the SDU and the key moments of its elaboration. These would include James "Ossian" Macpherson in the 1770s, his writings being taken up as a European vogue; Sir Walter Scott throughout his active life and beyond, his works likewise being taken up universally, not least in North America (Mark Twain hyperbolically blamed Scott for the outbreak of the American Civil War); Queen Victoria and Prince Albert and their placing of the royal imprimatur on the Highlands, resulting in the emergence of "Balmorality"; those masters of Victorian regional sentimentality the Kailyard writers (particularly J. M. Barrie, S. R. Crockett, and "Ian McLaren," the pen name of John Watson) and their popularity in the late nineteenth and early twentieth centuries, especially their being lionised in North America; and Harry Lauder and his rise to dominance in the Edwardian music hall and, from the early 1900s, his celebrity status in North America. As to why the ball should have been set rolling by Scotland's emerging cultural visibility two centuries ago, Malcolm Chapman offers a convincing, if partial, answer:

Perhaps the most significant intellectual trend of the eighteenth century was that towards what we now label "Romanticism." Within this often rather monstrous historical figment of retrospective definition, one of the commonest of theoretical concerns was to speculate on the nature of society, and on the nature of social development. Theories of Man's primitive nature blossomed, and the Romantics looked both to nature and to this primal human essence for their poetic and intellectual inspiration. At the same time as British intellectuals were becoming more and more interested in the nature of primitive man and primitive society, they had within their own national boundaries a fitting object for their attention. The Scottish Gael fulfilled this role of the "primitive," albeit one quickly and savagely tamed, at a time when every thinking man was turning towards such subjects. The Highlands of Scotland provided a location for this role that was distant enough to be exotic (in customs and language) but close enough to be noticed; that was near enough to visit, but had not been drawn so far into the calm waters of civilization as to lose all its interest. (1978, 19)

Listing the points of articulation of the Scottish Discursive Unconscious in no way conveys the nature of its operation, its mercurial, hydra-headed, shape-shifting quality; its capacity to reconfigure and rearticulate all or part of the sub-discourses of which it is constituted; its ability to refurbish itself by appropriating parts of existing or emergent discourses. The sub-discourses constituting the SDU go some way beyond the discourse of Tartanry and Highlandism, which this volume rightly sees as hegemonic among transatlantic Scots. Indeed, part of my purpose in this chapter is to thicken the discursive soup in which Scots, transatlantic and indigenous, swim, to suggest that they are prey not only to Tartanry/Highlandism but also to some of the other sub-discourses making up the SDU. But first, some clarification of the nature of these sub-discourses. Many of them do, of course, have a conscious dimension—Catholicism or Calvinism, for example—but what I am concerned with here is their quotidian dimension, that part of them that is invoked unthinkingly in day-to-day utterances. Clearly, as has been indicated, the sub-discourse of Tartanry/Highlandism is central to the SDU, a "structure in dominance" to use the Althusserian terminology that is again problematic on account of the impression it gives of fixity. This recognition is writ large over several of the essays in this volume. The most curious absence, however, is any reference to the Kailyard or, in its discursive mode, Kailyardism, arguably the next most important sub-discourse in the SDU bricolage. That it tends to be overlooked may be due to the fact that, unlike Tartanry/Highlandism, which supplies the visual iconography of Scots "identity," Kailyardism rather supplies a range of moods, tones, and verbal registers. For example, Cairns Craig famously described Harry Lauder as

"Kailyard consciousness in tartan exterior" (1982, 13). Thomas Knowles has offered a succinct account of that group of Kailyard novels and stories that flourished primarily in the decade 1888–1898:

> In its "classic" form the Kailyard is characterized by the sentimental and nostalgic treatment of parochial Scottish scenes, often centred on the church community, often on individual careers which move from childhood innocence to urban awakening (and contamination), and back again to the comfort and security of the native hearth. Typically thematic is the "lad o' pairts," the poor Scottish boy making good within the "democratic" Scottish system of education, and dying young as a graduated minister in his mother's arms with the assembled parish looking on. The parishioners themselves, their dialogue sometimes translated for an English audience, sprinkle their exchanges with native wit, and slip easily from the pettiness of village gossip to the profundities of rustic philosophising. (1983, 13–14)

My wish to foreground Kailyardism is due to its electrifying effect on North America at the turn of the nineteenth to the twentieth century and thereafter and its probable influence on transatlantic Scots, of which more presently.

Although closely associated with Tartanry/Highlandism, Scottish militarism, as a discourse, is not wholly to be identified with it. It is discernible throughout Scotland as an exorbitant pride in the exploits of Scottish regiments, in periodic, well-supported campaigns to save them from amalgamation or extinction, in popular songs like "The Scottish Soldier," and as a trope of verbal intercourse. I recall being accosted by a drunk Orangeman in a Glasgow pub. Looking for trouble and judging me, mistakenly, to be of Irish extraction and therefore Catholic, he opened aggressively with "I say there's naebody like the wee Scots sodger." How should religion figure in the SDU? It should probably be represented as two separate traditions, Catholicism and Calvinism, not in their theological but their *ideological* aspects, those aspects of the traditions that translate into quotidian mental furniture to emerge as oaths, sayings and saws, and unthinking historical identifications. For example, the Catholicism of the Stuart dynasty seems to have been a strong attraction to latter-day Jacobites such as Compton Mackenzie and to the handful of cranks who, even today, entertain the delusion of the Stuart dynasty being restored to the British throne. As for the Calvinist tradition, although almost wholly eroded among young Scots, its influence is still discernible in older generations in the sense that the cadences of the "authorised version" may resonate within their heads and in their utterances. I suspect that such resonances are evident in my own writings and certainly my thoroughly secularised progeny throw puzzled glances my way when I refer to certain aspects of popular culture as "a sounding brass and a tinkling cymbal" (1st Corinthians 13:1–2) or when I describe a particularly unctuous politician or media celebrity as "a whited sepulchre" (Matthew 23:27). The vestiges of religion in the SDU are somewhat separate from what might be called the Sectarian Discourse, also part of the SDU, which Scotland shares with the north of Ireland. In the Scottish context it ranges from bitter, violent insult ("We're up to our knees in Fenian blood!") to mild banter and jokes ("Did you hear about the Catholic window cleaner? The sash came down on his fingers"). As Celeste Ray notes in this volume, organised sectarianism was imported into North America by, primarily, the Ulster Scots. Although it survives in Scotland sometimes as a lethal practice but more usually as a historic narrative Scots still live within, it is doubtful whether organised sectarianism is nowadays significant in the identity narratives of transatlantic Scots.

Another sub-discourse, which the sectarian discourse sometimes combines with, is Clydesidism. A heavily masculine and working-class discourse, its polar points are taciturnity, heavy drinking, devotion to football, and the banishment of women to the margins of life. Its historical evolution can be tracked from the myths generated by nineteenth-century urban planning and public health reports that revealed Clydeside to have the worst slums in Europe (Spring 1990), through interwar popular journalism about razor gangs with picturesque names (the Baltic Fleet, the Cheeky Forty, the San Toy), through novels such as *No Mean City* (1937) to the near-contemporary television plays of Peter McDougall. The journalism and novels of William McIlvanney are to some extent articulated within Clydesidism, but it is a version inflected toward Red Clydesidism, itself a discourse within which the Clyde Valley has been, is, and always will be a socialist-inclined place. It was this discourse that manifested itself in the "Workers' City" movement, set up to counter Glasgow's embourgeoisement implicit in the "Glasgow's Miles Better" public relations campaign and the designating of Glasgow as "European City of Culture" in 1990 (Spring 1990).

The Great Scots sub-discourse is discernible in any Scottish antiquarian bookshop—shelves of tomes celebrating Scots who have "made it" in the world beyond Scotland. It survives mainly in Scots journalism, Sir Sean Connery currently being the jewel in its crown. What could be called "the Scottish Enlightenment" sub-discourse—sometimes appropriated, in terms of particular personalities, by the Great Scots discourse—attempts to construct Scotland as rationalist, scientific, and progressive. The Scottish Development Agency (now Scottish Development International) reanimated this discourse in its advertising campaigns of the early 1990s to lure industrial investment to Scotland. Clearly the SDA/SDI and the Scottish Tourist Board are caught in a contradiction, the Tartanry/Highlandism the latter characteristically deploys in its publicity sending out quite the opposite message to that of the SDA/SDI. Finally, there is Anti-Englishness. Doubtless arising in the medieval Wars of Independence, it still flickers to life today, as with other discourses, showing itself in the lethal form of occasional physical violence against figures perceived to be English, but more usually at the level of banter among, for example, football supporters. It has to be said that an analogous anti-Scots discourse has deep roots in English culture, possibly peaking in 1902 with T. W. H. Crosland's book *The Unspeakable Scot*. It is nowadays much less common than Scottish Anti-Englishness, although it too survives in, for example, metropolitan murmurings about the disproportionate numbers of Scots holding high office in the Blair government.

These, then, are some of the sub-discourses making up the Scottish Discursive Unconscious. Clearly some—particularly Tartanry/Highlandism and, I would argue, Kailyardism—are more pertinent to the identity narratives of transatlantic Scots, while others (e.g., Sectarianism and Clydesidism) are more influential on (some) indigenous Scots. The unstable, mercurial nature of discourse means that, like the Blob in the film of that name, the SDU constantly assimilates (parts of) emergent discourses, even those most apparently in contradiction with it. Certain breast-beating instances of the SDU have included a dash of ecologism. For instance, there is an ecological flavour to the ambitions of the Wallace Clan Trust—battle reenactment group and praetorian guard to Mel Gibson during the making and premiering of *Braveheart*—to reinhabit "the traditional Wallace lands" as non-modern "clansmen." It is perhaps worth recalling the not insignificant "green" strain in German National Socialism (Biehl and Staudenmaier 1995). Analogously, Paul Basu, in his essay in this volume, draws attention to the New Ageist rhetoric informing some of his informants' utterances, and the following statement, from the same essay, clearly appropriates the emphases of feminism: "As the boat approached Lewis, I could almost 'see' years of Scottish women on the shores and bogs. I got my first real sense of the female side of the Scots . . . and I suddenly felt like I acquired a lineage of strong Scots women" (cited by Basu in ch. 11 of this volume).

A respect for the real gains of feminism should not blind us to the extent to which the phrase "strong women" is the premier shibboleth of vulgar feminism, cranked out by virtually every female film director, screenwriter, and actor to "explain" what drew them to particular projects or characters, another example of discourse "on automatic pilot." It is the vulgar feminist equivalent of the "positive images" phase of black discourse that, whatever its progressive historical role, is now somewhat discredited (Hall 1989). Celeste Ray has demonstrated, in this volume and elsewhere (Ray 1998 and 2001), the extent to which Tartanry/Highlandism may be merged with Celtic spirituality, and I would hazard a guess that it will not be long before the subalternist preoccupation of certain postcolonialisms (Bhabha 1984; Spivak 1988) is brought to bear on the historic experience of that, in all likelihood fanciful, construction, the "Celtic" peoples (Chapman 1992).

Perhaps this is the point at which to tease out the implications of this chapter. In the introduction to the present volume, Ray makes the following tactful observation: "While some cultural studies scholars and anthropologists (especially those leaning toward ethnopoetics) would privilege what people *believe* about their past, the historian privileges 'facts' and the deconstruction of myths. If not through individual essays, then as a whole, this volume attempts to balance a respect for both and to offer both the 'natives'' perspectives with those of the outside observer." While appreciating the respect shown by the anthropologists toward their informants' utterances and practices—a respect that always makes me feel guilty about my own writings as sanctimoniously judgmental—confronted with these utterances and practices, I feel akin to Tom Nairn at that point in *The Break-Up of Britain* when he describes the interlocking of Kailyard and Tartanry:

> Kailyard is popular in Scotland. It is recognizably intertwined with that prodigious array of *Kitsch* symbols, slogans, ornaments, banners, war-cries, knick-knacks, music-hall heroes, icons, conventional sayings and sentiments (not a few of them "pithy") which have for so long resolutely defended the name of "Scotland" to the world. Annie S. Swan and Cronin provided no more than the relatively decent outer garb for this vast tartan monster. In their work the thing trots along doucely enough on a lead. But it is something else to be with it (e.g.) in a London pub on International night, or in the crowd at the annual Military Tattoo in front of Edinburgh Castle. How intolerably vulgar! What unbearable, crass, mindless philistinism! One knows that *Kitsch* is a large constituent of mass popular culture in every land: but this is ridiculous!" (1977, 162)

Clearly most of the ethnographic work in this volume takes some distance from the North American version of "the tartan monster," but this is not always the case. Some subjects come perilously close to being fashioned from within the Scottish Discursive Unconscious. For example, it is hard not to hear in Jonathan Dembling's informants' accounts of Cape Breton fiddling the macho tones of a kind of rural, North American version of Clydesidism. One is not condemnatory of "the tartan monster," and its centrality in transatlantic Scots' identity narratives, because it is popular. One is concerned about the heavy *political* cost of tolerating it, a cost recognised by some of the pieces in this volume. As Michael Vance's chapter in this book makes clear, it is principally the blacks of Nova Scotia who have had to pay the psychological price for the hegemony of "Scottishness" there. One wonders also what the transatlantic Scots' "webbing" with other Scots distant in place and time implies for their capacity to "web" with their ethnically diverse North American fellow citizens in the here and now, whether there might not be lurking under the filiopietistic utterances the kind of identity-shoring Paul Gilroy condemns as "ethnic absolutism" (1993). This essay's reservations about certain aspects of ethnographic practice reflects the beady eye that anthropology and cultural studies have been keeping on each other for some decades. I have reason to be grateful to ethnographers (e.g., my pillaging of Celeste Ray's work on southern American Scots for my book on *Brigadoon* and *Braveheart*), but, *pace* Clifford, Geertz, and others, there is a lingering suspicion that ethnography's humanism and empiricism remains in many cases largely unreconstructed, particularly in its fetishising of "the field." Also, ethnography's tendency to political quietism is noted by that most ethnographically inclined of cultural studies practitioners, Paul Willis, in a book designed to promote dialogue between anthropology and cultural studies: "[T]he approach to the field, the reasons you go to the field, the chain of logic that leads you to the field, what you admit to knowing and being before you're in the field—all these things are far more contingent and related to, in my own version of cultural studies, some form of intervention rather than to the continuing assumption that the field can stand by itself" (1997, 187).

Broadly sharing Willis's position—doubtless exacerbated by the indigenous Scot's exasperation at the flagrant invention of tradition at play—may help explain my impatience with the utterances of transatlantic Scots and their respectful transmission by some ethnographers. I see the revealing of the workings of the Scottish Discursive Unconscious as a *political* act, a necessary ground-clearing operation that will help both indigenous and transatlantic Scots form an identity adequate to the real.

The specific proposition of this essay, then, is that however passionately transatlantic Scots experience their connection with Scotland, however much they feel their utterances and practices come out of the deepest core of their being, these practices and utterances are always already textual and discursive; if my argument is correct, they are emerging primarily from reconfigurations of the Scottish Discursive Unconscious. Although the fictive nature of these phenomena is recognised by the ethnographers writing in this volume, their respect for their informants, while not crediting their utterances as proclamations from the Ark of the Covenant, tends to push that recognition to the background. Perhaps much of the ethnographic work herein is caught in the contradiction highlighted by Ella Shohat and Robert Stam—"theory deconstructs totalising myths, activism nourishes them" (1994, 342). Though not wholly analogous to the ethnographic work in this volume, Annette Kuhn's work on the production of "cinema memory"—based on interviews with cinemagoers of the 1930s—yields a model that more clearly foregrounds the fictive element in ethnography:

> [E]thnographic enquiry was undertaken in full recognition of the fact that, in dealing with events of 60 and more years earlier, informants' accounts are memory texts, or recorded acts of remembering and that particular questions arise concerning the evidential status of accounts which rely on remembering—and thus also on forgetting, selective memory and hindsight. However, memory is regarded here as neither providing access to, nor as representing, the past "as it was"; the past, rather, is taken to be mediated, indeed produced, in the activity of remembering. When informants tell stories about their youthful film-going, they are producing memories in specific ways in a particular context, the research encounter. In other words, they are doing memory work; staging their memories, performing them. (2002, 8–9).

Mutatis mutandis, this might be applicable to what transatlantic Scots do in constructing their identity narratives, with the important addition, if my argument is correct, of the hegemonic positioning power of (parts of) the Scottish Discursive Unconscious.

What, then, might be the mechanisms whereby the SDU exercises this power continuously on the transatlantic Scots throughout their history in North America? What follows is a series of—doubtless far from comprehensive—notes for empirical research into the question. Andrew Hook, in his chapter in this volume, alludes in passing to Sir Walter Scott as model for indigenous American novelists such as Thomas Dixon. In an earlier work Hook goes more deeply into the influence of Scott on the American sensibility in the course of which he offers the following statistic: "[I]n 1823 C. J. Ingersoll asserted that 'nearly 200,000 copies of the Waverly [*sic*] novels, comprising 500,000 volumes, have issued from The American press in the last nine years" (1975, 145).

Ted Cowan, in his essay, cites the even more startling statistic of five million copies of *Waverley* being printed in America between 1813 and 1823. Although we have some sense of the overall effect of Scott's work on American sensibilities, particularly in the South, we are missing any sense of how the works circulated among transatlantic Scots and to what effect on their identity narratives. Even less documented is the considerable impact of the Kailyard novelists on North America, particularly in the decades spanning the nineteenth and twentieth century. Thomas Knowles has talked about "a Kailyard fever" in America:

> For at least a six year period from 1891 until 1897, Barrie, McLaren and to a lesser extent Crockett ranked high on the lists of American bestsellers: *Beside the Bonnie Brier Bush* and *The Days of Auld Lang Syne* gave McLaren first and sixth place in 1895; the former novel was in tenth place in 1896, and *Kate Carnegie and Those Ministers* and Barrie's *Sentimental Tommy* in seventh and ninth places respectively; while in 1897 Barrie's tale of Tommy Sandys had risen to eighth position immediately after *Margaret Ogilvy*, the story based on the author's mother. (1983, 66).

The same author cites the account, by the Chicago correspondent of the *New York Observer*, of McLaren's lecture performance there in 1896: "'Ian McLaren' has just closed his engagement in the city, and it is fair to say that no foreigner has been more popular in Chicago than he. People of all classes have sought to do him honour . . . The audience . . . was decidedly Scotch, who thoroughly appreciated the speaker's analysis of Scotch character. The gross receipts of those lectures are not below 8000 dollars" (Knowles 1983, 79–80). Another writer on the Kailyard has noted its influence in Canada: "[T]he familiar authors are freely available second-hand in Ontario, in the districts settled by Scots, and among the most fascinating of Canadian novels of the early years of this century are those by such writers as Robert Knowles, Minister of Galt in Ontario, who reproduces the formula of Barrie and McLaren exactly, but applies it to rural Ontario" (Campbell 1981, 119). These passages suggest that transatlantic Scots were avid consumers of Kailyardism, but the wider research question is the extent to which the tones and values of the Kailyard helped shape the identity narratives of this community.

Although the strictly literary phenomenon of the Kailyard would be eclipsed by the turn of the century, as Campbell's account of its Canadian impact makes clear, its influence lingered on. Barrie's success as a dramatist was initiated by a theatrical adaptation of *The Little Minister* that, following its New York success, toured the United States. The first cinematic adaptation of *The Little Minister* was in 1912 (with subsequent adaptations in 1915, 1921, 1922, and 1934), and cinematic versions of *Beside the Bonnie Brier Bush* and *The Lilac Sunbonnet* appeared in 1921 and 1922. Throughout the twentieth century the cinema, particularly Hollywood, has appropriated several of the Scottish Discursive Unconscious' sub-discourses, individually and in combination: Tartanry/Militarism—*The Black Watch* (1929), *Bonnie Scotland* (1935), *Wee Willie Winkie* (1937), *The Drum* (1938), *Gunga Din* (1939); Tartanry itself—*Rob Roy* (1911, 1953, 1996), *Bonnie Prince Charlie* (1923, 1948), *The Swordsman* (1947), *The Master of Ballantrae* (1953), *Kidnapped* (1917, 1938, 1948, 1960); Kailyardism—the numerous adaptations of the Kailyard novels referred to above, *The Green Years* (1946), *Bob, Son of Battle,* the Disney films *Greyfriars Bobby* (1961) and *The Three Lives of Thomasina* (1964); plus that melange par excellence of Tartanry and Kailyard, *Brigadoon* (1954) (McArthur 2003b). These titles—which exclude the extensive number of adaptations from Sir Walter Scott's works—are a mere fraction of the list, running from 1898 to 1990, compiled by Janet McBain (1990). Once again, the research question— ethnographic work on the model of Annette Kuhn's would be appropriate here—is, How did the transatlantic Scots relate to this diet of films representing Scotland and/or the Scots, and to what extent did it shape their identity narratives?

There are three other phenomena that require investigation in relation to the construction of these identity narratives. Harry Lauder—"Kailyard consciousness in tartan exterior"—took North America by storm on his first visit in 1907 and was to return there twenty times. He was never in any doubt about the role played by transatlantic Scots in his triumph:

> While the native Americans certainly rolled up in their thousands . . . there is no doubt in my mind that the exiled Scots in the States had more to do with my success than many people imagined . . . The expatriated Caledonians sure rallied to my support during my earlier trips to Dollar-land. Not only so, they turned up at my shows in all manner of Scottish costumes—in kilts, with Balmoral bonnets, wearing tartan ties. And many of them brought their bagpipes with them. They imparted an enthusiastic atmosphere to my appearances everywhere; their weird shouts and "hoochs" and skirls provided good copy for the journalists, and next-day talking points for the natives. In the first twenty weeks I spent in the

States I must have met personally ten thousand people who claimed acquaintance with me . . . I shook hands with them all . . . and presented signed postcards to one at least out of every fifty! (1928, 160–61)

It is likely that Lauder's onstage success translated into extensive sales of his recordings and, at a time when family music making was still a significant social activity, sheet music of his songs, both among transatlantic Scots and beyond. Yet again, the research questions relate to the construction of Scotland offered by these songs and their role in shaping ideologically the transatlantic Scots community.

In the period before extensive intercontinental travel and telephoning, the major means of contact between transatlantic and "homeland" Scots was the letter or postcard. The same questions posed about the other utterances and activities of transatlantic Scots might be asked of their letters—to what extent are they always already textual and discursive and informed by the Scottish Discursive Unconscious? Postcards pose an additional question. As well as their written messages, which might be interrogated in terms similar to the letters, what visual messages did the cards carry? Austria in 1875 is usually cited as the point of origin of the picture postcard, although the period 1900 to 1918 is spoken of as "the golden age of the postcard" (Byatt 1978), the period when postcard production, collection, and transmission were at their height. A significant number of "Scottish" postcards were produced, collected, and sent during the "golden age," some manufactured within Scotland, many manufactured elsewhere. A particular postcard "genre" is especially interesting in relation to transatlantic Scots—the "Hands Across the Sea" card. Although not restricted solely to "Scottish" cards (there are English and Irish variants), it is a significant presence in the Scottish context, and there is even a subgenre that foregrounds the Scotland-North America connection (see frontispiece images). I have written elsewhere (McArthur 1981–1982) of "Scottish" postcards frequently displaying "semiotic overkill," that is, the insistent signification of "Scottishness" being carried redundantly in several dimensions. Thus on the bottom left cover image there is not only the tartan, the lion rampant, and the Kailyardesque written sentiment, but also that other icon of Scottishness, the purple heather in the corners of the card. The Kailyardesque element is more explicit in the top right cover image with its invocation of Burns and the use of the Scots language. The central point, however, is the hegemony of Tartanry and Kailyard in "Scottish" postcards, and the research question is yet again, What was their circulation in the transatlantic Scots community and their contribution to the formation of identity narratives?

Finally, the rearticulation of discourses relating to Scotland in mass circulation magazines should be considered, assuming that the magazine-buying habits of transatlantic Scots did not differ significantly from those of other hyphenate communities in North America. The leading critical work on *National Geographic* describes its rise to mass circulation status since its founding in 1888 as "a 'slim, dull and technical' journal for gentleman scholars [evolving] into a glossy magazine whose circulation is the third largest in the United States," reaching a peak of nearly eleven million in the mid-1970s (Lutz and Collins 1993, 16). *National Geographic* has offered constructions of Scotland in two ways. Virtually since its inception the magazine has run intermittent pieces on Scotland (sixteen substantial articles, always lavishly illustrated, between 1917 and 1996). It would be an oversimplification to suggest that Tartanry and Kailyardism are indisputably hegemonic in these pieces, but they are substantially present, constructing Scotland as an additional exotic Other, the delivery of which to bourgeois Americans is the central function of the journal. Also, apart from its articles on Scotland, *National Geographic* has, at least since the 1930s, carried adverts for Scottish tourism that invariably invoke Tartanry. Other North American mass circulation magazines (e.g., *Life, Saturday Evening Post, Colliers*) have also been a channel for the circulation of discourse relating to Scotland, occasionally in their articles (e.g., "They *Like* to Dress That Way," *Saturday Evening Post*, 1944, and "Robert Burns: These Scottish Scenes Inspired His Poems," *Life*, 1949), but more centrally in their adverts. Apart from the frequent (but not invariable) recourse to Tartanry in these magazines' adverts for Scotch whisky, they consistently offer the common melding of Tartanry and Kailyardism. An enormous number of their adverts invoke the legendary thrift of the Scots. Within Scotland itself this is a lowland discourse, with jokes being made about the meanness of people from places on the east coast such as Aberdeen and Fife ("It taks a lang spoon tae sup wi' a Fifer"). As such, it is a Kailyardesque discourse. This lowland linguistic element is retained in many of these North American adverts, but so hegemonic is Tartanry in the worldwide representation of things Scottish, that they invariably include a tartan-clad, Lauderesque figure, or some splash of tartan, to reinforce the message that the product is keenly priced. I have counted over thirty products in the period 1930 to 1960 deploying this strategy. Once again, the research questions are, To what extent did transatlantic Scots partake of these magazines, and to what effect?

Margaret Bennett's piece on the Québécois Scots displays both the sophistication of the ethnographic work in this volume and its key potential lacuna. On the one hand, it is entirely aware of the fictive, performative dimensions of the transatlantic Scots' identity narratives: "In the New World, descendants of immigrants keep alive images of Old World identity constructed from descriptions perpetuated in oral tradition (usually of individual characters and their specific traits); from written accounts in popular books and journals; and also from stereotypical images such as Scotland's mountain glens, heather, tartan, whisky, and oatcakes." On the other hand, Bennett cites with approval the words of Alan Dundes: "I am interested in folklore because it represents a people's image of themselves. The image may be distorted but at least the distortion comes from the people, not from some outside observer armed with a range of *a priori* premises. Folklore as a mirror of culture provides unique raw material for those eager better to understand themselves and others" (1980, viii, cited by Bennett in ch. 4 of this volume).

The material of folklore is, in my view, far from "raw." It is highly processed and, in the case of the transatlantic (and, indeed, the indigenous) Scots, the key blender is the Scottish Discursive Unconscious. Like other writers in this volume, I am reluctant to deny the transatlantic Scots the dignity of agency and the support of cultural identity; but so compelling, in my view, is the evidence of the shaping power of the SDU that this concession has to be provisional, interrogatory, and denying of fixity. Having opened with a quotation from Stuart Hall, let me close with another: "Identities are . . . constituted within, not outside representation. They relate to the invention of tradition as much as to tradition itself . . . not the so-called return to roots but a coming to terms with our 'routes'" (1996, 4).

Works Cited

Bhabha, Homi K. 1984. "The Other Question: The Stereotype and Colonial Discourse." *Screen* 24: 18–36.

Biehl, Janet, and Peter Staudenmaier. 1995. *Ecofascism: Lessons from the German Experience.* Edinburgh: AK Press.

Byatt, Anthony. 1978. *Picture Postcards and Their Publishers.* Malvern, UK: Golden Age Postcards Books.

Campbell, Ian. 1981. *Kailyard: A New Assessment.* Edinburgh: Ramsey Head.

Chapman, Malcolm. 1992. *The Celts: The Construction of a Myth.* Basingstoke, UK: Macmillan.

———. 1978. *The Gaelic Vision in Scottish Culture.* London: Croom Helm.

Clifford, James. 1988. *The Predicament of Culture: Twentieth-Century Ethnography, Literature, and Art.* Cambridge, MA: Harvard UP.

Craig, Cairns. 1982. "Myths Against History: Tartanry and Kailyard in Nineteenth-Century Scottish Literature." In *Scotch Reels: Scotland in Cinema and Television,* ed. Colin McArthur, 7–15. London: British Film Institute.

Crosland, Thomas W. H. 1902. *The Unspeakable Scot.* London: Grant Richards.

Fanon, Frantz. 1952. *Black Skin, White Masks.* London: McGibbon and Kee 1968.

Geertz, Clifford. 1988. *Works and Lives: The Anthropologist as Author.* Stanford, CA: Stanford UP.

Gilroy, Paul. 1993. *The Black Atlantic: Modernity and Double Consciousness.* London: Verso.

Gunn, Neil. 1937. *Highland River.* London: Porpoise Press.

Hall, Stuart. 1996. "Who Needs Identity?" In *Questions of Cultural Identity,* ed. Stuart Hall and Paul Du Gay, 1–17. London: Sage.

———. 1990. "Cultural Identity and Diaspora." In *Identity: Community, Culture, Difference,* ed. Jonathan Rutherford, 222–37. London: Lawrence and Wishart.

———. 1989. "New Ethnicities." In *Stuart Hall: Critical Dialogues in Cultural Studies,* ed. David Morley and Kuan-Hsing Chen, 441–49. London: Routledge.

Hook, Andrew. 1975. *Scotland and America: A Study of Cultural Relations, 1750–1835.* Glasgow: Blackie.

Knowles, Thomas D. 1983. *Ideology, Art, and Commerce: Aspects of Literary Sociology in the Late Victorian Scottish Kailyard.* Gothenburg, Sweden: University of Gothenburg.

Kuhn, Annette. 2002. *Everyday Magic: Cinema and Cultural Memory.* London: I. B. Tauris.

Lutz, Catherine A., and Jane L. Collins. 1993. *Reading National Geographic.* Chicago: U of Chicago P.

McArthur, Colin. 2003a. *Whisky Galore! and The Maggie.* London: I. B. Tauris.

———. 2003b. *Brigadoon, Braveheart, and the Scots: Distortions of Scotland in Hollywood Cinema.* London: I. B. Tauris.

———. 1996. "The Scottish Discursive Unconscious." In *Scottish Popular Theatre and Entertainment,* eds. Alasdair Cameron and Adrienne Scullion, 81–89. Glasgow: Glasgow University Library Studies.

———. 1993. "Scottish Culture: A Reply to David McCrone." *Scottish Affairs* 4: 95–106.

———. 1981–1982. "Breaking the Signs: Scotch Myths as Cultural Struggle." *Cencrastus* 7: 21–25.

McBain, Janet. 1990. "Scotland in Feature Film: A Filmography." In *From Limelight to Satellite: A Scottish Film Book,* ed. Eddie Dick, 233–53. London: British Film Institute.

McRobbie, Angela. 1999. *In the Culture Society: Art, Fashion, and Popular Music.* London: Routledge.

Nairn, Tom. 1977. *The Break-Up of Britain.* London: New Left Books.

Noble, Andrew. 1981. "Machismo in Retrospect." *Bulletin of Scottish Politics* 2: 72–81.

Pendreigh, Brian. 1992. "Myth and Mystique in a Cruel Glen." *The Scotsman* (Feb. 19): 15.

Prebble, John. 1961. *Culloden.* London: Penguin.

Ray, Celeste. 2001. *Highland Heritage: Scottish Americans in the American South.* Chapel Hill: U of North Carolina P.

———. 1998. "Scottish Heritage Southern Style." *Southern Cultures* 4, no. 2: 28–45.

Said, Edward. 1978. *Orientalism.* London: Routledge and Kegan Paul.

Shohat, Ella, and Robert Stam. 1994. *Unthinking Eurocentrism.* London: Routledge.

Spivak, Gayatri Chakravorty. 1988. "Can the Subaltern Speak?" In *Marxism and the Interpretation of Culture,* ed. Cary Nelson and Lawrence Grossberg, 271–313. London: Macmillan.

Spring, Ian. 1990. *Phantom Village: The Myth of the New Glasgow.* Edinburgh: Polygon.

West, Cornel. 1990. "The New Cultural Politics of Difference." In *The Cultural Studies Reader,* ed. Simon During, 203–17. London: Routledge, 1993.

Willis, Paul. 1997. "TIES: Theoretically Informed Ethnographic Study." In *Anthropology and Cultural Studies,* ed. Stephen Nugent and Cris Shore, 182–92. London: Pluto.

Contributors

Paul Basu

Basu is a lecturer in anthropology at the University of Sussex. His forthcoming book, *Highland Homecomings: Genealogy and Heritage Tourism in the Scottish Diaspora,* results from several years' research exploring the relationships between landscape, memory, and identity in the Scottish Highlands and Islands.

Margaret Bennett

A folklorist, Professor Bennett has taught in the School of Scottish Studies at Edinburgh University and is now a Research Fellow in Scottish History at the University of Glasgow. Her books include *Oatmeal and the Catechism: Scottish Gaelic Settlers in Quebec* (1999) and *Scottish Customs from the Cradle to the Grave* (2nd ed., 2001).

Edward J. Cowan

Cowan is chair of Scottish History at the University of Glasgow. In addition to popular culture, his interests span Viking history and the Icelandic sagas, the Scottish Wars of Independence, Scottish political thought, and Scottish identity at home and abroad. He has written or edited fifteen books, including: *Alba: Celtic Scotland in the Middle Ages* (ed., 2002); *Scotland since 1688* (2000); and *The Ballad in Scottish History* (2001).

Jonathan Dembling

Dembling is a PhD candidate in anthropology at the University of Massachusetts, Amherst. A Gaelic-speaker, Dembling has published Gaelic music reviews and articles on the Gaelic revival in Canada.

Andrew Hook

Hook is Bradley Professor of English Literature at the University of Glasgow, where a Center for American Studies has been named in his honor. His ten books include *From Goosecreek to Gandercleugh: Studies in Scottish-American Literary and Cultural History* (1999); *The Glasgow Enlightenment* (1995, co-edited with Richard Sher); and *Scotland and America: A Study of Cultural Relations, 1750–1835* (1975).

James Hunter

Formerly chairman for the Highlands and Islands Enterprise, Hunter is a freelance writer and historian. His ten books include *A Dance Called America: The Scottish Highlands, the United States and Canada* (1994); *The Other Side of Sorrow: Nature and People in the Scottish Highlands* (1995); *Scottish Highlanders, Indian Peoples: Thirty Generations of a Montana Family,* (1996); *Last of the Free: A Millennial History of the Highlands and Islands of Scotland* (2000); and *Culloden and the Last Clansmen* (2002).

Grant Jarvie

Jarvie is chair and head of Scotland's first Department of Sports Studies, at the University of Stirling. His most recent book is *Sport, Revolution, and the Beijing Olympic Games* (2005). He has written extensively on both historical and sociological aspects of sport in society, including *Sport, Scotland, and the Scots* (2000); *Sport in the Making of Celtic Cultures* (1999); *Scottish Sport in the Making of the Nation: Ninety-Minute Patriots?* (1994); and *Highland Games: The Making of the Myth* (1991).

Colin McArthur

Formerly a senior executive with the British Film Institute, Colin McArthur is now a freelance teacher, writer, and graphic artist. He has written extensively on Hollywood cinema, British television, and Scottish culture. His many books include *Brigadoon, Braveheart, and the Scots: Distortions of Scotland in Hollywood Cinema* (2003); *Underworld USA* (1972); *Television and History* (1978); *Scotch Reels: Scotland in Cinema and Television* (1982); *The Big Heat* (1992); and *Whisky Galore! and the Maggie* (2003).

Celeste Ray

An anthropologist, Ray is associate professor and chair at the University of the South. Her books include *Highland Heritage: Scottish Americans in the American South* (2001); *Southern Heritage on Display: Public Ritual and Ethnic Diversity within Southern Regionalism* (2003); and *Signifying Serpents and Mardi Gras Runners: Representation and Identity in Selected Souths* (2003).

John W. Sheets

Chair of the Department of History and Anthropology at Central Missouri State University, Sheets has published on topics in biological anthropology and genetics and began publishing on his ethnographic research in Scotland in the 1990s. His Scottish research, appearing in journals such as *Current Anthropology* and *Scottish Studies,* considers biography, demography, migrations, and folklore.

Michael Vance

Vance is associate professor of history at Saint Mary's University in Halifax, Nova Scotia, with particular interests in identity politics, migration history, and memory. His publications include several articles on Lowland migration to Canada and an edited book on Scottish ethnic identity in Nova Scotia titled *Myth, Migration, and the Making of Memory: Scotia and Nova Scotia c. 1600–1990* (1999).

Index